THE GLORY OF THE PERFUMED GARDEN

THE MISSING FLOWERS

An English Translation from the Arabic of the Second and Hitherto Unpublished Part of Shaykh Nafzawi's Perfumed Garden

PANTHER
GRANADA PUBLISHING
London Toronto Sydney New York

Published by Granada Publishing Limited
in Panther Books 1978

ISBN 0 586 04222 9

First published in Great Britain by
Neville Spearman Ltd 1975
Copyright © Neville Spearman Ltd 1975

Granada Publishing Limited
Frogmore, St Albans, Herts AL2 2NF
and
3 Upper James Street, London W1R 4BP
1221 Avenue of the Americas, New York, NY 10020 USA
117 York Street, Sydney, NSW 2000, Australia
100 Skyway Avenue, Toronto, Ontario, Canada M9W 3A6
Trio City, Coventry Street, Johannesburg 2001, South Africa
CML Centre, Queen & Wyndham, Auckland 1, New Zealand

Made and printed in Great Britain by
Richard Clay (The Chaucer Press) Ltd
Bungay, Suffolk
Set in Linotype Juliana

CONTENTS

		page
	Introduction	7

Chapter

I	On Lesbianism and Those who First indulged in it	19
II	On Sodomy and the Tricks of Sodomites, their Love for Boys and their Preference for Boys over Good-looking Girls	32
III	Pretty Girls are Superior to Boys	59
IV	On Pimps and Procuration	72
V	On Women, Sex and Marriage: Illustrative Stories, Unusual and Humorous Anecdotes and Comical Tales	97
VI	On Cosmetics and Perfumes and Grooming	131
VII	The Rights and Duties of Husbands and Wives	150
VIII	On Concubines and Wives and Plurality of Wives	161
IX	On Women Fat and Thin	184
X	On Colouring and Complexion in Women: The Question "Fair or Dark?"	189
XI	On Beauty and Attractiveness and the Natural Liking that all Mankind have for these Two Qualities	197
XII	On Diverse Matters relating to Sexual Intercourse	212

Contents

XIII   On Motitation in Coitus   240

XIV   On whether a Man may Gratify himself by Using
        Other Parts of a Woman's Body than her Vagina   247

XV   On Jealousy: The Case For and Against   251

XVI   Diverse Entertaining Tales and Anecdotes   264

XVII Conclusion   311

        Appendix: Genealogical and Dynastic Tables   316

        Index   321

INTRODUCTION

Translator's Notes on the History of "The Perfumed Garden"

Outside scholarly and academic circles *The Perfumed Garden* is perhaps the best known of all Sir Richard Burton's literary productions. Since the story of the book is told at some length by Alan Hull Walton in his introduction to the Neville Spearman edition of 1963,[1] there would be little point in retelling it in all its detail here. It will be enough to pick out the salient points and to make such corrections and additions as seem necessary.

In essence the work is not the product of Burton's imagination; it is the creation of a man whom, for the sake of brevity and convenience, we are justified in calling Shaykh Nafzawi.[2] The name Nafzawi suggests that our Shaykh was a native of that part of the Arab world which we know today as Tunisia, and indeed such an impression is fortified by the fact that, as we shall see, he wrote his book for a minister in the service of a ruler of Tunis. The first translation of his Arabic *Garden* into a European

[1] *The Perfumed Garden of the Shaykh Nefzawi* [sic]. Translated by Sir Richard F. Burton and edited with an Introduction and Additional Notes by Alan Hull Walton (London, 1963).

[2] Since readers unacquainted with Arabic are baffled by names and titles and their different forms a word of explanation is necessary. "Shaykh" (more familiar in English as "Sheikh") is a title of respect accorded to a wide variety of people in different stations in life and with widely differing functions. In the society in which Nafzawi lived it would be borne by religious dignitaries and scholars versed in the traditional sciences of religion and law. As regards "Nafzawi", Walton has already drawn attention to the forms *Nefzawi*, *Nefzaoui*, *Nefzawih* and *Nafzawi* (*Perfumed Garden*, p. 19). The correct form according to modern scholarly transliteration (from which we may drop distracting diacritical strokes and dots) is *Nafzawi*, and this will be the form used throughout the present work.

language is contained in the French "autograph edition" of 1876.[3] This very limited edition—irregularly lithographed on French government machines by four spirited officers serving in Algeria—eventually caught the eye of the great writer Guy de Maupassant, who was so impressed that in August 1884 he urged a publisher to produce a reprint of it.[4] To which publisher he was writing is not clear, nor does the question concern us here. What is more important is that in 1886 Isidore Liseux, a noted publisher and scholarly bibliophile with a taste for the unusual, corrected and revised the text and produced an attractive printed edition. Although limited to 220 copies, the Liseux text has been reprinted many times since his death.[5]

In this context the Liseux edition is of interest solely because it was anonymously translated by Burton and privately issued in London in 1886 by the so-called Kama Shastra Society, which in the same year produced a second edition. As is clear, Burton did not translate the *Garden* from the original Arabic, but rendered the French version into English, and, in so doing, left all the French forms of Arabic words as they stood—possibly in an attempt, at that stage of his career, to cloak his identity—thereby bequeathing, in the matter of transliteration, a legacy of what readers unacquainted with French can only regard as confusing balderdash.[6] Be that as it may, Burton had no intention of letting the matter of the *Garden* rest as it then stood. For, in 1888, with far less concern for anonymity than he would have shown in his less distinguished years, he embarked upon a new translation, this time apparently from an Arabic manuscript. The rest of the tale is soon told. In 1890 Burton died before he could complete his task. "As is now well known," writes Alan Walton, "his wife immediately burnt the book, thus incurring the wrath and (quite

---

[3] This first appeared in Algiers (see *Perfumed Garden*, p. 12).

[4] Ibid., pp. 13 f.

[5] Ibid., p. 16.

[6] In this connection it is interesting to reflect how English monoglots pronounce the words *chate*, *heub*, and *ouarde* (ibid., pp. 137, 150, 167). In the transliteration currently accepted by British and North American scholars these words would emerge as *shāṭ*, *ḥubb*, and *warda* respectively, and, if we ignore the long stroke and the dots we come very much nearer to the actual Arabic pronunciation than if we try to wrestle with outdated French forms.

justifiable) exasperation of innumerable eminent scholars throughout the world."[7]

What was the reason for the new English version? Walton's
suggestion is that Burton's main motive was to include "the
whole of the very considerable portion of the twenty-first
chapter[8] concerning homosexuality, which had been eliminated
by the modest and anonymous French translator".[9] This may
well be true, but no Arabist familiar with the original— in whatever recension—can avoid the suspicion that the inaccuracies and
adaptations of the French version left ample room for improve-
ments. Of course there has been much speculation over the
question whether much has been lost by Lady Burton's precipi-
tate action, and the matter has been complicated by the fact that
comments made by one of Burton's friends, Dr Grenfell Baker,
who was in close and regular contact with him during the period
he was engaged on his new translation, have led to judgements
which may be wholly erroneous. "There is no reason," says
Walton, "to doubt Dr Grenfell Baker's statement that the burnt
manuscript ... was simply a revision of the translation from
the Liseux edition, considerably expanded by many additional
footnotes, and with the long section on pederasty restored—in a
translation made by Burton, direct from an Arabic manuscript."[10]
But was Baker's assessment right? Did Burton tell him everything? Did he understand everything Burton told him? Certainly,
if Burton was producing a full translation of the Arabic recension
on which this present book is based and in which there are
obvious breaks indicating lacunae, there is every reason to believe
—as any reader will see for himself—that the text he had before
him may well have been very much longer than supposed by
Baker, though not perhaps as long as that with which the curious
Charles Carrington claims to have been familiar.[11]

What we have lost in the way of Burton's own annotation is
naturally an entirely different problem, and on this point one can

---

[7] *Perfumed Garden*, p. 20.

[8] i.e. of the *Perfumed Garden*, in which it constitutes the last chapter.

[9] Loc. cit.   [10] *Perfumed Garden*, p. 21.

[11] Ibid., p. 23. Carrington spoke of "four large royal octavo volumes of
about 500 pages each".

do no better than quote Walton and the authorities on which he draws. "Baker," he writes, "continues: 'The [sc. *Arabian*] *Nights*' had contained many curious and extremely interesting notes, but there was still a large amount that had not been published, and such a work as *The Perfumed Garden* offered a good opportunity for putting on record what remained partly in Burton's private note-books and partly in his great brain.' '... To give an example, Burton had already ... written a long note on the history of eunuchs. Some time after he discovered an article by G. Carter Stent in the "Journ. North-China Branch Roy[al] As[iatic] Soc[iety]," N.S. XI, 1877 (pages 143–84), on Chinese eunuchs. This is a most interesting article ... The information contained therein was certainly new to Burton, and it is marked (in his copy in the Kensington Library) ready for amalgamation in the new edition of the *Garden* ... There was also a new, and very full Introduction by Burton, said to consist largely of extracts translated from the works of Numa Numantius, a learned German legal official, himself sexually inverted, who spent the greater part of his life in the exposition and defence of homosexual love.' "[12]

A Note on Nafzawi and the Date of his Work

Before anything is said of the Arabic text of which this present book is essentially a translation, a few words about the author and his work are more than desirable—they are indeed necessary. As regards Shaykh Nafzawi, the first thing that needs to be said is that most of what we read about him in the French translation and, consequently, in Burton's version of the latter, is such a comedy of errors that the quality and accuracy of the translations are immediately suspect. While our author's name certainly seems to have been Abū 'Abdullāh Muḥammad ibn 'Umar (al-) Nafzāwī,[13] the patron for whom he wrote his *Perfumed Garden* was certainly not Mohammed ben Ouana ez Zonawi (which in the modern and more acceptable system of transliteration would emerge as Muḥammad ibn Wāna az-

[12] Ibid., pp. 21 f.   [13] Ibid., p. 71, n. 11.

Zunāwī) of the Kabyl tribe of Zonaoua (Zunāwa), who was alive in the early sixteenth century.[14] He seems, rather, to have been Muḥammad ibn 'Awāna az-Zuwāwī ("of Zuwawa"), a minister of the seventeenth ruler of the Hafsid kingdom of Tunis, Abū Fāris, whose reign extended over the period 1394–1434.[15] As to the work dedicated to him by Nafzawi, this was written around 1410,[16] and it seems in fact to have started its life as a comparatively small treatise, of which we have quite a number of published texts (Fez, Tunis, Cairo, etc.)[17] The use of the words "started its life" is deliberate; like many technical treatises of much more limited interest, the *Garden* seems to have been developed and extended or trimmed and modified by various hands. To the uninitiated such "tinkering" savours of fraud, forgery, or some kind of dishonesty or malpractice such as plagiarism. But it must be remembered that modern criteria must not be applied to medieval literary production, especially in the technical and scientific fields. Just as Gray's *Anatomy* and *Salmond On Torts* are modified and expanded from time to time by various anatomists and lawyers, so also were certain medieval works expanded and modified. Modern practice, however, differs in one impotant respect from that of medieval Islam: whereas the editor of today will normally identify himself and indicate, even if only in the broadest terms, the scope of his contribution, his medieval Muslim counterpart, honest or otherwise, did not always feel the need to do likewise—and very often did not. We need not feel at all perturbed, then, if the *Perfumed Garden* exists in several recensions or versions—as in fact available evidence suggests that it does.[18] Without our plunging into a mass of detail that can be of

[14] Ibid., p. 74.

[15] As Nafzawi himself tells us (ibid.), the name of Abu Faris was 'Abd-ul-'Aziz, and the translator of the autograph edition came near to a correct identification, but was misled through ignorance of certain historical facts.

[16] See R. Brunschvig, *La Berbérie orientale sous les Hafsides* II (Paris, 1947), 372 f.

[17] See C. Brockelmann, *Geschichte der arabischen Literatur* (Leiden, 1937–49), II, p. 257, and *Supplementband* II, 368.

[18] It is enough to consult entries in the catalogues of various major libraries throughout the world to note that there are manuscripts of greatly differing lengths.

little or no interest to the general reader it is sufficient to say that on the basis of preliminary investigations the original *Garden* seems to have been a comparatively small work—and indeed a most distinguished French Arabist has no hesitation in describing it as "short".[19] Whether Nafzawi himself revised and enlarged his original it is difficult to say without close research into the problem. What is certain is that it was enlarged and that other hands had fingers in the pie; this much is clear from internal evidence.[20]

The Present Translation

The present translation of the missing portion of the *Garden* has been made on the basis of one manuscript, the text of which has been made available to me in a private modern copy. Such investigations as I have felt obliged to make leave me in little doubt that it does represent the recension used by the author of the French translation which Burton rendered into English. One does not really have to go far to suspect as much: the Arabic text of the missing portion and the existing French and English translations overlap, and a comparison of text and translation in the overlapping chapters gives no cause for any suspicion that the two parts do not constitute a single work.

Ideally, any translation of a work of medieval Arabic literature should be made from a critical edition based on all known manuscripts and any published texts reproducing a lost recension. Since it has been no part of my duty to the publisher to investigate the Arabic text or to prepare a critical edition, the ideal has not been achieved—which is all the more regrettable since there are obvious lacunae in the text which lay before me. What I have done, on the other hand, is to correct, solely on the basis of my own knowledge and experience, innumerable textual corruptions, some of which would have given rise to gross errors. Since Nafzawi and his later "editors" have largely drawn on other

---

[19] Brunschvig, op. cit., p. 372. The Tunis text (1897) is in fact in sixty pages.
[20] For instance, Dawud Antaki, who died towards the end of the sixteenth century, is quoted on p. 214 and Suyuti (d. 1505) on pp. 226 f.

sources, some of them well-known classics long in print, I have been able in parts to restore the text. In other places, however, this has not been possible since our text is either lacking in the published editions or is at variance with them, sometimes considerably so. Those parts of my translation, then, which can be easily traced and checked against a printed text may sometimes appear incorrect. But in such cases—and this I stress—it must be understood that where my text has made sense (and, in the case of poetry, also presented no metrical anomaly) I have translated what I saw before me and ignored the published version.

Notes Relevant to the Content of the Missing Portion of "The Perfumed Garden"

As regards the content of this missing portion of the *Garden*, few comments are called for since the essential subject-matter speaks for itself. Moreover, Walton has already had something to say on the *Garden* generally which is also applicable here.[21] Some points, however, must be made, the first of which is that attitudes to sexual matters in the Islamic society of the Near and Middle East should not be judged by standards that are totally alien to that society. Segregation of the sexes, eventually carried to extremes, should not mislead us into supposing that sex was a matter for shame and not to be discussed. In the early days of Islam the subject was treated by the Prophet Muhammad—a deeply religious man of undoubted sincerity—and his Companions in the most blunt and forthright terms, and, during the formative period of Islamic law, men of religion and unfeigned piety entered into most detailed and serious discussions of sexual practice which many of the older generation of today would still consider highly indelicate. Of course, this is not to say that the concept of indecency did not exist or that sexual behaviour, notably that of the rich and leisured urban classes, did not with the passage of time incline to debauchery and excesses that would be considered outrageous by any but wholly amoral standards.

21 *Perfumed Garden*, pp. 27 ff.

A second point to be made is that the Christian ideal of sacramental marriage must not be equated with matrimony as conceived in Islam. From the outset polygamy and divorce had a lawful place within the framework of the Islamic religion. Moreover, concubinage with slave-girls was permitted, which, in practice, meant that, while the average free man of any standing would, in the first place at least, marry a free woman (usually his cousin on the paternal side of the family) and beget offspring by her, it was to slave-girls that he would turn for his real sexual enjoyment and entertainment. Acquired from all quarters of the known world, these girls were often highly sophisticated and well versed in all facts of the art of love, including singing and dancing.

In the wake of the masculine society that came to characterize the towns and cities of Islam, with their rigid segregation of the sexes and the seclusion of women, there inevitably followed widespread homosexuality. Not every young man was rich enough either to marry a wife or to have slave-girls, and most of those who sought to advance themselves by education and learning often spent long years as students. If not residents of the centre in which they were studying, such students often lived and slept together in colleges. Under these conditions they, not unexpectedly, fell into unnatural ways of living and developed homosexual tendencies. As masturbation was generally accounted the worst sexual offence, there were few ways of satisfying the male instinct. To many, boys, because of certain resemblances to girls, proved more attractive than other adult males, and, not surprisingly, pederasty became part of a scheme of things which, though not by any means approved (indeed religious teaching condemned it), was not at the same time frowned upon by society. From what Nafzawi has to say, however, it is clear that few boys found their experiences enjoyable. Most, we may be sure, submitted only under duress or out of economic necessity, or both.

As regards Lesbianism, it is quite clear that in the harems of the rich and powerful no less than in those of kings and princes women lived in conditions conducive to the formation of homosexual relationships. Leading lives of enforced idleness and necessarily neglected by a lord and master who could not possibly satisfy the sexual demands of all the women at his disposal, whether wives or concubines or both, they tended to form attachments either among themselves or with women who dressed and groomed them and therefore had close physical contact with them, especially when it came to removal of hair from the pubis and other parts of the body.

In the pre-modern Muslim world male homosexuality and prostitution were facts of urban social life, to which segregation of the sexes, arranged marriages, and, in the case of the rich and powerful at least, ready access in the harem to a cloying surfeit of women must have contributed in no small measure. Looking beyond, or perhaps even overlooking, such factors, our present author offers his own explanations—medical, social, and psychological—of the facts (pp. 39–42) and has socio-economic categories for the kind of individual likely to be found playing the passive role (pp. 51–3).

Apart from homosexuality characterized by straightforward substitution of the male for the female person, a man's intercourse with a woman *per anum* is virtually the only other sexual aberration discussed by the author and then primarily, it seems, for the purpose of giving a ruling on a disputed point of law (p. 249). None of the vicious and outrageously obscene forms of sexual gratification of the kind practised by the more unhealthy elements of Western society are mentioned, though what we ought to conclude from this is uncertain.

Intelligent readers ignorant of the history of Arabic literature will not know exactly what to make of the *Garden*, and they are almost sure to ask themselves whether, as Walton maintains,[22] it has a serious purpose, whether it is classical literature, and, if so, whether it is typical. To the first question the answer is that its purpose is as serious as that of, say, *Studies in the Psychology of Sex* by Havelock Ellis. This much is quite clear from the space devoted to entirely serious matters in the fields of medicine (the observations on eugenics on p. 107 are of special interest), psychology, law, etc. Lest the Western reader be misled by what he may see as an unnecessary and irrelevant, but yet liberal, admixture of lascivious frivolity descending at times to the crude and coarse, he must be forewarned that the aim of the admixture is to combine entertainment with instruction. Such a combination is far from alien to the Arabic literary tradition, and the technique, of which salient features are the frequent quotations of appropriate poetry and the recounting of illustrative anecdotes, derives from a highly respected genre of classical *belles-lettres*.

Is the *Garden* classical literature? If so, is it typical? Both questions can be answered together: the *genre* to which it belongs is certainly one of classical writing, but not in the mainstream of Arabic literary endeavour and therefore not typical. What must be stressed, however, is that the bulk of material that has gone into the making of this encyclopedia of sexual behaviour—for such it is—is drawn from a wide range of classical literature from religious and legal writings to the works of well-known poets, prose writers, anthologists, physicians, philosophers and philologists. If at times the subject-matter is gross and even offensive to good taste, at others it reveals a sensitive understanding of human emotions,[23] a respect for chivalry and justice,[24] and a keen awareness of the need for spiritual and physical harmony between marriage partners, based on mutual affection, tenderness, loyalty, devotion and consideration.[25] This much said it remains only to point out a merit of the work that will soon become obvious: it is an absorbing social document that can be read for both information and diversion.

H.E.J.

Arabic Words, Names, etc.

Notes on the transliteration of Arabic words and names together with dynastic tables will be found on pp. 317 ff. The reader is advised to look at them before starting to read the book.

[23] See *inter alia* pp. 100 f., 106, 251 ff.
[24] See *inter alia* pp. 92 ff., 104 ff., 148. 150 ff.
[25] See *inter alia* pp. 58, 104 ff., 117, 120 ff., 132.

SUGGESTIONS FOR FURTHER
READING

On the Arabs and Islam

To most English-speaking people the world of Islam and the Arabs is virtually a closed book, and many would like to know more of it but are uncertain where to seek out their information. Readers of Nafzawi will no doubt wish to acquaint themselves with the history and civilization of that world of which he was a product since the attainment of knowledge will not merely help them to acquire a better understanding of his book but it will also reveal to them the many facets of a great civilization which was at its height in the ninth and tenth centuries A.D. and to which the West owes more than it has ever been prepared to acknowledge. For the benefit of such persons the following items—selected for price and accessibility —are recommended for further reading:

COULSON, N. J. A *History of Islamic Law*, Edinburgh U.P., 1964. An excellent introduction to the subject from which information on women, marriage and divorce may be derived. A very reasonably priced hard-back.

GABRIELI, F. *The Arabs: a Compact History*, New York, 1963.

—— *Muhammad and the Conquests of Islam*, London, 1968 (Paperback).

GIBB, H. A. R. *Arabic Literature*, 2nd. revised edn., Oxford U.P., 1963.

——*Mohammedanism* [i.e. Islam], 2nd edn., Oxford U.P., 1969 (Paperback: Opus 17, being a revision of the hardback of 1953).

LANG, D. M. (ed.), *A Guide to Eastern Literatures*, London and New York, 1971. Chapter 'Arabic Literature'. This section is divided into three parts: Historical Background; Main Trends in Literature; Individual Writers. The sections on Persian and Turkish literatures are also recommended.

LEWIS, B. *The Arabs in History*, 4th edn., New York and London, 1966 (Paperback).

NICHOLSON, R. A. *A Literary History of the Arabs*, London, 1969 (reprint of Cambridge, 1930 edn.).

WATT, W. M. *A History of Islamic Spain*, Edinburgh U.P., 1965.

——*What is Islam?* London and Beirut, 1968.

On Sexual Matters

A. H. Walton gives numerous references in his introduction to *The Perfumed Garden* (1963 Spearman edn.) and has a select bibliography, pp. 57–59. By far the best work on the theory and practice of sex in Islam is unfortunately in French: G.-H. BOUSQUET *L'éthique sexuelle de l'Islam*, Paris, 1966 (Paperback). The author is both a jurist and a sociologist with many years of experience in Algeria, and the book merits translation into English. For the English reader interested in the tradition of Arabic writing on the subject of human love the following publication may be recommended: L. A. GIFFEN, *Theory of Profane Love among the Arabs*, London U.P. and New York U.P., 1971. On the Harem as a royal Turkish institution one can do no better than recommend N. M. PENZER, *The Ḥarēm*, London, 1966 (2nd impression of a reprint of 1935 edition). A fundamental work on Muslim marriage is E. Westermarck, *Marriage Ceremonies in Morocco*, London (Curzon repr.), 1972. Medical aspects of sexual behaviour are currently dealt with in periodicals such as the *British Journal of Sexual Medicine*.

CHAPTER 1

On Lesbianism and Those who First indulged in it

Lesbianism is an ancient female practice in which women find sexual gratification and which in their opinion minimizes the risk of infamy and notoriety. According to commentators on the Koran, the practice made its appearance some years before pederasty. The Prophet declared it an unlawful sexual practice.

The first Lesbian was the daughter of Hasan Yamani. This woman had gone on a mission to Nu'man ibn Mundhir, who lodged her in the apartments of Hind, his wife (sic).[1]

Now Hind was the most beautiful woman of her day, and she it was who was called "The Naked One" because of her beauty in the nude. At any rate, Hasan's daughter would not let her be, but kept on putting wrong ideas into her head and extolling the virtues of Lesbianism to her, saying that in a Lesbian union there was to be experienced a delight such as had never been known between a man and a woman and that there was no risk of disgrace, no danger of pregnancy, and only supreme ecstasy in the indulgence of carnal desire without the fear of any imputations or the need to beware of any consequences. And so at last they came together in sexual union, and Hind found a delight in it

[1] Nu'man (d. 602) was the last Lakhmid ruler of the Christian Arab principality of Hira, a city on the Euphrates a little to the south of Kufa in the region of ancient Babylon. In pre-Islamic times the Lakhmids—vassals of the Persian Empire—and their capital were of great importance, not only because they attracted to their patronage some of the great Arabian poets, but also because they were one of the channels through which Christianity reached the Arabian Peninsula. Of Hira's famous pre-Islamic Christian poet 'Adi ibn Zayd and his relationship with Hind we shall learn something later (p. 274).

far beyond what she had been led to expect from her companion. The couple reached a stage of infatuation with each other such as had never before been known between two women. When in the end Hasan's daughter died, Hind devoted herself only to tending her grave, and her devotion became proverbial. Hence the poet Farazdaq says:

> Unstintingly you have fulfilled your pledge even as
> Hind did hers towards Al-Hasan's daughter.

Then, in aftertimes, there came Raghum and Najda. These two fell in love with one another, and so notorious did their love become that Raghum's brother suffered nothing but insults and taunts because of his sister's conduct. So he lay in wait for them one day as they were bedding together and slew Najda and made off with his sister. But Raghum set about urging Najda's tribe to take vengeance on her own brother, and war broke out between their peoples. Therein lies a proof of the great delight that women can experience in Lesbianism and of the measure to which it can outweigh the delight to be found in men.

There are two kinds of Lesbian. First, there is the kind of woman who loves tribadism, yet is not averse to the penis. Any one of four reasons may induce her to take up the habit. She may, for instance, suffer from insatiable lust or take an inordinate delight in a sexual appetite that no man can satisfy, in which case the desire to play the man drives her to Lesbianism and the practice of rubbing labia against labia. This will bring on an orgasm and satisfy her urge. All that is needed to put such a woman on the road to normal sexual behaviour is a resourceful gay deceiver who can offer her every imaginable kind of performance until he can see where her choice lies and what sort of coitus will meet her sexual needs and then serve her accordingly.

To illustrate, we have all seen a hen who has had no contact with a cock for some time play the cock on other hens and mount them and actually crow like a cock. Yet when such a bird meets a cock, hears him crow, and experiences natural treading, she will revert to type, her crowing will cease, and no longer will she tread a hen. In exactly the same way I have seen a notorious Lesbian with an overtly masculine voice give up her habit on marriage and acquire feminine traits.

Another reason for Lesbianism is ignorance of the sweetness of true coitus and an unawareness of what it really has to offer. Where this is the cause of a woman's trouble, she will be quick to grasp the proper way of doing things and very soon get back on the right road. There is in fact a story about a Lesbian who, once she had seen a man's penis, exclaimed, "To think that for this last twenty years I've been beating on my door with the palm of my own hand when there is a knocker like this about!"

Another reason for Lesbianism is its value as a contraceptive measure for the sort of woman who has an aversion to children. At the same time it safeguards her against the risk of scandal. And so she turns to Lesbianism as a substitute for the more usual ways of satisfying her urge. Then there is the woman who starts her life as a Lesbian by helplessly submitting to another who is too strong a character for her to resist and deludes her with glowing tales of the pleasures of tribadism.[2] And so, once having tasted the delight of the experience, she goes on in the same way and wants only to do the same thing with some other woman because she craves the delight she now knows. She then develops the habit of knocking her partner up in just the same way as a catamite[3] who, once having been knocked up, never again cares for anything but sodomy.

The second kind of Lesbianism is found in the sort of woman whose natural disposition is perverted. This phenomenon shows

[2] "Tribadism" (from the Greek *tribas* "a woman who practises 'pounding', 'grinding', 'rubbing', with another woman") is a more accurate translation of the Arabic *siḥāq* "pounding", "grinding" than "Lesbianism" (from the name of Sappho of Lesbos, whose vice is also known as "Sapphism").

[3] A catamite is defined in the *Shorter Oxford English Dictionary* (Third ed., 1970) and the *Oxford Illustrated Dictionary* (1962) as "a boy kept for homosexual purposes" and "a boy kept for homosexual practices", respectively. In the present translation, however, it will, for the sake of convenience, also be used in the sense "a boy or young man used for unnatural purposes".

itself right from childhood. A girl like this will compete with men, imitate them, and scorn submission to them. She will be the sort of girl who will refuse to couple with a male, despise the penis, refuse to yield to a man's advances, become as jealous as men of other women and protect her partners. She may well end up by copulating with catamites, changing places with them and getting an erection.[4] Some people say that such women are able to get an erection by means of some kind of organ under the clitoris like a cock's comb. But this is not so. All there is there is the fine bone which lies above the point where the penis should go in[5] and is very much the same sort of thing as the bone in the nose. What the woman does in this case is to put this part between the legs of her passive partner and rub it up and down. When she does so, they both experience a delight far beyond anything that natural copulation can produce. But the woman, who is the active partner, experiences the greater sensation, for when she rubs up against the parts of her passive partner her clitoris juts out like an infant's penis except that it is long and not so thick. From this performance the two partners derive, as I have said, a far more delightful sensation than that experienced

[4] The erection referred to is that of the clitoris, which is the rudimentary analogue of the penis and accordingly enters into erection when sexually stimulated. In the normal woman, however, it is far too small to be used penetratively. In the average British woman the clitoris is only a little over 1 cm., expanding to no more than 2 cm. in erection, and it will only be of any reasonable size (about 5 cm., say) in hermaphrodites or other persons presenting signs of trans-sexualization. In some races it may be *relatively* large and be a focus of great sexual sensation, and for this reason infibulation —so-called "female circumcision", but more properly amputation of whole or part of the clitoris and stitching together of the labia—has long been a common, but cruel and often dangerous practice in the Nilotic Sudan. Fatalities and serious illness following the operation, performed by unskilled and ignorant women in unhygienic circumstances, have in the past prompted legislation to put an end to infibulation, but it still goes on in some parts and among certain strata of society.

[5] Anatomically, this is termed the "symphysis pubis". In some women who are not naturally well-padded, this bony prominence can cause a man discomfort during intercourse. Moreover, if the junction of the two bones which form the symphysis by fusion has taken place at an angle (as the result of a bone disease or some other contingency), the prominence can jut outwards quite markedly and be used to good effect by a Lesbian.

in normal coition. If a man's penis finds the same spot in a woman, it will also protrude to meet it,[6] and the truth of what I have said will be proved by the ecstasy the man will feel as she gives herself to him in complete abandon.

Sometimes a Lesbian will draw blood from a catamite's orifice as she is copulating with him, so that he actually imagines that it is some secretion from her vulva. But the truth is that the sensation is just the result of abrasion produced by the roughness of her pubic hair and the friction of her parts against his in this tender spot.[7]

In her practice of tribadism a Lesbian behaves with her partner in much the same way as a man does with a woman—she hugs, kisses, embraces, uses the sideways positions, squats between her legs with her thighs against her belly and her arms around her knees, and so on. The only thing they don't do is to perform from the back. A Lesbian will only adopt this method in copulating with a catamite.[8]

If a Lesbian of this kind ever couples with a man and conceives, it will not be because of any passion she has for relations with men in general; it will be because she has developed affection for that particular man and finds delight in him alone because of that affection or because it suits a purpose that she will achieve through him and makes copulation with him gratifying for that purpose alone.

A Lesbian once wrote a letter to a respectable sort of girl in

[6] This is something of an exaggeration. What happens is that the woman, once sexually excited, will do her best to press the clitoris hard against the penis or pubic bone of her partner.

[7] As is well known, the anus is an erogenous zone which, if titillated, is capable of providing voluptuous sensations. The blood drawn by the Lesbian is easily comprehended: a rough and bony pubic prominence would very quickly abrade the tender mucous membrane of the anus. The term "draw blood" may also conceivably be taken in the sense of "cause suppuration". A catamite's anus and rectum would be very subject to inflammatory conditions producing a mucous discharge such as one often finds in cases of piles. The latter condition would scarcely be helped by unnatural uses of this part of the body.

[8] In the frustrating conditions of the harem, catamites and eunuchs would often play the part of a Lesbian for a woman who had no access to mature or uncastrated men.

which she sent the following message introduced by the verses I quote:

> "My life I would gladly give for you! So see what I
>   write in this note of mine and take it well to heart.
> May fortune never treat you ill! What I have to say
>   you may reveal or keep it to yourself—it matters not.
> If you think my words are sound, then act upon them if
>   you will; otherwise ignore them.

"Betake yourself to one who dearly desires you and is the soul of discretion—so that I may show you a slave-girl. I am that slave-girl—a girl as beautiful as you and no less perfect. I have hair as black as charcoal, a soft bosom and swelling breasts, largish bottom, slenderish waist, a vulva bulging like the forehead of a hornless bull[9]—a girl graceful, lissome, flirtatious, craving love. These verses bear on Lesbian love:

> A girl who is slender, not clumsy and flabby, will show
>   you how to rub and grind.
> So quickly come and lose no time in savouring true delight.
> And then you'll know that all I say about the joy that
>   Lesbians feel is right.
> How wretched and unhappy the vagina that a penis
>   splits!
> It loses all the ecstasy that another girl can give and
>   entails, to boot, the infamy and shame
>   that fall on girls who lie with men.

"The game of love may well repel you, whether it be played with a man or with another girl, but at least you must confess that the second of these options is the lesser of two ills. The second is a moderate course to take, the first an excess. The one is a blameless act in law, while the other is proscribed.[10] I have

---

[9] See *The Perfumed Garden* (Spearman, 1963), p. 188: "Some women have this sort of vulva, which is very large, with a pubis prominent like a projecting, fleshy forehead." On the same page Nafzawi speaks of a plump woman whose "vulva stands out like the head of a calf".

[10] In Islamic law unlawful intercourse between a man and a woman

given you advice, so act upon it. I must see you are not disgraced.

Her more respectable friend wrote back in the following vein:

> "Your note which I hold in high regard has reached me.
>   So dear are you, my friend, that I would gladly give
>   my life for you.
> I grasp the meaning of the words you write and all that
>   you explain in prose and poetry.
> Now you, who are to me the dearest friend in all the
>   world—may I always have your counsel—just give
>   an ear to me.
> Be fair to me and don't be silly.

"I am surprised, dear friend—may God prosper and uplift you!—that you so thoughtlessly reproach me, that you are unfairly importunate, that you overstep the mark in speaking as you do and describe my way of life as wrong. You regard your own caprice as respectable, lawful and moderate and something to be proud of. You illustrate your point with examples and quotations. You harass me with arguments for your case and persist in showing me your way. You have strayed from the straight and narrow path and invite me to do something of which I disapprove in the same way as you disapprove of the course of my choice. I shall now answer your case point by point so that you will come to know that those very things which make tribadism attractive to you make normal coitus desirable to us, and that

---

(*zinā*: intercourse between persons who are neither husband and wife nor master and slave-concubine) is a heinous offence proscribed and sanctioned by punishment in the Koran. The more severe penalty for the offence is lapidation, i.e. stoning to death (in the case of a free person who has concluded and consummated a valid marriage with a free partner, but see below Ch. V n. 72 p. 129), the lesser being 100 lashes for persons outside the last mentioned category (for a slave this penalty is halved). Because of the severity of the penalties, the requirements of Islamic law with regard to proof and witnesses are so exacting as to make conviction of the offence very difficult indeed. Many modern systems of penal law in Muslim countries have modified the sanctions. It is worth noting here that in Islamic law there is no concept of adultery since a woman has no exclusive right to the person of her husband. Moreover, the woman's offence is only punishable as a crime against religion.

those things which make your pawing so charming to you make men's embraces so charming to us. Inkpots without pens are no use, nor can a filly be held in check without a bit on the bridle. The palm is the best of trees, and fresh ripe dates the sweetest fruit.[11] The pen interprets the feelings of the heart, and no mill-stone is turned without an axle through its centre. No collops roast without skewers, no sails rise without a mast. Without a stick no eyeblack can be applied to the eyes, without a fire no oven will roast. And so this mortar of ours is designed for their pestle; our clean-shaven hill of Venus[12] for their smooth-tipped stave; this expandable fissure for their unyielding rod; this pierced hole for their penetrating length; this noble portion of our bodies for their exalted verge; this plaintive part of us for that of theirs which sheds its flowing tears; this denizen of darkness for their bold adventurer; this levelled pathway waiting calmly to be trod by a lively traveller striding out uphill—this is indeed our answer to all men's prayers. On this theme take the following lines of mine:

> Say to a girl who prefers the cleft, 'Cleft on cleft is a
>   barbarous thing!'
> In the penis she found happiness, but then she wandered
>   from the right and proper path.

"I am ready to forgive you without any reproaches, for you have condemned that of which you have no knowledge and pro-scribe that of which you have no experience. If a man has never tasted honey or had a whiff of camphor, he has no appreciation of their true worth or excellence. Were that which *you* proscribe

[11] The point here is that the palm is a sexual species and the female can only bear fruit if fertilized by the male.
[12] Translating the Latin term *mons Veneris*. This is the pubic prominence which is the cushion of fat above the vulva and which is covered with hair after puberty. It is customary for Muslim women to shave the pubis, com-plete depilation being the rule (see pp. 141 ff. below for further details). This practice is originally connected more with hygiene and ritual cleanliness than with the ugliness of body hair. In the Middle Ages returning Crusaders brought back the practice to Europe, and for a time it was fashionable amongst the aristocracy.

not universally accepted as the most exquisite pleasure, no woman would ever wish to experience it again after all the discomforts of lochial discharges[13] or ever return after bearing a child to indulge in the same fancy again.

"As for men, we find that there is not one who will not stint himself to lavish his substance on his bride. Suffice it only to take the case of any lover of time past. There have been those lovers who lost their reason, lovers who lost their family, lovers who took their own lives in grief, lovers who died of pain and chagrin, passion and anguish. Do you suppose that they fell in love merely to lose their senses? Or gave their affection to lose their lives? Never! How wrong you would be to think so! Oh no! they were denied what they strove to attain; their hopes were deferred, and they lost their reason; they were debarred access to their hearts' desires and were consumed with the flames of passion; they tasted the sweetness of love and yearned the more; they beheld their beloved and burst with helpless rage; they burned with the flame of passion. And so each lover in his turn became enraptured or mad, crazy or dazed; each pined or wasted, wept or moaned. And yet all of them persisted all the more in the pursuit of their desire and struggled long and hard to unite their bodies with those of the women they loved.

"It is a well-known fact and universally agreed that in all the world there is no delight more pleasurable than that of union between a man and a woman. My dear friend, in all the world there is nothing quite so odd as fire taking pride in fire. You have described a girl to me and invited me to have her to my bed, but, let me now assure you, my alternative is better. Questions like this are not solved by correspondence but by open discussion. But if your desire is sexual pleasure, then slip some man's penis between those lips that lie between your legs. Now I have in mind for you a good-looking and well-built young man with a winning smile, alluring eyes, and considerable culture and talents—a most desirable boy. He is as smooth as ebony; his temples are as those of a bride; his cheek is as radiant as your very

---

[13] Vaginal discharges after labour. During the first few days the discharge is sanguineous, but from about the seventh day the flow is whitish.

own; in build he is as slim and lithe as you. He is as the poet says:

> Subtle in coquettish ways, astonishingly handsome, a
> man of charming traits, pleasant, easy-going,
> A noble soul with a healthy appetite for bedding,
> ever-willing to oblige,
> Of radiant countenance and winsome smile, of pleasant
> ways and slender build.
> Jovial and jolly, exquisite to lie with, not one to take
> to quarrelling with those he falls in love with.
> A man he is of splended stature and mellifluous
> speech, a man as comely as the moon at full,[14] whose
> ardour for the couch is never quenched,
> Strong, patient, affectionate and jealous of his darling,
> yet a tyrant with his burning wand.[15]
> Effortlessly five times he'll copulate, then five times
> more press on and take it in his stride.
> Come on now! welcome such a man. Away with your
> other pastime! Away with Lesbian love!
> Keep well away from that, for such love is utter vice.
> Come, give me your ear—don't turn aside and you will
> see that all I say is right.

"Dear friend of mine, don't think I'm taking liberties—I'm only making a suggestion such as you have made to me; I'm confiding in you as you've confided in me. If the thought I put before you is to your fancy, take it for what it is in the spirit in which it is given. But, if you opt for Lesbian love, then fare you well!"

With this she sent her friend a present of a citron which had grown in such a way that it looked like a woman's parts with a penis set within, and on it she wrote these words:

> When I beheld this gift, dear lady, these words I spoke,
> "More than anyone alive this charming friend of
> mine deserves this most.

[14] The full moon is the conventional Arab image for a beautiful face whether of a girl or a boy.

[15] i.e. in a state of sexual excitement with penis erect and hot, he imposes his will without any restraint.

Here is a vulva like a fire whose flame rises in the
   centre like a penis. Consider well and learn.
A vulva such as this lies in the centre of a girl I
   know who is more lovely than the moon,
   a girl of fair complexion, sweet-scented just like
   musk—the loveliest of comely girls."[16]

The Lesbian replied in the following vein:

"You have made me a present of a citron that glitters
   like gold and diffuses the scent of perfumed amber.
For me it has a beauty all its own—its adornment is a
   cleft unharmed by the thrust of a verge.[17]
Were there anything so beautiful as this, God would
   not have made of it an ornament for trees."[18]

Once a girl of normal inclinations portrayed a young man
coupling with a slave-girl whose legs he had parted above her.
This she sent to a Lesbian with these verses inscribed beneath:

"This, I swear to God, is the manner I prefer! No Lesbian
   love for me!
I have a graceful lover, and flirtation and coquetry are
   the very games for me.
I have a lover who strikes at a woman's heart with
   glances that fly like arrows straight and true."[19]

[16] The girl in question is her Lesbian friend, and the suggestion to the
latter is that she take a lesson from the mis-shapen citron—a fruit somewhat
resembling a lemon—in which the pointed extremity had obviously been
telescoped into the body of the fruit.

[17] What is meant here is that no real penetration has taken place since the
citron's peel is intact and that in actual fact the fold with its protrusion
resembles a vulva with its clitoris.

[18] The idea is that if there had been anything to equal this particular
citron's beauty, God would not have made it—the citron—the wonder of
nature that it is, but would have put the other creation there instead.

[19] In Arabic poetry the comparison of the beloved's glances to arrows is a
commonplace.

> He is graced with a forelock black as night and a blaze
>   like the crescent moon
> And a stature like a stave whose beauty is its straight
>   unbending form.
> He is my source of comfort, the height of my desire, and
>   for him I'd give my life and all that I possess!
> By what I say I hope to stir your heart, so take me not
>   to task for what I do.

In her reply the Lesbian drew a picture of a slave-girl locked in love with her, she lying on the top with her parts between the slave-girl's vulval lips. To the picture she appended the following lines:

> My source of happiness is a soft-skinned girl whose
>   beauty lies in her cheeks and a mole
> Like a spot of musk that glistens on the crescent moon.[20]
> She'll flash you a smile from a mouth clean and fresh,
>   a smile adorned with pearls—
> The moisture of her mouth is sweet and fresh to those
>   who care to taste it.[21]
> Between her legs a fissure lies as pretty and alluring as
>   the neck of some gazelle.
> And when her beauty was first laid bare to me I said
>   what I felt in my heart:
> "Praise be to Him who has moulded such beauty from
>   the driest clay
> And so created a shapely creature fashioned from
>   loveliness itself!"
> My night was one of sucking at her mouth and throat,
> And if to love a girl in such a way is sinful, to love a
>   man's unlawful.[22]

---

[20] The cosmetic value of the mole has long been known in Europe, where there can be few who are not familiar with the beauty-spot, or small patch placed on the face as a foil to the complexion. Sometimes silver nitrate was used to create a more durable black spot.

[21] The flashing smile, the intoxicating, healing or soothing power of the beloved's saliva are commonplaces of Arabic poetry.

[22] That is to say, if Lesbianism is a vice, at least it is not proscribed as a crime against religion as illicit intercourse wth men is (see p. 24, n. 10).

Abu Nuwas writes:

> What sense is there in tribadism? None—I know that
>   game full well!
> It's fat rubbed up by fat, and nothing more.[23]
> And rub as one may, when down to bare skin, there's
>   nothing to rise in response.
> There's no wicked shaft that is smooth at the tip to
>   drive itself home and sink into place.

Another poet says on this same theme:

> God's curse on that foolish red flower![24] It has led
>   ladies of honour and repute into shameful and
>   scandalous ways.
> They have stirred up a war in which there are no arms—
>   just shields against shields nothing more![25]

I myself have written:

> They were taken aback by her Lesbian ways and asked,
>   "What pleasure can open wounds[26] desire from one
>   another?"
> "Her poor little fissure," I said, "is sick and needs the
>   soothing balm of a man's embrace."

[23] The reference is to the cushion of fat on the *mons Veneris*.
[24] i.e. the vulva. Cf. *Perfumed Garden*, p. 196: "As to her vulva, it was
white ... the centre of it was red ..."
[25] The male member is compared to an active, or offensive, weapon, the
female to a passive, or defensive, shield.
[26] That is to say, what satisfaction can one vulva expect from another?

CHAPTER II

On Sodomy and the Tricks of Sodomites, their Love for Boys and their Preference for Boys over Good-looking Girls

Nowadays a boy who prostitutes himself is known as an 'ilq, a term which normally denotes an object that is greatly treasured and jealously guarded—in other words "a precious thing".[1] Now, some fraudulent character who makes a show of mystical piety will approach a lad, pinch his nose, pull his lips and boldly and unashamedly accost him with the words, "Ah, my precious one." Then if the lad yields and gives him a little encouragement, the man will quickly seize the opportunity and have his way with him.[2] But if the boy snubs him or rounds on him or is apprehensive of the outcome of his evil intentions or shows his displeasure, the fraudulent mystic will desist, sigh, and, shaking his head, say, "Ah, it seems you don't know what 'precious one' ('ilq) means or what it is. The word denotes a person

---

[1] In order to understand this opening paragraph it is important to realize that there is word-play which cannot be brought out so easily in translation. In Arabic every primary concept is linked to basic consonants—in most cases three—which form what we call the "root". In this case the root letters are 'LQ, which convey the notion of "attachment".

[2] Rasputin was not a phenomenon peculiar to Czarist Russia: the exploitation of religious sentiment for personal ends is as old as religion itself. In medieval Islam the respect gained by genuine Sufis (mystics) of deep devotion and profound spirituality was only too frequently abused by scoundrels who, donning the garb of holiness and poverty, moved easily among all strata of society and took short cuts to ecstasy that were far from religious.

who continually holds fast to[3] the mercy of Almighty God. My old Mentor[4]—may God have mercy on his soul—used to say, "A handsome countenance denotes that the Creator cares for those who are blessed with one. He for whom the Creator cares is beloved by His creature, and he whom such a creature loves is shown thereby to have the Creator's love, and he whom the Creator loves will hold fast (*ta'allaq*) to the mercy of Almighty God. He, then, who holds fast to the mercy of God is an *'ilq.*" The "mystic" will then go his way crying, "O God, make me one of those who hold fast to Thee!"

Many great rulers of old, to say nothing of men of culture and letters, poets and other great men in all walks of life, have had a penchant for boys and become known far and wide for their passionate love affairs with them. They have described their loves at length in verse and, on wings of song, have spread abroad the story of their passions. The captain of them all and grand master of their craft was, despite his exalted position, his grandeur and high-ranking office, Yahya ibn Aktham, the judge. It is he who said:

> Food and catamites and wine are all that life is made of.
> If the truth of this eludes you, your life is not worth living.

The story goes that the secretary Burdan, who was a handsome young man, was once writing something for Judge Yahya when the latter pinched him on the cheek. Blushing with embarrassment, the lad flung down his pen. At this Yahya turned to him and said, "Pick up your pen and write as I dictate." So Burdan did as he was bid, and the judge dictated as follows:

> O beauty that you are! I nipped your face, and angrily
> you started back in pride.

---

[3] Here the idea of "attachment" inherent in the root 'LQ is brought out in its derivative *muta'aLLiQ.*

[4] In Arabic "*shaykh*" (whence the English "Sheikh", often with a different sense). In organized Sufism (Islamic mysticism) the Shaykh (Pīr, or *Murshid* in Persia and India) is the personality arround which his particular fraternity revolves. He has absolute authority over his disciples in spiritual and secular matters.

Now, if you have no taste for nips and bites, don't go
unveiled about the market streets.[5]

Be not so fetching with those locks about your temples;
don't let them form a scorpion curl above those
cheeks of yours.[6]

For, by so doing, you only do to death a soul who
longs for you; you only tempt a lover all the more
and leave in torment the Lord Justice of Islam.

According to another version he said:

O ink-well never entered by the pen! O earth as yet
untrodden by my foot![7]

The Caliph Ma'mun once teased Yahya by throwing up a
poet's lines about him. "Who," he asked, "is the author of the
verse that runs, 'A judge who enforces sanctions for adultery,
but sees no harm in sodomites'?" To which he got the answer,
"The man who said, 'No end to injustice can I see while some
descendant of 'Abbas rules over this community.'[8]" "I was only
teasing you," said Ma'mun.

One day Yahya went to visit Ma'mun, and when he reached
the centre of the courtyard he saw some youths indulging in
behaviour which really took him aback. "Had it not been for
you," he cried, "we would have been Believers!"[9] Whereupon
one of them rejoined, "Was it we who kept you from the Guidance after it had reached you? No, it is you who were sinners."[10]

---

[5] Like a woman, he should wear a veil to conceal his tempting beauty. The
judge, Yahya ibn Aktham, was a friend of the Caliph Ma'mun and died in
847.

[6] What we would call a kiss-curl is regarded as a mark of beauty. In Arabic
literature it was often compared to the curl in a scorpion's tail.

[7] In Arabic the verb "to tread" also means "to copulate" with a woman in
the same way as in English it is used with reference to cock birds.

[8] The Caliph Ma'mun (813–33) was a member of the Abbasid dynasty, which
takes its name from the line of 'Abbas, uncle of the Prophet. It is with
Baghdad that this dynasty was most closely associated.

[9] Koran (Fluegel ed., 1883/repr. 1965), xxxiv, 30.

[10] Ibid., 31

Ma'mun heard this exchange and asked Yahya the story. "Oh," came the answer, "I was a little stuck over a point in my study of the Holy Book but I have just been enlightened." Ma'mun smiled and took the point.

In Ma'mun's time there was a man who claimed to be a prophet, and one day the Caliph said to Yahya, "Come on, let's go in disguise and have a look at this fellow. We may find he's got something worth hearing." So off they went and, once in his house, Ma'mun seated himself on the man's right hand and Yahya on the left. "Are you a prophet?" asked Ma'mun. "I am," said the man. "Then what miracle can you work in support of your claim?" asked the Caliph. "Well," said the fellow, "I can do no better than tell you that just before you arrived the Archangel Gabriel appeared to me with the message, 'Two visitors are about to call on you. One will sit on your right and the others on your left. The one who will sit on your left is the greatest sodomite God ever created.' " He had of course recognized them. Ma'mun just burst into laughter and said "I bear witness to the truth of what you say." Those were his very words, and with that they both left.

On another occasion when Yahya was with the Caliph Wathiq, there was one of the serving boys there who was extremely good-looking. Yahya stared at the lad and smiled. Whereupon Wathiq turned to Yahya and said "Kishkanat" which is a distorted form of the question in Arabic,[11] "Have you been up him?" "Yes, indeed," came the answer. "Just once, that's all."

Some person or other once asked the question, "What are the most pleasurable things in life?" The answer he got was, "A yellow garment, red wine, and a boy with the eyes of a houri."[12]

Contrasting boys with the opposite sex, Abu 'Anbas once remarked, "A boy is less troublesome and more helpful. With a boy there is no danger of truculent turbulence or guile, nor does

---

[11] The word is evidently some kind of acrostic. The Caliph Wathiq reigned 842–47.

[12] Houri: a nymph of the Islamic Paradise and therefore voluptuously beautiful.

one run the risk of the full rigour of the law or of lapidation.[13] When you are alone, he is a good boon-companion; when you have boon-companions, he is an old friend, and when you have to travel, he is a good helper and a servant."

Among the best known practitioners of the art of sodomy we have Abu Nuwas[14] whose poems on the subject abound. It has been said, however, that his interest in women was actually his strongest passion and that he was fonder of them than of boys. It is Mubarrad's view that there is a certain class of poets who convey of themselves an impression that this is the very reverse of what they are seen to be. For instance, Ibn Hazim was notorious for his cupidity, yet he specialized in poems on the theme of peace and contentment with a simple life and actually identified himself with such. There was also Abu 'Atahiya, who wrote ascetic verse and dispraised the world, but was nevertheless a very dubious Muslim. Yet another example is Ibn Abi Hakima the Secretary, who went out of his way to stress his impotence in verse, yet there was no one who copulated more than he except Ibn Mu'tazz. Again, there was Jahshawayh, who exhausted all his literary talent on descriptions of youths who play the passive role and spoke of himself as such, yet he was a greater bugger than a bear.[15] Finally, we come back to Abu Nuwas. Here is a man who writes passionate poems on boys and recklessly depicts himself as a sodomite. Yet what a man he was for the women! Here are some examples of his verse:

> By God, a slap from the hand of a smooth-faced boy—
>   a slap that will crack my eye and jaw—
> Is a greater delight than a musk-filled apple from the
>   hands of a coy, young belle!

[13] See Chapter I, n. 10. Islam did not allow pederasty, however (see below n. 20).

[14] One of the most famous of all Abbasid poets, Abu Nuwas (c. 747–813) was regarded by the Arab critics as the doyen of the "modernist" school of classical literature. He was exceptionally gifted, but his name has become synonymous with pederasty because of his frank and realistic poems.

[15] The bear is proverbial for its lust.

Again:

> Make for smooth-faced boys and do your very best to
> mount them, for women are the mounts of devils!

The following lines are also his:

> Those who go up boys I'll truly love, but those who go
> up whores shall have my hate.
> No decent young fellow—nor even a man in mid-life
> with a head full of dye—would go up a strumpet girl.

He also wrote:

> I set my heart on a whore—how many a hope is doomed!
> —but, when I saw her, I said, "Quick! Cover your
> face with your veil.
> Go hire me a boy and be off and do your job with
> someone else. No finger of mine will I put in a hole
> where a scorpion lurks!"[16]

Now Abu Nuwas married a woman whom he deserted on the
very night of their marriage, and upon his departure he left the
following lines:

> O you who are dressed for your wedding night, abandon
> hope! Be on your way, you're now divorced.[17]

[16] Scorpions tend to conceal themselves in crevices and strike at any unwary
intruder. I have been told by a doctor that he once treated a patient who was
drying his penis against a wall after urination when a scorpion unexpectedly
struck out and stung his penis. (The custom of drying the penis after urination
is a practice connected with ritual cleanliness—on which see below, p. 56
n. 40.—and is dealt with by Tournefort in A Voyage into the Levant, II, 49
(London 1718): "When they make water, they squat down like women, for fear
some drops of urine should fall into their breeches. To prevent this evil, they
squeeze the part very carefully, and rub the head of it against a wall ...".)

[17] In the first half of this verse we have a reference to the customary recep-
tion by the bridegroom of his sumptuously dressed and heavily made-up bride.
This would often be their first meeting unless, as was often the case, they
were cousins and had known each other as children. As regards the divorce

There's many a good lass like you who tried her luck
    with me, I'm not one to trade gazelles[18] for hares!
No, menses and the sort that shed them have no charm
    for me. Another mount, more to my desire than you,
    I'll find.
Yes, now—if you lust as I do and act according to my
    rules, then give a cooling cup to me.
Not willingly will I poke inside a crevice, for I fear
    snakes and scorpions![19]

Among the poet's outrageous lines are these:

Follow Abu Nuwas in his recklessness and beat him at
    his game just as, and how, you will
Let not fear stand in the way of delight lest you be the
    first to deny Muhammad's prophethood.[20]
May the manhood of the jinn brought forth on the
    Day of Reckoning be measured in terms of a catamite's
    rump.[21]

mentioned in the second half of the line, the husband could, if he chose not to consummate the marriage, pronounce a definite (as opposed to a revocable) repudiation.

[18] In Arabic literature women of extraordinary beauty are regularly compared to gazelles. Even in the West, the gazelle is renowned for the softness of its eyes and the grace of its movements.

[19] See n. 16 above.

[20] According to tradition, Muhammad loved three things above all others: the ritual Prayer, women, and perfume (see opening paragraph of Chapter III). The point in this verse would seem to be that to condemn sexual pleasure would be to condemn the Prophet. Or else it could be an oblique reference to the boys of eternal youth who are to wait on the Faithful in Paradise (Koran, lvi, 17 f.). Whatever the true interpretation of the verse, it must be stressed that only lawful heterosexual pleasure was approved by Muhammad since there is specific condemnation of homosexual relations between males in Koran, vii, 79 f.

[21] In orthodox Islam the *jinn* (singular *jinnī*, whence the "genie" of Aladdin's lamp) are bodies consisting of smokeless flame and are an order of imperceptible beings lower than the angels. They are, however, capable of assuming different shapes. Like men, they will be called to account on the Day of Judgement and, according to works, some will be sent into Paradise, while others will be thrown into hell-fire. In Arabic literature and folklore there are numerous tales of love affairs between jinn and human beings. The meaning of the present verse would appear to be: when on the Last Day the

Even more scandalous are the following lines:

> O the joy of sodomy! So now be sodomites, you Arabs.
>   Turn not away from it—therein is wondrous pleasure.
> Take some coy lad with kiss-curls twisting on his
>   temple and ride him as he stands like some gazelle
>   standing to her mate.
> —A lad whom all can see girt with sword and belt,
>   not like your whore who has to go veiled.[22]

Some other poet writes:

> Listen, my fool, to a word of advice from a friend who
>   pities you:
> Taste not a vulva, be it as sweet as a nut;
> A clean-shaven vulva is no match for a hairy anus.[23]

Adherents of this cult of sodomy have different reasons for their predilection. There are those who follow medical opinion and argue that sexual union with boys is less harmful to health than coitus with women. They say that homosexuality imposes less strain on the body and is less apt to be followed by the harmful effects that result from coitus with the opposite sex. This opinion is shared by rulers, men in high places and all well-to-do persons who are concerned to keep their bodies fit and take care of their persons.

Others there are who retain boys as servants to see to their needs when they are travelling or journeying away from home. These boys are constantly in their company, and when they are alone and in close contact with them, they are impelled by their sexual urge to have intercourse with them, especially when they are relaxing or are alone with them in bath-houses or when they

jinn are judged, let the criterion of their manliness be the extent of their homosexual activities.

[22] Cf. Genesis, xxxviii, 15: "When Judah saw her, he thought her to be an harlot; because she had covered her face." It is interesting to note that at the present day whores of Baghdad cover their faces.

[23] See above Ch. I, n. 12.

are drinking in company or are in a state of intoxication which induces an awareness of the charms, grace, suppleness and fine deportment of a stripling.

Others use boys because they are reluctant to beget children or to bear the responsibility of a family or because they fear the disgrace of having daughters.[24] There are also those who like to lord it over boys, use the sexual act to assert their superiority over them and force them into submission and experience a sense of superiority by so doing.

Abu Nuwas says:

> Rape the boy who is your father's sister's son and the
>   son of your mother's brother and your mother's
>   sister's son
> And anyone else that is in the house at the moment you
>   are there. Rape him and devour his substance!

One of my own pleasantries on this same theme runs thus:

> There are three sorts you simply must ride to give
>   comfort to your heart:
> The arrogant to humble him, the catamite for pleasure,
>   the jealous to bring him to book.

The following lines are also mine:

> If only those who censure me were fair, they'd see that
>   laying boys is only right and proper.
> Instead, with haughtiness and frowns they greet me.
> But I know how to strip whores' sons of haughtiness.

---

[24] In desert life female progeny was not welcome amongst the Arabs because a girl could not contribute to the fighting force of a tribe and could in fact be an economic burden as well as a military impediment. The prejudice against girls was carried over into urban civilization, and one of the reasons for its survival may well have been the fear that a daughter's sexual misconduct might expose a family to shame and dishonour. Even to this day, the birth of a son is, in most Muslim circles, more welcome than that of a daughter, though it should not be supposed that daughters are unloved by their parents.

Again, I am the author of the next two lines:

> I'll have my cup from a lad of gazelle-like grace with
>   houris' eyes, dark lips and down just sprouting
>   round his mouth and temples,
> And then I'll rape him and strip him of his manhood!
>   To vanquish a victor is the only source of pride.[25]

I also composed the following:

> "Leave the boys alone," they say, "and ride them no
>   more. Sodomy is a vicious trait."
> But I reply, "I have an organ with ambition—it just
>   won't let me mount a girl."

A muezzin—so the story goes—was once caught red-handed laying a Christian lad in a mosque. "Shame on you!" they cried. "How could you do such a thing in a mosque?" "I am out to earn a reward in heaven," he protested. "Have you never heard the word of God in the Koran: 'Neither tread they any place of treading, thereby enraging the infidels, nor make they any gain from some foe but some righteous deed is lodged to their account in Heaven.'[26] So," he went on, "what place of treading[27] is there that can enrage the infidels more than a mosque? What gain more satisfying can there be than submitting an enemy to your sexual will?"

Then there is the sodomite who will take to boys to have old debts repaid. Let me explain my meaning. As a boy he will have served his apprenticeship under some pederast, and, once grown up, he will have no thought of anything but boys and enter the craft his master practised; for a pupil who follows in his master's steps will be best versed in and most knowledgeable about the intricacies and secrets of his teacher's art and have a

---

[25] In other words, he has vanquished me with his beauty, but now I will vanquish him, and to vanquish a victor is an achievement to be proud of.

[26] Koran, ix, 121.

[27] There is a play on the word "tread", which also means "copulate". See n. 7 of the present chapter. The Koran is, of course, quoted wholly out of context and the sense there is "tread".

keener eye than others when it comes to breaking in lads who prove difficult to handle. He will be so qualified simply because of his first-hand knowledge and experience of the craft and because he will have acquired his training as a boy and thus remembered every detail. And so, in manhood he will embark on his career by practising on others what was practised on him.

Another type of sodomite is the sort who, for some purely fortuitous reason, will have had a boy and, on this single occasion, have found the experience pleasurable. The memory of that delight once tasted will spur him on to continue the practice until he has acquired the habit of it and become addicted to his vice. His motivation is the memory of the pleasure he experienced on the very first occasion that he came to know of it. It is as Abu Nuwas says:

> How many a cup will make a lad endearing if he takes a
> liking to it![28] For the last taste will ever be to him
> as sweet as he found the first.

The Vicious Practice of "Crawling"

"Crawling" is a term used to denote sexual assault on insensible persons.[29] To begin our treatment of the subject, we may tell the tale of a man who once crept on a Christian boy as he lay dozing. Just as he finishes and the lad woke up, this man recited the following lines:

> The most pleasurable form of union is that which you
> snatch in secret without interference from rival
> or watcher.[30]

[28] Or "How many a cup will conquer him who takes a liking to it."

[29] This practice is termed *dabib* in Arabic from *dabba* "to creep, crawl" of reptiles, etc. The use of wine or hashish or a combination of both was a common means of breaking down a boy's resistance, weakening his will, rendering him torpid or insensible and at the same time relaxing the anal sphincter. On the use of hashish by pederasts see F. Rosenthal, *The Herb* (Leiden, 1971), pp. 82–6. Other references to the subject may be found by consulting Rosenthal's index under the word "sex".

[30] Towards the end of the seventh century the malicious "slanderer"

Damn that Christian boy! Yet how many a boy as
    pampered as he has made himself my partner!
The twist and turn of his waist is as a supple branch
    that sways atop a sand dune.[31]
I slipped my arm around his waist just where his
    girdle rests, but he drew himself away, for he'll not
    give nor respond to love.
He denied me what I sought from him, though the
    eyes of the watcher were not on him.
But there was the orifice between his buttocks all
    laid bare for me! Oh, the delight of his softness
    and fragrance!
My urge grew strong and drove me on, and the tickle
    of my rod soon roused him.
He awakened when roused by my ejaculation, and
    with disapproval he observed what I was and how I
    had leapt upon him.
He began to revile me and point his finger at me, but
    I said, "Be kind to me, my darling."
"You have played a dirty trick on me!" he shouted,
    "You've pushed in me that wretched rod and all the
    milk it stores!"

It should be noted that a man who crawls on a woman is safer
and more secure against the consequences of his action than if
he chooses a boy; for, if a woman feels the penis inside her she
will relax and yield because she is then stirred by desire. She is
unable to push the man away because of the overwhelming urge
she has within her. We have yet to hear of a woman who removed a man's penis from her vagina out of dislike of it, or who
ever succumbed to anger in such a situation or at such a time.
There is a Tradition of the Prophet which runs: "Between their
legs they find their satisfaction."

(wāshī) and the prying "watcher" (raqīb, often translated "censor") became
conventional figures in Arabic love poetry representing the ever-present threat
of killjoys bent on the undoing of lovers. On the "watcher" as a reality see
below Chapter IV, p. 89.

[31] The slender branch swaying or shaking above a sand-hill is a convention
of Arabic poetry. The idea is that of a slim and graceful torso surmounting
plumpish thighs. Such a figure was the ideal.

If a man obsessed with the desire to crawl on lads is wise, he should confine his practice to some young boy or youth not as strong as himself. But if he cannot help himself and so crawls on someone whose resources are greater than his and is something of a risk to handle, he must be circumspect, careful and absolutely certain. Otherwise, he is walking into danger and will either get what he wants or risk a beating-up. It is imperative that a man bent on crawling on a youth who is liable to turn on him should neither give him the glad eye when sober, nor smile at him, nor should he offer him a cup of wine or anything like that, nor should he snuggle up to him when asleep. Any one of these actions will put his intended victim on his guard, and make it difficult for the sodomite to have his way when he wants it most. Moreover, if some other member of the party should crawl on the intended victim, suspicion would only fall on the one who had made the gestures, and it is he who would pay the penalty.

If the victim is sleeping off his wine, the sodomite should not go near him in either the first or the last stages of his drunken sleep; for, at the beginning he might only be half-asleep and still able to take in all that is being said in the gathering. Nor should the sodomite be misled by the extent of drunkenness he observes in his victim, for mere drunkenness will not deprive a man of his senses; he has to lapse into unconsciousness before that happens. Towards the end of the victim's sleep is also a bad time because he will be near to waking and regaining his lucidity, and the least thing will bring him to his senses. In my view the best policy is to try out the intended victim in a way that could be thought accidental. For instance, the sodomite can get up and step on him heavily as if he did not see the recumbent body. He can then fall on the lad with all his weight as though tripping over him by accident. This approach will give him an excuse, should the other wake up. But such a plan should only be adopted if there are only the two of them in the room. If others are present, he should jump up in alarm as if struck by some falling vessel, and in so doing, go out of his way to tread on the object of his attentions. If the latter does not move, he should not be deceived by his slow reaction since there are people who are relatively insensitive to pain and who, out of cunning or timidity, can bear it if they are aware that there is someone in the party out to have them by force and with confident hope of success. And so the sodomite should proceed slowly by degrees. His best approach will be to leave the lad alone while he makes preliminary tests. He can then go back to him and, taking care to keep a distance, very cautiously bare his bottom by raising his shirt. This is the first point at which trouble is liable to arise since the sleeper will quickly wake up when his clothes are pulled away from his bottom, for such will be his natural reaction. The clothes once lifted, the sodomite should take it easy for a while and wait to see what happens. If the sleeper covers himself up again, he should leave him for a short while and then come back and do the same thing again. But if the victim goes on sleeping with bottom bared, the assailant, still keeping his distance, may now apply some spittle to his anus. If the sleeper does not budge, the other should next blow on the moist spittle. Then, if the victim does not wake up under the stream of cold air on his anus he will certainly not feel the penetration of a penis, and the sodomite can be sure that he is fast asleep and well under the influence of drink. He can now get on with his business.

Now, if the lad is wearing trousers, the thing to do is to slit them just above his anus. To try to loosen the cord would be a long and tiresome chore, and the victim may well have been clever enough to knot the cord, or it could, in any case, have got tangled without the wearer's knowledge. Do just as Abu Nuwas recommends:

"Slit their trousers—don't wait to undo their cords."

If the perpetrator of this deed succeeds in attaining his end, he should neither flag in his determination to continue nor be misled by what he has so far learned of the sleeper's condition. In preparing to effect an entry he should first lay the sleeper on his side, and, lifting one of the latter's thighs, bend it as far up to the lad's belly as he can. He then brings the lad's hands together on his chest and, having set one on top of the other, clasps them tightly with one of his own hands, at the same time placing the other under and behind his victim's back. Finally, he gets his lower leg up under the lad's lower buttock as he slips his own other leg up under the thigh of that leg which he has man-oeuvred into position towards the sleeper's belly.

While about his business, he should take great care not to let his head go anywhere near his victim, for he is liable to be seized by the hair and be unable to get away. And if he has no hair, he will certainly get such a crack on the head that he will be too dazed to make good his escape. The very least that can happen is that the other party will have gained some inkling of his assailant's identity by having touched his head and either snatched a hair or felt evidence of recent shaving or something similar. And it could be that there would be no one else in the company with a shaven head, or alternatively, a head of hair. Again, the assailant might be wearing a head-cloth and let it drop in the confusion, thus leaving behind him a means of identification. Another hazard is that he could be left with scratches on his face that would expose him to scandal—unless, of course, he is an utterly shameless character who cares noth-ing for scandal or exposure and therefore needs not to bother about such precautionary measures as I have just recom-mended.[32]

Crawling is the sort of thing that can only be done when the lamps are out and there is no moonlight. Now there exists a special kit of tools for the job, and the character who developed them claims that the equipment is essential for the right results. It consists of a scroll, a waterskin, a hook, some string, dust, sumac and a pair of scissors. The scroll is rolled tight like a straight trumpet and used to blow out the lamp. Our operator next takes the waterskin or bag and blows it up until it is fully inflated. Putting his clothes over it, he leaves it in the place where he is sleeping so that the man next to him will not miss him, but think that he is still there. Another explanation of the bag, how-ever, is that the user, finding that someone has bedded down next to the boy who has taken his fancy, inserts his bag between the

---

[32] The observations in this paragraph will doubtless be of interest to historians of forensic medicine.

two bodies and blows it up so as to separate them. Each will think that the push caused by the inflated bag is coming from the person next to him and so move over. At this stage the crawler removes the bag to make room for himself.

Now to the hook. This item is fastened to the victim's bed-clothes and a thread attached to run from the place occupied by the crawler to the place where the other fellow is sleeping, the idea being that he will be able to find his way back without his falling on any of the other sleepers who might then wake up. Some offer a different explanation and say that the hook is secretly slipped into the intended victim's clothing before he beds down for the night. The hook should be as small as a needle and the thread sufficiently long for the job in hand. The crawler will then find his way in the dark.

The dust is for sprinkling on the sleeping man's eyelids so that, should he wake up, his attention will be diverted from his assailant. Another view, however, is that the reason for the dust is this: the crawler, finding the sleeper on his back, sprinkles the dust on his face so that he cannot but turn on his side—thinking all the while that it has dropped from the ceiling.

As regards the sumac, the crawler puts a little in his mouth to stimulate a flow of saliva, which contains a lubricant that will help him to slide his penis in.[33] Finally, the purpose of the scissors is to cut the trouser cord or to snip a hole in the seat. Generally speaking, to carry things of this kind will soon expose and disgrace the owner even before he uses them. The scissors and the dust, however, are not so bad. In fact they are indispensable for anyone who makes a profession of the kind of practice in question.

According to Abu 'Anbas Saymari, a crawler once turned up at a social gathering organized by Yahya ibn Salih ibn 'Abd-ul-Quddus carrying a nose-bag slung round his shoulder. His host took a look inside and found it contained a small pillow, a cushion, dust wrapped up in one rag and fresh brains in another, a small case containing marshmallow, a wooden phallus with a

---

[33] Muslims, like Jews, are circumcised, and so penetration would be difficult without a lubricant.

smooth head, some mucilage, a ring, a pair of soft felt slippers and a small pad with a narrow tab. Ibn 'Abd-ul-Quddus ordered his men to shrink the fellow's head in a wooden press unless he declared his trade. Whereupon his prisoner came up with the answer. "Spare me and God preserve you, Emir!" he cried. "Certainly," replied the Emir, "if only you'll tell me what I ask. Tell the truth and you have nothing to worry about." "I'm a crawler," said the man, "and I use this tackle for crawling." "But," insisted the Emir, "you simply *must* tell me what you do with all these various things." "Well, I will," said the other. "When I've made up my mind to crawl on some lad and want to see how deeply he's sleeping and just how drunk he is, I fling the little pillow at him. If he wakes up I exchange some joke with him and say, 'Do allow me, my dear friend. Put this under your head.' He then thanks me for this gesture and I have absolutely nothing to fear. As for the dust here, if I find the fellow sleeping on his back, I sprinkle some on his face and he turns right over face downwards, which is just what I want. If, on the other hand, he turns on his side, I sprinkle it in his ears and he just has to turn on his face. The brains are for scattering all around him so that if he wakes up, turns nasty and comes at me, he'll slide across the floor. The soft felt slippers I use when I first make for my prey so that no one will hear my footsteps. Into this ring I pull the loose fold of his trousers covering his anus and cut it off with scissors, thereby gaining access to his bottom, which I lubricate with the marshmallow and spittle. The phallus is merely a decoy which I keep to hand for my own protection in case he wakes up at this point and makes a grab at my penis or my hand. But if all goes well, I get on with my job. Finally, I carry this little round pad with me for two reasons: firstly, I can stuff it over the lad's mouth to prevent him shouting, should he wake up, and secondly, I can press it to my own mouth if I have to sneeze."

The Emir marvelled at the craftiness of the fellow and laughed himself to the ground. He then called upon him to mend his ways and put him on oath to behave himself in the future and treated him well.

It is a sound idea not to crawl on anyone who is a member of company to which one is new or on anyone who has a retinue to protect him, even if one has the opportunity, for, even if the victim does not wake up during the act, he is certain to realize sooner or later that he has been the object of a sodomitical assault. Suspicion is then bound to fall on the newcomer, and in the long run retribution is sure to follow. On this theme Abu Nuwas writes:

> It grieved me sorely to behold it in frenzied search for
> beauteous partners in pursuit of love.
> Some slept, some dozed; but one there was who stayed
> awake to guard his sleeping wards from wolves.
> When, bewildered. I could no longer bear the strain, I
> sprang in overwhelming anguish
> At a boy who moved my passions—a boy as handsome
> as the moon, for whom I'd searched both hard and long.
> Successfully I loosed his trousers' cord and thought
> myself more cautious than a crow.
> Then, when I said, "I've got him!" with the pride of
> a drunken sot,
> He jerked himself away and cried out to his friend "By
> the Lord of the Holy Koran, I am ravished!"
> Had I not risked myself that night, my life with young
> folk would be happier now.

There is one trick which affords a crawler a greater chance of security. What he does is to take some money [in a purse] and, having assured himself that his intended victim is sleeping deeply and well under the influence of drink, he fastens it to the sleeping man's clothes. Then, proceeding with all the care and attention we have seen to be needed, he rapes the fellow. If his victim is still asleep by the time he has finished, he retrieves his money. If, however, he is unlucky enough to be caught, he rounds on the lad with the words "How dare you do this to me when you've had my money!", taking care to mention the exact amount. If the lad denies the charge on oath and then the money is found tied to him as stated, the rest of the company will think little of his word. The crawler is bound to feel ashamed of the ruse, but it will help him extricate himself.

In the company there may be someone who is plagued with the dreadful disease of sexual passivity and does not much mind being crawled on. He will pretend to be asleep and not budge when tested. But what will give him away will be his sensitive reactions, his gentle breathing and the erection of his penis during the performance. On this theme Abu Nuwas composed the following lines:

> . . . a guest awakening from his slumber to find that his
> host had crawled on him without the cupbearer's
> knowledge,
> And thrust in him the like of a black, sliding serpent,
> hard and solid, with no charmer to hold it in check.
> Yet, when his host approached him first, the other
> only stirred and turned aside and held his head
> well down while being used.
> I said to him, "You should never be caught failing in
> a way such as this and showing affection where
> none is expected."
> For I found his anus tight and his silence just the silence
> of a lad longing to be ridden.
> Had he not been wide awake, his verge would never
> have risen, nor, when being ridden, would he have
> tightly crossed his legs.

Any intelligent man who reflects on the habit of "crawling" will find that the sweetness of conquest does not make up for the bane of having to exercise great care and that to flee the immediate consequences of his actions will not repay him for the loss of reputation. Let us take, for instance, the case of Farazdaq,[34] who once stayed with a certain Bedouin. His host extended a most generous welcome to him, but when the man had gone off to sleep, Farazdaq crawled on his wife. Her husband, however, awakened and drew his sword. The poet slipped through his fingers and made good his escape. Yet for all that he could

---

[34] Renowned Arab satirist and panegyrist of the Umayyad period (d. 728 or 730). Vigorous and often obscene, his poetry is essentially Bedouin in spirit.

never shake off the disgrace, and in the long run Jarir[35] threw it up at him in one of his satires:

> Whenever you have stayed in a house of repute, your departure has been marred by disgrace and you have left a stain on your name.

The safest way for the crawler to gratify his desires is to find a willing partner and to have his co-operation in eluding detection by the guard.[36] In this connexion it should be noted that there are various types of young lad that can be tried. In the first category we may place the sons of the well-to-do who enjoy both rank and fortune. To have your way with a boy of this class is an easy matter, requiring little effort. The greatest measure of success is to be attained with those whose servants are lax. The low fellows with whom such boys mix because they are not denied their company will readily win their submission with any bit of a toy or plaything, and in this respect pigeons are the most corrupting enticement of all because they are far dearer to a boy's heart than money. By means such as these, men of this ilk will get their prey into their clutches.

Access to boys in the top stratum of society can only be attained by bribing servants to act as procurers. Tutors are also in a commanding position to have their way with them. It often happens that conflict will develop between a tutor and servants, each of them guarding their young master from the other. With assistance, however, they will succeed either in their plan to do the lad or procure him for someone else. Hammad 'Ajrad, so the story goes, was tutor to the son of a notable. At the time Abu Nuwas was forever hanging about the boy's study and accosting him. Hammad accordingly put his charge under close surveillance.

---

[35] Like Farazdaq, a classical poet (d. c. 730). Of central Arabian origin, he went to Iraq to meet his rival, Farazdaq, in Basra. He was particularly famed for his devastating satire against Farazdaq, whose scandalous ways contrasted with his own irreproachable life.

[36] For fear of seducers and sexual assailants the better classes of Muslim society would have their women and children under close surveillance. See below Chapter IV.

So Abu Nuwas wrote a note to the father and, having sealed it, asked Hammad to give it to the boy to deliver. The contents were verses advising dismissal of the tutor. They run as follows:

> Abu Fadl, do not sleep—the wolf has fallen on the sheep!
> A wicked old man is Hammad 'Ajrad, a man who burns
>   with lust.
> Between his thighs there lurks a spear sheathed in a
>   scabbard of skin,
> And if he only find the chance he'll lodge it in another
>   sheath!

As soon as Abu Fadl set eyes on these lines he relieved Hammad of his duties as mentor to his son, and the way was then clear for Abu Nuwas.

The *second* class of boys for sodomites are sons of rich merchants and their like, who are out for gain and spurred by avarice. They are a class of people enthralled by a love of money and a fascination with lucre. Anyone who so desires can reach this type without having any need of a procurer's services or needing to bribe some guardian simply because avarice and love of money predispose them to fall in with the wishes of anyone who has got the necessary wherewithal and is ready to lavish on them all they desire. Moreover, they have no difficulty in associating with the common people, frequenting the markets, and spending long hours sitting about there and mixing on intimate terms with the mob. On the contrary, they consider it a means of earning money and doing business—and that's just what they like. Anyone, therefore, who wants to have his way with them will find it easy provided he is generous with his money. It makes no difference whether he acts for himself or through an intermediary. Money will break down any barriers and pave the way for action. It has been rightly said:

> Were the right amount of money put on a tooth of iron,
>   the iron would largely melt,
> And were it put on a lion's tooth, the whole would
>   melt completely.

Speaking on the same theme, another says:

> If the lad with shining cheek draws back, smack his
> face with twice ten shining pieces.
> For were he even on a rainbow, he would drop from
> the sky for them and grovel on his belly.

With folk of the kind we are discussing do not trouble to deal in bribery. Nor will you have any need of a pimp. However, it is better not to confront a boy openly, when speaking to him, with anything likely to embarrass or startle him at the very first instant. He should not be given money without some preliminary to let him know what is desired of him. His seducer should first approach him with something that will put him at his ease, dally with him, and throw out some veiled allusions which he thinks he may be clever enough to interpret. If the boy has any aptitude for interpreting slips of the pen or tongue, one might begin by trying a somewhat tricky phrase.[37] If that fails to work something simpler can be tried. For instance, "kisses are a comfort to the heart" can be disguised in Arabic as "killing grieves the heart".[38] And so on and so forth.

The *third* class of likely lads is made up of illegitimates, artisans, down-and-outs, and orphans who have come down in the world because they have no one to care for them. Most of these will openly solicit and accost without so much as a blush of embarrassment and turn up at drinking parties fully expecting to be used for immoral purposes. Of these, some will be spoken for and stick to one particular partner provided he can compensate them for their trouble and make them independent of others. A wink or a gesture is all that is needed to attract them. One of their kind will soon follow a man who has given him the sign. Indeed, one has only to tread accidentally on such a boy's foot in

[37] The phrase is actually given in the Arabic, but it is incomprehensible because of textual corruption.

[38] In this case the desired effect is achieved by manipulation of the dots—termed diacritical marks—which differentiate Arabic consonants. In both sentences the consonantal outline of the words is the same, but the sense is altered by misplacement of the dots.

a crowd and he will follow unbeknown to one until in the end one has to ask him what he wants.

For all the degradation of these characters you will find the odd one among them who is remarkably good-looking and easily won. One can soon be taken by lads of this type because they are in the habit of showing their bodies off and wearing a skirt[39] in place of a shirt. All their physical charms can therefore be exposed to view and be there for all to see at a single glance. There are others, however, who are hard to get, difficult to make contact with and not easily procured.

Lads of all the classes mentioned above have guile and cunning which they do not hesitate to use on those who seek their favours. Some tempt a client and stimulate him for the sole purpose of defrauding him. Once they have his money, they resist his advances, put him off, and make false promises. And so he waits indefinitely for the fulfilment of his desires and spends long days and nights in hopeless expectation. What is more, a lad of this sort is apt to mock and laugh at his client if he knows that he is acting under cover, has a sense of guilt, and is afraid of the scandal. In such an event he will thrust him aside in the sure knowledge that he will not be asking him to return any money or presents he has already got his hands on.

A boy may well create trouble between two men by transferring his affections from one to the other either because of his aversion to one of them or because of a preference for the more generous of the two. This sort of thing is a very frequent cause of strife between sodomites. Then there is the type who will put himself at the disposal of some individual and, having done so, will try all sorts of dodges to make things difficult for him. He will worry and fidget and moan and groan. Unable to get his penis in, his partner will think that, not being used to it, the boy is incapable of going through with the performance and that he is making his first attempt. Anyone who is unfamiliar with

[39] In Arabic *izār*. This would be a garment somewhat like a woman's skirt running from the waist to well below the knees. It could be lifted to expose the lower part of the body. A shirt, on the other hand, would have long sleeves and cover the upper half of the body completely and, furthermore, be worn over trousers.

such types and is stupid enough to believe them will acquiesce. Accepting the lad's story, he will be content to rub his member between his thighs and ejaculate in that position without ever effecting an entry. But the shrewder type of sodomite who knows their ways will not be deluded or tricked. Nothing will satisfy him but full penetration right up to his testicles, and this he will achieve by cajolery, trickery or sheer force. Here are some of my own verses on the point:

> Let not the tightness of a catamite deceive you
>   merely because he fears a splendid staff—
> What he has there is just a travelling-bag drawn
>   tightly at the neck, or a purse with a top that expands.

If a boy, when asked for services, means well, he will do all he can to help his partner and urge him on as he wriggles on his member. On this very theme a poet says:

> Between his buttocks I thrust home, and tears streamed
>   from his eyes. "Why not drive it hard?" he cried.
> "Out of pity for you, my lad," I said, "Oh, to hell with
>   that!" he cried.

There are some boys who will squeeze their buttocks tight to hinder penetration, and anyone with a slack penis will be unable to get it in. He will be led to believe that he himself is to blame and has failed for all that the boy has given freely of himself. Only a man with a really hard staff well smeared with plenty of spittle will be able to reach his target. If, in addition, he is the kind of man who secretes prostatic fluid in erection, the boy's ruse will fail because of the rapidity with which his partner will slide inside. (The same thing will happen in coitus with a woman who, to tighten her vagina to discourage penetration, makes use of astringents such as gall.) The kind of secretion to which I refer is that known as *madhy*, a clear fluid, which will ooze without any accompanying sensation from a penis that is fully engorged and erect. It is secreted in greater or lesser quantities according to the individual. Men can secrete this fluid so profusely that they actually think, in intercourse with a woman, that it is she who is streaming. But this is not so. The emission of fluid of this kind, which is liable to occur during petting or when one thinks of sexual pleasure or is stimulated by the sight of animals copulating, does not entail the performance of the greater ablution.[40] There is a Tradition that 'Ali[41] said of himself, "I was a man given to excessive secretion of seminal fluid and therefore wanted to raise the question with the Prophet, but was too embarrassed to do so because of my marital bond with his daughter. So I asked Miqdad ibn Aswad to inquire on my behalf. This he did, and the Prophet's answer was that I need only wash my penis and perform the lesser ablution."

The story goes that once a Bedouin called on Mazini and asked him to explain the meaning of two verses which he recited. What they actually described was his penis, and they run as follows:

> The morning found me with such an intractable beast
> —Oh, what a head to control as the sticky moisture
> flowed!

[40] Presumably because there is no ejaculation. Since we are going to encounter frequent references to the ritual ablutions of Islam, it is worth our while to explain them here. Before doing so, however, we ought to note that prostatic fluid is not secreted in the great quantities indicated by Nafzawi—he is guilty of gross exaggeration.

The greater ritual ablution (ghusl) is the complete uninterrupted washing of the body in water that is ritually undefiled. In the absence of water the body may be rubbed down with fine sand. The ghusl is performed after major ritual pollutions. Sexual intercourse (in whatever manner), emission of sperm, menstruation, lochial discharges, etc. entail a state of major ritual impurity (janāba) to which certain taboos attach (a man may not, for instance, perform his ritual prayers, recite the Koran or go to the mosque, nor may he have sexual relations with a woman who, after menstruating, say, has not herself performed the ghusl). The ritual of the lesser ablution (wuḍū') is defined in Koran, v. 9: "... wash your faces and your arms up to the elbows and wipe your heads as also your feet to the ankles ..." The lesser ablution is strictly enjoined before the ritual prayers. The state of ritual impurity which calls for it is termed ḥadath and it is incurred by contact with unclean substances which soil clothing or the person (e.g. urine, sperm, fermented drink) or by the emission of any substance—even gaseous—from the anus, urethra or vagina, additional to those connected with the ghusl.

[41] 'Ali, when mentioned without qualification in the present translation, is to be taken as the husband of Fatima, daughter of the Prophet. His full name was 'Ali ibn Abi Talib. and he was assassinated in 660.

A lusty creature, brisk and foaming—skin-tight it was
and near to bursting.

"Why, the lines describe a horse, of course," explained Mazini.
"Let's hope you mount it then!" was the Bedouin's retort.

A similar tale is told by Asma'i.[42] "I was once," he said, "on
my way to Mecca in the company of friends, and suddenly a
Bedouin passed us shouting, 'Has anyone by chance seen a red
camel go by with plenty of thick, firm flesh on its neck and with
two young brown ones trailing behind—it was last seen near the
well?' 'God keep you,' we replied. 'We've not spotted any
camel that would fit that description.' Just then the Bedouin
met a desert girl by a cistern and asked her the very same question. 'Go to the devil, you dirty wretch!' she cried. 'How,'
we asked in our simplicity, 'can you treat a man like that when
he's only asking after his lost camel?' 'Blast his filth!' she
retorted. 'He's on about his penis and his testicles—that's all.'"

The way to lay a catamite is to get him first on his side. You
then lift the lad's thigh as you would with a pregnant woman
and crouch down in a squatting position with your penis poised
towards his anus. If you like, you can kneel over him with your
forearms resting on the floor. Alternatively, you can get him to
lie on his belly and then go belly to back. This last position is
better with the younger rather than the older male because, if a
man lies face downwards, he can contract his buttocks and make
penetration difficult. If you lay the boy on his back, you cannot
be sure that he will not excrete onto you. There are some sodomites, however, who maintain that that heightens the sensation
and ensures a more vigorous performance.

Let us conclude with lines of Abu Nuwas, who speaks of his
predilection for boys in the verses which follow:

Supreme joy was never known by any but the sort of
man who takes a drink with catamites.

[42] Asma'i (d. 828) was one of the most notable of all Arab philologists, and
later Arabic scholars owed much of their knowledge of poetry and lexi-
cography to his labours.

For this lad here will sing to him and that one offer him
a cup with words that spell devotion.

And when he yearns for kisses from a smooth-cheeked
boy, he'll have them showered on his mouth.

God bless the time I drank with such as these! How
sweet those days when we would quaff

A vintage wine from vats till then unbroached and
stipulate that each would ride the boy with whom
he slept!

CHAPTER III

Pretty Girls are Superior to Boys

Women would have just cause for pride if they could boast of nothing other than the Prophet's words "In this world of yours three things have been made dear to me—women, perfume and comfort in the ritual prayer to God." Justification resides in the fact that nothing but the best was ever made dear to the Prophet.

Women have five qualities to commend them—qualities which a catamite just does not have. First, the body of a young woman as opposed to that of a boy is cool in summer and warm in winter. Secondly, when a girl reaches the age of puberty she develops a fineness of physical features, and the lustre of youth glows in her face. Her countenance blooms and her voice grows sweet. The exact opposite is the case with a boy. Thirdly, a woman falls in love with a man in the same way as he does with her and finds the same delight in sexual union with him as he finds in union with her. Supreme delight is achieved when love is reciprocated by the one who is loved and each acts in harmony with the other. It is as the poet says:

> Life is this: you love and are loved in return.
> But the only thing a catamite loves is cash.[1]

Fourthly, in sexual union a woman will co-operate with her partner, giving embrace for embrace and kiss for kiss—and this

---

[1] To judge from this observation and other remarks in the chapter as well as evidence from elsewhere, the catamite, far from enjoying pederasty, found his role as passive partner in the act repulsive, painful and unpleasant. In other words, it is quite apparent that economic necessity drove him to the way of life he lived.

is part of the pleasure. A boy, on the other hand, has no time for that, nor is he interested in co-operation. The most he can offer is his back. Union with him is about as good as separation[2] and his good pleasure is tantamount to anger. The poet rightly says:

> When a catamite entertains you, he turns around and
>   spoils your pleasure!
> To hope for better from a catamite shows weakness in
>   your head.

Fifthly, a woman is by nature disposed to obey a man, to confine her attentions to him alone and to be his constant companion in patient seclusion. Not so a boy.

Catamites have five contemptible characteristics, none of which is found in a woman. First, hair will eventually grow on a boy's face and body, making him thoroughly disgusting to men and women alike. Praise will then turn into blame, as we see in the poet's lines:

> O passionate, tortured lover, you have there neither
>   vinegar nor wine.
> The pink of his cheeks has turned to black, those
>   embers' glow to charcoal.

And another says:

> They say of the place where the lad's beard sprouts,
>   "By 'shame' one means the part where the hair grows
>   on his cheek."
> There is no glory in a beard; a growth of hair's no
>   ornament, for, were it so, it would be found in the
>   Everlasting Garden.[3]

[2] In Arabic poetry separation of the lover from the beloved, and, indeed, separation of a man from his tribe or family, is regularly represented as an occasion for sorrow.

[3] By this expression (taken from Koran, xxv, 16) the poet means Paradise. In Koranic descriptions of its delights there is no mention of bearded men. The righteous admitted to the Garden are promised "wives purified" (Koran, ii, 23; iii, 13, etc.); they will be espoused to houris, the black-eyed virgins of Paradise (lii, 20), who will have "swelling breasts" (lxviii, 33) and be beautiful,

Another poet, in condemning facial hair, has this to say:

> What fire does to iron is the very same as what hair
>   does to the cheeks.
> Even as you behold a beardless and seductive lad as
>   beauteous as a moon at full, set in a night of stars,
> You see the hair turn black upon his cheeks and boy
>   turned into monkey!

Again:

> There's blackness now upon his face; his colour's changed,
>   decay's set in.
> He's like the traces of a desert camp with only ashes left
>   to tell its tale[4]

Another tells the tale of a lad just growing a beard who accosted a girl who had tried to seduce him before his beard grew but met with no success. And so she said:

> Why did you not do this while your face was still desirable
>   during your early youth and you had but little hair
>   upon your cheek?
> It's like the grape's first juice pressed into wine that started
>   sweet and then grew sour, and is now a vinegar.

Of a smooth-faced boy whose beard sprouted, another poet says in condemnation:

> Why did you not act thus when, in your youth, your face
>   was still desirable and you as yet were spared the
>   ravages of years?

modest, chaste, and loving. The function of the immortal youths of Paradise will be to circle round as attendants serving the blessed as they recline on couches with their houris (lii, 24).

[4] In old classical Arabic poetry the deserted encampment and the traces and relics of habitation play a conventional role: the poet regularly opens his ode by halting at the site of a desolate camp where he recollects the happiness of days when a girl whom he loved had dwelt near by and departed when her tribe struck camp.

For now grim Time[5] has veiled you with a beard—and
    what a plucking does it need!
A front and back your head once had, but now you turn
    your head, and face and neck are all the same.

Now to our second point: A catamite will abuse a pederast
disgracefully. To put it bluntly, he will continually insult him
and make a fool of him, especially if the two of them are in a
group at some drinking party, and he may even go so far as to
attack him physically. Hence the lines of a certain pederast
which run:

Their noses are pierced with degradation,[6] yet they scorn
    us and revile us.
If this is so when *we* ride them, what would it be like if
    they rode us?

Thirdly, the pederast can expect to be fouled by excrement,
and that's the quickest way to spoil his pleasure and make a
public scandal of his intimacy with his boy.

Fourthly, a pederast is the talk of the town and a public
scandal. His vice is no secret. It is just not the same as being a
womanizer—the latter may be doing wrong, but what he does at
least is natural and entails no notoriety.

Fifthly, you have only to look into the face of a boy who is
being buggered to witness the most dreadful expression as he
screws up his eyes and twists the corners of his mouth on account
of the pain that he feels.

One curious proof of the superiority of women as partners for
the opposite sex is the fact that the best-known name for their
sexual parts is ḥirr,[7] for, if you give the constituent letters of this

---

[5] Allusions to Time as a personalized entity determining man's destiny are
frequent both in pre- and post-Islamic poetry.

[6] To take the spirit out of a refractory and truculent camel, his nose is
pierced and a ring fitted by which he can be led. He is thereby made submis-
sive and so "degraded".

[7] Currently, the best-known name for vulva in Arabic is *kuss*, which is
given at the end of the paragraph. There is scarcely any serviceman who has
served in the Middle East who does not know the term!

word their numerical value,[8] you will find they add up to 208.[9] This total is the same as that given by the words *ni'ma jammuhu* "how beautifully made!" Another designation for their private parts is *farj*,[10] the numerical value of whose letters is the same as that given by the expression *ni'ma ḥusnuhu* "how lovely it is!" Again, we have the synonym *ḥann*, in which the letters add up to 55 as in the sentence *huwa ḥarr* "it is hot". Finally, there is the term *kuss* who letters total 90 as is also the case with the words *mawāhib ṭayyiba* "fine gifts".

A sodomite and a womanizer once had an argument. "I am on a higher plane than you," contended the pederast, "because I do those who do, whereas you only do those who are done." "Ah, but if that were something to boast about," countered the other, "men would rush to mount goats. But take me—now when I perform I kiss cheeks and press breast and suck cool moisture from a woman's lips. But what do you do but ram from behind, grasp hairy chests and collect a load of excrement?"

Once a catamite and a singing-girl engaged in a dispute at a drinking-party. "We," boasted the lad, "are superior to you because we have beardless cheeks, naked bodies, lithe figures and exquisite down such as is lauded by poets. We are free from the ritual impurities peculiar to women and the bane of menstruation and parturition,[11] and we don't have to bear the burdens of

---

[8] To each of the twenty-eight consonants in their alphabet the Arabs assigned a numerical value according to position. In the case of certain letters the system used in the East differed from that employed in North West Africa and Muslim Spain. It should be noted that according to neither system is it possible to accept the last two examples (relating to *hann* and *kuss*) given in the text. While it is true that *hann* adds up to 55, *huwa ḥarr* does not. Similarly the letters in *kuss* neither add up to 90 nor in any way equal the total to be derived from the words with which it is paired.

[9] In the original we have 108 resulting from an obvious scribal error.

[10] Literally, "opening". Occurring in the Koran, *farj* is a perfectly respectable term.

[11] See above Ch. II, n. 40, p. 56. It is worth noting here that the laws of Islam relating to menstruation are less severe than in Judaism. Sexual relations with a menstruating woman are forbidden in Koran ii, 222, but failure to comply with the injunction is not a punishable offence. Moreover, contact with a woman who is menstruating does not entail a state of impurity. Regulations relating to lochia are very similar to those relating to menstruation. The state of ritual impurity can be terminated by the greater ablution as soon as discharge has ceased—there is no fixed term.

child-bearing and pregnancy. It is we who have most often been the subjects of poetry and love-lyrics. We are loved by both men and women, and it is from our ranks that the 'eternal boys' in Paradise are drawn.''[12]

The girl answered the case in the following vein. "You wildly exaggerate and your boast has no basis in fact. If you can bear the truth, I can answer you." "Just answer me," he rejoined. "Can anyone with vision deny the light of the moon or the glory of the dawn?" "It would have been better," came her answer, "if you had never pressed for an answer to your case. Let us first take the question of tender cheeks, naked bodies and lithe figures. Here your claims are without foundation simply because all such things are *our* heritage—these are the gifts with which *we* are endowed. *You* are utterly devoid of them. The pinnacle of beauty is your attribute only so long as you bear any resemblance and have any affinities to us, and the time when you are most loved is just as brief. Your proudest boast is simply this, that you should be compared to us. Some sage of old is reported to have said: 'Avert your eyes from the sons of the rich, for their countenances are those of maidens.' In other words, your looks are compared to ours. This being so, remember this, that that which sets the standard of comparison is superior to the object compared. The poet says:

> In manner and in mien beauty reached perfection in this
> boy; in neck and figure he had all the features of a
> pretty girl.

"When you catamites are stripped of your borrowed likenesses to us [and lose your charm] by the sprouting of down which to you is a source of pride, your features grow ugly, your forms change, and the market for your goods is gone. Your lovers then come to loathe you and cast you aside. Your consorts shun you and your panegyrists turn to satire. Your poet Abu Nuwas[13] has this to say on the point:

[12] See n. 3 above, pp. 60 f.

[13] Al-Hasan ibn al-Hani' is the name actually given in the Arabic, but as this is Abu Nuwas, substitution of the latter will cause less inconvenience to the general reader.

A comely boy delights me when I behold him slender-bellied
    with bottom full and round
And then I see his beard, and that's the end of that!

"Another poet has accounted the sprouting of a beard one of
your misfortunes and offered his condolences on that account:

> God compensate you for your loss in this your tragedy and,
>   granting patience, hold back the tears now welling
>   in your eyes!
> We have heard the news of the affliction you have suffered
>   through the sprouting of a beard.

"It was not enough for you that they should have accounted it
your misfortune; so they went so far as to regard it as your death.
One says:

> Once his cheeks are clothed with hair, the boy is dead
>   albeit that he lives among us still.

"Another says:

> O you there slain by a fine black beard, the death of
>   beardless lads lies in the sprouting of their beards!
> God recompense your lover! Now you are dead and stand
>   stripped of the garb of your beauty.

"Another gives us the following lines:

> If you were as you used to be, we would praise you in
>   our verses.
> But your face has now grown swarthy, and swarthy
>   faces die.

"One of your crowd still plucks his beard to cling to what's
past and seeks to recapture what's gone for ever. But how stupid!

How absurd! For now the growth of hair on his body shows him up for what he is, and the stubble of his beard is thickening. Can there be any reason for his actions apart from the fact that hair is ugly and far removed from anything that's good? On the other hand, if any of you lot grows only a scanty beard and it doesn't really flourish, his face grows thin, and his comeliness fades, and he then starts doctoring it and treating it with anything that'll make it grow as he flees from what's already ugly to something even worse. And so you see that all that's comely about you stems from us—all that's ugly harks back to you. As for your silly talk about all this menstruation and the mess of parturition—well, by God, if you were to clean your bottom . . . need I say more? Menstruation and parturition are only with us for a matter of days, and God Almighty willed that they be use to purify and cleanse the womb. When it's all over, we're once more better than we were before we started.[14] But you—if you'd just take a look at what comes from your bottom twice a day, to say nothing of the soil you drop on your partner, you'd need to blush for shame! And if you argue that that's something that puts us on equal terms with you, well have another think! We hardly match you in unloading excrement such as you unload by accident on your partner's penis—that's a fine way to kill his zeal and wreck his fun. There are you crawling from under him, your head held down in shame as he, with frowning face, then heaves himself from off you, caked in filth! Which, then is the dirtier—that sort of thing, or menses and parturition? If you don't know the answer, well, go and ask and folks will tell you.

"As for your argument that more poems and lyrics are sung in your praise, well that just shows how ignorant you are and betrays your utter lack of knowledge. Have you never yet learned, you ignoramus, that it's the practice of poets and indeed a poetic convention, to use the masculine for metrical convenience? For *qāla* ('he said') and *fa'ala* ('he did') are shorter than the feminine forms *qālat* ('she said') and *fa'alat* ('she

[14] The period just prior to menstruation was not considered healthy. See below, p. 217.

did'.) And what's more, poets will also use the masculine to conceal identities. For example, take the lines:

> His garment clothes a sculpted form that enthrals the
> hearts of many. And how soft that gentle waist
> wrapped round!
> It were as if two rounded jewel-caskets lie upon his breast,
> well-shaped and set there high above his belly but
> just below the neck.

"In these lines the masculine form is used, but applied to the description of a woman. By 'rounded jewel-caskets' the poet means the breasts. Now, I ask you, is it you, the boys, who have the breasts, or girls?

"Now, to another point of yours. When you claim that both men and women love you, I can tell you that no man's love for any single one of you extends beyond the satisfaction of his lust and the discharge of his semen into your rectum. If a man is driven by his lust to fondle a boy like you, he's only just to penetrate—or even less than that—for the lad to frown and glower and grimace. Then come long gasps and moans, a gaping mouth, blinking eyes and a screwed up mouth, and the boy sounds and looks the most revolting thing God ever made. Indeed, if the sodomite were not wild with unbridled lust, he'd run away.

"Now let's take another point. What lover ever achieved renown for his love of catamites? Or ever died for them? Name just one man who ever loved one of your sort as desperately as Qays ibn 'Amir loved Layla, or a Qays ibn Dharih loved Lubna, or as 'Urwa ibn Hizam loved 'Afra', or as Jamil loved Buthayna, or as Kuthayyir loved 'Azza, or as Yazid ibn 'Abd-ul-Malik loved Hababa.[15] For us it's a satisfying source of pride to have been

---

[15] Yazid (*not* Walid as in the Arabic text) was an Umayyad Caliph (reg. 720–24). The names of all the men indicated in this sentence are inseparably linked in Arabic literature with those of the women with whom our author pairs them. Qays ibn 'Amir is better known as Majnun ("crazed"). The Layla-Majnun legend is not merely a celebrated literary theme; it is also a favourite with the miniaturists of Islam. A well-loved scene inspired by the story may be seen in D. Talbot Rice's *Islamic Painting* (Edinburgh U.P., 1971), p. 142. One scene or other can be seen in most works on Islamic miniatures.

loved and desired by prophets and indeed sufficient indication of our superiority over you.[16] For women, love is a thing that grows out of harmony with their partners. When their hearts are in close and constant contact with another human being and natural harmony follows, attachment will result. It is as the Prophet says: 'Hearts are like enlisted troops, and those of them that are known to one another will stick together, whereas where there is no mutual acquaintance the ranks will fall asunder.' And so there was not a single one among the women I've spoken of who didn't reciprocate the desperate love of her lover and cherish him as he did her. Not one of these men was a catamite. If by some freakish chance a woman does fall in love with a catamite, she falls into utter disgrace—and human nature has no time for sources of shame and feels only contempt and loathing from them.

"Now we come to your argument that it is from your ranks that the eternal boys of Paradise are drawn. This is just not so. They do not come from your ranks at all—nor you from theirs. However, if we're making comparisons of this sort, houris are females and in a higher class. For God Almighty says in the Koran 'Houris cloistered in cool pavilions' and He also says 'Eternal boys shall move around them'.[17] In other words, He has appointed them to move around and dance attendance. Now surely a master is superior to a servant.

"You and your boasting remind me of the goat and the ewe. When the ewe's tail came up, the goat turned to her and said, 'Thank God, we both look the same from behind!' "

At this the catamite got up and left in shame, quite unable as he was to find any reply to her case.

Ibn Hajjaj is the author of a poem in which he says:[18]

---

[16] See below, p. 70.   [17] lv, 72; lxxvi, 19.

[18] A Shi'ite of Baghdad, this poet (941 or 942?–1001) was the author of two entirely different kinds of poetry: neo-classical panegyric and a new genre to which he gave the name *sukhf*. The latter is totally unconventional and is characterized by lewdness, vulgarity, cynicism, and the use of language and ideas drawn from the gutter. Because of the outrageous nature of this genre, his *diwan* has not so far found its way into print, though manuscripts of it do exist.

I'm wholly convinced and know in my heart that the
    vulva is our curse.
Thus spoke my boy, and I in answer said, "I'd give my
    life for you!" as he lay upon our bed
In all his beauty like a bride displayed upon her bridal
    chair.

Later he was taken to task by a Persian. "Why," asked the
latter, "did you say that the curse of all the world lies in the
vulva? That doesn't make good sense to me! For on this very
point you say:

'When that gorgeous woman snubbed me and I spent the
    night consumed with ardent love
My penis jumped beneath my garb and sang, "Ambition
    can reduce a man to nought."
"You mean *ḥirṣ* without the *ṣ*?"[19] I asked. "You take
    the point," my penis said.' "

The following verses are those of a poet who said in a challenge
to Abu Nuwas (though some say that they are actually the lines
of Abu Nuwas himself):

Many a poet unawakened to the light of truth has,
    through his ignorance, persisted in misguided ways,
Extolling in his lines the superiority of boys. His poetry
    and that of others of his ilk astound me.
He claims that boys have coquetry and can be trusted
    not to menstruate or find themselves with child.
Anyone, I say, who flees from girls and has his needs
    supplied by catamites has little need of folly— he
    has enough!
No lecher slyly sunk in sodomy, eschewing righteous
    ways, can be compared
With some gay gallant who makes himself a slave to
    girls and, loving, never wakes from rapturous
    dreams of love.

[19] By dropping the ṣ from the Arabic the word for "ambition" can be read
as "vulva".

There is no lad you loved for a span—yes, at the time
 it seemed as if the full moon lived in all its beauty
 in his clothes,[20]

And then when your hands had won him and the
 weary business of delays and pretexts palled,

An unsightly beard was there upon his cheeks repelling
 lovers from his kisses—

There is no lad, I say, to compare with a tender girl,
 one half of whom is a sandy dune and the other a
 curving branch

That lies above the waist like a straight spear's shaft
 bent wildly by the wind.[21]

Has the boy with whom you are in love a bashful
 blush like hers?

Or has he locks and curls like hers? Or a slender waist
 that blossoms on his buttocks?

No, love of girls is right indeed, even though it brings
 a lover close to death.

Their beauty captivated Joseph, and David was
 enthralled so much that he deeply wronged a man;[22]

For he slew him that his wife might be a lawful spouse
 unto himself, and thus debased himself for love.

And even Moses—he who spoke with God—fell, by
 chance a prey to love despite his fear of God.

And Abraham, the Friend of God, fled with Hagar to the
 curtains of the Kaaba's sanctuary.[23]

---

[20] On the full moon as the symbol of beauty see above Ch. I, n. 14, p. 28.
[21] On this image see above Ch. II, n. 31, p. 43.
[22] These are the biblical Joseph (son of Jacob) and David, who are Koranic as well as Old Testament figures. The man whom David wronged was Uriah (Samuel, II, xi). The theme introduced by this line is the compelling power and superiority of natural heterosexual love. The point is demonstrated by reference to men whose names are venerated in Islam by virtue of their connexion with God's scheme of revelation. It should be noted that in the Koran, Islamic Tradition, and legend, details relating to biblical figures are not necessarily identical to those offered in the Scriptures. In Koranic commentaries and histories of the Prophet their lives and deeds are much embellished with material drawn in part from non-biblical Jewish sources. It almost goes without saying that popular story-tellers not only distorted such material, often beyond recognition, but also confused one personality with another.
[23] In Islam Abraham of the Bible plays a vital role: he is the primitive pure monotheist who stands at the head of a line of prophets of whom Muhammad

And even Zaynab enthralled our Lord Muhammad,
  and so Zayd left, and the Prophet took his place.[24]
God fashioned Adam, and Adam, feeling deep desire,
  set his heart on women.
For us did God contrive and wondrously create the
  other sex and make their lovely eyebrows bows
  wherewith to shoot the shafts of love.
A young she-camel is the camel's natural mate—no
  other male for him!
And so do not, in folly, heed the Devil—sodomy is
  just another of his tricks.

On the same theme I myself say this:

Away with sodomy, and all will perfect be; for coitus
  use a woman's parts, for they are best by far.
And what is more, I'll tell you this: two penises
  beneath the clothes are greater trouble than they're
  worth!

was the last. In the Koran Islam is identified with the "religion of Abraham"
(ii, 129; iii, 89, etc.), who was "neither a Jew nor a Christian", and who was
taken by God as "a friend" (iv, 124; cf. Isaiah, xli, 8). It was he who, with
Ishmael—his son by Hagar (see Genesis, xvi)—established the Kaaba (Koran,
ii, 119), that is the Islamic "holy of holies" at Mecca. The Kaaba is a cube-
shaped building of stone and mortar normally covered nowadays with a black
curtain decorated in gold with Koranic verses. In its corner is set the Black
Stone, a relic from the original construction erected by Abraham.

[24] The Prophet married Zaynab daughter of Jahsh, the divorced wife of his
adopted son, Zayd ibn Haritha, a freedman who had been one of the first to
embrace Islam. The justification for the marriage—which was most probably
of a political rather than a romantic nature, as often suggested by Christian
polemic—is given in an *ad hoc* Koranic revelation (xxxiii, 37). To most people
this is perhaps the best-known event in Muhammad's life and it has often been
used to denigrate the Prophet's character. The Koranic revelation was necessary
because, it would seem, an alliance with a woman who had been the wife of an
adopted son would have been taboo according to old Arabian ways of thinking—an adopted child would have been equated with an actual child of the
blood.

CHAPTER IV

On Pimps and Procuration

Although the very word "procuration"[1] is accounted loathsome and the deed quite infamous, we have here a fine art and a subtle vocation which can only perfectly be practised by a person of wit, skill, shrewdness and guile, who can insinuate himself with delicacy and extricate himself with speed—in short, an able practitioner of his art. For it is his business to bring together in love and affection hearts that are strangers to one another, to blend in harmony temperaments that clash, and to join in concord diverse kinds of person. For he is the sort of person who must flow like magic into people's hearts and bring lover and beloved together. He must act as wine upon the heart and subtly infiltrate the system like water infiltrating trees through roots. Often his task may be to sow the seeds of love in two persons before they have even seen each other by putting into their ears words calculated to enchant the hearer and bring tears to the hearer's eyes.[2] All the while he must act with the speed of flashing lightning, working through the magic of the words with which he wins the hearts he seeks to captivate as he depicts the lover to the object

[1] In Arabic *qiyāda*. In medieval Muslim society procuration was not quite the same thing as it is in modern Western society. Women living in purdah and, if neglected, deprived of regular sexual satisfaction would welcome any opportunity to gratify their natural inclinations. Such women were not prostitutes since, unlike the pimp, they did not necessarily derive any financial advantage from their activities. There were, of course, those who did, and these can be rightly described as prostitutes.

[2] Needless to remark, there were no photographs in medieval times, and, since there were few, if any, opportunities for the sexes to meet one another licitly, it was up to the pimp to make an appeal to the imagination through the medium of words.

of his love and so enraptures her. He is like the Devil, who, when he sets out to play the tempter, sets before his victim's soul that which he knows will find favour in its sight. And so the pimp brings lovers together and they are then in his debt.

People may feel the pangs of love through hearing about them as well as by seeing them. It is as Bashshar ibn Burd says in his verse:[3]

My ear, my kin, is enamoured of a girl in the camp—
at times the ear may love before the eye can see.

Proofs of the shrewdness of the practitioner of this art are the way he can produce the beloved of a man in love and the way he can ply to and fro by day and night and infiltrate like magic. He will expose himself to danger and embark on enterprises fraught with dreadful hazards. Then, reaching for remote objectives, he will summon down results that fall more quickly than the rain. He will bring out a girl from purdah and unite the lover with his beloved. Difficult tasks are no trouble to him at all: he can humble the headstrong and make them his prisoner; he can demean the virtuous and leave them no respite. Yet in all he does he acts with great circumspection and is careful to be neither heard nor seen; for he has to contend with the trials of truculent characters who can land him in trouble, enemies who may come upon him, elusive rascals who may try to deceive him with pretences, guards who may take him unawares, avengers who are out for his blood, and watchers who need to be watched.

The art of procuration was first revealed to man by the Devil, who—God curse him for it!—is a great seducer of women. The children of Noah, so it is said, multiplied in great abundance after the Flood, and every corner of the earth was filled with

---

[3] The son of an Iranian freedman and native of Basra, Bashshar (c. 714–84) was the first major Arab poet of non-Arab extraction. In the present context the most important point about him is that he is blind. Sightless from birth, he depended on rhapsodes to circulate and transmit his poetry. Above all a master of love-lyrics, he was a trend-setter in this branch of poetry.

them. Some dwelt in the plain and others inhabited the moun-
tains, and their story is proverbial. Now the women of one group
were more comely than their menfolk, and the men of the other
group more comely than their womenfolk. The two groups,
however, never met until the Devil—God's curse upon him!—
contrived to unite them and have one lot fall in love with the
other. Taking up a flute, he played it, and when they heard
strange but pleasant strains, they were transported with joy.
Attracted by the music, the mountaineers went down to the
plain and were tempted by the Devil, the accursed fiend who
tempted Abu Jahl.[4] The women looked at the men, and the men
at the women. Enraptured by each other, they fell to adultery
as their clothes were shed. A certain poet says of them in this
connexion:

> I am astounded at the Devil and his pride and the
>   shameful revelation that he made.
> Too proud he was to bow to Adam, yet not too proud
>   to play the pimp when it came to Adam's offspring.

Procuration, then, is an ancient practice. At the same time it
is vicious and fraudulent. Women have a far greater aptitude
for it than men and are indeed the most skilful of all operators in
the field. They exert more subtle power and get their victims
more easily into their clutches, for craft and guile are part of a
woman's nature. It is the older woman who is the specialist of the
profession. If such a woman has been a whore and whoremonger
in her younger days, she is an unbeatable practitioner and a
snake who cannot be charmed. These female pimps have quite a
range of tricks and different ways of plying their trade. To illustrate, I will take one or two examples of their behaviour, for if a
man has any wit and determination and would be on his guard
against falling foul of women's wicked wiles, he must know what

---

[4] This man was the leader of Makhzum, a clan of the Prophet's tribe,
Quraysh. Shortly before the emigration of Muhammad from Mecca to Medina,
Abu Jahl seems to have tried to have the Prophet killed because he felt him
to be a threat to his commercial and financial interests. At any rate he perished
fighting the Muslims in the battle of Badr in 624.

he is up against. As the saying goes, "He who knows not evil falls prey to it."

Some procuresses profess Sufism,[5] carry rosaries, wear woollen clothing and carry staffs. A woman of this type will enter a house with her rosary dangling from her hand and make a show of self-abasement and humility. If she spots a woman as old as herself but of better class, she will approach her, though cautiously at first for fear she might turn on her. She will shake her intended victim by the hand and ask her how she is in a friendly and familiar way as though she had known her for many a year. The other woman will be taken aback. "But don't you know me?" our procuress will ask. "I'm the daughter of Shaykh so-and-so,"[6] dropping the name of some well-known Sufi. Without stooping to the indignity of begging she will continue "I only dropped in to bid you the time of day." With that she begins by telling the woman all about her father, the Shaykh, and all his feats and miracles. She tells false tales of dreams he has communicated to her and insists that her present visit has been motivated entirely by some dream that she has had in connection with the particular woman she is talking with or about the girl she is really after. (She will, of course, need to have got hold of the woman's name and that of her mother.) She will now go on to recount what she saw her saintly father do when he came to her in her sleep—the sort of thing that women are apt to fall for. This much done, she will make the victim a present of a rosary or a prayer-mat or a staff or some other appropriate article, refusing either any payment or gift in exchange. In her dream, she will protest, her father instructed her to make the gift in question. From that very moment she will treat her victim just like a sister. At the same time she won't stay too long, but will leave before she becomes boring or arouses displeasure. However, she will make a point of paying a second visit and behave more familiarly than on the first occasion, and thereafter be for ever in and out with increasing familiarity, effusive at times, self-effacing at others, now mouthing pious invocations and prayers, now playing all the

[5] See above Ch. II, nn. 2 and 4, pp. 32 f.
[6] See above Ch. II, n. 4, p. 33.

tricks that Sufis play, and so on. Next she'll be back to her self-effacement and pious invocations and go on in this fashion until in the end she feels that the other woman is friendly enough. She then casts her spell on her and works her guile, and at that stage only those who have God's own protection can hope for deliverance from her clutches. Should the other shun and snub her and it become obvious that persuasion is of no avail, she will then adopt a threatening attitude and a policy of intimidation, terrifying her victim into the belief that she will suffer condign punishment for the death of the lover for whom she is acting and that the wrath of God will fall upon the unfortunate woman if she does not take steps to deliver the man who is so plagued by the agonies of love. When means such as these are used to gain one's ends, there are very few who can extricate themselves from the net of a procuress simply because they are too timid, weak willed, and witless to challenge her. It is as the poet says:

> As a learned physician she came to her and time after
> time mixed jest with earnest.
> Raising her voice when the other gave in, she would
> use soft words when anger raged.

When Ibn Abi 'Atiq heard these two verses used to describe a procuress, he is said to have commented "Men have been looking for a Caliph of such a character as this ever since 'Uthman ibn 'Affan met his doom, but they have never yet found one."[7] The key to the understanding of the verses lies in Mu'awiya's words, "If there were but a single hair between myself and my people, it would never be severed." "How so?" he asked. "I would let it go slack," he replied, "if ever they tugged it, and I would tug it myself if ever they slackened it."[8]

[7] 'Uthman was the Prophet's son-in-law and third "Patriarchal" or "Orthodox" Caliph (reg. 644–56). His misguided policies aroused such widespread disaffection that they culminated in his assassination. The Ibn Abi 'Atiq referred to was the great grandson of the first Caliph, Abu Bakr (reg. 632–34).

[8] Mu'awiya was the first Umayyad Caliph (reg. 661–80). The sense of the words attributed to him here would appear to be that he would keep a tight rein on his subjects but not be so foolish as not to know when to let up. In the present context the inference seems to be that 'Uthman had alienated his

Some procuresses are house-to-house saleswomen,[9] and women of this particular kind can exercise the subtlest influence of all because they can get to girls in purdah who are unwatched and unsupervised by any sort of guard. Moreover, they can obtain access to any place they like at any time they choose on the pretext of showing them dress material and clothing. They are always in a position to be alone with them and they have every conceivable opportunity for playing their crafty games. Hence if a procuress of this type observes that a woman has taken a liking to and begun to bargain over some garment or piece of jewellery which can give her an opening such as she is looking for, she will seize the opportunity to make it easy for her customer to get what she wants without payment and tempt her with the offer. It will not then be too difficult for the procuress to manipulate her victim because of the power she derives from the customer's eagerness to secure the goods she so much desires. It may also be that the procuress will bring gifts of one sort or another for the sole purpose of encouraging her victim. At all events, once the first contacts have been made, women of this type are for ever on the doorstep and sending little notes through accomplices. In all this they act quite shamelessly. They may well win over guards, male or female, and insinuate themselves into people's favour by cheap sales of anything their victims want to buy or alternatively grant them easy terms for payment.

Next there are the women known as *mudarmikāt*, whose business is the sale of scents and perfumes and who can therefore worm their way into people's houses by means of their occupation. Such a type may take with her rare and costly scents and manipulate her victims in the same way as the saleswomen do.

Then we have fortune-tellers, commonly called "destiny-decree-

people and been so blind or stubborn as to let matters get out of hand. He should have been like the procuress and known when to tighten and when to relax his grip.

[9] In Arabic *dallālāt*. In the Muslim West the singular of this word denotes a woman who deals in women's clothing and visits the houses of the more well-to-do with clothes, fabrics and jewellery. This is the sense in which we have it here.

ing amulet ladies", who practise the profession of prediction by casting beach pebbles.[10] They have their own ways and means of getting women into their clutches and of being able, through long and regular practice, to read what is in their minds.[11] Women are given to reposing unshakable confidence in such characters. They hold them in esteem and believe everything they say. Meanwhile, their manipulators subject them to continual indoctrination. Once a person in this line of business has made up her mind to procure a woman, but cannot immediately achieve her end, her first move will be to cast pebbles for her intended victim and tell her something she wants to hear. "And in this line here," she then goes on, "I see unexpected good fortune coming your way and its one and only source is a certain man who is passionately in love with you." She then describes him in glowing terms, telling of his good looks, wealth and charming manners. At the same time she warns her not to throw away her chances with him—"him", of course, being the man for whom she has set out to procure. She leads her victim to believe that it will be greatly to her detriment to turn down her chances with this man when she has before her the prospects of a happy home, children and prosperity. Acceptance, on the other hand, will result in riches. The fortune-teller's words stick in the woman's mind and she tells herself that she will take up with the man in question either because her heart is set on the good looks she has heard of or because she finds the prospects of his wealth alluring. All this comes about because, unless they are preserved from their own folly by the grace of God, women are lacking in wit and the observance of religion. At all events, the victim then begins to look for the moment she will receive the letter of invitation and grows restless as time passes. If she feels like it, the old

[10] The term translated as "destiny-decreeing" is uncertain; it derives from a verb *aḥamma*, the subject of which is normally God. It is, however, possible that its use here is frivolous or sarcastic. Pebble-casting is in essence analogous to the reading of tea-cups in that predictions were made on the basis of fortuitous configurations. Pebble-casting is mentioned by Ibn Khaldun as a popular means of telling fortunes (F. Rosenthal, *Muqaddimah* (New York, 1958), I, 216; II, 201).

[11] Text uncertain, but this seems to be the sense.

fortune-teller will bring the message herself. But if she feels like demonstrating the accuracy of her prediction, she will say "It won't be long before you get the message from the man who figured in the line of pebbles—and he won't come empty-handed. You must let me have a share." At that juncture she sends an accomplice with the message from the man she wants to meet up with the woman. She then comes to demand recompense for the good news because her prediction has come true, and naturally enough her victim's mind will be firmly fixed on the prospects of riches still to come and everything else that has been prophesied.

Procuration is also practised by hairdressers.[12] They are more artful than any other sort of pimp and can exert a more powerful and penetrating influence over women. This is because they have them very much under their control and are so often alone with them. What is more, they know all that is good or bad about a woman and, because they groom her, they are in a position to take liberties. And so it is that a hairdresser can get her way without all the trouble that others are put to, and the more so in cases where a woman has been prepared for marriage by her as a girl. Another class of women who get up to much the same sort of tricks as hairdressers are the henna beauticians[13] who know almost as much about the secrets and private lives of their clients.

"Slave-girls-on-the-run" constitute another category engaged in the business of procuration. A girl of this sort will select a house and get into it on the pretext of seeking refuge from her

---

[12] Or, more archaically but more properly, "tire-women" (in Arabic *māshiṭāt*). One particular function of such women was to groom a bride for her wedding and to attend her on the actual day of marriage. Since their functions included the removal of all body hair, their contact with and knowledge of their clients was very intimate.

[13] Henna—shrub whose leaves yield a reddish-orange dye—was, and still is, widely used in many parts of the Muslim world as a cosmetic (even by men who feel the need to dye their beards). It may be used as a hair dye (giving a reddish brown, if used alone, or black, if mixed with other substances). It is also commonly applied to the fingers, backs of the hands and the feet. In particular, the dyeing of a bride's hands and feet is one of the rituals associated with the festive activities leading up to the wedding.

own household. In simulated fear and trembling she will beg that every effort be made to secure her freedom for sale. Tears flow freely until she calms down upon finding herself with the one she is after. She then confides in her and tells her the true purpose of her being there. If things turn out as she hopes, all well and good. If not, she spies her opportunity and runs off as if making a dash for safety. There is, incidentally, the kind of slave-girl who will get into houses for purposes other than procuration: often her business is to act as a spy for thieves. She gets to know the plan of the house, its entrances and exits, and all the goods and chattels it contains. Then off she goes to her accomplices with a description of the lot. Knowing all they need to know and working with a precise plan of action, the thieves can now effect an entry.

A procuress may very well come from a high-class family of some standing and comfortable background. In her case the reason for her occupation is that she lives a life of luxury and ease and has too much time on her hands to indulge her fancies. Accordingly she is inclined to let the less desirable side of her nature draw her into evil ways and prompt her to derive pleasure from having men see and admire her beauty. This she does without having any need for any material recompense. Women of this sort consider it a waste not to turn their beauty and physical attractions to advantage. Moreover, if they can make friends with some other woman who can be persuaded by reason, they will talk her into joining in the game and co-operating with them. If, however, the woman has no wish to participate, they will abuse and deride her with some such taunt as "Why you're no better than we are!" They then take the unfortunate woman and play on her psychology, abusing and coaxing her alternately until in the end they reduce her to the same level of depravity as themselves. This sort of corrupt practice is worse than anything mentioned so far.

Among other types of person engaged in procuration are old female wine-vendors[14] and impecunious women who beg for bread and ex-slave-girls who, having gained their freedom, are

---

[14] The reading of the Arabic text is doubtful.

always able to return to their former masters' houses and procure. Men and effeminate homosexuals sometimes procure, but they do not have the same access to places as older females do. They can only solicit flashy dolls and women on their way to and from weddings, funerals and similar gatherings.[15] All in all, they are better able and qualified to procure boys.

To make a success of procuring, one must be able to break down resistance and win over a stubborn and difficult character by the use of skilful tactics and a sound knowledge of the game. One poet says of a drab:

> No mercy did God show her in her childhood, nor will
>   He pardon her the day she dies.
> By virtue of her skilful tactics she can lead a thousand
>   mules, stubborn though they be,
> By a spider's slender thread.

One who, without the need for persuasion, brings two lovers together is not a pimp, but merely a messenger or go-between. To quote the poet:

> " 'Amr's a pimp," says many a one. "Oh no!" I retort.
>   "That's going too far—'Amr's no pimp at all.
> He's merely a man who will rent you his house for
>   just a copper or two and whatever's left over from
>   supper!"

There are, however, two meanings to these verses, the first of which is the obvious one as set out above. The other lurks behind the second verse, for when the poet declares that 'Amr "will rent you his house", he levels against him the gravest charge in the calendar of procuration. In the first line he acquits him on the lesser count, but then in the second, by the use of the word

[15] Such occasions often afforded women the only opportunities of leaving the house.

"merely", he qualifies his previous statement and indicts him on the higher count. To illustrate my meaning, let us take the following verse:[16]

> In them there is no fault to find; it is merely that their
> swords are notched from raining blows on squadrons.

Here we are at first led to suppose that there is some fault in the persons referred to because the words "it is merely that" are introduced. But what follows next transforms the whole statement into a perfect compliment.

The old drabs and queers who practise procuration have many crafty ways of extracting money which can easily fool many an old hand. For instance, the pimp, whether male or female, will approach some man and say, "I'd like to pair you off with the daughter—or wife—of so-and-so." The name of some high-class lady never before aspired to is dropped, and then comes a description attributing to her all the qualities that will induce the victim to set his heart on her. The story will be continually hammered home until the man in question finally calls on the procuress to fulfil the promises she has made. She, for her part, has him believe that she is risking her life for him, all the while drawing the matter out with promises. With each new promise and every detail added to the picture of things in store for him the man's eagerness mounts as the pimp all the while extracts money from him first for her hairdresser, then for her slave-girl, and so on all along the line. She will make him believe that she, the procuress, is the go-between essential to the attainment of his end. A type such as this may also deceive her client by feeding him the sort of tale or hopeful message that he unwittingly leads her to suppose he will believe. She follows this up by saying, "Just see now what you can send the lady." He then finds himself in such transports of delight that he is quite unable to think what to give and has to ask. In the end he asks the pimp, and she tells him exactly what she wants. When the old drab has got all she wants out of

[16] At this point our author steps momentarily into the field of literary criticism and the art of rhetoric.

him, she goes off to find some really low-class whore who is not too well known, but who at the same time is not too bad looking or has some of the characteristics to which she has committed herself with her client by telling him the girl is tall or short, slender or buxom, of such-and-such a complexion or with eyes that are such-and-such. Then, engaging her services for a night for a couple of dirhams, she hires such jewels and finery as the whore may need and sprinkles her with the most exquisite scent, at the same time telling her the name by which her client will know her. Nor will the old pimp be averse to embellishing her tale of the whore by supplying additional details for which no proof will be asked of her, but which will convey the impression of her high social status. She next hands the girl over to some other old drab who will take her to her client's house. The man will not, of course, have the slightest doubt that he has in his grasp a prize which no one ever won before.

One story that will illustrate the kind of trap that a man can fall into concerns an individual who went and stayed for a time in a certain town. Wishing to marry, but having no contact with any woman to whom he could propose,[17] he complained of his plight to an older man in whose good intentions he misguidedly believed. "Yes," said the old fellow, "I know just the right woman for you." And at that he went into details about how beautiful, intelligent and religious she was, and so on and so forth. "The only drawback," he ended, "is that she has a job which keeps her busy through the day. However, she will be home at nights. If you're prepared to put up with that sort of arrangement, she'll give you very little trouble in other respects." Whereupon he went off and came back with a woman who really did appeal to the man. And so the latter married her on

---

[17] To mix freely with the opposite sex and to make a direct proposal of marriage to a respectable woman would have been out of the question in medieval Muslim society. Normally, a man or a friend of his would approach a girl's nearest male relative, and he, in his capacity as her legal guardian (wali), would conduct all legal business relating to the marriage. The suitor would very often be well known to the family, if not in fact even a member of it. To marry in a strange town where one had no friends, relations, or acquaintances would present obvious difficulties.

mutually agreed terms.[18] Now it so happened that the bridegroom had a friend whom he told of the favour the old man had done him and how he had found him a wife who was devout, beautiful and charming. Impressed by his story, the friend begged him to ask the old man to do the same for him. So the man did as he was asked. "Yes, indeed," said the old man to his friend, "I know a very fine woman who would be ready to marry you. The only trouble is that she has a job which keeps her busy at night. However, you'll have her during the day." The man was delighted with the idea, and so the older man brought him a woman who met with his approval and whom he married as agreed. In a very short time, however, it dawned upon the two younger men that the older had married them both off to one and the same woman. Whereupon they laid into him, reviled him and dragged him before the local governor. When he could see that he was in real trouble, he broke down in tears. "What are all the tears about?" they demanded. "This," he sobbed, "is all the thanks I get for having married you both to a good-living woman from a most excellent background!"

Pimps and procuresses share the pleasures both of those whom they procure and of those for whom they act, quite apart from any money they earn for the job. For the pimp will often bed the woman—or boy, as the case may be—whom he procures. One poet says:

> Procuring yields a fine return: "Well done! Well done!",
> they cry, and then there's pleasure and delight as well!

Here are some of my own lines on the same theme:

> If you want to find life sweet, then pimping is your
> game. No pimp ever tasted bitterness in life.

---

[18] In Islamic law a wife has a right to a "dower" or nuptial gift (*mahr, ṣadāq*) and maintenance. The nature (money, property, etc.) and value of the dower as well as the method of payment (immediate payment in full or a down payment with postponed payment of the remainder) are matters for negotiation between the contracting parties.

For all that you scorn and deride him, he has you in
   his hands.
He'll have his pleasure laying some fine lass, and
   then you'll skim the cream of his delight.
Food and drink are the harvest that he reaps with
   catamites and whores thrown in as well.

Pimps and procuresses have various tricks that can be played
on couples they pair off, and indeed they can be vicious to them if
they do not get the kind of fee they expect. They will set rowdies
on them who will make an utter nuisance of themselves by
hammering on the door and throwing stones. They will indulge
in all sorts of disgusting behaviour to frighten the life out of the
couple until in the end they get them out. Sometimes the owner
of a bawdy house will fling himself from the terrace to give them
the impression that they have more on their hands than they can
cope with and leave them in such a state that they consider it
best to clear out. Again, the pimp is quite likely to turn them out
just as they are coming to the moment of rapture, declaring that
he has a client who is far more profitable than they are and is
wanting to use his services immediately. He makes them believe
that unless they leave forthwith, he will burst in upon them and
make a public scandal of them.

There is also the type of pimp who will keep glass bottles and
containers that have cracks and breaks carefully concealed
beneath the outer casing.[19] Then when the lovers ask him to
bring them some wine, he will take their money, pick up the
carafe or whatever and disappear.[20] When he gets back his
clothes will be wet, and just a drop or two of wine will be left
in the container. Making a pretence of anger with the pair, he
will launch into excuses: "I tripped and dropped the bottle—it
got broken and everything ran out!" Or he might tell some tale
about being caught in a crush and moan about being half dead

[19] The bottle would be encased in wicker- or rush-work or something
similar rather after the fashion of a demijohn.

[20] Since wine-drinking is a punishable crime against the Islamic religion,
the pimp could reasonably claim that it was necessary to go out to purchase
it, his plea being that it would be dangerous to keep wine on the premises.

as a result. "And it's all your fault for sending me," he will complain. As he puts down the bottle with the fragments clattering inside the outer cover, he will vow and declare that that is the last favour he will do for them. For their part, the lovers feel under an obligation to pay the price for what, though lost, would have made their joy complete. And so they beg and plead with him not to be cross and coax him back to good humour. He then gets out of them as much as they gave him in the first place and he comes back with wine that is watered down by half its volume. The lovers realize they are being fooled, but they accept it and say nothing because they have no option but to acquiesce for the sake of peace. Another of his tricks is to divert their attention and filch some of their wine when they are not looking. Having tricked them into believing that there is none left, he will sell back to them what he has actually stolen from them. There is, of course, one way of getting in with faded drabs and old queers, and that is to lay them.

There is a story about Mazyad which runs as follows. "I hear," someone said to him, "that you had so-and-so and so-and-so together in your house yesterday." "Yes, that's right," he said. "But just listen to this. When they'd had their meal and chatted for part of the night, they asked me to bring them some wine. 'It's a bit late,' I said, 'for getting anything like that, and I just don't have any in.' 'By God!' they threatened, 'If you don't do as you're told, you've got it coming to you!' And they meant it. At that point I remembered I had a purgative that someone had given me. 'Oh, I know where I might get some wine,' I said. So I took their money and went off and got the purgative, which I then put in a bowl. I poured some water on it and softened it up until it dissolved. I then took it in to them in a bottle. They tasted it and said, 'This really is superb, but it's a bit on the bitter side.' When they'd had two cups of it, they got the gripes and were taken short. Now the lavatory's at the top of the house and you've got to go up stairs. Well, all they saw of each other for the rest of the night was a fleeting glimpse as they shot past one another on the stairs, and they didn't come round till morning!"

A poet says of a procuress:

I sent her on my mission, a woman sharper than a sword
    in striking and swifter than a flood in spate at night.
Her gentle words, demeanour, and her guile sink deep
    and spread like wine as it permeates the limbs;
The stubborn and intractable are soon moulded to her
    hands. Unerringly she guides them to the very door
    of error.
The astute and quick witted will spot her for the
    dullard she is. Yet, the craftiest of the crafty is she.
For she'll lure forth those pretty girls with swelling
    breasts—for all the veils that hide them—when the
    curtains of purdah are drawn.
Her smooth, sweet words will unite the sheep with the
    lion and call down the stalk from between the fronds
    of a palm branch.
At will she could couple a lamb with a ravenous wolf—
    and that with the greatest of ease.
And even a stubborn male camel[21] that she sought to
    procure in its own despite would soon be a she-camel
    in her hands.
Her humility and modesty and the praises of God on
    her tongue from sunrise to sunset win the credence of
    all mankind![22]

Another poet says:

I plotted and planned with her, hag that she is— a drab
    worn with years and with bones poking through,
Whose sole asset left is a gentle approach on errands of
    love as now she tries her victims with warm-hearted
    gestures and knowing looks;
Who gets what she wants when in commanding position,
    but turns a deaf ear to all she dislikes.
And so, with guile and her witch's spells, she sidled up
    to the girl I had in mind, now dropping her hints, now
    fighting out in the open,
Now jesting as she talked, then going the limit and beyond.

---

[21] The camel is a spiteful and stubborn animal, and a rutting male is
possessed of extraordinary strength.
[22] She makes an outward show of piety to gain credibility.

On this very theme I have some of my own verses which run:

> Many a procuress of old has trod the crooked path, but
>   never have I yet held it against her.
> But this old drab is deaf—and yet, when I called, never
>   did any hear better—no, not in all the world.
> She knows her job and does it well—and proves it's
>   no fool's game.
> Never did the Devil hear tell of her unmoved—and, more
>   than that, he even smiled—and smiles.
> Many's the time she's raised a flag of vice[23] to haul
>   down one of decency!
> Many's the time she's set out to corrupt, yet never set
>   out to reform!
> Many's the time she's bewitched folk with the sorcery
>   of her guile and succeeded where others have failed!
> Many's the time she's got beyond curtain upon curtain![24]
>   Many's the time she has hunted a gazelle from its
>   sanctum![25]
> Many's the time she has slipped penis past vulva! How
>   many a small mouth has she joined with the mouth
>   of another!
> She leads the wolf of the wilds to the sheep, and couples
>   the pair in the dark.
> Were she to rise to the stars in heaven, even there she'd
>   have them copulate to the rules she formulates.
> Should the time of Prayer[26] conflict with a chance to
>   procure, she bids the Prayer "Be on your way!" Her
>   errand's more important.

[23] Possibly an allusion to the pre-Islamic desert custom whereby the prostitute indicated her whereabouts by means of a special flag or emblem flown above her tent.

[24] The sense is as follows: no matter how many curtains may have screened off the private quarters and recesses of a house separating the drab from her quarry, she has often got beyond them all. "Purdah", we may note, primarily means "curtain" (from Persian *parda*), notably that serving to screen the womenfolk of a household from the sight of outsiders.

[25] Once again, the term "gazelle" is used to denote a lovely girl.

[26] For the Muslim there are five prescribed ritual prayers each day: at daybreak, at noon, mid-afternoon, after sunset, and in the early part of the night.

On occasion, to allay suspicion, she'll perform the Prayer
 without the ritual ablution.[27]
Should her client wish to play mate to a lion and ask
 "Can you arrange it?" she'll say, "Indeed I can."
When tumult starts and voices rise, she'll affect a certain
 deafness, though she's anything but deaf.
How many a cunning practice has she mastered!
 How many, oh, how many a trick she knows so well!
Well past ninety now she is, but God still lets her
 have her way!
The Devil has written on her forehead, and the inscription
 reads as follows:
If you cannot get it with a girl in purdah, put this
 woman on her trail and leave it all to her.

A watcher appointed to spy on girls[28] as well as custodians and
trusted serving-women will, if bribed with things they badly
want, gladly play the pimp. A poet writes:

> Let the watcher have it first, and if you do a good job
> there, the watcher, however trusty, will then procure
> for you.

If the watcher is a woman who is getting on in years and keeps
close guard, and, if it is known that no help can be expected of
her in procuring her charge, the thing to do, I would say, is this:
The man should leave both the watcher and her charge alone
for some time and let them think he has little desire for the girl
so that the older woman will relax her vigilance and care. Then
one of his young servant boys or some other person who is
known to have no interest in the object of his desire can exert
his influence over the watcher by blandishing and cajoling her
and feigning affection for her. This will appeal to her, and she
will fall for her flatterer wholeheartedly. If she shuns him or
reviles him, he shouldn't be discouraged. It will only be a pretence to test him and a means of letting him know what she

27 See above Ch. II, n. 40, p. 56.
28 See above Ch. II, n. 30, p. 42.

wants. Then, when the two chance to be alone together in some convenient spot or other, he can rape her and she will love him all the more since, to her way of thinking, he will have proved his love by the use of force and provide her with a better excuse for letting him have his way with her. Once having had it, she will relax her tight hold on her charge, and he for his part will find it all very easy to get what he wants out of her. If, on the other hand, the interested party is willing to do his own spade-work and put himself out for the woman, he will be even more certain to succeed. I have composed some lines about this sort of thing:

> If one *kuss* spends the night keeping watch on another,[29]
>   give your penis the joyful news.
> Go first to the watcher, exposing your parts —your
>   organ will make itself known by such means.
> Lend her your penis time after time, and the loan will
>   bring your heart's desire quite within your reach.

I have also written the following:

> If you want to attain your desire, first perform with
>   the pimp as much as ever you can.
> It will not then be hard to have your way. So take
>   my advice—it is sound.

Many an older woman will procure you her daughter or her ward in the family either because she desires to get the man she loves or because she is by nature depraved. She will often corrupt girls behind their husbands' backs and impart a desire for vice, even where they are not short of sexual satisfaction. And certainly no pretty and attractive wench is likely to go short. What the older women really wants to do is to compete with her cronies who brazenly flaunt their depravity.

It is related that Asma'i recounted the following incident:

"I once went out into the open country and while I was

---

[29] That is, if one woman keeps watch on another. *Kuss* is the commonest vulgar term for vulva and may, like its four-letter English equivalent, be used of a person in obscene abuse.

ambling along I suddenly spotted a tent all on its own.[30] So I went up to it, and there inside was an older woman sitting with a girl as pretty as the moon at night. I asked for a drink, and the older woman told the girl to go and get me one. So she brought me out a cup of milk, and I drank it. As I looked at the girl I was smitten with her, so much did her beauty delight me. I motioned to her that I wanted to kiss her. But she held back and drew away from me. 'What's the matter with you?' asked the older woman. 'He was wanting to kiss me,' came the reply. So the older said, 'Dear child, haven't you heard these verses:

> If one human being kisses another in longing for his
>   mouth, he is no sinner. Nay, he will have his reward
>   therein.
> The thicker and faster the kisses, the greater the number
>   of good deeds that God will add to his record to erase
>   the bad.[31]?

Asma'i said, "So the girl came back to me, and I gave her ten kisses. 'Mother,' she said. 'This is the reward you named for one who gives two kisses. What is the recompense for one who puts it in right up to his testicles?' I laughed and went on my way longing to couple with her because of the way in which the older woman had given me the opportunity with those two verses of coming into contact with the girl."

If a man is after a girl who is co-operative, he will have no need to go to any great trouble to exert himself in any way. If she is closely guarded, he can get in touch with her by some very brief message or by dropping the slightest hint. One charming story I heard about the wit of both a messenger and the recipient of a message centres on Dhu Rumma.[32] This great poet decided he was

---

[30] Since Asma'i (above p. 57 n. 42) collected his philological information from desert Arabs, this excursion is understandable.

[31] In the Koran we are told that angels keep a record of men's actions and give witness for or against them at the Day of Judgement.

[32] A celebrated Arab poet (d. 735 or 736). Of his love affair with the girl called Mayya, we have little certain knowledge. From about the ninth century, however, he is assigned a place among famous Arab lovers whose love was unrequited.

going to pay Mayya a visit. Accordingly he got a Bedouin friend of his to go with him. When they got near to her tribe Dhu Rumma commented, "I've heard that Mayya's folk guard her jealously, and I can't think how I'm going to get in touch with her unless you can go to the camp by night and have the goodness to arrange an assignation." "But how," asked his friend, "am I going to manage that?" "You must use your wits," rejoined the poet. "If you don't, I'll just die of passion and anguish!" "So," said his friend, "I put my camel down, dismounted, and made my way to the tribe in a casual kind of way just like a passer-by. When I eventually found myself in front of Mayya's tents I recited the following lines:

'I drew near her yearning for union with her. Yet what
   is the good of being near the dwelling without so
   much as a guide?
I'll do anything for anyone who will take my message to
   her, and I pray that when he comes back he'll have
   arranged an assignation.'

"When the woman heard me she cried, 'Be off! Be off!' 'Whatever's the matter?' her father asked. 'Oh, it's a dog,' she replied, 'that comes to us every night at this time just when we've eaten.' So I went back and told Dhu Rumma that I'd arranged a meeting at the time indicated. He was overjoyed at the news and asked me how I'd managed it. So I told him the tale. Off we went for a day and a night, and after supper on the second night we secretly entered the encampment and made for the spot that they were to meet in. In due course she arrived with a young slave-girl of hers. The two lovers then spent the night immersed in the delight of the sweetest conversation and chafing and complaining of the pain of separation. I was with them all the time, yet did not see my companion even so much as put out his hand towards her with any base intent. There they stayed together until almost daybreak when the poet bade her goodbye and we went our way."[33]

[33] The ideal of chaste love and the sadness and tears of those who were martyrs to it are favourite themes with Arab—and also Persian and Turkish—poets and romancers. Such themes appear to have had their origins in a kind

I have actually come across this same story in a different version and with different lines of poetry. It is related with a chain of authorities going back to one of the sons of Hasan, son of 'Ali.[34] The narrator was a Bedouin of some eloquence who had been hauled before the Caliph Mutawakkil, imprisoned and subsequently released. This man says he was told the story by Nusayr ibn Tahif of Hilal. It runs as follows: "We had a young man called Bishr ibn 'Abdullah, better known as Ashtar.[35] Now, he was in love with a young slave-girl of his tribe by the name of Jayda', who happened, however, to be married. When the story of his love for her got round, he was kept well away from her, and things were made so difficult for him that he could get nowhere near her. So one day he came to me and said, 'My friend, I'm bursting with passion and can bear it no longer. Will you help me to see her?' I told him I would. So we got on our mounts and after two days' journey we stopped at a place not very far from the tribe. My companion found a spot to hide in and then said, 'Go to the tribe and accept hospitality but don't breathe a word about either me or her. Wait until you see a woman who is in charge of Jayda' '—and he told me what she looked like. So off I went and eventually came across the chaperon and had a word in her ear, whereupon she went to Jayda'. When she came back, she told me to tell Ashtar that an assignation had been arranged for such-and-such a time that night by a certain clump of trees. Whereupon I took myself off and told him.

"We sat down by the trees at the appointed time, and then all of a sudden Jayda' appeared. Ashtar leapt up to greet her and kissed her between her eyes. At this juncture I got up to leave them but they stopped me and begged me to come back. 'We've

of romantic nostalgia characteristic of detribalized elements as the Arabs became urbanized in the course of the eighth century.

[34] Hasan, son of Ali, the cousin and son-in-law of the Prophet, had a brother, Husayn who was killed in a revolt at Karbala' in October 680. Hasan himself abdicated the Caliphate to the Umayyad Mu'awiya. The Shi'ites accord the two brothers extraordinary veneration and include them in a sacred group of Five (of which the other members are the Prophet, 'Ali, and Fatima).

[35] The name means "having inverted eyelids" through a diseased condition of the eye.

nothing whatever to hide from you,' they declared. So I did as they asked. They sat talking, and then he said to her, 'Tell me, Jayda', can you think of any means whereby we can spend tonight in a really pleasurable way?' 'No,' she replied. 'Not unless you'd want me to go through all the misery and trouble that you know I've had to put up with before.' 'No,' he protested, 'I don't want anything to happen to you at all—but we *must* risk it even if we bring down heaven from above!' Whereupon she turned to him and asked, 'Is this friend of yours willing to do a good turn?' 'Yes, indeed,' I said. At this she got up and withdrew to a spot a little way away where she took off her clothes. She then gave them to me. 'Put them on,' she said, 'and give me yours.' So I did as I was asked. 'Now,' she said, 'go to my quarters and bed down in the place I normally sleep in. After dark my husband will come in and ask you for a bowl for milking the camels. Don't hand it to him, but just leave it down in front of you. That's what I do. He'll go away and come back with it full of milk and say, 'Here's your bedtime drink.' But don't take it first time. Wait till he keeps on insisting. Then take it or leave it. If in the end he puts it down himself, you'll not see it again till dawn. But if you put it down and he goes off, just drink a third of it and put it back in its place.' At that I left and did as she told me. Her husband in due course proffered the cup full to the brim, but I declined to drink, and, when he pressed me, I kept on declining. In the end, however, I leaned forward to get hold of the cup at the very same moment as he did. Our arms locked, and the cup got knocked over. 'Oh, this stubborn nonsense really is the end!' he shouted, and with that he grabbed a whip, seized me by my flowing hair and gave me a good thrashing across my back. At that point his mother and sister came and rescued me from his clutches just as I was about to knife him in an insane fury.

"They left, but presently Jayda''s mother came along. In she came and nattered to me until I was almost beside myself with rage. However, I held my tongue and kept on sobbing. 'Fear God, my child,' she urged me, 'and obey your husband. Forget Ashtar—how can he ever get to you? However, tonight I'll fetch your sister to keep you company.' With that she left and sent a girl who began to talk to me, calling down the wrath of God upon my assailant and weeping while I held my peace. When at length she lay down by my side, I clapped my hand over her mouth and said, 'Listen girl, your sister's with Ashtar. As I've had my back flayed for her, all the more reason for you to cover up for her. If you open your mouth you'll disgrace her, but it won't make any difference to me.' At this she shook like the branch of a tree with fright. Then she broke into a smile and spent the night chatting with me. At the crack of dawn she left, and I, for my part, went off to join my friends.

" 'What news?' asked Jayda' the moment I got back. 'Ask your sister,' I replied. 'She knows well enough, I assure you.' With that I gave her back her clothes and showed her my back. When she saw it, she was most put out and burst into tears. Tears also welled in Ashtar's eyes when I told him my story. We then went on our way."

The point of telling this tale is to illustrate that no guard will ever stop a woman once she has her heart on a man.

Some women will resort to all kind of tricks to arrange access for a man in whom they detect an inclination to co-operate. Such a one will have some old pedlar woman get him in her clutches. Here the commonest approach is for the go-between to ask a man to read her a note or a letter which she pretends she has received from her husband, alleging that she can find no one to read it to her and urging him to earn rewards from Heaven by doing her the favour.[36] But no sooner does he get inside the house than she bolts the door behind him and launches into a catalogue of the charms and attractions of her client and sets out to entice the man—may God protect him from her efforts! The situation is exactly the same as that exemplified in the well-known case of Bishr Hafi[37] and Hind.

Some men, of course, will scheme to bring lovers together and others will contrive to bring about a happy matrimonial match. But attempts of this sort are accounted part of chivalrous behaviour and not to be categorized as pimping. To illustrate, let us

---

[36] The assumption, of course, is that the woman is illiterate.
[37] A respected Sufi of Iranian provenance (c. 767–842).

look at the story of 'A'isha, daughter of Talha ibn 'Abdullah who was in love with Mus'ab ibn Zubayr. This woman was notorious for her unpleasant ways, her viciousness and bad temper. Mus'ab, however, was madly in love with her because of a beauty and loveliness that was unrivalled in her day and age. Now, one day she turned on him in a fit of rage. He, for his part, went off to tell his tale of woe to one of his friends. "What," asked his friend, "will you give me if I make it up with her for you?" "Just name your price," answered Mus'ab. "Ten thousand dirhams, then," said his friend. "It's a bargain," Mus'ab declared. Whereupon his friend went off to 'A'isha. "I'd give my very life for you," he began. "As you well know, I was once in love with you long ago, yet never had any recompense or profit for my pains. But now I have a request to make—you can do me a favour which will make up for what I never had and at the same time earn my gratitude." "What is it then?" she asked. "The Emir," he said, "has promised me ten thousand dirhams if only you will make it up with him." "How dare you! Never!" she cried. "Come now," he begged, "I beseech you by all that is sacred to me to make it up with him so that he'll keep his promise. After that you can be as ill-tempered as God made you." At this she smiled and made it up with Mus'ab.

It is said that this story actually concerns 'Amr ibn 'Ubayd and that the messenger was Ibn Abi 'Atiq. The latter was well known as a mediator who would do all he possibly could to reconcile married couples and bring them together again once estranged.

CHAPTER V

On Women, Sex and Marriage: Illustrative Stories, Unusual and Humorous Anecdotes and Comical Tales

One of Solomon's sayings is "Women epitomize a faltering tongue and laxity of morals. Cure, then, the one with silence and the other by confinement to the home." One of 'Umar's is: "Neither teach them to read and write nor leave them alone in rooms." There is also a saying, "Teach them the 'Chapter of Light' in the Koran, but keep the 'Chapter of Joseph' out of their reach; for in the latter they are told the story of Joseph and Zuleika, while in the former they are castigated for fornication and adultery.[1]

[1] The "Chapter of Light" is Koran xxiv, the essence of which is that unlawful sexual intercourse (see above Ch. I, n. 10, p. 24) must be severely punished (cf. verse 2: "A man or woman guilty of illicit union flog with a hundred lashes"). The "Chapter of Joseph" is Koran xii, the Joseph in question being the biblical Joseph of whom Zuleika, wife of Potiphar (Genesis xxxix), became enamoured. In the Koranic version Joseph no more falls prey to temptation than in the Old Testament, and the worst that is said of him is "She was taken by him and he by her [and would have succumbed] except that he saw his Lord's clear indication [that he should not yield]" (xii, 24). On the other hand, this chapter dwells on the wiles of women, and the story lost nothing in the telling by popular story-tellers whose aim was to titillate the imagination. The Koranic version was elaborated to the full by the great Persian poet Jami (1414–92), and in Persian the story is known as a great popular romance.

People also say, "What we gain in the 'Chapter of Light' we lose in the 'Chapter of Joseph' " which means that one gains on one thing, one loses on another.[2] The history behind the saying is that there was once a story-teller who would wait for women at gravesides[3] and recite the "Chapter of Joseph" to them and describe in great detail what went on between Joseph and Zuleika. So popular did he become with the women that they took to gathering round him in large numbers. In this way he amassed a fortune and became notorious for having women around him. In the end he was summoned before the town governor, who had him beaten and forced him to recite only the "Chapter of Light" from that time onwards. When asked how he was going on, he replied, "What I gained on the 'Chapter of Joseph' I've lost on the 'Chapter of Light'. "

Among other sayings are, "Keep women to the duster" and "A woman's best pastime is the spindle." In this connexion we may mention the story of the wife of Hajjaj,[4] who was asked on some occasion or other, "And does the wife of the Emir spin then?" To which she replied, "I once heard my father say that the Prophet observed that the woman with the longest thread shall have the greatest reward—spinning drives the Devil away and clears the mind of bad thoughts."

'Ali once asked Fatima,[5] "Who is best among women?" ''She who neither sees nor is seen by men," she replied. When the

---

[2] Or as we would say "What one gains on the swings one loses on the roundabouts."

[3] Because visits to the cemetery were among the few opportunities which many women had of leaving the house, graveyards were often the scenes of great sexual activity. Medieval censors of public morals frequently call for the strongest measures against those who transform cemeteries into places of sexual licence and debauchery. See, for instance, E. Lévi-Provençal's French translation of a treatise by Ibn 'Abdun (twelfth century): *Séville musulmane* (Paris 1947), pp. 57–60.

[4] Hajjaj ibn Yusuf (661–714), the most celebrated of all Umayyad governors and one of the most efficient administrators that the Muslim world has ever known. Cultivated, competent, and conscientious, he was widely detested for his unswerving and often ruthless devotion to duty and the Umayyad dynasty. Arabic literature abounds in anecdotes for and—mostly—against him.

[5] See above Ch. II, n. 41, p. 56.

Prophet was told of this observation his comment was, "She's a chip off the old block" meaning that, like him, she made wise pronouncements.

Someone else once said, "That a thousand men should see my wife uncovered would be easier for me to bear than that my wife should see just one man uncovered." By this he meant that women are quicker to mischief than men.

Akhyal's Layla[6] once tasted wine and said to the men who offered it to her, "Do your women drink this?" "Yes," they replied. "By God, then," she said, "they must sleep around and none of you ever know who your father is!"

Hutay'a,[7] who was a most jealous man once went off on a long journey. When asked, "Who have you left in charge of your daughters?" he replied, "Hunger, that they might not stray from home and Nakedness that they might not dress to kill!"

In similar circumstances 'Aqil ibn 'Ullafa was also asked, "Don't you feel any pangs of jealousy when you think of the womenfolk you're leaving behind?" "No, I'm leaving two good guards with them—Hunger and Nakedness," was his reply.

I personally see no sense in these tactics, for if a woman through poverty and need created by her husband or legal guardian is forced in consequence to seek alternative means of support, knowing full well that her spouse is capable of supporting her, she will readily keep the wolf from the door the best way she can and not mind dishonouring him and betraying his trust in her since loyalty does not come naturally to a woman. The evidence of their own eyes is sufficient inducement to women to yield to their craving for pleasure, and hunger will force them to cast modesty aside. No, the best thing is to steer a middle course and to have them keep themselves in check.

[6] Layla (flourished early Umayyad period and died 707 or 708) was a woman of great beauty of the line of Akhyal, a desert hero of old Arabia. A poetess of some beauty, she was distantly related to Majnun (see above Ch. III, n. 15, p. 67.

[7] Arab poet (born c. 582) whose work largely dates from the early Islamic period. In Arabic literature he is portrayed as a most unpleasant character and is listed as one of the top four Arab misers—miserliness being considered a major vice by the Arabs.

A man of good sense will not be fooled by his wife's pretence that she is not a jealous woman and does not mind him taking another wife or buying slave-girls. Many a man has foundered on this kind of rock. A husband would also do well to keep his secrets from women, for no sooner are they party to a secret than it is all over town and no longer a secret. Indeed any enterprise in which they are allowed any part is doomed to failure. It is said that the wife of the Caliph 'Umar ibn 'Abd-ul-'Aziz[8] was once offering gratuitous advice in some matter or another, but he took her to task with the words, "A woman is a fragrant flower and not a high steward."[9]

A man would be wise not to be deluded by the passionate and abandoned love his wife gives him when she is happy. She has only to have a fit of temper for her to withhold her favours and make life a misery for him. Moreover, if he has any sense, he will not trust a woman in any sphere or believe a single word she says; women are tricksters who have the ability to wriggle out of awkward situations which give their husbands room for suspicion. The following story will illustrate the point I am making.

There was once a man who used to collect all the anecdotes about women he could keep a record of the crafty and deceitful tricks they would play on their menfolk. "There's nothing I don't know about women," he would boast. Now, a certain woman got to hear of this and invited him to join her for drinks. Having got together an unimaginable array of drinks and snacks, she had him come to her house. The woman in question was noted for her beauty and much desired, and, as soon as our friend got his feet inside the house and saw her—she had groomed herself well for the occasion—he was enthralled by her extraordinary beauty. What he did not realize was that she had deliberately contrived the meeting to coincide with her husband's return— and this man was of a notoriously violent and tyrannical dis-

---

[8] Often called 'Umar II (reg. 717–20). Although an Umayyad, 'Umar was a pietist and is generally venerated as a noble character of scrupulous integrity whose policies were aimed at suppressing abuses and restoring Islam to its pristine purity.

[9] i.e. not a senior administrator, but a desirable adornment delighting the senses.

position who would not hesitate to shed the blood of anyone he caught in his house.

No sooner had they begun their carousal than they heard a knock at the front door. The hostess pretended to throw a fit of agitation and terror. "Oh God, here comes my husband!" she cried. And with that she pushed her guest, filled with dread, into a closet that opened into the room. Locking the door on him, she put down the key by the place where she was sitting and then opened the door to her husband. When he saw the drink and all the utensils, he demanded to know what it was all about. "Well, you can see what's there," she replied. "But whatever for?" he went on. "It's for a lover I have," said she. "And where is he?" he demanded. "In that closet," she said as she pointed to the spot. The answer infuriated her husband. Leaping to his feet, he made a dash for the closet only to find it locked. "Where's the key?" he thundered. "Here," she said as she threw it to him. But once he had the key and set about opening the door, she burst into screams of laughter. "What's so funny?" he shouted as he rounded on her. "I'm just laughing at your stupidity, poor discernment and the way you go about things, you silly man. Do you really think that if I'd have had a lover and let him into the house, I'd have been foolish enough to tell you about him and show you his hiding place? No, I've laid on this spread just for you. I don't care for anything before you get home, so I just thought I'd tease you to see what you'd do." With that her husband just left the key as it was and went back to his drink with the comment, "I was absolutely convinced that what you first said was true." The couple then got on with their drinking, and all the while the man languished in the closet until the husband finally went out. Whereupon the woman opened the door and let him out just when he thought his end was in sight. "Have you," she asked, "included a story like this in the collection you've made?" "I always knew women to be great schemers," he gasped as he took himself off as fast as he could.

It is good common sense not to go away and leave one's wife on her own for too long because, generally speaking, a woman will not go without sex for too long unless the fear of Almighty God holds her in check. In Ibn Jawzi's(?) book on the Caliph

'Umar ibn Khattab[10] the author recounts an incident on the authority of a chain of authorities going back to Sa'ib ibn Jubayr, the client of Ibn 'Abbas. One night, so he tells us, 'Umar went for a stroll round Medina[11] and heard a woman singing the following song:

> The nights are long and dark for me. No friend have I
> to dally with, and so I cannot sleep.
> By God, were it not for Him who has no overlord, the
> sides of this bed would shake!
> Throughout the night I'd stay awake and snuggle up to
> a carefree lad, lively, lithe and lean.
> But in my heart I fear a Watchful Guardian[12] of our
> souls whose scribe never sleeps nor rests.

She then heaved a deep sigh and said aloud, "Little does Caliph 'Umar care for my loneliness and my husband's absence on campaigns.[13] 'Umar was deeply moved by these words and went straight to his daughter's. "What brings you here at this late hour, Commander of the Faithful?"[14] asked Hafsa. "Just tell me," he asked, "how long can a woman do without her husband? That's what I came to ask you." "Six months," she replied. He then wrote a letter in which he instructed the woman's husband to return and look after his wife. Thereafter he never put an army into the field for more than six months at a time.

[10] 'Umar I (second Patriarchal Caliph, reg. 632–34) was largely responsible for the vigorous campaigns which gained for Islam the territories on which the foundations of the Arab Empire were raised.

[11] One of the two Holy Cities of Islam in what is now Saudi Arabia and the first capital of Islam. It was there that the Prophet died.

[12] i.e. God, for whom a record of men's actions is kept (see above Ch. IV, n. 31, p. 91).

[13] Her husband was obviously a member of one of the numerous armies which 'Umar I had to raise to break down opposition within the Arabian Peninsula and to maintain the steady spread of the early conquests beyond the Peninsula. See above n. 10.

[14] Although essentially incorrect ("Prince of Believers" even more so), this translation of the Arabic style adopted by 'Umar I and thereafter borne by the caliphs is that most commonly used in English and will therefore be retained.

A somewhat similar story is told by a Shi'ite,[15] who relates that one night 'Umar was strolling along a street in Medina when he heard a woman uttering these verses:

> Now that 'Amr, my spouse, has left me alone, my
>   roving eye as it gazes around invites me to pleasures
>   new.
> But I tell it my heart will not accept—and yet, if he
>   tarries too long, I know it must surrender.
> Yet if I surrender to you, my eye, I'll have to reckon
>   with the heat of a fire and disgrace that'll cover me
>   just like a veil.

'Umar then knocked on the door and asked her to repeat the lines. When she had done so, he asked her, "What prevents you from following your roving eye?" "Modesty," she answered, "and respect for my honour." "One who seeks modesty," commented 'Umar, "is faithful, and one who is faithful is God-fearing. Tell me, where's your husband at the present time?" "He's stationed at such-and-such a place," she said. 'Umar then sent a message to his commanding officer and the latter sent him home to her.

The Prophet was once asked, "What sort of woman is best?" He replied, "One who is pleasing to her husband's eye when he looks upon her, who obeys him when he gives an order and who gives him no displeasure by what she is or has."

Zayd ibn Haritha[16] was once in the company of the Prophet, who asked him whether he was married. When Zayd said that he was not, the Prophet gave him the following advice, "Marry

[15] The Shi'ites are a schismatic minority in Islam and in doctrine and law they differ from the majority group of Muslims (Sunnites). Within Shi'ism itself there are sects, of which the most important are the Imamites or "Twelvers" (see below p. 161, n. 3), whose religion is the official religion of Persia, having a following in India, Iraq, and Syria. The more extreme Isma'ilis, who, under the Aga Khan, have a following in India and East Africa. Shi'ism had its origins in the political claim that 'Ali, cousin and son-in-law of the Prophet was his true successor and that the first three Caliphs of Islam were usurpers.

[16] See above Ch. III, n. 24, p. 71.

and encourage chastity, but marry none of the following types —a *shahbara, lahbara, nahbara, habdara, lafūt.*" "By God," exclaimed Zayd, "I don't understand a word of all that, Messenger of God!" Where upon he received the following explanation, "A *shahbara* is a woman who is blue-eyed and gross, a *lahbara* is tall and thin, a *nahbara* is a withered old woman, a *habdara* is short and ugly, and a *lafūt* is one who has already borne children to some other man."

Abu Hanifa used to laugh whenever the following tale was told to him.[17] Some Arab once gave his son this advice, "Beware, my boy, of three kinds of women: the type who waits for her husband's death so as to inherit his wealth, the type who is quick to anger, and the type who is given to scowling."

A sage once gave his son similar advice. "Do not, my son," he said, "marry a moaner, a yearner or a benefactress. By a moaner I mean one who remarries after losing one husband and then forever moans to the second about having lost the first; by a yearner I mean a woman who has a son by a previous husband and is always yearning for him; by a benefactress I mean a woman of enormous wealth who plays lady bountiful to her husband."

While on the subject of moaners, let us take the case of Laqit ibn Zurara who married to Laghdur daughter of Qays ibn Mas'ud.[18] These two were very much in love, and after his death she was married by 'Umar ibn Jawz of Kinda, who for ever had to listen to her uttering her first husband's name, bewailing his death and singing his praises. One day he could stand it no longer. "Damn you, woman," he cried, "Laqit was no better than one of my slaves! Just tell me one thing about him that pleased you." "Indeed I will," she said, "I'll tell you. One day when the tribe had gone off to fight the battle of Dhu Zahr-wa-Zill he had sweetened himself with perfume. I was asleep at the time, and he hadn't wished to rouse me. So he sat there waiting for me to wake up and sipped the rest of a drink that he'd had. When at last I

[17] Abu Hanifa (699?–767) is one of the most important figures in Islam in that he was the reputed founder of one of the four legal systems recognized by Sunnite Islam.
[18] The full name given in the text is Q. ibn M. ibn Khalid ibn Dhi 'l-Jadir.

woke up, he picked me up and got on his horse, and away we went. All of a sudden we ran into a herd of wild asses. Setting me down, he charged them and slew one of the herd. He then came back to me smelling of musk and wine and the sweet scent of battle. I snuggled up to him, and he pressed me to him, leaving the smell of him lingering on me. Oh, how I wish I had died there and then!"

'Umar, having heard this story, was moved to do as his wife's first husband had done. So he sweetened himself with perfume, drank some wine and went off hunting. On his return he went straight to his wife, pressed her to his body and asked, "How do I compare with Laqit?" "Like a pasture, but not of the finest grass, like water, but not of the sweetest wells," she replied. At this he repudiated her, and she returned to her tribe and said, "Erect for me a widow's tent. May God never unite me with another man now that Laqit is dead!"

'A'isha daughter of Talha was another who exasperated her husband by dwelling on a former husband.[19] She would frequently give her then husband, 'Umar ibn 'Ubaydullah, detailed accounts of Mus'ab, the man to whom she had previously been married. She would enumerate all his qualities and tell of his good looks, his generosity and good nature until 'Umar almost died of chagrin. Mada'ini tells how 'Umar staggered in one day absolutely overcome by the heat and dust of the day.[20] Turning to 'A'isha, he gasped, "Wipe the dust off me." So she took a cloth and started to wipe him down. "I've never seen dust look better on any man's face than on Mus'ab's," she remarked. "I well

---

[19] This 'A'isha—not to be confused with the Prophet's wife whose name without qualification is to be taken as referring to her exclusively—was the daughter of one of his renowned Companions and one of the most celebrated of all Arab women. Noble and by nature imperious, she possessed great beauty and charm which she went out of her way to display and exploit. She married in succession 'Abdullah ibn Abd-ul-Rahman, Mus'ab ibn Zubayr (rebel governor of Basra (687) for his brother the anti-Caliph 'Abdullah ibn Zubayr), and, after his death, 'Umar ibn 'Ubaydullah.

[20] A student of Prophetic Tradition, Mada'ini (d. 840) was a noted scholar of Basra, who organized the historical material collected by his predecessors. His work is of capital importance as a generally reliable source of early Islamic history.

remember the day he came home after a great and victorious battle. We'd not seen each other for a long time, and so I went out to meet him as he stood there in his armour and congratulated him while the dust was still on his face. 'I'm sorry,' he said to me 'for filling your nose with the smell of this armour.' " And she went on describing him to 'Umar, who all the time was seething with rage and almost dying of jealousy and frustration.

In his *Songs* Abu Faraj[21] relates the following story: When Hajjaj married Hind, daughter of Asma' ibn Kharija, who had previously been married to 'Ubaydullah ibn Ziyad, he took her with him to Basra and built there for her the palace which was named after him.[22] When the building was finished, he asked her, "Have you ever seen anything to compare with this palace?" "It's really splendid," she replied. "Do you truly mean that?" he persisted. "Well then," she replied," since you don't believe me, I'll tell you quite truthfully that I've never seen a finer building than the Red Palace when 'Ubaydullah lived there,"—the Red Palace being the Emir's residence in Basra which had been built of red clay for 'Ubaydullah. This remark so incensed Hajjaj that he repudiated her and sent a message to Basra with orders to demolish the Red Palace. In its place he erected another building which was subsequently demolished and incorporated in the Great Mosque of Basra.

So much for women who bemoan former husbands. Here we have evidence enough that a suitor contemplating marriage should marry a virgin whose love for him will be enduring and who will never forget the man who took her virginity.

---

[21] As will become apparent later, the *Songs* of Abu Faraj Isfahani (897–967) is the source of many of our author's anecdotes and, as such, it merits an extended note. A monument of classical Arabic literature written over a period of fifty years, the work is a collection of songs selected by famous musicians on the orders of the celebrated Caliph Harun (al-) Rashid (better known to most readers of the *Arabian Nights* as the "good Haroun Alraschid"). More important than the actual songs is the information given by its author about the poets who wrote them. In short, it offers a rich and detailed picture of Arab life from pre-Islamic times to the end of the ninth century.

[22] 'Ubaydullah ibn Ziyad (d. 683) had been governor of Basra prior to Mus'ab (see above n. 19). The latter was defeated by Hajjaj in 691.

It is a good idea for anyone contemplating marriage to marry into a family of outsiders, that is to say persons who are not related by blood. This point is made by Ghazali in his *Revivification*,[23] where he quotes the Prophet's words: "Do not marry close relations, for your offspring will turn out to be puny." Moreover, we have 'Umar's words to the tribe of Beni Sa'ib, "You are too inbred—marry out of your tribe." The Arabs of old also used to declare that the child of closely related parents would turn out to be weakly. On of their sayings was, "Marry outside the family and you will not breed weaklings."

In this connexion some poet once said of Bilal:[24]

> Bilal's mother brought him no disgrace, for his kin,
> paternal and maternal, came of different stock.

On the same theme another poet says:

> . . . a lad not of a cousins' marriage and therefore weak—
> for often weakness springs from kin too close.

Another poet's words run thus:

> I chose my wife outside my kin to bear me healthy stock.
> She did just that and bore me a son graced with
> features like the moon when full.[25]

[23] The full title of this work—yet another major source utilized by Nafzawi—is *Revivification of Religious Sciences*. In it the great religious thinker and writer Ghazali (1059-1111)—known to medieval Europe as Algazel—expounds his concept of religion as a faith rooted in spiritual experience. In reconciling orthodox formalism with mystical idealism Ghazali treats of a wide range of subjects falling within the scope of religious law and therefore with marriage and sexual relations.

[24] A black African slave born in Mecca. An early convert to Islam, he was purchased from his master and given his freedom. He was highly regarded by the Prophet whom he accompanied on all his military expeditions. After the fall of Mecca he had the distinction of being the first muezzin to summon the Faithful to prayer from the top of the Kaaba. He died somewhere between 638 and 642.

[25] See above p. 28, n. 14.

Yet another poet says:

> I chose a wife outside my kin to bear me healthy stock.
> And so she bore me noble offspring as mothers will who
> lie outside one's kin.

Asma'i comments on the words of Ka'b ibn Zuhayr, who says in describing a she-camel:[26]

> A lean she-camel whose sire's her brother, born of a
> she-camel's mother with sire's brother as mother's
> brother—a camel meek and brisk.

Asma'i's commentary is that the animal described was a fine she-camel inbred because of pedigree. Abu Makarim, on the other hand, expresses disagreement and maintains that Asma'i did not know that inbreeding gives poor stock. In his book *The Pearls* Bakri[27] tells of a Bedouin who would say, "I'm just the offspring of nobility." He goes on to explain that the man's father married only within his own family and in consequence his son was puny.

Some other writer explains that the reason behind the condemnation of marriage within one's own family is the fact that a wife who is one's cousin will not appeal to her husband as much as a wife from outside. This is either because he is too closely connected with her and sees too much of her or because such a degree of modesty develops between the two that it produces indifference to sexual relations and weakens the husband's urge. What is more, no child will develop to perfection or attain to full strength unless he is the fruit of a perfect union based on desire. Hence the saying, "A man who is shy with his wife will not produce fine offspring."

In his *Songs* Abu Faraj recounts the following: Manzur ibn

---

[26] Ka'b—the author of a famous panegyric on Muhammad—was the son of one of the greatest of all pre-Islamic poets.

[27] Ranked with Idrisi (author of the famous *Book of Roger*) as the greatest geographer in the Muslim West, Abu 'Ubayd Bakri (d. 1094) was also the author of the work whose abbreviated title is given here and which is a commentary on Qali's *Dictations* (see below p. 170).

Zabban of Fazara[28] once went to visit his maternal grandfather, Hasan ibn Hasan, who said to him, "No doubt you're married by now, boy?" "Yes," replied Manzur, "I'm married to my cousin, the daughter of my paternal uncle, Husayn." "That's a bad thing," commented his grandfather. "Don't you know that unions between close kin weaken the strain? You ought to have married a girl more distant."

In his *Women* Abu Faraj writes: Someone once said to Hayya, "I would like to take a wife." "For what sort of dower?" he asked. "A hundred dinars," he said. "Don't do that," said the other. "Make it ten, and if she agrees you'll gain ninety, and if she doesn't, you'll be able to marry ten with the money, and out of ten there's bound to be one that'll suit you."[29]

Abu Yasir of Baghdad in his *Treatise on Perfume* relates a curious tale. According to him there have been two wedding feasts without equal or precedent in the annals of Islam. The first was the marriage of Harun Rashid with Zubayda daughter of Ja'far ibn Mansur.[30] We have this on the authority of Ahmad ibn Abi Tahir, author of the *History of Baghdad*. He tells us that when the Caliph Mahdi arranged for his son to wed Zubayda, he regaled her on an unprecedented scale with utensils, vessels, furnishings, carpets, clothing, perfumes, jewels, slaves and eunuchs. He also had made for his daughter-in-law a robe studded with priceless pearls of indescribable quality. (It is said that it was the robe which belonged to 'Abda . . .).[31] At all events, Harun was married at the Khuld Palace in the month of Muharram in the year of the Hegira 165 (A.D. 781). People

28 The Arabic text is corrupt and has been amended from the *Songs*.

29 On the dower or bride-price see above Ch. IV, n. 18, p. 84. Islamic law, of course, permits a man no more than four wives at any one time, and a Muslim could only marry up to ten by the use of his right to divorce.

30 As already noted (above n. 21), Harun (reg. 786–809) is the "good Haroun Alraschid" of the *Arabian Nights*. His wife Zubayda, whom he married in 781, was the granddaughter of Mansur, the second Abbasid caliph and virtual founder of the dynasty. As such, she was Harun's cousin. On her qualities, benefactions, and her position among the famous women of Islam see D. M. Dunlop, *Arab Civilization to A.D. 1500* (Longman, 1971), p. 257.

31 The text is almost illegible at this point, but appears to read "daughter of 'Abdullah ibn Zayd ibn Mu'awiya ibn Hisham ibn 'Abd-ul-'Aziz."

flocked from all over the Empire to attend the celebrations, and wealth such as no treasure-house could be imagined to contain was distributed. Golden vessels were filled with dirhams, and vessels of silver filled with dinars, and then presented to leading personalities in addition to sachets of musk, pieces of amber and embroidered robes of honour. Mahdi then summoned all the women of the Beni Hashim and gave each and every one of them an embroidered garment, a leathern bag of dinars and a bottle of perfume. It is also said that it was at these celebrations that Qamari aloes were held to be inferior to Indian; for, when the two scents were tested one against the other, the Indian was found to be better and proved to linger longer on one's clothes. Poets sang of the feast, and Mahdi and his son, Harun, received letters of congratulations from all quarters of the globe. It has been said that a more splendid wedding feast than this has never been recorded in the history of Islam. It drained Harun's treasury of 50,000,000 dinars.

The second of the occasions concerned was Ma'mun's indescribably splendid wedding. In the month of Sha'ban in the year of the Hegira 210 (A.D. 826) Ma'mun had left for Fam as-Silh,[32] where he assumed the office of ruler. For his wedding he did what no ruler had ever done before either in pre-Islamic times or in the history of Islam. He invited all the Hashimites,[33] military commanders and secretaries of state and showered them with pellets of musk containing pieces of paper on which the names of land grants and slave-girls were written as well as the right to personal gifts and presents of great value. As each guest laid hands on any of these things as they fell around them, he immediately opened his piece of paper and went straight away to collect his prize. On the rest of the gathering were showered dinars and dirhams to-

[32] Sha'ban is the eighth month of the Islamic year. Ma'mun was the eighth Abbasid Caliph (reg. 813-33) and the woman he married was Buran, daughter of Hasan ibn Sahl, his senior financial officer. The wedding festivities were held at Fam as-Silh on the River Tigris below Baghdad. See Dunlop, op. cit. (above n. 31), pp. 259-60.

[33] i.e. members of the Abbasid family. Sometimes the term also covers their supporters and followers as well. It derives from the name Hashim ibn 'Abd Manaf, the common ancestor of the Prophet and Abbas.

gether with sachets of musk and pieces of amber. Moreover, annual stipends and grants were assigned not only to each and every member of Ma'mun's armed forces, each according to his rank. It is said that quite apart from his army, which Abu Yasir puts at 90,000 strong on the authority of Hasan ibn Raja', there were 36,000 naval men.

When Buran was prepared for the nuptial couch, so we are told by Abu Faraj, special mats of gold thread were spread on the floor and a great vessel wrought of gold was brought in filled with pearls and emptied on the mat. Among the women who were present were Zubayda and Hamduna, daughters of Harun Rashid, and others—all daughters of the Caliphs. None of these picked up a single pearl. And so Ma'mun remarked, "Honour my wife by taking your choice. At this each and every one stretched forth her hand and picked one pearl, leaving the rest for all to see upon the mats. "Oh, what a poet Abu Nuwas is!" exclaimed Ma'mun. "He may well have been right when he said in praise of wine:

> It is as if bubbles large and small upon this liquid surface
> were tiny pebbles, little pearls strewn on a floor of gold.

Abu Yasir tells us that on that night a candle weighing eighty pounds was lit, but Ma'mun disapproved of it on the grounds of sheer extravagance. So Zubayda ordered that it be removed and replaced by ordinary candles. When Ma'mun in due course asked her the cost of the celebrations, the reply he got was "Between thirty-five and thirty-nine million." When Buran's father, Hasan ibn Sahl heard of her estimate, he protested, "You'd think she'd paid the bill. I did in fact tot up the amount and it came to thirty-three million."

Some four thousand mules were put to carrying wood for fuel for four months before the wedding, and, when they ran short of fuel during the actual celebrations, they burned flax for firewood.

Haytham ibn 'Adi recounts the following story: When Hajjaj married his son Muhammad, he said, "For his wedding celebrations I shall lay on such a feast as no one has ever done before or will ever do again." These words prompted someone to say, "God bless you, Emir. You may think it a good idea to send for someone who lived to see the Chosroes Parviz[34] and who could tell you what the Persian Kings did on such occasions, so that you may do things properly. For knowledge is the basis of statesmanship." Accordingly, Hajjaj sent for some aged survivor from the last days of the Persian Kings and asked him to describe to him the most delicious, the most lavish and most renowned dishes ever served by that monarch. "Yes, I can tell you," the old man replied. When Parviz decided to marry, he wrote to all his provincial governors throughout the Empire and commanded each to attend accompanied by his private secretary and a local notable. In all, four thousand gathered there, and for these guests he spread silk carpets embroidered with gold with cushions to match. Silver trays were brought in with rare delicacies served on gold plates. When the meal was over, each guest was presented with a miskal of musk with which to wash his hands.[35] The celebrations went on in this fashion for three days, and all carpets and utensils were divided among the guests. Their every need was supplied, and then they were sent their several ways. "This infidel," exclaimed Hajjaj," has spoiled it for us! Go and get camels for slaughter, and in every district of the city of Wasit slaughter a beast and divide it among its inhabitants.[36]

At this point we may usefully turn to various details relating to the unveiling ceremony on the wedding night[37] and the rules to be followed by man and wife at the time of their union as well as before consummation. In this connexion reference will be made to the work entitled *The Bride's Gift and the Heart's Delight*.

[34] Persian Sasanid ruler (reg. 590–628). He is often referred to outside Arabic sources as Khosrau Parvez II, son of Ormizd IV.

[35] Traditionally the Arabs ate with their fingers (many still do), using the right hand only. The need to wash one's hands at meals is necessary if this custom is followed. What usually happens is that a servant will bring water and a towel and pass from one guest to the next. A miskal is a measure of weight (Arabic *mithqāl*) which varied according to time and place, but which in this case would have probably been about 4.68 grammes.

[36] Wasit was located on the Tigris between Baghdad and the Gulf.

[37] This was the ceremony at which the bride's veil was lifted to display her to her husband. On this occasion the husband would present to her a wedding gift.

From the earliest times right up to the present it has been customary for the bride, prior to leaving for the bridegroom, to be displayed unveiled before members of her family and then again before the bridegroom after her arrival at his house. This custom is justified by a Tradition which most people quote and which they ascribe to Qasim ibn 'Ubaydullah, who, on the authority of Ibn Dinar and Ibn 'Umar, relates that the Prophet had his wife 'A'isha displayed unveiled before her parents prior to consummation of the marriage at his house.[38]

In his book *Inspection* Abu Qattan says that the implication is that it was the custom for the bride to be displayed before the womenfolk before she went in to her husband. Sa'id ibn Musayyib,[39] on the authority of Ibn 'Abbas[40] says that when the Prophet married his daughter Fatima to 'Ali, he first went round to his womenfolk and told them he had given his daughter Fatima in marriage to his paternal cousin, adding, "You are well aware of her standing with me. Now I shall hand her over to 'Ali. There you are, then—take your daughter." With that the womenfolk went up to Fatima, covered her with scents and bedecked her with finery. When the Prophet later entered the room, all the ladies leapt up in deference to him except Asma' daughter of 'Umays. "Who," the Prophet asked, "are you?" "I'm watching over your daughter, because a girl, on her wedding night, needs a woman near her in case she requires her or wants to have a word with her," was her reply. Whereupon the Prophet said to her, "May God watch over you and protect you from the Devil at every end and side." The full story is a long tale.

The woman in charge of arrangements for displaying the

[38] In medieval times custom demanded that the bride be conducted to the house of the bridegroom in a palanquin carried on the shoulders of bearers. After being welcomed by her husband, the bride would be taken into a room specially set aside for them, and the marriage would be consummated. Immediately afterwards a dresser appointed to the task would display a blood-stained cloth to the guests in the courtyard as evidence that the bride was a virgin. Great importance was, and still is, attached to the bride's virginity.

[39] One of the seven great jurisconsults of Medina (634–713).

[40] The Prophet's cousin (c. 619–87 or 678). He is generally recognized as one of the greatest of the first generation of Muslims.

bride to her husband should take care to show off all the girl's best points and bring out hidden charms by the use of cosmetic dyes and other beautifying agents. Should she overlook anything, the bride should draw her attention to it by pointing her hand or waggling her foot or using some other sign.[41]

Rughayb, the hairdresser, tells the following story: "It was I who performed the ceremony of displaying Rayya daughter of Jahhaf to her husband Qudama. She was a buxom girl with the eyes and neck of a gazelle, a girl of outstanding beauty and nature. Just as I was drawing her hands forward to show her husband the beauty of the colour which adorned them she stuck her foot out from beneath her robe, and I knew immediately what she meant and turned to showing him hand and foot alternately. The husband turned to me and said, 'Never have I seen any colour more beautiful than that which adorns the hands and feet of my bride. I can think of nothing else. Indeed I can look at nothing else, for every time I glance at her hands my eyes go down to her feet—and still I long to keep on looking.' This pleased the bride—I could see the joy in her face."

Rughayb also relates how she carried out the same ceremony for Umm Banin daughter of Musa ibn 'Iqal when she married 'Umar ibn al-Farîd, Mahdi's intendant: "She was a slave-girl of such comeliness that she had no need of adornment, though adornment enhanced what she had. Women everywhere forever spoke of her beauty, her perfection and her utter modesty. No sooner had I begun to hold out my hand to point out some physical quality of hers than she anticipated my action. Yet when her husband went in to her to consummate the marriage she hated him for his lack of desire. She never thereafter ceased to loathe him and have a detestation of sleeping with him until in the end he was forced to divorce her."

Haytham ibn 'Adi relates the following story: Mus'ab ibn Zubayr went in and found 'A'isha daughter of Talha combing her hair and reciting the following verse:[42]

---

[41] The bride's movements would in any case be restricted by her elaborate and carefully arranged clothes as she sat enthroned in her bridal chair.

[42] On 'A'isha and Mus'ab see above n. 19.

I shall never forget the way she looked at me there in
Hijr[43] when she was displayed by Umm Manzur.

Upon being told that Umm Manzur, an old woman of the
Arabian tribe of 'Udhra, was still living, Mus'ab sent for her,
and she came to see him. "Umm Manzur," he asked, "how
did you prepare Buthayna for her wedding?"[44] "I combed her
hair," she replied," and perfumed it with a scent of saffron called
khaluq. Around her body I draped a gem-studded sash and
around her neck a necklace from Balkh.[45] Then Jamil rode up on
his she-camel, looked at us for a while and left." "I beseech you,"
begged Mus'ab, "to do exactly for 'A'isha what you did for
Buthayna." She did as she was asked, then Mus'ab came and
stayed to look at her for a while and left.

A bride should preferably go in to her husband at night, for
night is the time for rest and peace, the time to shed one's cares,
whereas the day is the time when people take themselves off and
go about their business. God appointed night for rest and day for
reawakening and return to life. There are, however, some in-
stances of consummation during the day. 'A'isha once said, "I
was married to the Prophet for six years, and he consummated
our marriage when I was nine.[46] When we came to Medina I
was not at all well for a month or so. I remember I had a good
head of hair at the time. At any rate, my mother Umm Ruman
came up to me one day while I was on a see-saw surrounded by
my playmates. As she took me away from them, I didn't really

[43] Now a site of ancient ruins in the north-west of Saudia Arabia near
Mada'in Salih, but in antiquity an important commercial town.

[44] Buthayna was a girl whose name is always associated with that of Jamil
(c. 660–701), a love-poet of the tribe of 'Udhra. Although hopelessly in love
with Buthayna, whose parents married her to someone else, he for ever
lamented his loss tenderly and passionately in a poetry of sublimation exalt-
ing the nobility and purity of love.

[45] Once a great capital of Khorasan, but now a village in what is today
Afghanistan.

[46] The motive for the marriage was political, and it was only consummated
in April 623 or 624 when 'A'isha was around ten years of age. In Islamic law
consummation is a fact which may have a legal effect in the event of dissolution of the marriage, but it is not essential for its conclusion.

know what was in her mind. However, she got hold of my hand and took me to a house where to my surprise I found some of the Helpers' womenfolk. They greeted me with the words, 'Very best wishes and the best of luck!' My mother then lifted me up, washed my hair and groomed me. It came as a complete surprise to find that the Prophet had arrived before noon. My mother left me with him . . ."

In his *Perfection* Judge 'Iyad[47] states that the consummation of a marriage during the day is lawful and explains that this point is dealt with by Bukhari[48] in his section "The Lawfulness of Consummation during the Day without any Procession or Torches." Some, he says, take the view that the more public a wedding is made by a procession or torches, the better it is. Since the meaning is that a nuptial procession should be illumined with a quantity of lamps, the implication is that the ceremony can only take place at night. But it could be that the torches are only symbolic of wedding celebrations, for in another Tradition we find the words, "Let smoke be seen."[49]

Bukhari relates the following Tradition on the authority of 'A'isha: A bride was conducted to her husband, who was one of the Prophet's Helpers. "Oh yes, 'A'isha," said the Prophet, "they did indeed offer entertainment. The Helpers[50] are fond of enter-

---

[47] Great Malikite jurist of Ceuta (1083–1149). The work in question is the "perfection" of a commentary by a certain Mazari on the *Ṣaḥīḥ* (Corpus of Authentic Traditions) of the celebrated Traditionist, Muslim (d. 875).

[48] Author of the most venerated collection of Prophetic Traditions (810–870). In orthodox Islam (i.e. Sunnite Islam) his collection, called the *Ṣaḥīḥ* like that of Muslim (see preceding note), ranks second to the Koran. Muslim's work is held in almost equal esteem, and the two works together are known as the "Two *Ṣaḥīḥs*".

[49] It is more likely that this Tradition refers to the smoke of cooking. In the Malikite system of law (which was that of the Muslim West) particular emphasis is laid on the necessity of the marriage feast as a means of making the wedding publicly known. The two main means of doing this were the playing of the tambourine (*duff*) and the smoke of the fire on which the food was being cooked.

[50] "Helpers" (in Arabic *Anṣār*) is the regular name for the men of Medina who supported the Prophet when he emigrated from Mecca—in other words, his Medinese, as opposed to his Meccan, supporters who accompanied him in his emigration and are accordingly known as "the Emigrants".

tainment." Bukhari records this Tradition in the section "On the Women who Conduct a Bride to her Husband". Nasa'i[51] on the authority of Muhammad ibn Hatib Jumahi relates that the Prophet said, "Of all that is lawful or forbidden, nothing is more commendable than singing and the tambourine at a wedding." This Tradition is recorded by Tirmidhi[52] who declares it "good"; others pronounce it "sound". According to Shurayh,[53] it is traditionally accepted that before going in to his bride a husband should perform two *rak'as*[54] and have his bride do likewise, praying behind him as they seek God's blessing on their wedding night, and take refuge in Him against the evil thereof.

Ibn Sirin[55] relates the following: I married a woman of the tribe of Beni Tamim, and on our wedding night I went in to her and found her sitting at the entrance to her private apartment. I put out my hand to her, but she said, "Gently now— take it slowly." Whereupon I gave thanks and praise to God. She then said, "God implants knowledge wheresoever He wishes. I have heard it said that a husband is commanded to perform two *rak'as* when he goes in to his wife on their wedding night and that his wife is to do likewise along with him. When he has finished this act of worship, he should then say, 'O God, bless my wife for me and me for my wife; O God, nurture my love and affection for her and nurture hers for me. Inspire us with love of one another.' And so I rose to my feet and did as she bade me, and, when I had finished I put out my hand to her again, and this time she said, "Gently now. A man about to cover his bride's body with his is commanded to say, 'O God, drive the Devil from us and let him not come between us.' So I uttered these words, and I have

---

[51] A collector of authoritative Traditions (d. 915).

[52] A collector of authoritative Traditions (d. 892).

[53] Legendary judge of the first century of Islam (corresponding to A.D. 622–718).

[54] A *rak'a* is part of the Muslim prayer ritual in which one bends the torso from an upright position and then makes two prostrations. It consists altogether of seven movements with appropriate recitations. See H. A. R. Gibb, *Mohammedanism* (Opus 17), Oxford U.P., 1969 (paperback), p. 42.

[55] A Traditionist and the first famous Muslim interpreter of dreams (654–728), Ibn Sirin was noted for his piety and the reliability of the information he transmitted.

never since known anything but prosperity and good fortune."

This injunction regarding the performance of rak'as by man and wife derives from a Tradition expounded by Bazzar on the authority of Hajjaj ibn Farrukh ibn Shurayh on the authority of 'Ata' on the authority of Ibn 'Abbas on the authority of Salman, who said that the Prophet said," When any of you marries, let him perform two rak'as on the night of consummation and tell his wife to do likewise along with him himself; for God will then bestow His blessings on their house. As for the injunction about a man's covering his bride's body with his, this is a Tradition recorded by Bukhari on the authority of Ibn 'Abbas, who relates that the Prophet said, "Should any of you say, on going in to his bride 'In the name of God[56]—O, God drive the Devil from that with which you have blessed us,' and should God then decree that a child be born of such a woman, no devil shall ever do the child harm."

Judge 'Iyad comments in his Perfection that what is meant here is that the Devil will not fell the child born of such a union.[57] It is also said by some that he shall do the child no hurt at birth as is said in the Tradition. But no one has understood the Tradition in the general sense as meaning that the child shall not be exposed to the persuasion and temptation of the Devil or something in that order of things.

In his book For Muwaffaq Zubayr relates the following story on the authority of his uncle, who heard it from Haytham ibn 'Adi on the authority of Sadi ibn Isma'il on the authority of Sha'bi: Shurayh said to me, "Sha'bi, marry girls from the tribe of Tamim." He told me that he had indeed married one of their girls and added, "I adjured her people to have her sleep in my home as soon as the marriage contract had been completed." "But," they protested, "we beseech you to let us remove her pubic hair and give her a good grooming all over." "I'm satisfied," he went on, "I've seen all I need to see"—adding that he

[56] Called in Arabic the basmala ("the in-the-name-of"), this formula is pronounced by Muslims at the beginning of every important act so as to bring down God's blessing on it.

[57] At this point our author enters into the domain of scholarly interpretation of Traditions.

had already seen the girl before. So they just tidied her up and conducted her to him that very same night. "She stood there at the door of my quarters," he continued, "and I rose and said to her, 'It is customary, my bride, for a man receiving his wife for the first time to rise and perform the prayer along with his wife, for the two of them to ask God's blessing on their wedding night, and to take refuge in God from the evil thereof.' With that I arose to perform my act of worship, and there she was behind me. So I did as I intended and turned round, and there to my surprise saw her there on the bed. So I took her gently by the hair, uttered a private prayer, and asked God's blessing. I then put out my hand, to which gesture she responded with the words, 'Gently now.' She then went on, 'Thanks be to God—I praise Him, I seek His succour, put my trust in Him and rely upon Him. The blessing of God be upon our Lord Muhammad! Well now, I'm a stranger to you, and since you're a man whose ways I don't know, please tell me your likes and I'll gratify you—tell me your dislikes and I'll avoid them. That's all I've got to say' " "So," he continued, "I gave thanks to God, invoked His blessing on our Lord Muhammad and said, 'Well, you have made a most seemly entry, my bride, into the household of your husband, who is the first among its menfolk. You shall be its first lady. Now what I like is so-and-so, and what I dislike is so-and-so.' "

At this point I interrupted him, "Tell me about your wife's relations. Do you like them to visit you?" "I am a judge," he replied, "and dislike being bored by their company." "However," he went on, " I had an excellent wedding night and spent three days with my bride. I then went off to execute my duties as a judge and was away for a full year, each day of which that passed I found more delightful than the day before. When the new year came round and I got back home from the courts, there to my surprise was an older woman issuing orders to everyone to do this or not to do that. 'And how are you, Abu Umayya?' she asked me. 'Who,' I inquired, 'are you?' 'I,' she replied, 'am your mother-in-law.' Whereupon I greeted her appropriately and told her that I was well. 'What do you think of your wife?' were her next words. 'One of the best,' said I. 'A wife,' she went on, 'will only deteriorate in two situations. The first arises when she becomes a husband's darling, the second when she bears him a son. However, if my daughter ever gives you cause for complaint use the whip on her. There's nothing worse in a man's household than a spoilt and brazen wife.' 'Well,' I commented, 'she's certainly her mother's daughter. You've trained her well enough for my needs and brought her up well.' "

"My mother-in-law," he continued, "would come and go every year and give me the same advice. And this is the tale behind some verses I wrote:

> Whenever Zaynab's family come to stay, I do them
>   well and treat them regally;
> And if she visits them, then so do I, albeit that I've
>   scant delight in visiting my in-laws.

"I had my wife," he added, "for twenty years, and in all that time I lost my temper with her only once, and I was in the wrong. What happened on that occasion was that I had to lead the public prayer. I had performed the two *rak'as* of the Daybreak Prayer[58] when I suddenly noticed a scorpion in the house. But before I could kill it, I heard the muezzin's[59] call to worship and had to leave in a hurry. So I stuck some sort of vessel over it and told my wife not to touch it till I got back. Upon my return I found she'd removed it and been stung by the scorpion. Oh, you should have seen me sucking the blood from her finger to get the poison out and in between reciting the Fatiha!"[60]

The same man told me that he had a neighbour who was for ever beating his wife and that his behaviour moved him to compose the following verse:

> I have seen men beat their wives, but may my right
>   hand wither if I ever beat my Zaynab!

"How could I beat her if she'd done me no wrong?" he re-

---

[58] The number of *rak'as* in the ritual prayers is not uniform. They are as follows: 2 for the Daybreak Prayer, 4 for the Noon and Afternoon Prayers, 3 for the Sundown Prayer and 4 for the Prayer which comes in the early part of the night.

[59] The muezzin is the official at a mosque who calls the Faithful to prayer.

[60] The Fatiha is the opening chapter of the Koran. It is short and used somewhat in the manner that Christians use the Lord's Prayer.

marked to me. "And what plea could I offer if I'd sinned against her? Why, when she died, the world collapsed about me, and ever after that I had no further taste for women. I only wish I'd joined her there and then."

A similar kind of story is related by Malik who was told it by Yahya ibn Sa'id ibn Musayyib [as he heard it from his father, Sa'id].[61] "I once had a friend," he said, "who failed to put in an appearance for some days. He then turned up again, greeted me and sat down beside me. 'And where have you been recently, Abu Muhammad?'[62] I asked him. 'My wife fell ill,' he replied, 'and so I stayed at home to nurse her. Unhappily, she died and I've buried her.' 'But why,' I asked, 'didn't you tell us she was ill? We could have visited her. Or why didn't you tell us she was dead? We could at least have gone to her funeral.'" Sa'id then comforted his friend and said a private prayer for him and the wife he had lost. This done, he urged him to remarry and not to meet God as a widower. "God have mercy on you!" cried his friend. "Who's going to marry *me*?" "But glory be to God!" rejoined Sa'id. "Isn't it worth four dirhams to keep a good Muslim chaste?[63] My dear Abu Muhammad ['Abdullah], I'll give you my daughter in marriage if you'll have her." To this 'Abdullah modestly made no reply out of respect for his friend. "But why don't you answer?" insisted Sa'id. "Are you offended by my suggestion?" "God have mercy on you!" replied 'Abdullah. "How could I refuse you? By God, I know full well that you

---

61 On Sa'id see above n. 39, p. 113. (N.B. The narrative is confused; it is begun by Sa'id, but completed by his friend.)

62 In addition to his name an Arab will also have a *kunya*, i.e. a sort of agnomen consisting of Abu ("father of") followed by the name of a son (though the name of a son was not necessary—indeed the *kunya* was often given to a boy before he had begotten any sons). From the second century of Islam it became polite to address a person by his *kunya*—unless one was the Caliph. The practice is somewhat puzzling to non-Arabists since in historical narrative an author will often use his supject's name, but in recorded conversation use the *kunya*. Although names are used here, 'Abdullah is also called Abu Muhammad.

63 In other words, if you have as little as four dirhams to give my daughter as her dower, I will arrange a marriage with her on those financial terms and remove you from the temptation of unlawful intercourse. On the dower see above, p. 84, n. 18.

could, if you wished, give her in marriage for a dower of 4,000 dirhams." "Never mind that, 'Abdullah," Sa'id went on. "Just get up and call that group of Helpers over here." "So," said 'Abdullah, "I did as he said, and he had the group witness the marriage in consideration of a payment of four dirhams.

"We then moved off, and when we'd performed the last prayer of the day, I made my way home. No sooner was I inside than I heard a man knocking at the door. 'Who's there?' I shouted. 'Sa'id,' came the reply. I thought of every Sa'id I knew in Medina apart from Sa'id ibn Musayyib, for the simple reason that he was never seen leaving his house except to go to the mosque or a funeral. 'Which Sa'id?' I called. 'Sa'id ibn Musay-yib,' he called back. Trembling with emotion, I told him to move back to the door. As he stepped forward ready to welcome me. I dragged myself down to let him in. I opened the door, and there to my surprise was a girl wrapped in a darkish cloak accompanied by several riding animals carrying household effects and a fair-skinned handmaid. 'Here's your wife, 'Abdullah,' he said, as he greeted me. 'God have mercy on you!' I exclaimed with some embarrassment. 'I would have liked to leave it for a few days.' 'But didn't you tell me you had four dirhams?' he asked. 'Yes, indeed,' I replied. 'I do have what I said I had. It's just that I'd like to leave it for the time being.' 'Not if Maymuna has anything to do with it,' he protested. 'Nor shall God hold *me* responsible if you spend tonight as a celibate when I've got a wife for you here. This girl's your wife, these are the chattels that go with her, here's a handmaid to serve in your household—and in addition 1,000,000 dirhams for her upkeep. Take her, 'Abdullah, and put your faith in God—for, I swear by God, that you're taking a woman who's in the habit of fasting and observing her moral and religious duties and who is versed in God's Book and the Practice of the Prophet.[64] Fear God, and don't hesitate to correct

[64] Muslims derive guidance not merely from the Koran but also from the practice of the Prophet. What he is supposed to have established either through personal example or definite prescription or prohibition is called the *sunna*, which it is convenient to translate as Practice of the Prophet. The *Sunna* has come down in the form of short narratives traced back to one of the Companions. Such a narrative is a *ḥadīth* or "Tradition", and one versed

her if you think fit, simply because she's my daughter.' With that he handed her over to me and left. And truly I never set eyes on any woman better able to recite the Koran or better versed in the Practice of the Prophet or more God-fearing than my wife. She could solve thorny problems that would task the jurists—I would just put them to her and find her ready with a solution."

After a short pause he went on "And so I took her into my home and settled down with her, and in due course, by God's good grace, she conceived. Sa'id would often ask me about her and inquire 'How goes it with that girl of mine?' and I would reply 'Very well.' Or he would say 'If it's convenient to you, 'Abdullah, to have us visit her, please let us do so.' On the day of her confinement I went out to get some of the things a man usually does get for his wife in such circumstances, and, when I got back, there was someone with her I'd never seen before. So I turned on my heels to go away, but the woman called me back. 'Come on in, 'Abdullah,' she cried. 'You have God's permission to look upon me.'[65] 'Who on earth are you?' I asked. 'I'm the mother of this girl of yours,' she said. 'But tell me, how do you find your wife?' 'She's from a good home—may God reward you! You've given her a good upbringing, a good education and a fine training,' I replied. 'Now don't hesitate to correct her simply because she's our daughter, 'Abdullah,' she went on, 'and don't transfer to her any of her property—a woman is a fragrant plant, not a high steward.[66] And don't smile at her too much, otherwise she'll take you for granted. God bless you both, 'Abdullah, with your new-born child, and may He make him like his grandfather Sa'id, for I've been his wife for these forty years and never seen him ever sin against God. Here's the money he's sent you for this special occasion.' I took the money she offered me and there to my surprise were five dinars. With that she left, and I never cast eyes on her for the eighteen remaining years of her life."

in the science of the *sunna* and *hadith* literature we normally term a "Traditionist".

[65] Because, as his wife's mother, she came within the prohibited degrees as laid down in Koran iv, 27.

[66] See above p. 100.

Ghazali's comment on this story is as follows: The haste with which Sa'id took his daughter to her new husband 'Abdullah on the night of the very day the marriage was contracted is indicative of the overwhelming nature of sexual desire and the religious necessity of quenching its flame by rapid consummation of a marriage.

Abu Faraj relates the following story on the authority of 'Amr ibn Shu'ayb on the authority of his father on the authority of his grandfather, who quotes the Prophet as saying, "Whenever any of you takes a woman to wife or buys himself a slave-girl, he should recite the following: 'O God, I beg of Thee that she may be a good woman and that the disposition with which Thou hast endowed her be good.' "

Abu Zinad recounts as follows: I was a man with many daughters until I was advised to ask God's forgiveness before having sexual intercourse. I took the advice and was blessed with a number of boys.

It is advisable for a bride not to hold herself too aloof from her husband on her wedding night. (At the same time it is not a bad thing to offer just enough resistance to stimulate him and arouse his sexual desire.) For aloofness is apt to kill his desire and leave him incapable of deflowering his bride on the very night he should. If he cannot then perform, the girl will spend the night with him an untouched virgin. Since the loss of a husband's sexual appetite on his wedding night may well last some time, a woman should take great care in this respect.

Both the author of The Scattering of Pearls and Abu Faraj in his Songs relate the following story: When Na'ila daughter of Farasifa was taken to 'Uthman after being given in marriage by her brother, her new husband made a bed for her by the side of his own. When she sat down on it, he said to her, "Either you must come to me or I must come to you." To this her reply was, "Having crossed the desert of Kalb, who am I to withhold myself from you when only the width of a carpet lies between us?" And so she got up and moved over to him. Removing his headdress, he said, "Don't be too taken aback when you see my bald head—beneath it there are things more to your liking." "I am," she replied, "one of those women to whom the dearest thing about a husband is his maturity and his baldness." "Drop your cloak," he said, and she dropped it. "Remove your scarf," he said, and she removed it. "Take off your shift," he said and she took it off. "Loosen the band about your waist," he said—but at that she demurred with the words "That's your job, not mine." "Indeed you're right," he agreed. He then consummated the marriage and found his bride delightful. In due course she bore him his daughter Maryam. After 'Uthman's death, his widow was courted by the nobility of Quraysh, the Prophet's tribe, but she would marry none of them, and in the end died a widow.

In his *Women* Abu Faraj relates the following story on the authority of Ibn Majashun: Mu'awiya married his daughter Hind to 'Abdullah ibn 'Amir, and one day some time later he happened to hear two slave-girls of his talking and commenting that his daughter had denied her husband access to her though a month had gone by since her wedding night. Mu'awiya immediately got on his horse, rode off to 'Abdullah's house and went in to see him. As he did so, Hind retired to her quarters and let down the curtains to screen her. After her father had talked with her husband a while, he rapped the side of her closet with his stick and recited the following verse:

> A shy and comely girl is she, and to her it comes hard
>   to do what's forbidden,
> though she'll readily yield to what is permitted.[67]

With that Mu'awiya got up and left. Hind knew full well what he meant, and when 'Abdullah later entered the room, she gladly gave herself to him.

When about to have intercourse with his wife, a man should cover them both, for there is a Tradition related by Nasa'i on the authority of 'Abdullah that the Prophet said: "Whenever any of

[67] That is, she is not the sort to countenance illicit sexual union, but, once lawfully united, she will do what is expected of her as a wife. As already hinted, an Arab girl was expected to behave with suitable modesty on her wedding night and not show herself too eager to consummate the marriage. Mu'awiya's daughter, however, had gone too far, and her father made it his business to remind her in diplomatic terms of her duty to her husband.

you goes in to his wife, he should put something over his buttocks and hers as well and not to be as bare as a camel."

In the act of sexual intercourse a man should take his time so that his wife may experience the desired climax just as he does. For, if there is one thing that will strengthen a bond of love between a man and a woman, it is the achievement of an orgasm on her part and the quenching of burning desire. Indeed it is related that the Prophet said, "Whenever any of you has intercourse with his wife, let him not rush her, but rather see to it that she satisfies her need just as he would wish to satisfy his own."

In his *Revivification* Ghazali writes that a marital practice strongly recommended by the Prophet is this: If a husband derives satisfaction from the attainment of orgasm, he should go slowly with his wife so that she may also come to a climax, since in her case the orgasm is more slowly achieved, and to move away from her at the wrong moment is hurtful and harmful. If husband and wife do not reach the climax together, adds Ghazali, and if it is the husband who is always first there, this can give rise to conjugal friction. It will do the husband no harm, however, if it is the wife who comes first. The supreme delight that a woman can experience, on the other hand, is achieved when the couple reach the climax together. This situation, moreover, serves to distract the man's attention from a wife who may otherwise be shy.

Ghazali also observes that it is a good marital practice for a man to turn away from the *qibla*[68] during intercourse out of respect for the sanctity of the Holy Places. Furthermore, he urges a man to speak tenderly to his wife and to pet and kiss her before he couples with her. In support of his advice he quotes a Tradition of the Prophet: "Let none of you fall on his wife like a brute beast, but let there be some prior communication between husband and wife." "Of what kind, Messenger of God?" he was asked. "A kiss and gentle words," was his reply. The Prophet

[68] The direction to which Muslims turn in praying (towards the Kaaba in Mecca). The term also denotes the niche in a mosque which indicates this direction.

also said, "A man reveals his own inadequacy in three ways: by meeting a person whom he would really like to know and then leaving him without having learned his name, by refusing a favour proffered by a friend, and, finally, by making advances to a woman and winning her favour without first having conversed with her and courted her, and then satisfying his own need before she has satisfied hers."

According to Ghazali, there are three nights of the month on which sexual intercourse is regarded with disfavour—the first, the middle and the last; for on these three nights the Devil is said to attend the union. The disfavour with which such unions are regarded is reported on the authority of 'Ali, Mu'awiya and Abu Hurayra.[69] Some authorities are said to favour Fridays as the days for sexual union, and they base their opinion on one of two interpretations of a saying of the Prophet.

Muslim on the authority of Abu Sa'id Khudri relates that the Prophet said, "The person in the worst position on the Day of Resurrection will be the man who confides in a woman, who in turn confides in him, who then spreads abroad the secret she has entrusted to him."[70] There is another version which runs: "In God's sight the safest of men on the Day of Resurrection will be the man who confides in a woman, who in turn confides in him, who then guards the secret she has entrusted to him." Muslim has this Tradition on the authority of 'Umar ibn Hamza al-'Umari, but it is held to be weak by Ibn Mu'in.

In his *Perfection* Judge 'Iyad writes as follows: One of the things that is forbidden is that a man should communicate revealing details of his sexual behaviour, since to do so is to expose a woman with both eyes and tongue. But the mere use of the word "intercourse" and discussion of it in general terms is in no way objectionable if it serves some useful purpose or is at all meaningful. It is as the Prophet said, "Indeed I do it and so does she—but to discuss it idly is neither a noble trait nor a chivalrous deed."

[69] Unlike 'Ali and Mu'awiya, Abu Hurayra (d. 676 or 677) was not a Caliph but a Companion of the Prophet, who is best known for the vast number of Traditions attributed to him, many of which cannot be genuine.

[70] The "secret entrusted to him" is the way in which she makes love.

Abu Dawud[71] on the authority of Abu Hurayra relates that the Prophet, at the end of his prayers in the mosque in the presence of two rows of men and one of women—or it could have been the other way round—turned to the men and said, "Is there any man among you who will go in to his wife, lock his door, draw his curtains and take upon him the concealment enjoined by God?" "Yes," said they. ". . . and then," he continued, "sit in company and say, 'I did so-and-so?' " To this question they gave no answer, but held their peace. He then turned to the women and asked them if any of them had anything to say. But they in turn held their peace—except for a girl with swelling breasts who went down on one knee and stretched out her neck as if to catch the Prophet's eye and so obtain a hearing. When she succeeded in having his ear, she said, "But they do talk, Messenger of God, both men and women." "Saying what, for instance?" asked the Prophet. "Well," she replied, "it's just as if a female devil met a devil in the open, and he laid her while all the world looked on." The rest of this Tradition is related by Khattabi in his book *The Unusual in Traditions* on the authority of Abu Haytham and Abu Sa'id Khudri, indicating that the Prophet forbade talking behind people's backs, which in Arabic is called *sibā'*—a term which connotes bragging about one's sexual prowess and a man's disclosure of what goes on between his wife and himself. As I have said, there is no harm in speaking straightforwardly about sexual relations, but a man should not tell the whole world details of his own sexual life. There is nothing wrong, however, with asking a man the morning after his wedding night how he found his bride since this is an old established custom. Malik ibn Harith Ashtar is said to have raised this very question with 'Ali who gave him an answer and told him how he had found his wife. Should it be, however, that a husband finds some fault or blemish in his wife such as ugliness, he is recommended to keep his peace on this particular point and to make some general comment to the effect that she was not really satisfactory and was not his type. Again, if he finds her to

---

[71] Famous Traditionist (d. 888) whose main work *Book of Traditions* is one of the six canonical books of Tradition in Sunnite Islam.

be a woman of outstanding beauty or astonishing loveliness or remarkable comportment, he should not go into great detail and rhapsodize about her as many foolish men do. To do so is to betray a baseness and weakness of character. Moreover, it can give rise to a good deal of mischief. The following story will illustrate the point.

In his book entitled *Failings* Abu 'Uthman relates that Ma'bad Saliti had a wife called Hamida from the tribe of Rizam ibn Malik ibn Hanzala, and she was of outstanding beauty. Now her husband had been drafted to Khurasan by Hajjaj, and out there he talked so much about her beauty to his companions and so blatantly expressed a craving for her that he almost talked himself into deserting and returning home. As a result of all this one of his companions, Hawt ibn Sinan of the tribe of 'Atid(?) secretly fell in love with the woman of whom he had heard so much and said one day to Ma'bad, "I should like to be transferred to Basra." "In that case I can give you a letter to take to my wife, Hamida," exclaimed Ma'bad. When in due course Hawt reached Basra with the husband's letter he said to himself. "I'm giving this to no one but Hamida in person." And when he went to her house, he insisted on doing just that. When she came out to see him, he had a word or two with her and dropped a hint of the love he felt for her in his heart. After that he called again and again and kept enticing her until in the end she ran away with him. She went into hiding in his house, but then her family revealed her whereabouts when she was already pregnant. She was soon arrested by 'Abd-ul-Rahman ibn 'Ubayd Hajjaj's chief of police and duly stoned to death for adultery.[72] On this subject a poet wrote the following line:

"A girl from Rizam whom Ma'bad Saliti dearly loved
   since he had no fear of Fate . . ."

Even if a wife is faithful and not the type to go astray as in

[72] See above Ch. I, n. 10, p. 24. Lapidation for adultery is not prescribed in the Koran. The legal basis of the penalty is an alleged Tradition of the Prophet, but its soundness is highly questionable, especially since lapidation for adultery is actually later than the time of the Prophet.

this case, and even if a man looks to the vicissitudes of fortune to deliver her or waits for some lawful means of attaining her—such as might arise, for instance, from the death of her husband or his decision to divorce her— and then makes a dash for her, he will nevertheless be marrying her because her husband was misguided enough to prattle about her. A sensible man, then, should be extremely wary of speaking of his wife. Similarly a wife should not tell her husband of the beauty and outstanding charm of some other women since he is liable to be impressed. If so, it could well be that, once he has set his heart on this other woman, his wife will suffer either from his adultery or from his decision to divorce her or to take the other woman as a second wife.[73] The least that can happen is that he will always have this other woman at the back of his mind and spy his opportunity to marry her as soon as either his own wife or the woman's husband dies. So anyone with the least intelligence should take great care in this respect.

To round off the present topic I will now speak of the cosmetics and perfumes a woman would do well to use.

[73] In Islamic law a Muslim husband has the right to unilateral termination of his marriage at his discretion. Modern divorce law reforms, however, have aimed at restricting the husband's power of divorce.

CHAPTER VI

On Cosmetics and Perfumes
and Grooming

Such beautifying agents are essential for a woman if she is to enhance her position with her husband and to enjoy greater respect from him. Women, as 'A'isha said,[1] are men's dolls. So a man must make his doll as pretty as he can. The use of cosmetics by a wife will not only stimulate her husband's desire and catch his eye; they will show off her charms to the best advantage and so prolong love and companionship between them.

In his *Women* Abu Faraj has something to say on the subject: A woman will always find favour with her husband assuming that she is really good-looking and physically attractive and provided she pays scrupulous attention to make-up and cleanliness and is aware not only of the different kinds of necklace and apparel that will enhance her loveliness, and the various ways in which she can make herself attractive, but also the kind of thing that will suit her husband's taste and meet with his approval. A woman should also be extremely careful not to let her husband see anything with which he can find fault and she should take the greatest care to ensure that he can find nothing dirty, malodorous or untidy about her—and so on.

In *The Multitudes* Abu Rayhan[2] has much the same sort of

[1] The wife of the Prophet (see above p. 105, n. 19). Without further qualification the name " 'A'isha" may be taken as that of Muhammad's wife unless the context suggests otherwise.

[2] Better known in the West as Biruni (973–c. 1050), this man of Iranian origin was a wide-ranging and original thinker in various fields of learning, notably mathematics and astronomy and the physical and natural sciences. He is considered one of the greatest scholars of medieval Islam. He was, amongst other things, a keen and unbiased observer of creeds and customs.

thing to say. A wife, he writes, should present a beautiful appearance to her husband. This she can do by cleansing her skin, cleaning out blocked pores and heightening the colours in her body and all that goes with it (such as clothes).

As far as her body is concerned a woman can use gypsum cosmetic to whiten her skin; she can apply rouge to her face, especially if, for whatever reason, she is of sallow complexion; she can use a toothpick and clean her teeth; she can wash out her eyes and apply eye-black; finally, she can file her finger-nails. As regards all else, a woman's first and foremost care should be her apparel. She should wash her clothes and rub them well so that there is no dirt left in them. They should either be white, the generally accepted colour, or dyed according to the fashion of the time and place.

In his book *The Primary Feather of the Wing* Tifashi[3] tells us that stimulation of the sexual appetite and the attainment of total satisfaction are an impossibility unless the wife is in complete harmony with her husband and is prepared to enhance her attractions in readiness for the moment when he is in the mood for those things which will satisfy his desire and make his joy complete. This objective she will achieve by open expressions of affection, by drawing close to him and presenting herself with charming appearance and elegant apparel of a kind calculated to rouse the dejected and lukewarm and to intensify the ardour of the ardent.

A sensible wife, who, with good grace, is obedient to her husband, will observe all these rules and look to every other kind of thing that will satisfy and prolong his appetite, whether it be a matter of outward appearance or inward emotions. By all such means she can be certain that she will immediately catch the eye or nose of her husband on occasions when he has cause to grumble or express his disapproval of her. She will find that it is in her own interest to have her husband notice her and that failure to enhance her appearance will only rebound on herself

---

[3] This author is probably Ahmad ibn Yusuf Tifashi (d. 1253), who wrote a work on prostitution, sexual deviations, and other matters entitled *Hearts' Delight: Things Which No Book will Tell*.

since there is a danger that once he notices a fall in standards he will turn his attentions elsewhere.

The best safeguards a wife can have against this sort of hazard are astuteness in making love and the utmost care and preparedness for the occasions when she can expect her husband around her. For the most part, these are the occasions mentioned by God Most High in His Book—the occasions on which He forbids slaves and boys to enter into the presence of husband and wife without seeking permission to do so. On this point Almighty God has this to say, "O you who have believed, let those who are your slaves and those of you who have not yet reached the age of manhood seek permission of you three times, before the Dawn Prayer and when you have put aside your clothing at noon and again after the Evening Prayer—three unguarded occasions for you . But beyond these times no blame attaches to you for going about amongst each other."[4] On the subject of women and their adornment God says, "Let them not show their ornaments"[5] [except to their husbands and menfolk who are close relations].

On Eye-black and Henna

Umm Shayba once aked 'A'isha what was meant by outward adornment, and her reply was, "Eye-black and henna."[6] The following story, related on the authority of Mu'awiya ibn Yahya, bears on the same theme: A woman once called on 'A'isha, and the Prophet asked who she was, to which 'A'isha's reply was, "She is so-and-so the wife of so-and-so." The Prophet then commented, "I hate a woman to have eyes that are pale and weak for lack of eye-black and a buxom woman to have finger-nails that are not dyed with henna." In more than one Tradition women are counselled to darken their eyes with collyrium. In one such Tradition the Prophet says, "The best eye-black gives lustre to the eyes and stimulates the growth of lashes.

---

[4] Koran, xxiv, 57.   [5] Koran, xxiv, 31.

[6] Eye-black (in Arabic *kuḥl*, whence English "kohl") is used not only to line the eyebrows and lashes so as to enhance the beauty of the eyes, but also as a salve to protect and heal them. On henna and its uses see above Ch. IV, n. 13, p. 79.

On the day 'Abdullah ibn Ja'far[7] gave away his daughter to her husband, he counselled her, "Make yourself up and don't forget that the best cosmetic is eye-black and that the best perfume there is is water." Abu Aswad said the same thing to his daughter, and likewise Asma' ibn Kharija when he gave his daughter in marriage to Hajjaj.[8] All these men without exception advised their womenfolk to use cosmetics and laid great stress on eye-black. They also urged all women to use henna. The Prophet, moreover, did not like women's hands to look the same as men's (i.e. undyed). It is related by Awza'i on the authority of Mu'awiya ibn Salama that the Prophet once saw a woman with undyed hands and commented, "None of you should neglect care of the hands to the extent that they look just like a man's." Having heard this, the woman hennaed her hands till well after she was seventy, at which age she died. In connexion with this same point Abu Dawud relates the following story on the authority of Safiyya daughter of 'Isma, who heard it from 'A'isha: A woman once pointed a book or letter out to the Prophet from behind a curtain, and he put out his hand to pick it up. On seeing her outstretched hand, he remarked, "I don't know whether this is a man's hand or a woman's." He then heard a voice from behind the curtain saying, "It's a woman's." "If you were a woman," he remarked, "you'd have dyed your fingernails with henna." Another Tradition on this theme is related by Bazzar on the authority of Layth after Abu Salim, who heard it from Mujahid on the authority of Ibn 'Abbas: Once a woman came to swear allegiance to the Prophet without having dyed her hands, and he would not accept her oath until she had hennaed them. Another Tradition has it that 'Umar ibn Khattab forbade women to varnish their fingernails or tattoo themselves,[9] yet he orderd them to dye their hands with henna. 'Abd-ul-Malik contested

---

[7] Nephew of the Caliph 'Ali and son of Asma' daughter of 'Umays mentioned earlier (p. 113).

[8] See above p. 106.

[9] In many parts of the Middle East, as elsewhere in the Muslim world, Bedouin and peasant women have themselves tattooed on chin, temples, backs of hands, and elsewhere above the waist. Designs are usually symbolic and serve as talismans.

this, arguing that the Tradition is that nail-polishing and tattooing are permissible, and he cites the following in support of his
claim: Once the Prophet came upon a woman whose menfolk were
Helpers just as she was applying henna and he asked, "Why
haven't you done this kind of thing?" pointing with his right
forefinger to the back of his left hand as if to indicate tattooing.
Someone or other once said, "I saw a singing-girl with hands
that she had steeped in henna and then tattooed on them in black
the following verse:

> It is not the dye that has adorned my hands; it is my
> hands that have enhanced the dye.

Care of the Teeth

Now after the question of eye-black and dye we come to the
subject of the tooth-stick,[10] the use of which is as much a matter
of hygiene as of cosmetics. Great emphasis is laid on its importance in the Traditions of the Prophet, and its advantages are
stressed by physicians. It is said that to clean the teeth with a
tooth-stick will, if well done in moderation, brighten and strengthen the teeth, make the gums firm, and prevent the formation of
cavities. It will also sweeten the breath and loosen the tongue
[by removing the fear of bad breath].

It is related that 'A'isha once spoke of the tooth-stick and said,
"A tooth-stick," she said, "will give brighter vision and do away
with embarrassment. It pleases the Lord and gives joy to the
angels and multiplies the benefits achieved through ritual
prayer." In the Traditions of the Prophet it is related that one
ritual prayer with the use of a tooth-stick is more beneficial than
a thousand prayers without.

In his *Women* Abu Faraj writes: No practice was more widespread in the time of the Prophet than that of cleaning the teeth
with a tooth-stick. One saying is: "A man's mouth contains two

---

[10] In Arabic medical works there is frequent mention of the use of tooth-
stick for dental hygiene. Aloes-wood, for instance, is included in prescriptions
for the removal of decayed portions of the teeth, the elimination of bad
breath, and polishing.

possibilities for actions that accord with the practice of the Prophet, and both are of benefit to him: one is cleaning the teeth with a tooth-stick and the other is rinsing the mouth with water. No finer remedy exists for cleaning and restoring the health of one's teeth than these two practices; for water sucks out the dirt and washes, polishes and cleans. In a Tradition of the Prophet we find the words, "Rub your teeth from side to side as a precaution against the plucking of the gums that is liable to occur from picking and rubbing them upwards and downwards."

Tooth-sticks should be made from a bitter and astringent wood. The best kind of wood for cleaning purposes is the type that is made from arak wood. But, for the purpose of staining the gums and lips, one should use bark from the roots of the walnut tree. After using a stick on the gums it is essential to clean out the spaces between the teeth; otherwise bad breath will result and the teeth will go bad at the roots. All remnants of food should be gently eased out. On this subject of cleaning the teeth with a stick Abu-l-Hawari Wisati composed the following lines, which are recorded in Bakharzi's *Statue of the Palace* and are supposed to be the best ever uttered on the topic:[11]

> Good luck to the wood of a thorn-tree that has the
>   pleasure, in my despite, of serving as a tooth-stick
>   in the sweet mouth of a pretty snub-nosed girl!
> How its thirst has been quenched! It came to her teeth
>   as dry thornwood and returned from its visit as moist
>   wood of aloes.[12]

Abu Fath Kushajim once made a present to a slave-girl of a tooth-stick inscribed with the words:

> We send this gift that you may polish teeth
>   like moistened pearls of lustre and great price.
> So sweet a fragrance rose from it that it seemed to me
>   it had been watered from your mouth while still upon
>   the tree.

---

[11] An Arab poet of mediocre but often over-rated talent (d. 1075).

[12] The poet envies the tooth-stick (*siwāk*) its easy access to his beloved's mouth and its ability to assuage its thirst by absorbing her saliva.

O God, could it but know its fortune there with you,
   it would sing forth praise and gratitude!
Oh, would I were this gift that I might quench my thirst
   on the coolness of your teeth at dawn!

Scent and Perfume

And now to perfume. Law, both natural and religious, approves and recommends the use of scent. The Prophet did, in fact, declare, "Three things in this world of yours have been made dear to me," and then he went on to name two of them as women and perfume.[13] In another Tradition four things are said to be approved in Islam, namely henna, the use of scent, tooth-sticks and sexual intercourse.

Abu Dawud relates a Tradition on the authority of Anas to the effect that the Prophet had a perfumed compound he would use on himself. Among other Traditions we find the pronouncement, "The best of your womenfolk are the sort who keep themselves washed, clean and perfumed. Moreover, Judge 'Iyad in his *Perfection* notes that the use of scent is recommended in Islamic law, the main consideration being that here we have a means of enhancing Fridays and feast-days, for instance, of dispelling repulsive odours from one's person, wafting fragrant breezes among the Believers and using substances agreeable to the angels, for it is said that the angels find unpleasant odours noxious. The use of scent also affords a man the opportunity of displaying his cleanliness and manly qualities to his fellows and his family, of strengthening his heart and brain through the invigorating effect of perfume on these organs[14] and of succeeding with women since scent provides him with an effective persuader that does not meet with the disapproval of the Law.

In his discourse entitled *Treatise on Perfume* Abu Yasir speaks of the qualities of different kinds of perfume, and one of his

---

[13] See above p. 59.
[14] Because of their supposed drying, moistening or other properties certain substances were quite erroneously believed by medieval physicians to cleanse, strengthen, debilitate or otherwise affect the various organs. Camphor, for instance, was supposed to be a drying agent.

pronouncements is that scent is one of the greatest delights of mankind and among the strongest stimulants to intercourse and the attainment of sexual satisfaction. This is why, when Musaylima married Sajah,[15] he was given this advice, "Give her plenty of perfume, for when a woman smells perfume she will be put in mind of sexual intercourse and will crave for union."

A common saying is "After the wedding night scent is valueless", and the expression is used proverbially of something that comes too late. The story behind it, according to one version, is that a man once married a woman whom he found to be dishevelled and unperfumed. "Why no scent?" he asked. "I've put it on one side for some other occasion," she replied. Whereupon he remarked, "After the wedding night scent is valueless." There are other explanations besides.

On Jewellery

The wearing, by women, of jewellery of gold, silver and various precious stones is approved by some, though others prefer a woman who does not adorn herself in this way. Ibn Jahm tells the following story in this connexion: I once bought a slave-girl who would refuse to wear jewellery whenever I wanted her to do so. Her argument was that jewellery conceals a woman's natural charms as well as her defects.

In his work The Sharp-Witted Ibn Jawzi relates the following story, "One night I asked this slave-girl, 'How long is it till dawn?' 'As long,' she replied, 'as the embrace of a lover whose heart is torn by the pangs of separation.' One day this same girl looked at the sun in eclipse and commented, 'The sun feels embarrassed by my beauty and has therefore veiled herself.' " "One night," he continues, "I said to her, 'Come, let us sit in the

---

[15] Musaylima was one of several claimants to the gift of prophecy who appeared in Arabia in the early days of Islam. He was from a large tribal group in Central Arabia and aimed at establishing a power bloc in Yamama somewhere around 632. Sajah daughter of Mundhir made a counter-claim to prophecy and went to convert or do battle with Musaylima but ended by embracing his cause and marrying him.

moonlight,' and her comment was, 'Do you want to bring co-spouses together?' "[16]

In his *Women* Abu Faraj writes: Sukayna daughter of Husayn clothed one of her daughters in a garment of many pearls. "My only purpose in doing this," she explained, "is to put the pearls to shame with her charms. Malik ibn Asma' borrowed this idea to give us the following lines:

> When pearls are worn on faces, the pearls will have
> the beauty of your face to enhance their charms.
> You make the sweetest perfume sweeter, and if you but
> touch it how will its scent compare with yours?

In Ibn Mutayr's ode we find the following line:

> A slender-waisted woman put on her strings of pearls
> and gave to them a beauty greater than they gave to her.

Yazid ibn Mu'awiya[17] said of his wife Umm Kulthum daughter of 'Abdullah ibn Ja'far:

> When asked about her lineage she can say she comes of
> 'Abd Manaf and 'Amir ibn Lu'ayy,
> With forebears from Mutayyibin and others of exalted
> allied tribes.
> Even unbejewelled and dressed in shabby clothes you'll
> find her radiant as a sea-shell's pearl.

When Yazid heard of Umm Kulthum's outstanding loveliness and arresting beauty, he became enamoured of her. He wrote to ask her hand in marriage from her father, who by then had little in his pocket and great debts to meet. Though he had previously refused Yazid, he now consented and sent her to him in Damascus. When Yazid set eyes on her, he was all the more enraptured and in love with her.

---

[16] In other words "I am as lovely as the moon, which is beauty personified. Do you wish me to meet my rival? To do so would be comparable to making love to one wife in front of another."

[17] Yazid I, the second Umayyad Caliph (reg. 680–83).

On the theme of jewels Husri in his *Flowers* records the follow-ing lines:[18]

> They had no jewels to adorn them, but the beauty of their
>   faces; so, unbejewelled they yet had jewels.
> Chaste they emerged and, for concealment, hid behind
>   their veils; so, any slander of them by the tribe is false.
> Wise men will leave them well alone and only fools
>   desire them—they have no use for scandal.

On the same theme another poet has this to say:

> Life's comfort led them far astray, and in the end they
>   donned the garb of perfect beauty,
> Taking as their ornament the best a man may see, and,
>   unbejewelled, were yet not unbejewelled.

In *Martial Courage*[19] we have the following line:

> "If she wears no ornament, no beauty will she lose
>   thereby; but, if she so adorns herself, her looks will
>   gain in beauty."

'Abd-ul-Malik ibn Habib[20] records that the Prophet would bid women wear some kind of ornament on their hands and legs, and he also disapproved of their not wearing perfume. Hasin ibn 'Abd-ul-Rahman quotes 'Atiyya as saying: We received a letter from the Caliph 'Umar ibn Khattab telling us to have our womenfolk adorn themselves with silver and not with gold, and

---

[18] Abu Ishaq Ibrahim Husri (of Husr, near Kairouan, Tunisia) was in his day a famous litterateur (d. 1022). His *Flowers* is an anthology of belles-lettres compiled at the request of a secretary to the Chancellery in 1014 or 1015 on the basis of Eastern material. Not surprisingly Nafzawi—also a native of what is today Tunisia—seems well acquainted with his work and also quotes from another work of his, namely *Light of the Eyes*, a book similar to the *Flowers* in manner, substance, and execution.

[19] Rendering *Hamasa*, the title of a number of poetic anthologies of which the most renowned is that of Abu Tammam (d. 849).

[20] Noted jurist of exceptional erudition (796?–853) who played the leading role in establishing the Malikite system of law in Muslim Spain.

to teach them the "Chapter of Light" in the Koran,[21] simply because, it would seem, he detested luxury and extravagance; for otherwise there is no difference between silver and gold when it comes to the mere fact of adornment.

On Clothes

The subject of feminine adornment extends to fabrics in red and yellow dyes, which the Arabs would use to clothe their brides on the day of a wedding. It is this custom that gave rise to the practice of applying the term "bridal garments" to any dyed clothing. Hence Asadi gives us the verse:

> "Their leaders are now clothed in bridal garments—
> gone are their widows' weeds!"

'Abd-ul-Malik ibn Habib quotes 'A'isha daughter of Abu Waqqas as saying, "I remember the time when some of the Prophet's wives mainly wore garments of yellow brocade."
Bashshar says:

> Put on pretty clothes—the most splendid are dyed,
> And when you go out put on a red veil, for red is
> of beauty itself.[22]

On Depilatories

Another aspect of the subject of cosmetics is the use of paste to remove superfluous hair. Depilatory paste was first applied, we are told, by the Queen of Sheba. Popular story-tellers have it that when Solomon wrote to her and when, as part of God's plan, she went to see him, the jinn[23] said to themselves, "If Solomon sets eyes upon her, acclaims her loveliness and weds her and then begets a child with her, we shall be in bondage until the end of time." Now the Queen of Sheba had hairy legs, and, bearing this in mind, the jinn built a hall with a floor that was tiled with glass,

21 See above Ch. V, n. 1, p. 97. 22 See below Ch. X, p. 189.
23 See above Ch. II, n. 21, p. 38.

and in this floor they cleverly portrayed a creature of the sea. At the far end of the hall Solomon took his seat on a chair and invited the Queen to see and marvel at the sight. The jinns' aim in this was that Solomon should see her legs, for it is said in the Koran! "When she saw it she thought it was a pool and uncovered her legs"[24] so as to wade through it. Now when Solomon beheld her he was enthralled by her beauty and appalled at the hair on her legs. He therefore bade one of the jinn to instruct him how to remove it. Whereupon the jinn created the depilatory, and the Queen rubbed it on her legs. Solomon then married her after she had accepted submission to God in Islam. Such is the tale of the story-tellers.

It is said that there are four pleasures in life: the pleasure of an hour, which is sexual union, the pleasure of a day, which is that of the bath-house, the pleasure of a week, which is that of the depilatory, and the pleasure of a year, which is that of marrying a virgin. Another view, however, is that the fourth most pleasurable experience is for a man to have sexual intercourse after the pubic hair has been shaved off with a razor. In his book *The Perfect*[25] Mubarrad says, "I do so wish that one application of a depilatory were priced at 100,000 and that the cleft of a woman were set on a lion's forehead so that only the worthy might reach it and the valiant attain thereto."

[24] The Koranic story of relations between Solomon and the Queen of Sheba describes how the King came to know of her existence and of the sun-worship practised by the Queen and her people. It tells of the breakdown of negotiations leading to the Queen's visit to Solomon, alludes to the ruse described in our text, and closes with her conversion to Islam. Koranic commentators expand the story by adding that the jinn, or demons, at the King's court, fearing an eventual marriage between the two, spread the tale that the Queen had an ass's foot and hairy legs. To establish the facts, Solomon had a glass floor made so that she might raise her skirts in the manner described. Although enthralled by her beauty, the King disliked the hair on her legs and had a depilatory specially prepared. Some say that once he had had the hair removed, he married the Queen, while others say that he gave her in marriage to one of the South Arabian kings. There are popular variations on the theme, and details differ and sometimes conflict as is clear from the version given here where the ruse is conceived by the jinn and not by Solomon.

[25] Great grammarian of Basra and, later, of Baghdad (826–98), Mubarrad is one of the greatest of all Arab philologists.

There is a Tradition that a man once complained to the Prophet of an excessive sexual urge and was accordingly advised by him not to let his pubic hair grow too long.

Because depilatories come within the category of cosmetics the Prophet forbade a man, when on a journey, to go in to his wife at night [when she might be applying it]. Another piece of advice he gave to men was, "Comb your beards and shave off your pubic hair." There are different opinions about whether the Prophet himself actually used depilatories or not. But according to Lu'lu'i and Ramali as quoted by Abu Dawud in his *Book of "Mursal" Traditions*,[26] it seems that a man once applied a depilatory to the Prophet's body, but stopped when he reached the pubic region. At that point the Prophet himself took over the task and carried on. In another Tradition quoted by Abu Dawud, however, we are told that neither the Prophet nor the Caliphs Abu Bakr nor 'Umar nor 'Uthman ever used depilatories.

The reason why a man, when travelling, is forbidden unexpected access to his wife is that she must be given time to prepare herself for him. Touching on this kind of theme, Husri gives us the following lines in his *Light of the Eyes*:

> The world has now begun to give delight to him who
>   can see with vision clear
> And given praise to God for a few gentle drops of rain—
>   how wonderful she is!—drops, which, being favoured,
>   have expressed their gratitude.
> Like garments streaked with ink, the earth in gardens,
>   all shyness cast aside, has blossomed forth in bright
>   array—
> The lady's adorned, awaiting now her partner.

But just as a woman should adorn herself for her husband, so is it commendable for a husband to make himself as presentable to her as she is to him.

---

[26] A *mursal* Tradition is a report in which the evidence for the words or deeds of the Prophet in a particular situation is transmitted by a chain of authoritative persons in which the first link—namely the direct witness of what the Prophet said or did—is lacking.

On Dirty and Unsightly Men

It is forbidden to constrain a beautiful woman to marry an unsightly husband or compel a young girl to wed an old man. For this we have 'A'isha's authority in the following Tradition: A group of Companions were once waiting for the Prophet, and as he was on his way out to meet them, the Prophet set about grooming his hair and beard. "Whereupon," said 'A'isha, "I asked him, 'Is this what you do?' 'Yes,' he replied. 'When a man goes out to meet his friends, he should make himself presentable beforehand, for God is comely and comeliness is dear to Him.' "

In his *Women* Abu Faraj relates another Tradition in which the Prophet says, "A man should make himself presentable to a woman in just the same way as she must make herself presentable to him."

In this same book we find the following story: A woman once went to the Caliph 'Umar ibn Khattab with a complaint about being married to a dirty, untidy man. "Commander of the Faithful," she pleaded, "this man's not for me—please deliver me from him." 'Umar took one look at the man and immediately saw the reason for her objection to him. He then signalled to a man nearby and said, "Go and give this fellow a bath, cut his fingernails and trim his hair, then bring him back to me." The man did as he was told and, having carried out the instructions, brought the husband back. Whereupon 'Umar motioned to the husband to take his wife by the hands. But when he did so she did not recognize him. "Heavens above, 'Abdullah!"[27] she exclaimed. "How can you do such a thing in the presence of the Commander of the Faithful?" When she recognized him as her husband, she went back with him. 'Umar merely remarked, "That's the way to deal with women—they dearly love you to adorn yourselves for them even as they adorn themselves for you!" In this connexion certain commentators quote the Koran: "Women have such honourable rights as obligations also."[28]

[27] There is no contradiction here. " 'Abdullah" in this context is analogous to the English "Jack", i.e. someone whose name is not known to the speaker.
[28] ii, 228.

In his book on 'Umar ibn Khattab the author Ibn Jawzi quotes Hisham ibn 'Urwa on the authority of his father as mentioning that 'Umar said, "Don't force your daughters to marry unsightly men, for in this respect their desires are no different from yours."

In his *Women* Abu Faraj relates that once during the circumambulation of the Kaaba[29] 'Umar heard a woman reciting the following verse:

> Some women are given cool, fresh water to drink such as
>   that wherein you have found refreshment.
> Others are given green water that is tainted and brackish;
>   and had it not been for fear of God, they would have
>   fled from it!

'Umar immediately knew what her trouble was and had her husband summoned. Finding him unsightly, he gave him the choice of either 500 dirhams or a slave-girl from the spoils of war on condition that he should divorce his wife. The husband took the dirhams and divorced his wife.

Ibn 'Abd-ul-Mu'min in his commentary on the *Assemblies*[30] recounts the following anecdote: While Ma'n ibn Za'ida was sitting one day in the company of friends, a woman with a most lovely face from the tribe of Beni Sahm came up to him and said, "God prosper you, Emir! My father's brother has married me to a man who is not my equal."[31] "I must see her husband," he declared. The man—a fellow of most ugly features—was duly brought before him. "And what," asked Ma'n, "have you to do with a woman as lovely as she is?" "She is my wife," replied the husband. "Give her her freedom," said Ma'n, and he did. Ma'n

---

[29] To go in circuit round the Kaaba (see above Ch. III, n. 23, pp. 70 f.) is one of the traditional ceremonies of the Greater Pilgrimage to Mecca.

[30] i.e. Abu 'Abbas Ahmad ibn 'Abd-ul-Mu'min (d. 1222), better known as Sharishi ("of Jérez", Spain), was the author of the most famous and complete of all the commentaries on the *Assemblies* of Hariri on whom see below Ch. VIII, n. 28).

[31] The allusion is to the legal doctrine of marriage equality (*kafā'a*), which required the husband to be his wife's equal in lineage, financial position, etc. It is no part of Koranic teaching but a development stemming from urban class-consciousness in eighth-century Iraq.

then stared at the ground for a while and then came up with the verses:

> Like a gazelle you drove her before you—but how lovely
>   the led and how dreadful the leader!
> Upon my very life, you have failed to win her love, and
>   so now part from her as one stranger would part from
>   another!

In his *Articulations* Sa'id writes that he found the following verses in the handwriting of Ishaq ibn Ibrahim Mawsili:[32]

> To all mankind I do declare my heart's infatuation with
>   one who is, by far, the fairest of the fair, though
>   plagued I am by her ugliest of spouses.
> Each night he crawls across her belly like [the reptile
>   that he is].[33]

Another poet says:

> Many a black-eyed beauty is driven [by her family] to
>   the bed of some base and weakly dwarf of her tribe,
> And all they say is this, "She's dragged to him by ties of
>   kinship." Oh, how dreadful is the lot of virgins when
>   they are the kin of men![34]

In his *Dictations* Abu 'Ali gives the following lines:

> How many an Arab filly, 'Amr, can be plagued by some
>   weakly fellow from her tribe who leads her by the nose!
> He has her in his power, but cannot handle her and wants
>   of her things which *she* wants not.

In *The Sharp-witted* Ibn Jawzi writes: 'Amran ibn 'Attar called

---

[32] Son of the famous musician at Harun Rashid's court in Baghdad. He was himself a well-known singer and poet (767–850).

[33] The text here is so hopelessly corrupt that nothing but a conjectural translation can be offered.

[34] In traditional Arab society the preferred bride is the daughter of the paternal uncle or, failing that, the maternal uncle.

on his wife, Hamda, just after she had groomed and adorned herself. Now 'Amran was an ugly dwarf of a fellow, whereas his wife was a beautiful woman. As he gazed at her, then, the more attractive he found her, and indeed he could not take his eyes off her. "What's the matter with you?" she asked. "By God," he replied, "how beautiful you have made yourself!" "Rejoice then," she remarked, "for you and I are destined for Paradise." "How so?" asked he. "Because," she replied, "you're grateful that a man like you has been given a woman like me and because I've had the patience to bear a man such as you—the grateful and the patient are destined for Paradise!" On hearing this he was overcome with embarrassment and forbade his wife to repeat such sentiments ever again.

In his book *The Scattering of Pearls* Âbi tells the story of a man, who, on his way to Tufawa in Arabia, suddenly found himself in the company of the most beautiful woman. "Good lady," he said, "if you already have a husband, I wish you good luck, but if you haven't, please tell me." "What," she said in reply, "do you want from me when I have something I believe you wouldn't like?" "And what might that be?" he asked. "Grey hair," she answered. He then turned his mount aside and made off. Whereupon she called him back and said, "By God, I'm not yet twenty—just look at my head." Uncovering her head, she revealed luxurious locks as black as charcoal and went on to say, "And I noticed your hair is no different from mine, but I wanted you to realize that women dislike what men dislike."

In his work *The Unusual in Traditions* Khattabi relates that 'Umar said, "None of you should marry a woman who is not of a like age"—which would seem to indicate that he disliked an old man marrying a young wife and vice versa.

'Abdullah ibn Yazid quotes his father as saying that Abu Bakr asked the hand of Fatima from her father, the Prophet, but the latter declined on the grounds that she was too young. Yet when 'Ali made the same request, the Prophet consented, and 'Ali married her. This Tradition is recorded and elucidated by Nasa'i, who comments that at the time Fatima was fifteen and five months and 'Ali twenty-one and four months, whereas Abu Bakr was eighteen years older than 'Ali, and 'Umar eight.

The following story is related by Mawa'ini(?)[35]: As an oldish man, Harith of the tribe of Asad[36] asked the hand of the daughter of 'Alqama of Tayy. So 'Alqama said to his wife, "See what your daughter has to say about this." His wife did as he wished and went to her daughter with the question, "Tell me, child, which kind of man do you prefer, a waddly but open-handed chieftain of riper years or a fine young stripling who is reckless and tight-fisted?" "The young man," replied the girl. "But," observed her mother, "the young man will only make you jealous, whereas the older man will put you first in his life." "Oh yes, mother," came the reply, "but young girls love striplings even as shepherds love pasture fresh and green." "That may be, my child," went on her mother, "but young men will jealously restrict your movements and for ever be full of reproaches." "Nevertheless," objected the girl, "I dread the thought of an old man who'll stain my clothes, wear out my youth and drive away my friends." But the mother kept on arguing until at length she talked her daughter round to her way of thinking. In the end, then, Harith married the girl and took her off to his home.

One day some time later while he and his wife were sitting in the courtyard some young men of the Asad tribe appeared on the scene disporting themselves. Suddenly she heaved a deep sigh and started to cry. Harith turned to her and asked, "Why are you crying?" "What," she replied, "am I doing with old men who are so weak that when they try to rise they fall about like fledglings from a nest?" "Curse you!" he cried. "Many a battle have I fought in the past, and many a captive girl have I put behind me on my mount, and many a good draught of wine have I drunk! Get back to your own family—I've no use for you!"

In his *Women* Abu Faraj writes: Mu'awiya married his daughter, Hind, to 'Abdullah ibn 'Amir. One day she brought her husband a mirror and comb, for she always treated him with the utmost kindness. When he took a look at both their faces in the mirror, the husband realized how young and lovely his wife

---

[35] Conceivably Ibn al-Mawā'īnī of Seville, twelfth-century author of a work on belles-lettres.

[36] A great and important North Arabian tribe whose territories lie at the foot of mountainous country once inhabited by the Tayyi'.

was and how his own grey and ageing features marked him as an old man. Looking up at her, he said, "Go back to your own family." At this she went off to see her father and told him what had happened. "But should an honest woman of noble birth be divorced?" he asked. "The matter," she replied, "is not in my hands." Mu'awiya then sent to ask the reason why his son-in-law wanted to divorce his wife. The message that came back was, "I will tell you. God has been very good to me and made me a noble man. Therefore I do not wish anyone to do me a favour. Now your daughter by her good companionship has put me in a hopeless position. Having looked at myself and seen how old I am and how youthful she is, I realize I am in no position to make her richer or more noble than she has ever been. I have therefore decided to send her back to you so that you can find her a husband with a face as unwrinkled as the page of a book." This 'Abdullah ibn 'Amir to whom Abu Faraj refers was her first husband who had married her as a virgin.

In his *Revivification* Ghazali writes: During the Caliphate of 'Umar ibn Khattab a man married a woman, pretending to be younger than he was by dyeing his beard. But unfortunately the dye came off, and his in-laws sought redress of grievance and brought him up before 'Umar, claiming that they had contracted the marriage in the belief that he was a young man. 'Umar had him flogged and in sentencing him declared, "You deceived these good people."

CHAPTER VII

The Rights and Duties of
Husbands and Wives

Here I shall first indicate the rights and duties of spouses and
then quote the recommendations offered by certain scholars and
sages to their daughters when the time to conduct bride to bridegroom approached.[1]

It is a well-known fact that God commands the husband to
treat his wife with due consideration. Otherwise, he should repudiate her. In the Koran He says "Associate reputably with
them" and ". . . retaining them reputably or sending them away
with tenderness."[2] By such admonitions God gives notice that
men do have a right over women but only in accordance with
His prescriptions in the Koranic verses quoted.

A husband, then, should keep his wife and live on amiable
terms with her and should not impose upon her burdens which
she cannot bear. At the same time God has imposed upon a wife
the duty to obey and serve him and not to dispose of her property, if she has any, without his prior permission. Likewise she
may only observe those religious duties which are obligatory;
for supererogatory fasting and praying she requires her husband's
permission. The Prophet says, "The most faithful of all the
Believers is the one whose character is fairest, and the finest of
them is the one who treats his wife most generously." He also
said, "Let each Believer advise the other to be kind to his wife.
Some Traditions take the matter further by declaring that
women "are created from a crooked rib, and the most twisted

[1] See above Ch. V, n. 38, p. 113.
[2] Koran, iv, 23; ii, 229.

part of the rib is the top, for, if you try to straighten it, you will break it, but if you leave it alone, it will remain crooked. Therefore counsel one another to deal fairly with womenfolk." On this theme the poet has this to say:

> Here's the rib you should not try to straighten, for indeed
> the straightening of ribs is the surest way to break
> them.
> How then can women combine the weakness of their sex
> with domination over men? Isn't it strange they look
> so weak, but are in fact so strong?

Abu Dharr Ghifari is actually said to have recited these two verses from the pulpit.

The Prophet, in his sermon on his Farewell Pilgrimage,[3] declared, "I commend to you fair treatment of your womenfolk, for they are your captives. Of themselves they possess nothing, and you have them on trust from God and have lawful access to their bodies by God's own command. Men and women have rights over one another. Women have a right to decent food and clothing, and it is your right as husbands that no one whom you find distasteful should tread your carpet. Your womenfolk should allow no one access to your house without your permission or knowledge. If they do, avoid them in bed and beat them, though not severely. Do I make myself clear?" "Yes," replied the Prophet's audience. "Then God be my witness," he concluded.

The Prophet placed all these various restrictions on women because prior to the advent of Islam Arab men would converse freely with women whether their husbands were there or not without any blame or suspicion attaching to the character of the persons concerned. But after the "Curtain Verse" of the Koran[4]

[3] This was the occasion on which the Prophet led the Hajj, or Greater Pilgrimage to Mecca—an annual event in Islam—in March 632. The Farewell Pilgrimage is so called because the Prophet died in June of the same year. It has special significance in the history of Islam in that it was on this occasion that Muhammad not only delivered a famous sermon which marked the fulfilment of his mission, but he also promulgated various important ordinances.

[4] xxxiii, 53. "And when you ask them [i.e. the Prophet's wives] for any

had been revealed men were forbidden to behave as they had done in the past.

As regards the words "avoid them in bed" quoted above, the meaning is not that you should transfer the women in question to another room or keep them out of your sight, but merely that you should keep them away from you in their beds. According to one opinion, the intention is that the husband should sleep in the same bed but that he should turn his back on the offending wife and neither speak to her nor have sexual union with her. But another view is that the husband should leave her bed and sleep in another but still in the same room.

As for the beating which is mentioned,[5] the words "though not severely" may be interpreted in the light of another Tradition which runs "Do not flog your wife as you would a camel and then couple with her at the end of the day." In another Tradition related by Abu Dawud on the authority of Khalid ibn Zayd on ing, "There are three things that are not to be taken lightly: the training of a horse, shooting with a bow and arrow, and, lastly, making love to one's wife." According to some reports this Tradi-

---

article, ask them from behind a curtain." (The word for "curtain" (*ḥijāb*) may be interpreted as "screen" or "veil" since it denotes anything that is put before someone or something to conceal it.) This Koranic verse is of special importance since it supplied the basis for the seclusion of women despite the fact that its application is limited to the wives of the Prophet. In xxxiii, 59, however, we read: "Prophet, instruct your wives and daughters and women-folk of the Faithful to draw their veils (or 'mantles') close to them." The veiling of urban women spread rapidly, but the custom found no general favour with Bedouin and peasant women. Egyptian Muslim reformers in the nineteenth century launched an assault on the evils of the veil and the state of subjection that went with it, and in recent years the veil has been increasingly discarded, especially by the educated classes.

[5] Beating as a means of bringing a difficult, disobedient, and obstinate wife to her senses has Koranic sanction (iv, 38): "As for those women on whose part you fear disobedience, admonish them in their beds and beat them. But if they then obey, take no action against them." This is interpreted by many jurists as meaning that disobedient women should first be verbally admonished, that, if such a course fails, sexual relations with them should be suspended, and that in the last resort, when all else has failed, corporal punishment may be administered. For obvious reasons they have tended to consider corporal punishment inadvisable and urge the need for moderation if such a permissible sanction is the only course.

tion is recorded elsewhere as "All that a man undertakes lightly is to no avail save the training of his horse, shooting with a bow and arrow and making love to his wife."

'A'isha would say, "A woman is a plaything and, as such, a man should treat her well."

Sa'sa'a ibn Sahwan once asked Mu'awiya, "How can we credit you with sense when you are ruled by only half a man?" By the words "half a man" he was alluding to the female of the species, the reference in this case being to Mu'awiya's wife and sister. The reply was, "Women rule the magnanimous—it is only the ignoble who rule women."

In his *Revivification* Ghazali relates the following story: Once a man went in to Mu'awiya (?) and asked him about a husband's duties towards his wife. His reply was that a wife is entitled to kind treatment and decent behaviour from her husband, the implication of "decent behaviour" being that it is not enough for a man merely to protect his wife from annoyance. He should rather be prepared to put up with annoyance from her and to be forbearing in the face of her thoughtlessness and loss of temper by following the Prophet's example. For the Prophet's wives would not hesitate to answer him back, and one of them might, on occasions, ignore him all day. Once when a woman answered 'Umar[6] back, he cried, "How dare you answer me back! You wicked woman!" Whereupon she turned on him with the words. "The Prophet is a better man than you, and *his* wives answer *him* back." 'Umar's only comment then was, "Hafsa is the loser if she gives back answers to the Prophet." To Hafsa he subsequently said, "Don't be misled by the actions of the daughter of Abu Quhafa's son[7]—she's the Prophet's darling."

One of the Prophet's wives once gave him a push, and her mother rebuked her "Oh, let her be," said the Prophet. "That's not the worst my wives do."

On another occasion the Prophet had such a row with his wife, 'A'isha, that he had to call upon Abu Bakr to mediate. "Shall I,"

[6] The future Caliph 'Umar I.

[7] Hafsa was 'Umar's daughter and wife of the Prophet. By "the daughter of Abu Quhafa's son" is meant 'A'isha, Muhammad's favourite wife, whose father Abu Bakr, subsequently the first Caliph, was Abu Quhafa's son.

asked the Prophet, "speak to him first or will you?" "You go ahead," 'A'isha replied, "but mind you tell the truth." At this Abu Bakr gave her such a slap that he made her mouth bleed. "Now listen, you who are your own worst enemy," he stormed, "does he ever speak anything but the truth?" This attack sent her flying to the Prophet for refuge, and she cowered down behind him. "We did not," remarked the Prophet, "call you in for this, nor do we wish to have this sort of behaviour."

Once when 'A'isha was in a bad temper, she taunted the Prophet with the words, "And are you the man who claims to be a prophet?" But the Messenger of God merely smiled and put up with her temper because of his forbearance and magnaninity.

According to Ghazali, the ideal for a man is willingness to tolerate annoyance from his spouses and respond by coaxing, joking and playing with them, for moves of this sort will restore women to good humour and win them over. Certainly the Prophet would joke with his wives and come down to their mental level in his various actions and modes of behaviour. He is said to have gone so far as to take up racing with 'A'isha.[8] One story told by the latter is the following: "Once I heard the voices of a group of Abyssinians and some of their companions as they disported themselves on the Day of 'Ashura',[9] and the Prophet asked me whether I would like to watch their antics. I said that I would, and so the Prophet sent for them. When they came, he stood between the doors and put his hand on one while I rested my chin on his forearm and watched them as they began their sport. When he finally said, 'Enough now,' I told him to be quiet and gave the same answer on two or three occasions. At length he said, 'You really have had enough now,' and I said, 'All right then,' and he motioned to the group to leave."

Muhammad said, "Of all the Faithful the most perfect is the

---

[8] As noted earlier (p. 115) Muhammad married 'A'isha while she was still a child.

[9] The name of a non-obligatory fast day (related to the Hebrew *'asor*) observed on 10 Muharram (the first month of the Islamic year). The fast is observed by devout Sunnites throughout the Muslim world. With the Shi'ites the day is a festival with which quite different ceremonies commemorating the martyrdom of Husayn, son of 'Ali, are associated.

best tempered and most considerate to his spouses." 'Umar, despite his roughness, said, "In his relationship with his wife, a man must behave as a small boy; but when anything is required of him he should be seen to be a man." In the *Commentary on Tradition* it is related that God Most High detests a man who is haughty and cruel to his womenfolk. It is as God says in the Koran, "Gross but highly esteemed."[10] "Gross" in this context is taken to mean "harsh-tongued and harsh-hearted towards one's wife."

In his *Revivification* Ghazali also notes that a man should not be so expansive, frivolous and easy-going in his relationship with his wife that he loses his own dignity and ruins his wife's sense of decorum into the bargain. He should rather observe moderation and neither disregard dignity nor conceal his displeasure at conduct he thoroughly disapproves of—and he should certainly not encourage it. On the contrary, under such circumstances he should raise his voice in protest and vexation. Hasan, son of 'Ali, said, "No man ever obeyed his wife in her whims and fancies without God casting him down into the Fire."

Note also that a woman's mentality is modelled after the pattern of your own. If, therefore, you allow her a little rein, she will bolt, and if you slacken the bridle an inch, she will pull you a yard. But if you keep a firm hand on her, you will hold her to yourself.

Shafi'i[11] said, "There are three kinds of person who will abase you, but who, if abased, will treat you reverentially." One of the three categories he had in mind was the female sex, and what he meant was that if you treat women with pure respect unmingled with the occasional sharp word or deed, familiarity will breed contempt.

At one time Arab women would teach their daughters to see how far they could go with a husband. A mother would instruct her daughter in the following metaphorical terms, "Before

[10] lxviii, 13.
[11] Jurist (767–820) who has given his name to one of the four Sunnite systems of Islamic law. A man of powerful intellect, he has been rightly described as "the colossus of Islamic legal history" (N. J. Coulson, *A History of Islamic Law* (Edinburgh U.P., 1964), p. 55).

insulting your husband, first remove the sharp point from his lance, and if he says nothing, cut his flesh on his shield. If he still says nothing, break his bones with his sword, and if at this stage he is still unmoved, put a saddle on his back, for he's only your donkey." To be brief, it is by balance that heaven and earth subsist, and anything that moves out of place will slide to the other extreme of itself and revert to the opposite. One should therefore exercise moderation, whether it be a case of agreement or a matter of disagreement, and do what is right and proper in all things. And so a man would do well first of all to find out what sort of person his wife really is and then to treat her as the occasion requires.

As regards a man's rights over his wife, Shafi'i says that marriage is a form of bondage in which a wife is a slave to her husband. She must therefore render him absolute obedience in every lawful demand he makes upon her. Ghazali, however, does not admit the use of the term "absolute" here and declares that although *coitus interruptus* is lawful—particularly according to the views of the legal school to which he adheres—she is not bound to obey him [if she does not desire *coitus interruptus*].[12]

In the Traditions greater emphasis is laid on a husband's rights over his wife. For instance, the Prophet said, "Any woman who dies in the enjoyment of her husband's approval and satisfaction shall enter Paradise."

Among a woman's rights over her husband is the right to sexual union. On this theme Muhammad ibn Ma'n relates the following story: A woman once went to the Caliph 'Umar ibn Khattab and said, "Commander of the Faithful, my husband fasts during the day and sits up all night [in prayer]. I hate to complain to you about him when he is obviously serving God, but here I am complaining nevertheless." 'Umar's only comment was, "God be good to you," meaning "for praising your husband". She kept on repeating the same words and receiving the same reply until in the end Ka'b ibn Thawr of Azd, who hap-

---

[12] *Coitus interruptus* is not forbidden in Islam. By general agreement of the jurists it can be practised unconditionally by a man with a concubine who is his slave. There is not the same consensus of opinion where husband and wife are concerned since some hold that the wife's consent is necessary.

pened to be present, said to 'Umar, "Commander of the Faithful, give judgement in the case." "But is she in fact bringing a case for judgement?" he asked. "Yes indeed," said Ka'b. "Her complaint is that her husband does not join her in bed and she is demanding conjugal rights." "Well then," said 'Umar, "if that is your interpretation of her words, you deal with the case." So Ka'b had her husband summoned, and, when he appeared, Ka'b told him that his wife had a complaint to make against him. "But why?" asked the husband. "Haven't I maintained her as I ought?" "No," said Ka'b. Whereupon the man's wife recited the following lines:

> "Sagacious and percipient Judge, my life's companion has
> a mosque that comes between us both.[13]
> Day and night he never lays his body down, but,
> speaking as a woman, I cannot praise his virtue."

In answer the defendant spoke the following lines,

> "I am a man made sparing of his favours in the bed
> by fear of the words of God.
> In the 'Chapter of the Bees'[14] and seven long chapters
> more from the very Book of God lies a dreadful warning
> for those who would indulge."

Ka'b then himself declaimed,

> "She has a case against you, Sir. Anyone with any wit
> will see she has a quarter share.
> Such a judgement comes from God Most High Himself.
> So give her her due and leave aside excuses."

"God," Ka'b commented, "permits you four wives, and so you have three days in which to worship Him. Four nights and days remain, and each wife has an equal share in them."[15] 'Umar

[13] i.e. his devotion to religion comes between them.

[14] Koran, xvi, in which there are warnings (e.g. vv. 26–31) against the doom that awaits evil-doers.

[15] i.e. the Law permits a man four spouses, and, if he assigns a day to each, there will be three left for supererogatory devotions.

then commented to Ka'b, "I find it hard to know which is the more remarkable—your grasp of this woman's plight or the judgement you've just given. Go now—you are appointed Judge of Basra."

In his *Revivification* Ghazali offers good advice in the story which follows: Asma' ibn Kharija of Fazara married off his daughter, and when he was about to conduct her to her bridegroom, he counselled, "You are now leaving the nest in which you have slowly grown to womanhood and now you go to a bed of which you have no knowledge as well as to the company of a partner with whom you are unfamiliar. Be to him a plot of land, and he will be your heaven above; be to him a place of rest, and to you he will be a mainstay; be to him a bondmaid, and to you he will be a slave. Do not cling to him lest he rid himself of the burdens of your weight—yet do not keep away from him too much lest he forgets you. If he comes toward you, then you move close to him; but if he moves away, then keep your distance also. Pay careful heed to his nostrils, ears, and eyes so that he may never smell anything but fragrant perfume from your body and never hear of you anything but what is of good report, and never see in you anything but beauty.

In his *Multitudes* Abu Rayhan relates as follows: 'Amir ibn Dharib of 'Adwan gave his daughter in marriage to his brother's son and said to the girl's mother "Tell your daughter she should never be without water in a desert, for water will make her radiant above and keep her clean below. She mustn't starve her husband's sexual appetite, for happiness lies in harmony. Nor at the same time should she lie too long beside him, for if the body grows weary, so also does the heart."

On the same theme Abu Rayhan records this advice given by a mother to her daughter: "Be a bed to him, and he will be a means of sustenance to you; be a carpet on which he may tread, and he will be your coverlet. Never be sorrowful when he is joyful, or joyful when he is downcast. Let him not see you in anything ugly, and let him smell nothing but perfume, Reveal no secret of his lest you lose favour in his sight. Use water, unguents, and eye salve for these are the best cosmetics."

Another man said to his daughter on the night he gave her in marriage: "Be a handmaid to your husband and he will be a slave to you; be kind to him, for kindness speaks louder than magic. Lastly, use water, for water is the fountain of perfume."

In his book *For Muwaffaq* Zubayr[16] tells the following tale: Qays ibn Mas'ud ibn Qays ibn Khalid married his daughter to Laqit ibn Zurara ibn 'Adas for a dower of one hundred she-camels sick and worn with age. He then went to visit her and said, "My daughter, I've married you to a lad who's good and true. Don't always be on top of him lest he feels oppressed—yet, don't stray too far from his side lest he forget you. Overwhelm your in-laws with all kindness, and heap no ill upon them. Be a handmaid to him, and he will be a slave to you. Exhale perfume in your tracks wherever he follows your trail, and realize that a woman's best perfume is water." With these words he left her and said to those about her, "Adorn her for her husband and take her away." When she had been given in marriage she said one day, "Take me to my father's house so that I can greet him." So they took her round to her father's, and, after staying there a little while, she got up to go, and, as she did so, her father said to her, "May you never prosper, my girl, nor ever bear a son!" "Father," she exclaimed, "you humiliated me as a child, stood aloof from me when I came to womanhood, and now you've crowned it all by giving me the most appalling send-off!" "And," persisted the father, "may you go to far-off lands, bear children who'll be your foes, lose all your possessions and never have a friend!"

In his book *The Primary Feather of the Wing* Tifashi writes: Umama daughter of Harith of the tribe of Taghlib married 'Awf ibn Muhallim, and in due course she bore him a daughter, the future Umm Iyas whom her father married to Harith ibn 'Amr of Kinda. Before the mother decided the time had come to give her daughter away to Harith, she said. "Now, my girl, if the only advice I could give you could not go beyond the sphere of good name and breeding, I would leave it at that. But such advice

---

[16] Abu 'Ali Zubayr ibn Bakr Bakkar (773–867). His book *For Muwaffaq* was a collection of historical narratives in five volumes designed for reading by Muwaffaq, son of the Caliph Mutawakkil.

is intended to be a reminder to the intelligent and a warning to the reckless. So I tell you this, child, if a woman could do without a husband and need nothing but the wealth of her parents, you would not have wanted for anything. But the truth is that we women are born for men as they were for us. You now leave the abode in which you have been brought up and the nest in which you have grown by degrees until now at last you go to a home that you do not know and to a companion with whom you are not yet familiar and who, by taking possession of you, is now your lord and master. So be a bondmaid to him, and he will become your slave. If you but observe ten rules, you will be unforgettable and someone to be proud of. The first and second are: be a good and contented companion, and, in your life together, be a good and patient listener and obedient to boot; for peace of mind consists in living with him as a good listener, and obedience is pleasing in the sight of the Lord. The third and fourth are namely these: be attractive to his eyes and fragrant to his nose, so that he may never see in you anything ugly or ever catch the scent of anything but sweet fragrance. Realize that eye-black is the most beautiful thing in existence and that water is the rarest perfume. The fifth and sixth are as follows: be attentive to his meals and be quiet when he is asleep; for the heat of an empty belly inflames the temper and disturbed sleep is apt to irritate. The seventh and eighth are: look after his house and his money and show good humour towards his nearest and dearest. In looking after his money the fundamental principle is good housekeeping, while good humour towards his family is sound diplomacy. The ninth and tenth are these: neither divulge his secrets nor disobey his orders; for, if you divulge his secrets, you cannot be certain that he will not give you away, and, if you challenge his authority you will only infuriate him. Beware of being gay when he is gloomy and of being gloomy when he is gay. The first is a failing, the second an affront. The more agreeable you are to him, the pleasanter he will be to you. You can take it that you will not achieve harmony unless you put his likes and good pleasure before your own although it may not suit you to do so."

CHAPTER VIII

On Concubines and Wives and
Plurality of Wives

In his book The Perfect Mubarrad writes: Maslama ibn 'Abd-ul-Malik once said, "There are three persons I really admire: a man who cuts his hair short, then lets it grow long again, a man who tucks his shirt into his belt, then lets it down again, and finally a man who finds delight in his slave concubines and then returns to his free-born spouses."[1]

King Solomon had seven hundred concubines. In Islam 'Ali had nineteen. In urging men to take concubines 'Umar ibn Khattab said, "There is no smarter set than the sons of concubines: they combine the pride and power of the Arabs with the intelligence of non-Arabs." He also used to say, "Now, my fine men, if a man wants sexual congress, he should go for Berber girls; if he wants good service, he should go for Europeans; if he wants nobility he should go for Persians."[2] It is indeed said that the daughters of non-Arabs and outsiders are superior to all other women and that none can strike off the heads of one's peers better than the son of a non-Arab girl.

In his book Treasures of the Claimant Ibn Sa'id writes: Musa Kazim[3] once said, "Go for slave-girls—they have minds and intelligence."

---

[1] What he means to say is that he admires men with a sense of occasion and duty. To tuck the skirt of a flowing Arab garment into one's belt is to indicate that one is preparing for hard work or battle, the point being that the man who recognizes the need for action and addresses himself to the task but can relax when the occasion is past is to be admired.

[2] For various reasons it is unlikely that 'Umar I said any such thing.

[3] The Seventh Imam (d. 799) of those Shi'ites (above Ch. V, n. 15, p. 103).

In his *Women* Abu Faraj writes: The Caliph Hisham ibn 'Abd-ul-Malik[4] once wrote to a governor of his as follows: "The Commander of the Faithful, having seen what Musa ibn Nusayr was in the habit of sending to the late 'Abd-ul-Malik, requires of you the same. You have wide-eyed winsome Berber slave-girls such as we do not have in Syria or neighbouring lands. Take care to select the best and seek out the sort of girl who is possessed of pleasing looks, well-padded buttocks, ample bosom, soft body, slender fingers and long limbs, full legs, a good head of silky curling hair, large eyes, full cheeks, small mouth and lovely teeth, a body that is long but well proportioned and a voice that speaks in melodious tones. At the same time see to it that this kind of girl is of honest birth and well brought up, for such women make excellent mothers."

In the same book Abu Faraj writes—as also Ibn Kardabus in his book *Contentment*: Abu 'Abbas Saffah, the first Abbasid Caliph, had a wife by the name of Umm Salama, daughter of Ya'qub ibn 'Abdullah of Makhzum. He had fallen deeply in love with her, and she had found a tender spot in his heart. He therefore swore that he would never take a concubine nor marry another wife, and this oath he never broke. Now one day he was alone with Khalid ibn Safwan, who addressed him in the following terms: "Commander of the Faithful, I have been thinking of you and the vast kingdom you rule.[5] Yet you allow yourself to be ruled by a woman and take her only to yourself. If she ails, you also ail—even if she menstruates, you also menstruate. You

known as Twelvers and so called because they believe in twelve invisible Imams (i.e. authoritative sources of doctrine to whom the occult interpretation of the Koran is exclusively known). In their view the last Imam mysteriously disappeared in the ninth century, and they await his reappearance.

[4] Tenth Syrian Umayyad Caliph (reg. 724–43). Musa ibn Nusayr to whom this letter—chronologically and stylistically suspect—is addressed is a man of considerable historical importance since it was he who played the leading role in the Muslim conquests in North-West Africa and Spain between 705 and 713. The Berbers referred to were the indigenous inhabitants of North-West Africa. The Berber race constitutes the substratum of the population of this region.

[5] The Arab Empire reached its zenith under the Umayyads of Syria, extending from Spain in the West to Central Asia and the Indus Valley in the East. Such was the heritage of the first Abbasid—a heritage that was soon to be lost through regional fragmentation.

have denied yourself the pleasure of concubines and the enjoyment of slave-girls and all the various kinds of delight that you could find in them. They come in all sorts and varieties, Commander of the Faithful. There is the girl who is young and slender, or there is the silver blonde with fair complexion or the golden blonde with light brown skin or the brunette with dark brown colouring or the Berber girl with rounded buttocks. Again, there are half-Arab girls from Medina whose conversation makes them most seductive. And, Commander of the Faithful, if only you could see half-Arab girls from Basra and Kufa with their red lips, sweet tongues, slender bodies, slim waists and round protruding breasts—yes, if only you could see the shape and beauty of these women, what a gorgeous sight you would see! Why be bothered with noble, freeborn girls, Commander of the Faithful? Why be bothered looking at their shy bashful faces? What of the coquetry and perfumes?" Khalid went on with his descriptions at such great lengths and in such delightful terms that when he had finished the Caliph exclaimed, "You devil, Khalid! Never have I heard anything more delightful than what I've just heard from you. Give me the same all over again." So Khalid repeated all he had said and indeed added more. He then left the Caliph alone and deep in thought.

Not long after, Umm Salama, who was very devoted to him, came in. She would do her best to make him completely happy and to agree to his every wish. "Commander of the Faithful," she said, "How is it that I find you so depressed? Has something unpleasant happened to upset you? Or have you bad news to perturb you?" "No, it's nothing like that," he replied. "Well then, what is it?" she persisted. He then began to evade the issue, but she kept pressing him until at last he told her what Khalid had said to him. "And what," she expostulated, "did you have to say to that son of a bitch?" "Good God," cried the Caliph, "is my adviser to be reviled by you?" At this she left without further comment.

However, Umm Salama did not let it stay at that, but sent her slaves after Khalid with orders to beat him and inflict exemplary punishment on him. At this point Khalid takes up the story: "I'd made my way home highly delighted with the attentive audience I'd been granted by the Caliph and the pleasure my performance had given him. I was really expecting some gift from him in recognition of my services. Before long I saw these slaves coming towards me and I felt sure of my reward. When they reached me, they stopped and asked me who I was. But no sooner had I told them than one of them came at me with a cudgel in his hand. I fled into the house as fast as I could and closed the door behind me with a slam. I shut myself in and didn't budge for days during which the Caliph hunted high and low for me. Then one day I was surprised by a party who commanded me to appear before the Caliph. I was certain that my time had come and, saying to myself, 'As sure as fate my head will roll,' I mounted my horse and rode off to the palace.

"As soon as I got there I was met by several messengers and made my entrance. There I found the Caliph sitting waiting for me. When he motioned to me to take a seat I recovered my composure and sat down. While in the audience chamber I spotted a door covered by a curtain which had been let down and behind which I detected some movement. 'Khalid,' said the Caliph, 'I haven't seen you for the last three days.' 'Commander of the Faithful,' I mumbled, 'I've not been very well.' 'Well now,' he continued, 'I've never had a finer description of women and slave-girls than the one you gave me the other day. Do tell me it all over again.' 'Very well, Commander of the Faithful,' I replied. 'I told you that the Arabs derived the term for a 'second wife' from the word 'trouble' and that no man ever met with two women without his life being a misery.' 'You devil!' cried the Caliph. 'You told me no such thing.' 'And, Commander of the Faithful,' I went on, 'I told you that to have three wives would be like having a tripod on which a caldron continually boils, while to have four is to suffer the affliction of a compounded evil which gives great pain and suffering and brings on great debility. And what is more, I said that virgin slave-girls are nothing better than eunuchs.' 'By God,' declared the Caliph, 'If I ever heard any such thing from you, I'm no descendant of the Prophet.'[6] 'Oh, but I did say that, Commander

---

[6] The Abbasid Caliphs were descended from the uncle of the Prophet.

of the Faithful, and what is more I told you that Makhzum is the sweet myrtle of the tribe of Quraysh and that you have the best myrtle of all,[7] albeit that your eyes may turn longingly to the bondmaids and slave-girls about you.' 'You lie to me and make me a liar!' cried the Caliph. 'Do you want to kill me, Commander of the Faithful?' I asked the Caliph—and at this point I heard a chuckle from behind the curtains and a voice saying, 'How true your words are, my good man! The Caliph changed the tale and put words into your mouth that you never really uttered.'

"I'd barely left them to delight in each other's company than messengers came from Umm Salama laden with gifts and chests of clothes and said to me, 'Umm Salama's instructions are that, whenever you speak to the Caliph, you are to talk to him in the same vein as you did just now.' "

Ibn Kardabus comments that Umm Salama was the daughter of Ya'qub ibn Salama ibn 'Abdullah ibn Walid ibn Walid ibn Mughira of Makhzum and had been previously married to 'Abd-ul-'Aziz ibn Walid ibn 'Abd-ul-Malik ibn Marwan, who predeceased her. Others say, however, that she had been the wife of Maslama ibn Hisham ibn 'Abd-ul-Malik. The story goes that one day while she was sitting by her husband's grave, Abu 'Abbas,[8] who was an attractive and handsome man passed close by. She asked who he was, and someone told her his lineage. Whereupon she sent her maid laiden with presents to ask him to propose to her mistress. But since Umm Salama was a woman of substance with a store of precious stones, Abu 'Abbas at first declined the proposition on the grounds that he was in fact a poor man. But she insisted on making him a present of all her wealth that her maid had taken to him. He accepted the gift and went straight to her brother to ask for Umm Salama's hand. Her brother agreed to the proposal, and the marriage was consummated the same night.

When the bridegroom first entered Umm Salama's room, he

---

[7] An attempt to flatter Umm Salama, a scion of the Makhzum branch of the tree of Quraysh, the Prophet's own tribe.

[8] "Abu 'Abbas" is substituted for "Saffah" of the text for the convenience of the general reader. As we have already seen (p. 162), Saffah—the style of the first Abbasid—and Abu 'Abbas are one and the same person.

found her on the bridal couch and went up to her. To his amazement every limb was festooned with jewels. As a result, he was unable to achieve an erection when he attempted to couple with her. So she removed her jewels and changed her clothes, and he tried again. But once more he failed. His wife, however, dealt kindly with him. "Don't let this worry you," she said. "You're not the first man to whom this sort of thing has happened, and you won't be the last." With that he settled down and caressed her all night long until he succeeded in having intercourse with her. Thereafter she found great favour with him and accordingly exerted great influence over him when he came to power.

Someone—it was not Ibn Kardabus—asserts that Umm Salama's loyalty to the Caliph did not outlive him since she subsequently contracted a secret marriage with his uncle Isma'il ibn 'Ali, who on that account had to visit her in disguise. But the whole tale eventually got round to the new Caliph, Abu Ja'far Mansur,[9] and threw him into a rage. "He was loyal to her throughout his life," he thundered, "but she can't be loyal to his memory." He lost no time in sending for Isma'il, of whom he then demanded an oath that he would divorce his wife. "And if you don't divorce her," he threatened, "I'll have your head." And so Isma'il divorced her. The Caliph then stripped her of all the jewellery and other possessions she had acquired from Abu 'Abbas. "Had you been loyal to the memory of your husband," he told her, "we should have been loyal to you."

No one, so they say, ever had a pleasanter disposition towards his wife than Abu 'Abbas when the two were together in private. The following story is told of the Caliph by one of his protégés:[10] "I remember one night when I was young seeing the Caliph Abu 'Abbas sitting on his couch with his wife Umm Salama. Just at that moment the two most exquisite young slave-girls that I ever set eyes on happened to go by. At the time they were veiled as free women normally are, and this prompted Abu 'Abbas to call them over and ask them whether they were free or slaves. 'We're

[9] This second Abbasid Caliph (reg. 754–75) was the brother of Abu 'Abbas.
[10] More correctly "clients" (*mawāli*).

slave-girls,' they said in reply to his question. 'Then why are you wearing veils?' he asked. 'It's the custom in the country we come from,' came the answer. But it was really that they had been so commanded by Umm Salama, who had no intention of allowing their charms to be seen. 'Take off your veils,' ordered the Caliph. But the girls refused for fear of his wife's wrath. So he told a eunuch to take them off. And what a beautiful sight they presented! They had the most beautiful hair, smooth cheeks, perfect figures with firm protruding breasts like rounded ivory caskets. The Caliph looked at the girls intently and then said to one of his attendants, 'Take them to so-and-so and tell each to take one for himself and to look well after them, for I shall then know how they're getting on.' He did all this merely to please Umm Salama."

In his book *Discourse on Women* 'Abd-ul-Malik writes: I was told by Mutarrif on the authority of Malik ibn Anas[11] that Qasim ibn Muhammad ibn Abi Bakr Siddiq, Salim ibn 'Abdullah ibn 'Umar ibn Khattab, and 'Ali ibn Husayn ibn 'Ali ibn Abi Talib were all sons of concubines.[12] In his *Primary Feather of the Wing* Tifashi quotes Asma'i as saying, "The Medinese hated concubines until these men were born and bred among them and excelled all the Medinese in religious knowledge and piety. Thereafter all men of rank showed great zeal for concubines"

In *The Perfect* Mubarrad writes: A member of the tribe of Quraysh whose name is unknown to us relates the following story. "I used to keep company with Sa'id ibn Musayyib, who asked me one day who my maternal uncles were. When I had to say my mother was a concubine I felt as if I had dropped in his estimation. Before too long Salim ibn 'Abdullah ibn 'Umar ibn Khattab entered our presence and in due course went out again. 'Tell me,' I said, 'who's that man who's just gone out, Abu

[11] Malik ibn Anas (712–96), a native of Medina, has given his name to the Malikite legal system, one of the four such systems recognized by Sunnite Islam. Mutarrif, a Malikite jurist (745 or 746–c. 829), was a son of one of Malik's sisters.

[12] As can be seen from the names given, the three persons were descendants of the Patriarchal or "Orthodox" Caliphs Abu Bakr (often styled "Siddiq"), 'Umar I, and 'Ali.

'Abdullah?'[13] 'Good God!' he exclaimed, 'Don't you know a man from your own tribe who is as important as he is? That was Salim ibn 'Abdullah ibn 'Umar.' 'Who was his mother?' I asked. 'Some concubine,' came the reply. Then Qasim ibn Muhammad ibn Abi Bakr called on us. After sitting awhile he left. I asked my companion who he was. 'But what an extraordinary fellow you are!' he exclaimed. 'Don't you recognize a man from your own tribe as famous as he is? That's Qasim ibn Muhammad ibn Abi Bakr.' 'Who's his mother?' I asked. 'Some concubine,' he replied. Lastly, 'Ali ibn Husayn ibn 'Ali ibn Abi Talib joined us, and I asked who he was. 'A man every Muslim ought to know—he's 'Ali ibn Husayn ibn 'Ali ibn Abi Talib,' he replied. 'And his mother?' I queried. 'Some concubine,' came the answer. I then ventured to comment, 'Abu 'Abdullah, I felt as if I had gone down in your estimation when you learned my mother was a concubine. But tell me how I differ from the men you've just seen.' By this question I gained greatly in stature."

According to Mubarrad, the mother of 'Ali ibn Husayn was in fact descended from the ancient Persian king, Yazdagird.

In his *Women* Abu Faraj quotes 'Umar ibn Khattab as saying "At ten a girl is moody; at twenty she delights those who behold her; at thirty she is a pleasure to lovers; at forty she is soft and supple; at fifty she has had her share of sons and daughters; at sixty she is a woman of the past."

In his *Scattering of Pearls* Âbi tells the following story: Once a woman asked another "What do you think of a man of twenty?" "He's fragrance to the nose," she replied. "And of a man of thirty?" "Of strong and powerful thrust." 'And of a man of forty?" "A father of sons and daughters" "And of a man of fifty?" "Passable." "And a man of sixty?" "Coughing and moaning."

In his *Dictations* Zajjaj relates the following: Nu'man ibn Mundhir, King of Hira, once asked the poet Damra ibn Damra to give him a description of women, and he did so in the following lines:

13 See above Ch. V, n. 62, p. 121.

When you meet a girl of ten whose breasts already firmly
 show, a girl as gorgeous as some diver's pearl, a girl with
 gently swaying neck,
Her sparkle and vivacity will give you true delight as
 beauty still adorns her.
There's nothing like a girl of twenty, for she's a girl in
 whom a man, if sensible, will truly find diversion.
Now, a woman of thirty with soothing speech is life itself
 so long as she's slim and her body's not ravaged by time.
And should you meet with a woman of forty, she'll be a
 sheer delight (for the best about women is the love
 they give and the children they bear).
The woman of fifty has still some love life to thrill her,
 for the pole of the tent still solidly stands.
But the woman of sixty's no use at all, but if she's got
 money, she'll still draw the man who is greedy.

According to Zajjaj, Akhfash says that there have never been
better lines than these to describe the stages of a woman's life.
However, Zajjaj quotes some lines by Muhammad ibn 'Abdullah
ibn Tahir:

Between the years of ten and twenty girls make pleasurable
 mounts—but, twenty reached, rein in your mount.
But, if you go beyond that age, then slow the pace, just
 take it easy, and do not overdo it.
For, as the years go by, women grow harsh—and that,
 and the children they bear, become a source of woe.

The following story is related by 'Ata' ibn Mus'ab: Once
when we were in the company of Khalid ibn Safwan at a gathering in Basra a Bedouin of the tribe of 'Anbar suddenly descended
on us. "The best sort of woman," observed Khalid, "is the sort
who is sophisticated and mature in her judgement, flat in the
belly, full in the buttocks and able to fill the arms of her lover's
embrace." "Never mind the maturity of her judgement," interjected the Bedouin. "Get her between the age at which her
breasts first begin to swell and the age at which they are full—at
the age when she's no experience and still doesn't know what
is wanted of her." He then recited,

"If ever you marry, Ibn Safwan, go for the well-clad girl,
Of the kind with ample buttocks and a belly well
padded with fat,
And the flat-nosed sort of pubis as round as a bowl and
covered in fluff."

"Well done!" applauded Khalid. "An excellent description."
With regard to the words "when she's no experience and still
doesn't know what is wanted of her" we may note that in his
Dictations Abu 'Ali Qali quotes Niftawayh[14] as reciting verses
by Majnun:[15]

Ever since I first met Layla when she was but a girl
with no breasts that any could see
—We were both tending lambs and both were young.
Oh, how I wish we'd never grown up—neither those
lambs nor ourselves!

In his *Songs* Abu Faraj tells us that, as Abu Mulayka was
calling the Faithful to prayer in Mecca, he suddenly heard someone singing these two lines. He listened, and then instead of
uttering the words "Come to prayer", as intended, he inadver-
tently called out "Come to the lambs!" All Mecca heard him, and
then he found himself having to beg everyone's pardon.

Among verses of a similar kind to those by Majnun are the
following addressed to Buthayna by Jamil:[16]

Don't you recall the days and nights we spent at
Liwa-l-A'sur?
When you were some potentate's pearl and the tail of
your youth was still long,

[14] The name of this well-known grammarian is said by some to be
Naftuwayh (see B. Dodge, *The Fihrist of al-Nadim* (Columbia U.P., 1970), II,
1067 f., but Niftawayh seems correct (see C. E. Bosworth (ed.), *The Book of
Curious and Entertaining Information ... of Tha'alibi* (Edinburgh U.P., 1968),
pp. 63 f,

[15] Majnun, it will be recalled (above p. 67), is celebrated for his love of
Layla.

[16] Jamil, it will also be recalled (above p. 67), is renowned for his love of
Buthayna.

And I had a deep black forelock as black as a raven's
    wing and perfumed with musk and amber,
Two youngsters were we who grew up in one place
    together. So why have I grown older while you yourself
    have not?

Lines by Nusayb:

Were it not that men would say, "Nusayb's a man for
    the girls!" I my very self would say, "I'd give my
    life for young and pretty girls!
I'd give my life for a thin-waisted girl who would have
    to give in to a rake such as me!"

In his *Flowers* Husri attributes the following lines to Bashshar:

Batta marvelled at my words describing her. For how
    can the blind describe?[17]
A hidden pearl of the sea is she, a pearl unpolished by
    the trader's hand.
A girl of thirteen with three parts to her beauty—
    a branch, a sand-hill and a moon.[18]

In his *Women* Abu Faraj writes: To these words of his we may
add the observations of another author who has dealt with the
subject of women and their characters and their age differences
according to type:

"It is in the nature of the young girl whose breasts have just
begun to form to give truthful answers to any questions. She will
not be reticent, shy or bashful, and the opposite sex will cause
her no trouble. Then we have the growing girl with rounding
breasts who has not yet wholly emerged from childhood.
Although somewhat more retiring, she will at the same time
show off her charms a little since she still likes to be the centre of
attraction. At the age of puberty a girl is in the full bloom of

[17] As already noted (Ch. IV, n. 3, p. 73), Bashshar was blind.
[18] The parts referred to are the face (moon), torso (branch), and buttocks
(sandhill). See above Ch. I, n. 14 and Ch. II, 31.

youth; her figure is fully developed and her breasts are formed and large. Now she will try to attract the opposite sex. She will behave with decorum and speak in sweet and melodious tones. At this age she will find it hard to check her sexual passion. Of such a girl the poet writes:

> She is now fully grown or nearly so, and off come her
> garments in passion.

"Now we come to the woman who, as yet unmarried, is half-way through her youth. Her breasts will begin to droop, but her deportment and speech will be graceful. Flirtatiously she will display her charms and will like nothing better than to tease and banter men. At this phase her sexual desire is at its height. At the end of her youth a woman loves nothing more wildly than carnal connexion with a climax that is long drawn out. Once she is in the middle age and 'half-way through'—by which we mean over forty—her face will begin to lose its fresh, moist look, and her flesh will get flabby. It is as the poet says:

> 'And if they come and tell you that the woman's half-way
> through,
> You'll know the better half has gone.'

"At this stage in their lives women blandish men in their endeavour to retain their hold on them. And now at last we come to the old woman at the end of the road. She is the sort whom any man with wit will loathe and shun."

Asma'i recounts the following story: A man once brought an action against his wife before Ziyad,[19] who dealt harshly with him in the matter. In a plea to him the plaintiff said, "God guide you, Emir, as you hear me. The better of the two halves of a man's life is the second, for at this stage he is no longer a fool, his wisdom returns and his judgement matures. But for a woman the second half is worse, for now her mind deteriorates, her tongue long and her vagina grows too wide." Such was the impression

---

[19] Probably Ziyad ibn Abihi (d. 673), who was governor of Iraq under the Umayyad Caliph Mu'awiya.

these words left on Ziyad that he gave judgement in the husband's favour.

In his *Songs* Abu Faraj relates the following story: When Ramla, daughter of 'Abdullah ibn Khalaf, who was a co-spouse of 'Umar ibn 'Abdullah, came to middle life she would keep away from him as she would normally have done at the time of her monthly periods so as to let him think that she was still young enough to menstruate.[20] But she was as dry as the woman of whom the poet said:

> May God put every drop that flows from you in your
> courses in the inmost lining of my eye![21]

Doctors are right when they say "To wed a woman who is getting on in age is to take a poison that saps the body[22] and brings care and sorrow on her spouse." And this is what a certain poet says:

> If offered an oldish woman's hand, turn down the offer,
> and shed your clothes in faster flight to leave her well
> behind you!
> And, if they come to tell you that the woman's "half-way
> through", you'll know her better half is gone.

No poet ever took the older woman as a subject for amatory verse—apart from Abu Aswad of Du'il, whom Abu Tammam quotes in his book *Martial Courage*:

> My heart can only love Umm 'Awf and bear my loving
> her now she's getting on;
> Yet anyone, I know it well, who loves a woman in her
> later years is surely laughed to scorn.

20 See above Ch. III, n. 11, p. 63.

21 i.e. the amount of blood she would lose in menstruation would be so negligible that it could be accommodated in the spaces between the eyelids and the eye. In other words, she would lose not so much as a drop because her periods have ceased with age.

22 In medieval times physicians held various erroneous beliefs about the harm that would come to a man's health and potency from the state, nature, and secretions of the vagina. See below Ch. XII, notably p. 217.

But she is like a piece of linen cloth—well used, with a
texture as you'd wish it.[23]

'Asim in his commentary on *Martial Courage* writes that
Kharqa', Dhu Rumma's lady friend, asked Quhayf to write some
amatory verses in tribute to her. Quhayf, however, declined by
pleading that he never took the older woman as a subject for his
verses. But at that moment Kharqa' appeared before him and,
giving him a fetching look, completely won his heart. To him
she seemed the most beautiful of women, and so he said of her:

> Kharqa' sent to me a message to make me stupid as a man
> she's sent distracted.
> For Kharqa' grows in charm, and even if she lived as long,
> or longer, than the oak, her charm would ever grow
> the more.

On Virgins

In his *Revivification* Ghazali writes: A woman who is a virgin
is possessed of certain characteristics that are lacking in one who
is not. For one thing she will long for no-one but the man to
whom she is first married, since it is only natural for one to care
for the first person one grows accustomed to. The love that is
truest is, in most cases, that which is felt for the first beloved.
Another point about a virgin is that a man will really care for
her. For a man has a natural aversion to a woman with whom
some other man has had an intimate relationship—it gnaws at
him whenever he thinks of it, and, in this respect, some men
are worse than others.

Again, a virgin will generally accept all her husband's little
ways because, once married, she will have grown accustomed to
him and have no standard of comparison. A woman who has been
previously married, on the other hand, and has experience of
men and got to know their different ways, does not so readily
accept a new husband's ways if they run counter to those she is

[23] Linen wears well and improves with keeping as its initial stiffness gives
way to a softer texture.

already used to, and she may, on that account, reject him. God Himself has described the houris and women in Paradise as women whom He has created as virgins for His servants who obey him in this world. He says—and how excellent a speaker is He!: "Perfectly we formed them, perfect, and We made them spotless virgins, chastely amorous, all of like age."[24] Likewise He says in the Koran that they are "untouched before them by any man or jinn."[25]

The following Tradition of the Prophet is related by Farra': "Go for virgins when seeking a wife, for they have the sweetest mouths, the most fertile wombs, and the fairest complexions." To this Abu 'Ali in his *Dictations* adds: "and they are more content with small things."

One day 'A'isha said to the Prophet, "Messenger of God, were you to see two gardens, one with its trees and plants grazed upon and eaten and the other completely untouched, which of the two would you loose your camel on?" "The one that had never been grazed on," replied the Prophet.

"All your wives, Messenger of God, are comparable to gardens," she observed "as only one has never been married before." The point of her remark was that she herself was the only virgin the Prophet had ever married.

In his *Women* Abu Faraj writes: No woman ever forgets the man who deflowers her or the man who slays her first-born.

In his commentary on *The Assemblies* Ibn 'Abd-ul-Mu'min writes: The Chosroes Parvitz[26] was once asked, "What is delight for an hour?" "Coitus," he replied. "And delight for a day?" "A steam bath." "And for a week?" "A depilatory." "And for a year?" "Marriage with a virgin." "And for ever?" "To talk with friends in this world and the pleasures of Paradise in the next."

In *The Wise Fools* a fine story is told: Once a man, contemplating marriage, said to himself "What I'll do is to ask the advice of the first man who comes along and act on his recommendation." Now it so happened that the first to come along was

---

[24] Koran, lvi, 36.   [25] Koran, lv, 56.
[26] Persian king (see above Ch. V, n. 34). On *The Assemblies* see next page.

Habannaqa Qaysi mounted on a bullrush (like a child on a hobby-horse).[27] "I want to get married," said the man to Habannaqa. "What's your advice?" "Wed a virgin," he replied, "and keep clear of a woman who's been married before, and don't go near one who's the mother of a child. And watch what you're doing with my horse lest I spear you!"

In one of his *Assemblies* Hariri[28] writes: A virgin is like a hoarded pearl, an egg that is covered with a sitting bird, a first-fruit ready for gathering or a vintage wine in store, a fragrant flower-bed or a necklet that is costly and choice, one unsoiled by a touching hand, uncovered by a body that might clothe it, one unsubjected to a trifler's whim, unsullied by defiling touch. A modest face has she, a bashful eye, a faltering tongue, and a heart that is pure indeed. Moreover, she's a playful doll, a coquettish plaything, a frolicsome gazelle, a girl of perfect beauty. She's a bejewelled sash that is shining and pure, a bedfellow that will be ever young and age not.

On the other hand, Hariri takes another stand when he says: She's a filly who brooks not the reins, a mount that is slow to submit, a flint that is hard to strike, a fortress not easily reduced, a girl, to boot, who needs some keeping with little to give in return—one whose company is unfruitful, whose coquetry is painful, and whose hand is clumsy. Her mood is a snake that cannot be charmed, her nature is harsh and she makes nights

---

[27] In Arab lore a kind of Don Quixote so noted for his craziness that in some parts of the Arab world one says even to this day "Crazier than Habannaqa".

[28] A master of the Arabic language, Hariri (1054–1122) is renowned for perfecting a genre of classical literature known as the *maqāma* (loosely "assembly"). A kind of sketch in rhymed, assonantal prose, a *maqāma* is essentially a story told by a narrator who is supposed to have witnessed some scene in which a scholarly rascal of no fixed abode has, by his wit, erudition, and mastery of the Arabic language, literature, and lore, "conned" his audience into giving the supposed beggar the contents of their pockets. Hariri's *maqāmas* can most conveniently be read in English in *The Assemblies of Al Ḥariri* (2 vols. London, 1867, 1898; reprint Farnborough, 1969) translated and annotated by T. Chenery and F. Steingass.

The extract quoted here by Nafzawi is from the "Forty-Third Assembly" (II, 119 ff.). My translation does not wholly tally because, for one thing, I do not agree with certain readings or renderings acceptable to Steingass.

long and dark. To break her in is a burden, and to know her needs one must remove a screen. She will frequently bring sorrow to her adversary or wear a philanderer down or bring the most seasoned man to his knees. Moreover, she will say pretentiously "I shall dress and take my place (in the ranks of the great) and shall seek out the governor who has power to release or imprison."

This same author goes on to extol the woman who has been married before and ranks her above a virgin: A woman who has been married before is a tractable mount, a quickly-snatched morsel, a soon-gained desire, one who has gained knowledge by repeated practice, a loving companion, a truly close friend, an excellent keeper of households, a woman of discrimination and wit. Moreover she is the tasty snack of the rider, a slip-knot for the suitor, a litter for the enfeebled, a prize for the champion to snatch. Gentle by disposition, she is a shackle that is easily borne. Her intentions are open, and clear, and her service an adornment indeed.

Of the woman previously married he also writes: She is leftover food, the dregs of the watering-hole, a garment bedraggled and a vessel well-used, a creature that will taste every new morsel, an extravagant spendthrift, a brazen-faced shrew, an agitated malcontent. Moreover, all she can say is "I was this and was that and now I am such-and-such. Whenever in the past I was wronged, I was given help. What a difference between then and now—it's as great as the difference between the sun and the moon." If she is forever harking back to the past and doing as little as a kneeling camel and is withal an unsubmissive wanton, she is as painful as a burning thirst and a sore that never heals.

In describing a virgin as "a girl who needs some keeping with little to give in return" and the previously married woman as "the hasty snack of the rider, a slip-knot for the suitor" Hariri is alluding to the words of 'Umar ibn Khattab: "A virgin is like wheat that must first be milled, then made into dough and finally eaten (as bread), but a previously married woman is the hasty snack of the rider that consists of dates and barley paste." He refers, of course, to the ease with which a previously married woman can be handled, whereas the virgin has to be married off and the marriage consummated at great expense. As regards the hasty snack, the point is that Arabs, when being passed by a hurrying rider, would invite him to dismount for food, but he would refuse because of the urgency of his mission. So they would rush out to him something that could be easily prepared, and he would eat it without dismounting. As for the matron being a tractable mount, Abu Faraj says in his *Songs*: Fadl the Poetess who belonged to a slave-trader was bought by Muhammad ibn Faraj who gave her as a present to Mutawakkil.[29] She would sit unveiled in the company of men and converse with poets. One day Abu Dulaf Qasim ibn 'Isa[30] recited to her lines in which he alluded to the fact that she had only been bought as second-hand goods,

> "They said 'You've coupled with a girl that's but a child!'
> To which my answer was, 'One longs for a mount not
> ridden before.'
> What a difference there is between a pierced pearl once
> worn and one that is not yet pierced!"

To which she came back with the answer,

> "The mount that has not been bent to the bridle is
> certainly no pleasure to ride,
> And pearls are of no use to their owners until they're
> pierced and strung!"

On the same theme 'Abdullah ibn Qays has this to say:

> Well done for the Pilgrims and Pleiads and the folk here at
> Khayf and the meeting-place of men![31]

[29] Tenth Abbasid Caliph (reg. 847–61).

[30] Since Abu Dulaf—a general in the reigns of Ma'mun and Mu'tasim— died in 840 or 841, Mutawakkil cannot have been Caliph at the time of the incident about to be described.

[31] Out of context it is difficult to see the relevance of this verse to that which follows. It is, however, probable that the poet—obviously in Arabia at the time of the Pilgrimage—is saying how fortunate for everyone and everything that they should be blessed with the presence of some beautiful girl whom he admires. Khayf is on the slope of Mina near Mecca.

A pearl from the treasures of the sea is a virgin untouched
by the jeweller's drill.

An amusing story is recounted by Ibn Jawzi in his book *The
Sharp-Witted*: Once a slave-girl was offered for sale to the Caliph
Mutawakkil who asked her "Are you a virgin or what?" "I am
'what', Commander of the Faithful." she replied.

It is also recounted in the same book: Iyas ibn Mu'awiya,[32] who
was renowned for his acumen, once glanced at three slave-girls
and commented, "This one's a virgin; this one's pregnant, this
one's a nursing mother." The woman in charge examined them
and found this to be correct. "How did you know?" he was
asked. "When I looked at them," he said, "they were somewhat
taken aback, and each put her hand to the parts of her body
which were most significant. One put her hand between her legs,
and I knew her to be a virgin. The other put her hand on her
belly and I knew her to be pregnant, and the third put her hand
to her breasts and I knew that she was a nursing mother."

In the *Book of the Careless* another story is told: A man once
bought a girl for a virgin and took her home. But there his
womenfolk told him she was no such thing. He therefore took
legal action against the vendor. The judge directed that she be
examined by midwives, and put her in the care of the imam of the
mosque.[33] In the morning the imam went to the judge and said
with a deep sigh, "You can trust no-one nowadays." Whereupon
the judge asked for his report on the woman. "The purchaser of
that girl," he said "took the word of the vendor and bought her
as a virgin, but the vendor has done him down. I tried the girl
myself last night and found her already deflowered with a
passage as wide as they make them. My God, you can go in
without moistening your penis with spittle! Who can you trust
nowadays? Is there anyone you can rely on?"

In his *History* Abu Hasin writes: Qasim ibn 'Ubaydullah ibn
Sulayman ibn Wahb once saw a slave-girl and immediately fell

[32] 666–740. At one time this descendant of the Prophet was a judge at
Basra.

[33] The official in a mosque whose duty it is to lead the Faithful in prayer.

for her. He stopped at nothing to get hold of her and in the end bought her. When she had been groomed and prepared for the bridal chamber he was on the point of deflowering her when she started to menstruate. She told him what had happened and he left her alone. He told Abu Ishaq Zajjaj, the grammarian, of his plight and asked him to compose one or two lines on the theme, and the result was as follows:

> A lancer wielding javelin sharp and sure and accustomed
>   to thrust in the dark
> Aimed to draw blood with his lance point but she was
>   first to show blood.

A similar thing happened to the Caliph Ma'mun on his wedding night when he was about to deflower Buran[34] and she started to menstruate. She turned to him and said, "God's will is here—don't rush it." Whereupon he left her alone.

In his *Clear Exposition* Jahiz[35] relates that Mu'awiya ibn Marwan ibn Hakam married a girl of noble family. She was a virgin, and it was he who took her virginity. The following morning he was so indiscreet as to say to her father in front of the best people. "Your daughter showed us no blood last night." Her father, covered in embarrassment, said "She is the sort of woman who would conceal such a fact from her husband."

This Mu'awiya was the brother of 'Abd-ul-Malik, and this wife of his the daughter of Mu'awiya ibn Mughira. One of the most stupid things he ever did was this: he once saw a bell attached to the neck of a mill-beast and asked the miller what the bell was for. Said the miller "I sometimes doze, and if I don't hear the sound of the bell, I know she has stopped and I shout at her." "And what if she stands and shakes her head like this and this?" asked Mu'awiya as he began to waggle his head from side to side.

---

[34] On the wedding of these two persons see above, p. 110.

[35] The greatest essayist in Arabic literature, Jahiz (776?–869) became the finest scholar of his day, and he is recognized as a unique prose-writer. Though possessed of extraordinary intelligence and percipience, he was a man of repulsive appearance whose humble Arab ancestors had black African blood in their veins.

"But how, Commander of the Faithful, can my animal come by a brain like yours?"[36]

In his *Songs* Abu Faraj recounts the following story about Muhammad ibn Fadl[37] Sakuni: Hammad 'Ajrad once married a virgin. The morning after the consummation we went to inquire how things had gone and he replied with these lines,

> "After fierce resistance I conquered the stronghold
>   through a traitor who opens up forts.
> My arm gained its victory by scattering the foe, and that
>   scattering we gained by uniting in love.
> Our forces are only united when we shoot and so split."

This Hammad 'Ajrad was Hammad ibn 'Umar ibn Kulayb, a protégé of the tribe of 'Amir ibn Sa'sa'a, whose lifetime spanned the last days of the pre-Islamic period and the first of the Islamic.[38] He was a shameless profligate and reprobate, and the very word *'ajrad* means "stripped naked".

In his *Treasure* Ibn Bassam writes: The Vizier Abu Marwan 'Abd-ul-Malik ibn Shuhayd fell behind Mansur ibn Abi 'Amir on one of his incursions into Christian Spain.[39] Seeing that the general had gained a victory and seized a number of prisoners, Ibn Shuhayd wrote to him to ask him for a slave-girl from the booty. These were the lines he sent,

> "I am now old, and old men love young girls. With my
>   life I'd defend you against all mishaps!

---

[36] Our author's facts are somewhat confused: the fifth Umayyad Caliph Abd-ul-Malik had no brother Mu'awiya who became Caliph. It may well be that some copyist has inserted the caliphal style 'Comrade of the Faithful'.

[37] In the text we are given "Mufaddal", but reference to other sources suggests that "Fadl" is correct.

[38] The genealogy of this satirical poet of distinctly unsavoury character and reputation (d. c. 777) is uncertain, but almost certainly we should read Hammad ibn 'Umar *ibn Yunus* ibn Kulayb. As can be seen from the date of his death, his lifetime can hardly have spanned the period indicated in our text.

[39] Abu Marwan 'Abd-ul-Malik ibn Shuhayd (d. 1003) is not to be confused with his more famous son, Ibn Shuhayd, the well-known Spanish-Arab poet of Cordova (d. 1035). Mansur—best known to students of medieval Spanish history as "Almanzor" (Al-Mansūr)—was the *de facto* ruler of Muslim Spain during the period 981–1002 when the Umayyad house was in full decline.

God's Messenger delivered the booty to all who urged on
  mounts.''[40]

Mansur therefore sent him four virgin slave-girls and addressed him as follows:

"We send you these girls like the sun of the day; in these
    three gazelles you have three beauties lovely as the moon.
Now take your time, but do your best, for now you're old.
    Already has night ousted the brightness of day.
God preserve you from excess of zeal and weariness withal
    —for a nail that has a blunted point brings shame upon
    itself!"

Old as he was, however, Ibn Shuhayd deflowered the three in
the same night, and the morning after wrote to Mansur the
following lines:

"We have broken the seal of that heady wine and stained
    ourselves with dark red hues.
In life's young pleasures have we found supreme delight
    and freely played with pearls and radiant girls.
The old man has struck a decisive blow with a sharp-cutting
    keen-edged blade,
Which he used—God recompense you!—and chose as a
    stallion against the infidels!"

In his *Gems* Sâ'id quotes Abu Ziyad of Kilab as relating the
following story: We knew an old man by the name of Abu
Gharib, with whom we were on very friendly terms. Now this
man got married to a virgin without giving a wedding feast. So
we gathered together outside his door and shouted "For God's
sake give a wedding feast even if you only serve desert rat—we're
dying of hunger!" Whereupon he agreed to the proposal, and
we all went into his house. The morning after the wedding we
went round and called out—in verse,

---

[40] In other words, the Prophet allowed every participant in any of his battles,
no matter how insignificant his role, a share of the spoils—his example should
be followed in Mansur's campaigns against the Christian infidels of Spain.

"How we should love to know whether Abu Gharib, when
    he spent his night amid scent and fine clothes,
Embracing a girl as sweet as a doe, stuck the spade right
    into the well or whether the shaft hung limply!"

He then came out and said to us "By God, it hung limply—and
how!"

In his book *Light and Blossoms* Husri, touching on this theme,
quotes the following lines by Ibn Mu'tazz:[41]

The sun keeps glancing at us with a sidelong glance that,
    hiding, peeps behind a curtain,
Trying to break through the clouds as some impotent
    fellow might try to break through a hymen.

On the same subject Ibrahim ibn 'Ali ibn Hurrama gives us
the following lines:

"Abu Thabit's fond of praise, but hates the gift he ought
    to give to the man who's there to sing it!
He's like a virgin who loves sweet union but flees from the
    charge of him who'd gladly give it!"

[41] Celebrated neo-classical poet, son of the thirteenth Abbasid Caliph.
Although proclaimed Caliph himself, he was assassinated in December 908.

CHAPTER IX

On Women Fat and Thin

Mus'ab ibn Zubayr once said: "Women are like beds—the bulkiest are the softest." He also used to say "Make your beds as soft as you can."[1]

Ibn Shubruma once remarked "I have never seen any garment on a man more enhancing than eloquence and on a woman a garment more enhancing than fat."

According to Asma'i, Imrul Qays[2] was once asked "What is

[1] In Arab countries the concept of a beautiful woman was and, generally speaking, still is different from our own, notably with regard to build and figure. The old desert ideal is reflected in the comparison, frequently made by poets, of a beautiful girl to a slender tree (torso) on a sandhill (all that lies below the waist). General fleshiness, however, came to be much admired, and the beauties in the harems of the leisured urban classes could be expected to be nothing if not buxom (for a different view, however, see below p. 187). At the farthest limit the ultimate in obesity was aimed at. In North-West Africa, for instance, girls were often fattened up to enhance their matrimonial prospects. The situation is well described in the following account by a visitor to Algiers in the early nineteenth century:

"As to figure and person, the Moors do not regard it so much as we do, or more properly speaking, their ideas of beauty and ours are materially different. So far from bracing up ... to produce slenderness and grace, they are anxious to give full development both to the limbs and person ... So that among the Moors immensity of size and beauty are synonymous ... Women are, in fact, esteemed by their weight. It is on this account that infinite pains are taken to fatten up Moorish ladies: enclosed in a small room they are fed like pigeons and doves in Italy; one part of their diet consists of little paste balls, which are dipped in oil ... while the mother is constantly in attendance, to enforce their being devoured ... Thus a young woman who requires a camel to carry her, is considered as a superior beauty; while one who cannot walk without the assistance of a slave on each side, is considered to have only moderate pretensions to that title!"
(Pananti, *Narrative of a Residence in Algiers*, London, 1818, p. 233.)

[2] Or more properly, Imru'-ul-Qays—a transliteration which I avoid out of

the most delightful pleasure in the world?" "A fragile girl of fair
complexion draped in beauty, well-padded with fat, and drenched
in sweet-smelling scent." he replied.

In his book The Multitudes Abu Rayhan writes: 'Abda,
daughter of 'Abdullah ibn Ziyad ibn Mu'awiya who was married
to Hisham ibn 'Abd-ul-Malik[3] was a very heavy woman and, in
order to get up, needed the assistance of three or four slave-girls.
Now, one day the pairless pearl, an heirloom, was presented to
Hisham. Weighing three miskals,[4] it possessed all the qualities a
pearl should have such as purity, lustre and roundness. "If you
can get up on your own," he challenged 'Abda, "without any
assistance at all, it's yours." 'Abda laboured and struggled in a
great effort to rise, and hardly had she staggered to her feet than
she fell flat on her face, and blood streamed from her nose.
Hisham got up to wash the blood away and gave her the pearl,
which remained in her possession until after the fall of the Umayyad dynasty when 'Abdullah ibn 'Ali took it from her and then
put her to death lest she should tell the tale to the new Abbasid
Caliph, Abu 'Abbas Saffah.

In his work known as the Treatise on Perfume Abu Yasir gives
a different reason for her death. According to him, 'Abdullah ibn
'Ali[5] did not much care for women, but seeing 'Abda, he saw in
her astounding beauty and extraodinary prettiness and, so it is
said, made overtures which met with no success. When he asked
'Abda to marry him, she declined, and this, it would seem, was
the strongest motive for putting her to death. What he feared
was that she might tell the Caliph of what had gone on.

The poet 'Umar ibn Abi Rabi'a[6] said of 'Abda:

'Abda, my heart can never forget, and neither joy nor
   sorrow can take my mind off you.

consideration for readers unacquainted with Arabic. This man was one of the
greatest, if indeed not the greatest, of pre-Islamic poets (d. c. 540). There is a
study of him and his great ode in A. J. Arberry, The Seven Odes (London, 1957).

[3] The tenth Umayyad Caliph (reg. 724–43).

[4] On the miskal see above Ch. V, n. 35, p. 112.

[5] Uncle of the first two Abbasid Caliphs (d. 764).

[6] The archetypal Arab love-poet (644–712). A product of Mecca and Medina,
he is the sensual man-about-town and playboy. (It should be noted that in this
'Abda narrative the names and identities of women are confused.)

White-breasted 'Abda, so tender and soft, you rouse the
passions of cool-blooded men and never feel passion
yourself.

In his *Songs* Abu Faraj quotes Abu Burda as saying on the
authority of Abu Musa: I was sent by Hajjaj[7] to ask for him the
hand of Hind, daughter of Asma' ibn Kharija. When I put the
proposal to her father, he accepted in her presence. She was
wearing a black silk dress at the time, and when she got up somewhat hastily I noticed her dress got caught in the fold between
her buttocks and her back. She could hardly stand unaided without leaning so much to one side that she bent double. Upon my
return I told Hajjaj all that I had seen and done. He then sent
her thirty slaves, each with 10,000 dirhams and thirty slave-girls
each of whom took with her a chest of clothing. His message to
her was that he disliked spending the night alone when he had a
wife. Her message to him was that there was nothing to keep
a woman from joining her husband once he had taken possession
and had paid the dower and given her a wedding present. With
this she made herself presentable and joined him forthwith.

Mada'ini, quoting the woman who was in charge of the bridal
procession, writes as follows: We went round to the place where
Hajjaj lived and went in. He was in a vast room at the far end of
which was a curtain. It was there in front of the curtain that
Hajjaj was reclining on his couch. On entering the room I greeted
him, and he motioned to me with a stick that he had in his
hand, whereupon I sat down at his feet. For some time he uttered
not a single word. Meanwhile we waited, and then at last Hind
gave him a slap on the thigh. "This is no time for rudeness," she
exclaimed. At this he smiled and moved towards her. He then
took a seat and sat up straight. We then wished them both well,
let down the curtain and left.

Abu 'Ubayd recounts the following story: Malik Ashtar called
on the Caliph 'Ali the morning after the night of his marriage to
one of his wives. "And how did the Commander of the Faithful
find his wife?" he inquired. "Excellent," he replied. "The only

[7] See above Ch. V, n. 4.

thing is that her breasts are too small and her waist too slender."
"But what else could a man wish for?" asked Abu 'Ubayd. "It's
not that," replied 'Ali. "It's just that he needs the sort of woman
who will keep him warm in bed and feed his infant well."

This story demonstrates, first, that 'Ali was partial to big
buxom women, and secondly, that he liked an ample bosom.

In his *Songs* Abu Faraj writes: 'Iqal ibn Shabba once entered
the presence of the Caliph Mahdi, who put the following question
to him, "What kind of woman do you like best, Abu Shayzam?[8]
One as slender as a horse's reins who sways like a ben-tree in the
wind? Or one who is fleshy, plump and buxom?" "Commander
of the Faithful," he answered, "the type I like best is the sort
described by Abu Nukhayla.[9] He had a sweet young slave-girl
presented to him by your uncle Abu 'Abbas Saffah. So small was
she that when he laid her, she was too tiny for him and was
dwarfed beneath his body. His feelings he put in the following
lines:

> I've found this miserable mount an impossible ride!
> Bring me something that shakes when it's shaken."

So Mahdi then made him a present of a plump and buxom
wench, and the day after 'Iqal went to thank him for his gift.
As the Caliph went out to greet him, he had a grin on his face.
"What are you laughing at, Commander of the Faithful?" asked
'Iqal. "The fact that I've just had a bath," he replied, "for as I
washed myself I cleaned 'something that shakes when it's
shaken,' and I just couldn't help thinking of your line."

In his *Women* Abu Faraj writes: Those who have the sharpest
eye for ideal women and are the most perceptive judges in these
matters prefer slender women who are neither fat nor thin—they
must have flesh on their bones—and that is why men compare
the ideal woman to the branch of a ben-tree or a bamboo cane
or the slenderness of a horse's reins.

The same author says that the best part of a woman lies in

---

[8] Abu Shayzam is 'Iqal's additional name (*kunya*; see above Ch. V, n. 62, p. 121).

[9] An eighth-century poet.

the sway of her body as she walks. This feature is incompatible with obesity. Abu Nuwas put it brilliantly in the following verse:

> She's taller than short, but not so tall as the tall;
> She's not so plump as the plump, nor yet so lean as the
> lean.

Qays ibn Khatim[10] says:

> Different women are of different shapes, and she is short
> in build and neither thin nor fat.

Raqashi[11] tells us, "Obesity in women is a sign of sensuousness and in men a great misfortune." In this same connexion Hasan of Basra[12] is quoted as saying, "Don't fatten your womenfolk, but, if you must, then guard them closely. Jahiz writes: Abu Ma'shar used to say, "I can understand a man with a long penis desiring a fat woman, but I can't understand a man with a short one feeling quite the same way."

The poet Farazdaq[13] preferred his wife Hadra' daughter of Ziq ibn Bistam to his wife Nawar, for Hadra' was slender-waisted whereas Nawar was a barrel of a woman. He speaks of her in the following terms:

> A girl from the desert as lovely as a wild gazelle or a
> diver's pearl, who almost shines like the sun as the
> world revolves about her—
> A girl dearer to us than that beefy heap who sweats the
> very moment she puts aside her fan!

[10] A pre-Islamic poet of Yathrib.

[11] Probably Abu 'Abbas Fadl ibn 'Abd-ul-Samad, a poet of Basra in the reign of Harun (reg. 786–809).

[12] A famous Umayyad preacher (642–728) of Basra. Few specimens of his work have survived, but what has come down to us shows him to have been an outstanding orator. He is often quoted as a model stylist.

[13] See above Ch. II, n. 34, p. 50.

CHAPTER X

On Colouring and Complexion in Women: The Question "Fair or Dark?"

Fair Complexions

'A'isha is on record as having said that a fair complexion is half way to beauty. Moreover she once remarked to some members of the tribe of Tamim "I understood you deal in slaves, and you never go wrong in your judgements. Well, you'll certainly never go wrong with the tall and fair since tallness and fairness are the ingredients of beauty."

Mu'ammal ibn Jamil gives us the verse:

> May Mu'ammal bear witness on the day he meets his Lord
> that a fair complexion is the ornament of beauty!

The Prophet is said to have had a fair complexion with tinges of red. Such is 'Ali's description.

In his *Women* Abu Faraj writes: A tinge of red or yellow will enhance the beauty of a fair complexion. A tinge of red brings out the delicacy of a fair complexion and shows that the blood is healthy. In *The Pearls* Bakri tells us that the Arabs apply the adjective "red" to beautiful women. For instance, Jarir was once asked his opinion of Akhtal.[1] "He is the most descriptive of us all when it comes to wine and lovely women,"[2] he observed, using the term "red" to express the notion "lovely".

---

[1] Celebrated Christian Arab poet (c. 640–710) in the pre-Islamic tradition. He was much admired for the formal perfection of his odes. With Farazdaq he long fought a satirical war against Jarir (on whom see Ch. II, n. 35, p. 51).

[2] In the Arabic it actually says "red woman".

A Bedouin was once asked "What is your desire?" "A lovely languid noble girl," he replied using "red" to express the notion "lovely". The whole idea behind this use of the term stems from the colour that the blood imparts to the skin, thereby enhancing the fairness of the skin. Sibawayh[3] comments that the frequency with which the adjective was applied to women transformed it into a noun in its own right, as it were. Bakri writes: When a woman is compared to fire it is this notion of redness in the sense of loveliness that underlies the comparison. The saying "Beauty is red" is also connected with this concept. It derives from the poet's line:

> She has a tinge of redness in the fairness of her skin, a
>   tinge that makes her eyes shine clearly. Beauty
>   indeed is red.

Again:

> If ever you go out, my girl, put on a veil of red. Beauty
>   indeed is red.

Yellowish Complexions

As for the yellowish hue in skin, this occurs in women of fair complexion who keep themselves in seclusion and constantly drench themselves in scent. Through excessive contact with perfume they acquire a yellowish tinge just as milk-white pearls and ivory do. This is substantiated by the poet who says:

> I've never fallen for a woman with a faded fair complexion,
>   a woman who, like ivory, has been yellowed by purdah
>   and perfume.

Abu Faraj writes: It is said that a woman of mature loveliness and soft and tender body changes colour through the day: from dawn to dusk her complexion has a reddish tinge, but from

---

[3] Although a Persian, this man became the author of one of the most celebrated works on Arabic grammar (d. between 793 and 796).

dusk to the end of the day it inclines somewhat to yellow. Such a one is described by A'sha:[4]

> Fair in the forenoon is she, as yellow as an oxeye by dusk.

Another poet says:

> She is known to be fair and yellow—so I'll be
> as happy as any man alive.

Abu Faraj's idea is that a woman with a fine skin and clear complexion changes colour with the air around her, and that a child's complexion will turn to yellow in the yellow of the sun, reverting to it's whitish hue with dawn. All this, of course, is hyperbole and it is merely a question of a literary device to emphasize the comfortable and untroubled life a woman leads. In reality, there is no such condition as that described, despite what is said in the verse of A'sha and in the subsequent line in which the lady is said to be dark at night and then to wash in the morning and to be white in the forenoon.

Abu Faraj quotes Dhu Rumma in praise of the yellow complexion:

> White is her skin and wide her black eyes, of yellowish hue
> her musk-scented skin.
> Indeed she is silver rubbed up against gold.

In the same vein another poet recites:

> White and yellow—silver and gold—strive for mastery in
> her skin.

Qays ibn Khatim speaks of "a slender girl as beauteous as the sun when it rises and sets".

---

[4] The name of several early Arab poets of whom the most renowned was A'sha of the Arabian tribe of Bakr (*c.* 570–625). Among others so named were A'sha of Hamdan (d. 702), A'sha of Sulaym (eighth century) and A'sha of Taghlib (d. 710).

And yet another poet says:

> The whiteness of her skin is suffused with yellow, and she
> is soft and slender, to boot.

Bashshar offers the following two verses:

> Yellowish and meek and well endowed with charms from
> nature's store of beauty she left, and with her took
> my heart.
> Like a garden bright with blossom she fills the air with
> fragrance and is lovely to behold.

Here, it will be noted, the poet associates yellowness with fragrance.

Brown Complexions

On women with brown skins there are as many opinions as there are on those with fair. In his *Dictations* Abu 'Ali writes: A man once went to Hasan's daughter to ask her advice about the type of women he should marry. She told him to go for a well-built woman with ash-brown complexion or a comely girl with fair skin, and, in either case to see that she came of a house famed either for its wealth or its courage.

Abu Faraj, in his *Songs*, tells a different story. He writes: Ghaylan ibn Maslama said on his death-bed to his sons, "My sons, marry into great Arab families, for they are the stairs to noble character. Marry a girl of ash-brown complexion and quiet manners or a girl with fair skin who has poise, and in either case see that she comes of a family famed either for its wealth or its courage, meaning by this a family that either has wealth as well as breeding or is content with little and satisfied with the bare necessities of life and fellowship and companionship.

A post-classical poet has said:

> Many a brown-skinned girl there's been whose face, when
> shining through a night of curling locks, has rivalled
> dark patches on the moon—

A girl beloved of men with skin as dark as the black spot
that lies within the heart, a girl fashioned from musk
and amber and roses.

In his *Treasure* Ibn Bassam gives us the following lines:

A body, slim and straight as a stave, a face as comely as the
moon at full, yet dark, a mouth of pearls and eyes as
lustrous as an antelope's
—My heart is smitten with a girl with all such qualities.
What man, be he ever so patient, can long resist
such gorgeous glances?
Her radiance and dark brown skin I see as musk soaked
deep in liquid camphor.

Black Complexion

Black women are distinguished by no appealing qualities
apart from the cleanness of their teeth and the heat of their
vaginas. The bad qualities far outweigh the good—their lips and
extremities are marred by cracks, and they have hard-skinned
bodies, small vaginas, fetid sweat and ill temper. It is said, however, that the women of Ghana are free from all such defects,
whether of body or of character.

In praise of black women the poet 'Abbas ibn Ahnaf says:[5]

Because of Buktum black women are my love, and all
things black I've come to love—and that because of her.
Show me, pray, a scent as sweet as musk; show me, pray,
repose more calm than night.

'Abbas borrowed the first verse from a Bedouin poet, who also
gives us the line:

How can my heart and eyes miss one who is as the eye's
black centre and the heart's black spot?

[5] Arab love-poet of Persian background and connections (d. after 808). A
great favourite at Harun's court in Baghdad.

Muhammad ibn Yunus gives us some fine verses on a black woman whose name was Durra, that is to say "Pearl":

> How many a black girl there is called Pearl![6] But what a
>   rarity it is to find a pearl that's black!
> To be with her is to turn the blackness of dark night to
>   white, and what a rarity it is to find a night that's white!

On the subject of the excessive heat and tightness said to characterize the vaginas of black women Ibn Sukkara offers us the following lines:

> Black she was—good luck to her cleft, may it come to no
>   harm— for how tight a fit it was!
> I threw myself upon her, not knowing what a burning lay
>   within that part of hers.
> I nearly roasted from the heat, and the tightness
>   almost choked me!

'Abd-ul-Malik ibn Habib in his *Discourse on Women* quotes the Prophet as saying, "A women who is black and fertile is better than one who is beautiful and barren."

On Height: Should Women be Tall or Short?

The height a women ought to be is a subject on which there are different opinions. Khalid ibn Safwan says, "Height is the pillar of beauty," and Ibn Zubayr advises, "Marry tall women, for it is they who bear sons." 'Urwa ibn Zubayr also says, "I never loved anything in a woman but her *sharaf*," and, according to Qasim ibn Thabit, Asma'i said that what 'Urwa meant by *sharaf* here was height, and not nobility. Moreover, in his book *The Perfect* Mubarrad observes, "Height is much praised by the Arabs, whereas shortness is despised and never mentioned except by those who defend this defect in themselves. Certainly nobody praises it."

---

[6] By antiphrasis (use of words in the sense opposite to their true meaning). Cf. English "Tiny" as a common nickname for very tall men.

Some people prefer a girl of medium height. Ibn Rumi[7] gives us the lines:

> It is as if she were moulded from a molten pearl—her face
>   on every side as lovely as a moon.
> Created to her heart's desire she was, and when the
>   work was done,
> She was perfect in stature and neither too short nor too tall.

Likewise Baha'-ul-Din Zuhayr[8] says:

> I fell in love with her—by then, a girl whose charm was
>   absolute, a girl whom none could take to task for
>   being tall or short,
> With hair reaching down to her anklets and her ear-ring
>   now perturbed at the length of the drop if it fell.
> She resembled the season of spring in a shapeliness
>   so lovely that night and day were truly matched.

In *The Perfect* Mubarrad writes: Men of perception and vision, whether Arab or non-Arab, are in complete agreement that perfection lies in moderation, and no sage has ever been reported as expressing any other view.

Qasim ibn Thabit relates that a tall and ugly Bedouin was once looking for a wife. "I'm looking," he said, "for a woman who is short of stature but yet beautiful, so that any son she bears me will have my height and her beauty." He did in fact marry just such a woman, but his son turned out to be as ugly as he was and as short as his mother.[9]

[7] A popular and highly individual classical poet of Byzantine extraction, Ibn Rumi (836–96) whose talent as a lampoonist led to his murder by a vizier.

[8] Celebrated Arab poet (1186–1258) of the Ayyubid period. His poetry is available in English translation: E. H. Palmer, *The Dīwān of Bahā' al-Dīn Zuhayr* (Cambridge, 1876).

[9] This story puts one in mind of an incident in the life of George Bernard Shaw. When invited by a certain lady to contemplate the possible combination of her beauty and his brains in any offspring born of their union, he suggested that she might consider the catastrophe of a child born with his looks and her brains!

On this very theme Kuthayyir[10] has this to say:

> You are the one, my girl, who made short women dear to
> my heart without their knowing it.
> I wanted brides of stature short, though never ones whose
> steps were short, for dwarfs are the very worst sort.

In his *Women* Abu Faraj writes: On seeing a very small man the Prophet once remarked, "If any of you should see a man with some affliction and remark, 'Praise be to God who has spared me such a fate and thus set me over many another creature of His!', he will be preserved by God from a like affliction, be it what it may." From this it is clear that the Prophet accounted shortness of stature an affliction from which one should beg God to deliver him.

[10] Medinese poet (d. 723) living in Egypt and celebrated in Arabic literature for his love of 'Azza (see above p. 67).

CHAPTER XI

On Beauty and Attractiveness and the Natural Liking that all Mankind have for these Two Qualities

It is reported on the authority of 'A'isha that the Prophet said, "God is a beautiful Being who loves beauty." And on this theme we have the lines:

> Thou didst create loveliness, O God, to try us, and hast
>   told us in the Book, "Beware and fear Me."
> Thou art a Being beautiful who lovest beauty. So how can
>   Thy servants help but fall in love?

Ibn Mas'ud[1] gives us the following Tradition: A man once went to the Prophet and said, "I really love to have my clothes well washed and the straps of my sandals looking nice." He went on in this vein, touching on one thing after another until he finally came to the thong of his whip-handle.[2] "Now would you call this pride?" he asked. "No," replied the Prophet. "This is beauty—pride is the insolent violation of what is reasonable and fair; it is the unjust treatment of one's fellow men."

The Prophet also said, "Three things delight the eye: greenery,

[1] A Bedouin of humble origin who became one of the best known Companions of the Prophet, Ibn Mas'ud (d. c. 653) heard the Koran directly from the Prophet himself and knew it by heart.

[2] i.e. until he came to the heart of the matter. Cf. Our "getting down to brass tacks".

water and features that are comely." The poet echoes his words
when he says:

> Three things will drive away grief from the heart:
> they are water and greenery and a beautiful face.

The Prophet also said: "To look on a lovely face will bequeath
a legacy of joy; gloom is the legacy one inherits from beholding
a face that is ugly." In the *Shooting Star* the Prophet is reported
as having said: "To look upon a beautiful girl will strengthen
the vision." To this comment a certain scholar adds the observation that, if this is so, it necessarily follows that to look upon
an ugly countenance will weaken one's sight.

In his *Revivification* Ghazali writes: A woman of comely attributes and character endowed with large eyes and jet-black pupils
—a woman who is loving and tender to her husband and keeps
her eyes only on him, such a one has the qualities of a houri.
God says in the Koran at the point where he describes these
maidens of Paradise: "In them are damsels good and comely,"[3]
by which He means damsels of good character and comely attributes. God also speaks of them as being "loving and of like
age",[4] by which he means that they will love their spouses and
desire sexual union. Herein lies the consummation of delight.
He also says: "In them are damsels with glance restrained."[5]
The commentators say this means that the houris will look only
upon their spouses and see no other men but them.

The Prophet once said, "If ever you send me a messenger, see
to it that he is good-looking and well spoken." There is also a
Tradition in which he is quoted as saying, "Seek goodness from
the good-looking." In allusion to this the poet says:

> You are just as the Prophet commanded when one day he
> said, "Seek goodness from those whose looks are good."

Ja'far ibn Muhammad used to say, "God will have mercy on

[3] lv, 70.
[4] lvi, 36.
[5] lv, 56.

beauty" and "Comeliness is an acceptable intercessor." We also have the verses of Ibn Qanbar Mazini:[6]

> How I sadden after him who slept too long and so could
>   not be reached! My heart had one more pain to add to
>   those it bore already.
> It was as if the sun shone splendidly within his garments
>   and the moon rose full from out his button-holes[7]
> To welcome those who loved him. And even if his sins
>   are legion, he's forgiven all he's done.
> For in his face he has an intercessor which, everywhere
>   it intercedes, obliterates from all men's heads the
>   thought of the wrongs he's done them.

Yahya ibn 'Ali Munajjim[8] recounts the following tale: One day I was in the company of Mu'tadid[9] when he was in a foul temper. All of a sudden his client Badr, who was extremely handsome, appeared in the distance. As soon as Mu'tadid spotted him he smiled and, turning to me, asked, "Who was it, Yahya, who said 'in his face he has an intercessor'?" "Ibn Qanbar," I replied. "Excellent," he exclaimed, and then he asked me to recite the verses in which the phrase occurred. By the time I had finished his wrath had turned to smiles and joyfulness. On this sort of situation Mutarriz[10] has this to say:

> If she speaks and his beauty meets my eye, I surrender
>   eyes and ears to him.
> If he gazes with delight at me, I say his gaze is that
>   of some gazelle.
> And if he walks, my comment is "Just like a beautiful
>   ben-tree that would put the moon to shame."
> When his face shines in its morning glory, his locks
>   bring down dark night in envy.

[6] Minor poet of Basra (fl. eighth century). Sometimes the spelling Qunbur is met with.

[7] i.e. he is radiantly handsome. Once again the full moon is the symbol of beauty.

[8] Theologian and court poet of several Abbasid Caliphs.

[9] Sixteenth Abbasid Caliph (reg. 892–902).

[10] Probably a singer *c*. late seventh/early eighth century.

> Never does he do some unintentional wrong but his
> handsome features plead his case and win.

In his *Primary Feather of the Wing* Tifashi recounts the following anecdote: When the 'Alid[11] laid siege to Damascus, he came to within a hair's breadth of taking it. Among the besieged was a woman noted for her beauty, who said to her fellow citizens, "Just leave him to me, and I'll deliver you." She then asked to be taken to him. When ushered into his presence, she asked him, "Aren't you the man who spoke these verses,

> 'We are a people so strong that we can bend steel, but
> yet succumb to wide, black eyes.
> You'll find us freeborn heroes in the face of cutting swords
> and yet, in secret, slaves to loveliness.'?"

"Yes, I am," he replied. Whereupon she snatched the veil from her face and said, "Now, tell me what you see—beauty or ugliness?" "Beauty," came the answer. "Then," said she, "if you are slaves to beauty, hear and obey and take your laws forthwith." Immediately he gave orders to his men to strike camp and depart. "But," objected his generals, "we're in sight of victory—the town's in our hands!" "I've no alternative," he answered—and he proposed to the woman and married her.

Hakam ibn 'Abdullah relates that he once saw Shurayh standing at the gates of the Great Mosque of Mecca and asked him what he was doing there. "I'm just hoping," he said "to catch sight of a good-looking face."

The author of *The Calices*[12] writes: Muhammad ibn 'Abd-ul-Rahman ibn 'Amr, who was nicknamed "Brocade" because of his good looks, was once asked by a woman, "And do you take pride in your good looks when only women have that right? Men should only take pride in good deeds." "Yes, I do," he countered. "For if handsome is as handsome does, a man pos-

---

[11] Since the Fatimid rulers of Egypt were 'Alids (descendants of 'Ali), the reference is probably to some Fatimid operation against Damascus, which was in and out of their hands in the tenth an eleventh centuries.
[12] See below Ch. XV, n. 37, p. 278.

sessed of good deeds and good looks will have reached the acme
of perfection."

Hammad ibn Ishaq quotes his father as saying that 'A'isha
daughter of Talha[13] was the most gorgeous creature God ever
made, but she would never veil her face. Once when she was
reproached for this practice by her husband Mus'ab ibn Zubayr,
her defence was, "God most High has marked me with the
stamp of beauty, and so I want people to look at me and recognize how superior I am to them. That's why I'm not one to veil
my face. Had I been aware of any blemish in me that required
covering up, I would certainly have hidden it from view." If,
however, Mus'ab ever insisted on her veiling herself, she would
obey; but, if he said nothing, she went unveiled and mixed with
everbody.

According to Ibn Hazm,[14] whenever 'Umar ibn Khattab saw
a veiled woman, he would order her to take off her veil. If he
found her good-looking, he would tell her to replace it. If, on the
other hand, he found her hideous, he would not allow her to
wear a veil. Apropos of the idea behind this, Zubayr ibn Bakkar[15]
gives us the following verses:

> Would that women were forbidden the veil that the ugly
>   might never deceive!

In his *Songs* Abu Faraj writes: 'A'isha daughter of Talha once
had a dispute with her husband in front of Abu Hurayra. Off
came her veil, and, as soon as Abu Hurayra saw her face, he
exclaimed, "My God, how exquisitely beautiful you are! By God,
one would think you'd just come from Paradise!" When her
husband heard these words, a wave of jealousy swept over him.
So he got up, tried to calm her down by placating her and took
her by the hand. He then did as she had requested before the
argument began.

In his *Flowers* Husri writes: Abu Hazim[16] once set out in the

13 See above p. 105.
14 Outstanding Spanish Arab author, scholar, and thinker (994–1064).
15 Medinese religious scholar and sometime judge of Mecca (d. 870).
16 On whom see what our author has to say later.

company of a group of ascetics with the intention of throwing
stones at the Devil.[17] As he was chatting with them, they suddenly came upon a most beautiful woman who was looking first
left, then right as she walked along. Their attention distracted,
the men walked into one another as they gaped at her in utter
stupefaction. "You there," called out Abu Hazim to her, "fear
God, for you've roused my appetite and bewitched us all! Throw
your scarf over your bosom, for God says, 'Let them throw
their scarves over their bosoms.'"[18] At this she went over to
him, laughing at what he had had to say. "Look," said she,
"I am one of those women of whom Harith ibn Khalid has
said:

> "She removed a silken cover from her cheek and slipped
> 　　a finely woven garment from her loins.
> From those who have not veiled themselves such women
> 　　desire account, but they catch an honest man off guard and
> 　　when they do they slay him."

Rejoining his companions, Abu Hazim said, "Let us pray to
God that such a beautiful face may never be punished with the
fire of Hell." Whereupon he began to pray with the assent of his
companions, who added their amens. Sa'id ibn Musayyib's
comment on the episode was: "Had Abu Hazim been one of
those beastly Iraqis he would have told the woman to get lost
and have cursed her. But he was a polite and God-fearing man
from the Hejaz."

The Abu Hazim in question is Abu Hazim Salama ibn Dinar,
one of the most important of the Successors, whose authority
was accepted by Malik and Ibn Abi Dhi'b and men of their
calibre.

Asma'i relates: Once during the circumambulation of the

[17] At a place called Mina between Mecca and Mount 'Arafat in Saudi
Arabia there are three stone pillars representing three positions where, in
Islamic belief, Satan tried to prevent Abraham's sacrifice of Ishmael in obedience to God's bidding. Temptation was resisted and the Devil was driven off
with stones. To this day Pilgrims throw stones at these pillars to symbolize
the rejection of Satan's promptings.

[18] Koran, xxiv, 31.

Kaaba at Mecca[19] I caught sight of a slave-girl as lovely as any gazelle. Everyone was entranced by her beauty, and I myself even stopped and stared at her to fill my eyes with visions of beauty. "And what's the matter with you?" she called out to me. "Is there anything wrong in looking?" I countered. To this she replied in verse,

> "If you send your eyes as a scout for your heart, then
>   what they see will wear you out.
> You have looked on one whose heart you cannot
>   conquer and whose dislike you can't renounce."

There is another version of this incident; it runs as follows: I—Asma'i—was once in a Bedouin watering-place when I heard people say, "Here comes Saqil ('Burnished')[20]". Everyone got up to look, and so did I. To my amazement the most beautiful slave-girl I had ever seen, incomparable in features and figure, had come to draw water. When she noticed everyone staring at her intently, she pulled her veil across her face, and it was then as if a cloud had crossed the sun. "Handmaid of God," I cried, "how I wish you'd let us continue enjoying your lovely face!" It was at this point, according to this version, that Asma'i tells of the girl reciting the two verses quoted above.

Sukayna daughter of Husayn once literally clothed one of her daughters with pearls.[21] "I have only done this," she explained, "that her beauty may heighten that of her pearls."

Ghaylan, the singer, relates, "I once went into the palace of Harun and saw there a most beautiful slave-girl on whose cheek was inscribed in a special ink two rhyming lines presenting a temptation to the servants of God as woven into His pattern. They read as follows:

[19] Pilgrims to Mecca make seven circuits of the Kaaba (see above Ch. III, n. 23, pp. 70 f), starting from the corner of the Black Stone, which they kiss, touch, or venerate by raising their hands towards it. During each circuit each Pilgrim recites prayers in praise of God. The rite is called *ṭawāf* in Arabic.

[20] i.e. bright and beautiful.

[21] Cf. p. 139.

> They say that a lovely woman is one who catches the
>   eye from afar,
> While a woman of charm and attraction is one who
>   catches the heart at close quarters.

In his *Songs* Abu Faraj relates: Sukayna daughter of Husayn once challenged 'A'isha daughter of Talha with the words, "I'm more beautiful than you." To this 'A'isha replied, "Oh no you're not!" So in the end they went and argued their case before 'Umar ibn Abi Rabi'a.[22] Passing judgement, he said to Sukayna, "You're the more attractive." To 'A'isha he said, "But you're the more beautiful." Sukayna then commented, "Your judgement's in my favour then."

A woman once said to Khalid ibn Safwan,[23] "How handsome you are!" "How so?" he asked. "I've none of the attributes of beauty, for I have neither its mainstay nor its garment nor its hood. Its mainstay is build and proportion, and I am short of stature; its garment is a fair complexion, which I do not possess; its hood is black curly hair covering the head, and I am bald. Had you said 'How charming you are!' you would have been nearer the mark."

In his *Women* Abu Faraj writes: Both Muhammad ibn Mundhir ibn Zubayr and Muhammad ibn 'Abdullah ibn 'Umar ibn 'Uthman ibn 'Affan[24] were nicknamed "Brocade" because of their splendid looks. The latter asked for the hand of the same woman as 'Abd-ul-'Aziz ibn 'Abdullah ibn 'Umar ibn Khattab.[25] The lady therefore began to make inquiries about them both, and then one night while on her way to perform the prayer in the Prophet's mosque, she saw them standing in the moonlight wrangling over her. She could see only the face of 'Abd-ul-'Aziz. Struck by his fair complexion and height, she said to herself, "I doubt if I'll find anyone more handsome than you." And so she decided to accept him. Among those invited to the wedding was Muhammad ibn Mundhir, who was accorded

---

[22] See above Ch. IX, n. 6, p. 185.

[23] Flourished late seventh century and was at the court of the first Abbasid Caliph.

[24] The great grandson of the Caliph Uthman.

[25] The grandson of Caliph 'Umar I.

special treatment and given the seat of honour by 'Abd-ul-'Aziz. After the meal Muhammad thanked his host and took his leave. The bride saw him depart and bitterly regretted the handsome face she had missed. It is said that she died broken-hearted from the loss.

A Bedouin once said of a handsome man, "By God, if only the lutes had seen him, their strings would have played for him, and had a woman of piety seen him, she would have slipped off the cloth from around her waist."

A Bedouin is the author of the following lines:

> What do you think will come of Salma if her path is
>   crossed by a man with flowing locks, urbanity, and
>   complexion fair and clear,
> A man with a turban made of silk, endowed with
>   humour sweet and carrying a key that's a spell from
>   the Devil himself?

The Arabs have a proverb that runs "How many a brother you must have that is not your mother's son!" The story behind it is as follows; Luqman ibn 'Ad[26] once saw a man and a woman making love. The woman had with her a small boy who started crying when no attention was paid to him as the two were copulating. Later, Luqman asked the woman who it was that he had seen her with. "Oh, that was my brother," came her answer. Whereupon he commented, "How many a brother you must have who is not your mother's son! He may be your brother in the sense of friend or lover, but certainly not by birth."[27]

It is said that the Persians used to take a good-looking person as a good omen and say that good looks are a man's main blessing. For God Most High, in the subtlety of His wisdom, the nobility of His inventiveness and artistry, created nothing in vain. Nor did he ever fashion a countenance endowed with all

[26] Legendary king of the "second 'Ad", a South Arabian people said by Muslim chroniclers to have had settlements in the Yemen in the region of Saba. To them is attributed the construction of the well-known Ma'rib Dam.

[27] The word *akh* in Arabic may mean either "brother" in the biological sense or "dear friend" or "fellow man".

the marks of loveliness and free from blemishes that did not receive the favour as a special mark of divine honour.

It is also said that one rarely encounters character not matched by comeliness. In his book *The Multitudes* Abu Rayhan Biruni writes: Good looks are in the countenance and beauty in the form, and all members of the human race love and yearn for both. Even the Prophet would seek to derive strength from lovely names and faces and would change ugly names of places and people to ones that were agreeable. We have already seen that he said "If ever you send me a messenger, see to it that he is good-looking and well-spoken." Anas is quoted as saying, "God never sent a prophet who was not endowed with good looks and a pleasant voice—and your Prophet was the best-looking of all and had the pleasantest voice."

In the *Science of Language* [by Tha'alibi][28] the author says that grace pertains to the face, clarity to the complexion, sweetness to the eyes, charm to the mouth, wit to the tongue, grace to stature, decorum to behaviour and perfection to the hair. Another author adds: "distinction to the neck and slenderness to the extremities".

The author of *The Bride's Gift*[29] goes into the attributes of women in general, and indeed he is worth quoting here. In the time of the Prophet, he tells us, there were three effeminates, who were allowed access to unveiled women. These men were called Hit, Haram, and Mati'. Now Hit was in the habit of calling on the wives of the Prophet, and one day he happened to call on Umm Salama[30] while the Prophet was there. On this occasion, then, he took up with Umm Salama's brother, 'Abdullah ibn Abi Umayya ibn Mughira, and in conversation remarked, "If, with God's help, you conquer the town of Ta'if[31]

[28] A well-known scholar and teacher from eastern Iran (c. 961–1038).
[29] Probably the work of Muhammad ibn Ahmad Tijani (d. after 1309) dealing with feminine attributes.
[30] One of Muhammad's wives.
[31] A place near Mecca.

tomorrow, you would do well to seek the hand of Badiya daughter of Ghaylan ibn Mughith[32]—she's supple, slender and full of fun, and she has lovely eyes as well. When she stands she sways curvaceously, and when she sits, she holds herself as erect as a building. When she speaks, she sings, and though she comes with four, she will go away with eight. Her teeth are as white as daisies and her breasts as round and full as pomegranates. Above she is as slender as a reed and below she spreads as a sand-dune. Between her legs nestles a pubic prominence as striking as an upturned cup."[33]

When the Prophet heard all this, he remarked, "You show great perception. I didn't think you were so artful." Prior to that the Prophet would laugh at what Hit said, thinking it stemmed from want of wit. But when he heard what he did on this occasion, he forbade his wives to let him visit them and gave orders for him to be banished to a place called Khakh. There he remained until the death of the Prophet when someone pleaded with the new ruler, Abu Bakr, to let him return. The request was turned down, but subsequently put to 'Umar when he succeeded to the Caliphate. 'Umar also refused to have him back. "And what is more," he added, "if I ever see him in Medina, I'll have his head struck off." When 'Uthman in due course succeeded 'Umar, he was likewise approached, and once more the petition was rejected. Upon being told, however, that Hit had grown old and feeble and was in great need, 'Uthman allowed him to come into town on Fridays to beg and then return home the same day.

Such is the story as related by the chroniclers, but there is another version which is shorter and transmitted by Muslim on the authority of 'A'isha. It runs as follows: There was once an effeminate fellow who used to call on the Prophet's wives, and this was permitted because they thought him ingenuous. But

[32] The evidence of other sources suggests that we should read Ghaylan ibn Salama ibn Mu'attib, this last name having been misread through lack of diacritics.

[33] Cf. *Perfumed Garden*, p. 196: "As to the vulva, it was white, prominent, round as an arch; the centre of it was red ... When she walked it showed in relief like a dome or an inverted cup."

one day the Prophet got home to find this effeminate there describing a woman in the following terms; "When she comes, she comes with four, and when she goes, she goes with eight." On hearing this the Prophet remarked, "This man's got all his wits about him. He mustn't be allowed in here again." And so thereafter they kept him out. The expression "to come with four and leave with eight" is said by Mazari on the authority of Abu 'Ubayd to mean that when a woman approaches she is seen to have four folds in her belly and, since each one has two edges she will be seen to have eight as she turns around and goes away. But such an interpretation is unintelligible, and the commentators ignore it.[34]

In his *For Muwaffaq* Zubayr writes: Harith ibn 'Amr ibn Hujr of Kinda[35] came to hear of the perfection and beauty of Khansa' daughter of 'Awf ibn Muhallim of Shayban. He therefore dispatched a woman called 'Isam from the tribe of Kinda to make inquiries about her. "Go," he said to her, "and find out all you can about this girl." Her account of this mission runs as follows: I went as I was bidden, and there, to my surprise, I found a woman as lovely as a gazelle of the wild surrounded by girls as sweet as antelopes. I told her what I'd come for, whereupon she sent for her daughter and said to her, "This lady, my child, has come to see you and find out about you. So don't conceal anything from her. Just talk to her when she talks to you." The girl agreed, and I went in. When I scrutinized her, I could see she had the most beautiful face and body. As I left she commented, "To put off one's veil leaves no room for deception."

Upon my return I called on Harith, whose first question was, "Well, what news, 'Isam?" "God prosper you, Prince," I started. "I'll tell you the plain and simple truth. The face I saw was as bright and as smooth as a mirror and crowned with locks of dark hair as sinuous as lizards' tails. Her eyebrows are as perfect as if they had been traced with a pen or blackened with charcoal

[34] The author offers no explanation, however. (At this point there also seems to be a lacuna in the text.)

[35] Harith (d. 528) was king of the powerful Kindite tribal group which constituted one of the three major Arab client-kingdoms of pre-Islamic times. It flourished in north Arabia in the late fifth and sixth centuries.

and they arch over eyes like those of a graceful fawn. They dazzle the onlooker and defy his powers of description, enhancing with their curves all that lies below them. Between her eyes is a nose as fine as the edge of a burnished sword—a nose that is neither too short nor too long, and hence unmarred and unblemished. On either side are cheeks like crimson set in white as pure as that of silver beads. Her face is adorned by a sweet-smiling mouth with teeth that are sharply cut and as white as pearls and a tongue that speaks with clarity and eloquence. This face crowns a slender neck and a soft bosom from which there spring two breasts as full and as round as any pomegranate as they thrust forward through a dress that barely hold them back. Beneath, there lies a belly as beauteous as embroidered linen with folds like scrolls encompassing a navel like an ivory unguent phial. All this leads down beyond a slender waist beneath which lies a bottom like a rounded sandy hillock,[36] which lifts her when she rises and seats her when she settles. Next come shapely thighs above fair-skinned legs. The whole is carried on two tiny feet that are so small that only by God's grace do they serve their purpose. And with that, my Prince, I take my leave. The rest you must see for yourself." Harith did in fact send for the girl and marry her. In due course she became the mother of his princely sons.

In his *Songs* Abu Faraj writes: Mus'ab ibn Zubayr, 'Abdullah ibn 'Abd-ul-Rahman ibn Abi Bakr and 'Amr ibn Sa'id ibn 'As held a meeting to ask 'Azzat-al-Mayla' to look for a bride for each of them.[37] She asked Mus'ab whose hand he sought in particular, to which he replied, "That of 'A'isha daughter of Talha." She put the same question to 'Abdullah and he replied, "Umm Qasim daughter of Zakariyya' ibn Talha. Finally, she asked 'Amr ibn Sa'id, and the name he gave was that of 'A'isha daughter of 'Uthman. Armed with this information, she went off to have a look at each of the women named, beginning with

---

[36] See above Ch. II, n. 31, p. 43.

[37] On Mus'ab and 'A'isha see above, p. 105; 'Abdullah was the grandson of the Caliph Abu Bakr; 'Amr rebelled against the Umayyad Caliph 'Abd-ul-Malik and perished *c.* 689; 'Azzat was a singer of some reputation in the Hejaz.

'A'isha daughter of Talha. The latter welcomed her and took to her. She then came round to asking her what she wanted. "I've been with a party of ladies from the tribe of Quraysh," she said, "and they were talking about beautiful women and their charms. I thought of you, but I didn't know how to describe you." "Well now," asked the other, "what exactly do you want me to do about it?" "Oh, just let me see you from the front and the back." So 'A'isha did as she was asked, and every portion of her body quivered as she did so. 'Azzat then asked her to remove her gown. This she did, and 'Azzat saw one of the most gorgeous and best-looking creatures she had ever set eyes on. She said a prayer to protect her from the Evil Eye[38] and exclaimed. "I just don't believe God ever created anyone on this earth more gorgeous than you!" She then said goodbye and went off to Umm Qasim.

At Umm Qasim's, 'Azzat repeated the performance, and her comment was, "I never saw anyone more lovely than you. With that she took her leave and went off. Calling on 'A'isha daughter of 'Uthman, she went through the same procedure. She then went back to the men to deliver her report. Looking expectantly at her, they asked. "Well, how did you go on?" "Mus'ab," she began, "I've never seen anyone like your 'A'isha, whether she be viewed from the front or from behind. She has a plump bottom, a full and ample bosom, shining teeth and a clear complexion, a thick head of hair, well-padded thighs, trim waist, flat belly with neat folds and a largish navel. Moreover, her entire body from top to bottom quivers as it should. She only has two faults:

---

[38] It has long been a superstition in Islamic countries that the action of a jealous eye can bring evil upon all that is exposed to the assaults of envy (e.g. beauty, happiness, riches, fine children). The eye is motivated by a desire to do injury, and its action operates through a hateful or envious look. Moreover, its power can be reinforced or replaced by a word of praise. Hence parents of a child do not always welcome complimentary remarks about its looks or its intelligence lest misfortune follow. To ward off the evil eye various charms are used, especially the stylized hand with its five fingers. Many visitors to North-West Africa and other Arab countries will have bought jewellery of this kind without realizing its prophylactic significance. It is thought by some that the veil worn by women had its origins in a covering to ward off the maleficent looks of other women, etc.

her ears and feet are far too large. However, the first are hidden by her head-scarf and the second by her footwear."

She made her next report to 'Abdullah. "Umm Qasim is as slender as the bough of a ben-tree or the rider's end of a rein— and indeed you could, if you wished, knot her at the ends.[39] She is however, fat in the bosom, but then you are broad in the chest."

To 'Umar she observed, "I've never seen such a well-made woman. You'd think she'd been cast in the very mould of beauty. The only thing is that her face is . . ." And here the expression she used has been taken to mean "not as lovely as her body", though some say the sense is "spoiled by a jutting chin".[40]

---

[39] Reins consisted of two equal lengths of leather so tapered that they could be knotted at the rider's end. Their ends were not sewn.

[40] The text breaks off suddenly at this point, and a lacuna of unknown length may be suspected.

CHAPTER XII

On Diverse Matters relating to Sexual Intercourse

The topics with which this chapter will be concerned include discussion of the beneficial and harmful effects of coition, opinions on the frequency of indulgence in sexual relations and Arab views on whether day or night is better for sexual congress.[1] Some mention will also be made of Arabic terminology relating to the sexual act.

The sexual act affords man one of the greatest of all physical sensations and is one of the most powerful animal appetites. This appetite pervades one's whole being and is not localized in a single organ. When God created woman out of a man's rib and made the one attractive to the other, the two partners tried to discover how they might draw closely to one another and unite,[2] and, in the process of propagating the species, they found nothing to excel sexual union.

Physicians attribute to coition a number of beneficial effects. They hold that it enlivens and gladdens the spirit, increases vitality, dispels irascibility, drives away unwholesome thoughts and morbid preoccupations and even cures melancholia. They

[1] Needless to say, medical fact is compounded with fiction in this chapter. Much of the fiction has its origins in folklore, on the one hand, and the erroneous physiological concepts of Hippocratic and Galenic medicine, on the other.

[2] It is interesting to note that the Kabbalah—a Jewish system of theosophy —claims that each soul, prior to its entering this world, consists of a male and female potency united into a single spiritual being. When a soul descends on this earth, the two parts are separated and animate two different bodies. At the time of marriage God unites them again and they constitute one body and one soul. In traditional Christian thinking we find a similar idea: those whom God hath joined together man must not put asunder.

say that it quenches the ardour of the passionate if such a one frequently indulges his passion, even though the act may be performed with a partner who is not the true object of affection. This is because it affords relief to a body under pressure.[3]

Coitus is highly beneficial to strong, full-blooded persons of heavy build, but harmful to those who are the exact opposite. Rhazes in his well-known work *The Book of Mansur*[4] writes of sexual intercourse and its effects in the following terms.[5] Those whose bodies are of the dry type should treat coitus with the same caution as they would an enemy, for over-indulgence may lead to tuberculous wasting. The same applies to those who are frail or thin or of lean and slender girth or persons of puny muscula- ture. To such people frequent intercourse is positively harmful. In one of his books Galen tells us that seminal fluid is one of the superfluities of the body which should at all costs be discharged;[6]

---

[3] This paragraph contains much that is factually sound.

[4] Because Rhazes (865–925) is well known in the West, it seems best to retain the Latin form of his name (from Arabic "(al-) Razi", i.e. "of Rayy" in Persia. An outstanding physician of Iranian origin, Rhazes was, even by today's standards, a most percipient clinician who made highly original con- tributions to our medical knowledge. (He should not be judged by his erroneous views on the effects of sexual intercourse on human health and constitution.) His *Book of Mansur* was a compendium of medicine in ten parts dedicated to (al-) Mansur ibn Ishaq, the governor of Khorasan, whose patron- age he enjoyed. It was translated into Latin by Gerard of Cremona in the twelfth century and was known to the medieval Western world as *Liber Almansoris*.

[5] Because it is essential to an understanding of certain physical types and certain aspects of sexual states and activities touched on in the present chapter, something must be said about the "humoral theory" which formed the basis of pathology in Arab medicine. This theory, which was borrowed from the Greeks, consisted in the belief that health depended on the harmony, or equilibrium, of *temperaments* and *humours*. There were four humours (blood, phlegm, black bile, and yellow bile) which were produced by food. There were three temperaments which could be simple, compound, or equable (*simple* being hot, cold, moist, and dry; *compound* being hot and moist, hot and dry, cold and moist, cold and dry; and *equable* being that in which there is perfect equilibrium signifying perfect health). The whole theory was without any foundation in fact, but it long dominated physiological thinking, so that even today we speak of "temperament" and "humour" in connection with states of mind, etc.

[6] Sexual activities, because of their excretory nature, were considered by

for, if it remains in the body, it will occasion disorders and serious illnesses. A man should therefore rid himself of it, though not immoderately. The type of person whose need to discharge semen is greatest is the man who, when sexually abstinent, is troubled by a heaviness in the head, clouded vision, dull wittedness and abnormally long hours of sleep. This is because coition or nocturnal emissions relieve them of complaints such as these. The type who most needs to abstain from intercourse is the man in whom the act is followed by languor and loss of appetite.

In his *Encyclopaedic Manual* Dawud Antaki[7] tells us that the term *jimā'* "union" is that most widely used to describe the sexual act, though there are more than 100 synonyms. *Jimā'* denotes the actual act, *bā'a* [*bāh*] "sexual potency" denotes the faculty which makes the act possible, and *inti'āz* denotes the engorgement of the blood vessels in the reproductive organs—though such an engorgement may, of course, be due to some pathological cause.[8]

Sexual union has curative properties. Those which it remedies include mental disorder, a sense of oppression in the chest, sensations of suffocation and epilepsy. It is particularly beneficial in cases where some discharge is occasioned by mere recollection of the sexual act or by unsatisfying nocturnal emissions. It is likewise indicated in the case of young people in whom youth has reached its peak of perfection where the body is fertile and the sexual drive is strong enough in itself to have no need of external stimuli such as kissing, embracing or the sight of animals copulating. If anyone belonging to any of the

medieval Arab physicians as part of the *expulsive faculties* of the human body (as defecation, urination, etc.) and therefore as leading to dryness of the wholesome moistures.

[7] Literally "David of Antioch", an Arab physician, who though blind, travelled widely and even learned Greek to study the medical writings of the ancients. Apart from his monumental reference work mentioned here, he edited a work on the art of love since the subject was still in his day considered a branch of medicine. He died in Mecca in 1599.

[8] Continual and troublesome erection of the penis is a condition known as Priapism. It is, as rightly observed, a symptom of certain pathological conditions (e.g. leukaemia, gonorrhoea). In the female the clitoris may be similarly affected. Priapism is seldom the only symptom of the disease in question.

categories indicated abstains from intercourse, abstention will expose him to some intractable disease.

Coitus may, on the other hand, generate a morbid condition, precipitating attacks of tremor, pain in the joints, pruritus and so forth. All this kind of thing is conditioned by factors in the active and passive parties to coitus, the frequency of intercourse, its timing or other precipitating circumstances preceding or following the act.

As regards the proper time for sexual relations, the most favourable occasion presents itself when the air is wholesome and the body is neither too hot nor too cold, nor too full nor too empty, and the time is correspondingly equable. For heat can lead to fevers and burning, cold to hypothermia and tremor, emptiness to loss of weight, atrophy and tuberculosis, and fullness to obstruction which may be coincidental with heat. Fullness of the body is less harmful than emptiness and not so pernicious or dangerous. In composition the four conditions of heat, cold, emptiness and fullness are governed by the same laws as govern those same conditions as simples. In other words, like the temperaments, we have here the possibility of simple or compound, and the same laws apply. A man should therefore carefully consider this point.

Another point for consideration is whether one is motivated by a genuine sexual urge. A mere erection is nothing to go by since this may be caused by flatus and pressure within the belly or indeed by an enema.[9] A spurious erection of this sort is particularly common in the early morning when a man may find himself physically ready for intercourse but have no real incentive to it. Nor are pruritus, engorgement and redness of the sexual organs necessarily signs of a genuine sexual urge since they may have a purely physical origin. Nor should a man see any real sexual significance in any urge prompted by anything he thinks or sees or by any erotic poetry he might hear or by the

[9] The observation is essentially sound. Such a condition is caused by pressure stimulating the appropriate nerve endings. Early morning erection is most often caused by a full bladder or a loaded rectum. It is common in cases of enlargement of the prostate gland in middle-aged men. Piles and—in children—worms are also common causes of spurious erections.

sight of animals copulating.[10] If, on the other hand, an erection follows physical activity, buoyancy or happiness, this results from a truly felt need for intercourse.

Physicians prescribe intercourse for older men because it removes excessive moistures and surplus heat. It is a better method of ridding the body of such superfluities than any other kind of exercise.

Sexual relations should follow meals consisting of foods which are conducive to the formation of wholesome blood to replace depleted reserves. Among such foods are fried dishes, sweetmeats, meat and eggs. For the sake of one's health food that is heavy, such as jerked meat and sour dishes, is contra-indicated, since food of this kind may bring on weakness in the muscles and joints. The particular rule to be observed is well known and is grounded in the fact that coitus after fish results in insanity, after milk in paralysis, after camel-meat, beef and lentils in varicose veins, gout and arthritis, after aubergines in burning humours. Pumpkins and fruit are harmful to a woman—though not a man—simply because they are too cold for her secretions. Intercourse before breakfast brings on tremor. Finally, it should be noted that what a man eats is largely expelled if his performance of the sexual act does not necessitate strenuous activity such as is the case when a rapid orgasm is achieved by both partners simultaneously or if the husband merely satisfies himself without caring for his wife's needs.

A man who wishes to enjoy matrimonial harmony and enjoy good health must have a good-looking partner with a pleasant voice, graceful deportment and lovable nature. Once he has such a partner, his first preoccupation should be to win the heart and ensure that he and his partner are in harmony, that their blood vessels are engorged and that their physical faculties generally are in a state of readiness for the act of reproduction.[11] Such conditions are attained by kissing, embracing, sucking of the mouth and lips, fondling of the breasts and the application, by each

[10] Actually the contemplation of coitus between animals is an almost normal symbol of sexual emotion, particularly in the young.

[11] It is automatically assumed that the man will wish to beget children right from the outset.

partner, of pressure and friction to the sexual parts of the other until finally the partners are worked up into a state or ardour and experience a passion to cling fast each to the other. At this point the husband should penetrate his wife as she lies on her back with him on top of her. This is the natural coital position,[12] and any other is bad, especially that in which the wife mounts her husband. That is the worst of all positions since it exposes the husband to intractable maladies even though his partner be young and lively and of moderate build. The reason why we insist that the woman should not mount the man is the risk that certain uterine secretions might drain into the meatus of his penis and thus lead to serious pathological conditions.

Coitus with girls under thirteen is bad.[13] It can harm or deaden the brain and bring on depression and morbid fantasy. This is because no secretion[14] is attracted. The same applies in the case of a woman who is too old. Intercourse with a menstruous woman can bring on eruptions of papules, pustules and ulcers (of the penis?) and result in loss of sexual appetite. The reason for this is that menstrual blood is tainted and has cooled off, and some of this corrupt substance may find its way into the erect penis. Intercourse with a virgin who is no longer young has a debilitating effect on the kidneys and may bring on a rupture because of the strenuous movements involved, on the one hand, and the coldness and debility of the vagina, on the other. Intercourse with an unsightly woman can produce the same ill effects as those we have already mentioned as resulting from coitus with young girls—and, in fact, the effects are even worse. Sodomy, too, is highly detrimental to health since it

---

[12] This observation is substantially correct if the purpose of coitus is reproduction. A pillow placed beneath the woman's buttocks will enable a man to make the deepest penetration and at the same time ensure that the semen is well retained. Although scorned as the "missionary position", this anterior approach in coitus appears to have been that most widely favoured by humanity. It is even depicted in ancient Egyptian tombs of the Twelfth Dynasty.

[13] A strange observation in view of the fact that the Prophet consummated his marriage with 'A'isha when the latter was only ten.

[14] In young girls Bartholin's glands are not fully developed with the result that there is insufficient secretion to lubricate the vagina for intercourse.

entails no attraction. Moreover, any sparing of the faculties it might offer is offset by the putridity of the residues. Coitus with a woman over forty should be less frequent than with younger woman and indeed discontinued once she is fifty for fear of ill effects on health.

The physical harm that women can cause impairs the health of the faculties. Men, on the other hand, occasion no harm to women unless they are too big for their partners, in which case their semen will extinguish the heat of the vagina, and this could well bring on the sterility or dropsy.

Apart from specific aphrodisiacs, erotic verses and pornography are sexually stimulating. Among literature of this kind in Arabic we have the *Guide to the Intelligent, The Return of the Older Man to his Youth.*[15] *The Sash* and *Fissures of the Citron.*[16] Sexual desire is also stimulated by mixing with women, by wearing clothes of a fine material and by inhaling the scent of perfumes, amber and civet. To watch animals in the act of copulation will also excite sexual desire. But the strongest stimulant of all when one has lost all hope of one's sexual urge returning is a change of woman. This is a well-tried and successful remedy for loss of libido, for to stick to the same thing all the time only leads to monotony and boredom.[17]

Over-indulgence in sex is physically debilitating and can lead to a loss in weight, a change in complexion and premature senility. The same results can follow from having intercourse when one is hungry or when one is in the bath or soon afterwards. In such circumstances coitus may even bring on sudden death. Moreover, men who prefer intercourse with women who are fat or are in early pregnancy or are nursing mothers—to say nothing of men who suffer from maladies of the heart or brain—should

---

[15] There is a nineteenth-century English translation, viz., *The Old Man Young Again, Literally Translated from the Arabic by an English Bohemian* (Charles Carrington), 2 vols. (Paris, 1898. Edition limited to 500).

[16] Such erotic works were written by men well versed in theology and religion, and were not intended to corrupt but to instruct. See Burton's "Terminal Essay" in the *Arabian Nights*, X, 201, where he lists a number of these works.

[17] A most accurate observation.

indulge their sexual whims as little as possible. It will be much better for their health.

As regards masturbation, this habit leaves only sluggish apathy and depression.

Removal of the pubic hair by plucking will entail diminution of libido, but the use of a razor will have results that will excite it.[18]

Some books tell us that the lesser ablution[19] revitalizes the sexual appetite, and Hippocrates avers that anyone seeking to replenish his resources for further coitus after a first performance should wash himself down in cold water; for cold water rekindles bodily heat and imparts new vitality to the faculties.

We have it on the authority of Anas that on a full bladder sexual intercourse will give rise to anal fissure, and, on a fully loaded rectum, to piles. This is also Galen's opinion. What inevitably happens in the first case is that urinary pressure causes congestion and consequent tearing of the membranes, while in the second the incarceration of solid faeces results in congestion of the rectal gut.

To derive true delight from coitus a man should go for nutriment that is hot and moist, take plenty of rest and sleep and make use of perfume. He should also eat meat dishes and make as much use of bezoar as possible. He should reduce the number of baths he normally takes and in particular consume fewer foodstuffs characterized by cooling properties such as lettuce, coriander and fish [...].[20]

The sexual appetite may be whetted by a number of dishes and preparations of one kind and another. One recipe is the following. Take equal parts of wild garlic, rocket seeds and Chinese ginger mixed to a paste in sesame oil. Another concoction you can try is a potion compounded of milk and the rubbed pizzle of a siring bull and prepared in a glass utensil. Alternatively, you may try celery seeds mixed with fat. Another compound consists

[18] Although the plucking of pubic hair was painful and tedious, it is said by Penzer to have been "largely favoured by women", notably in Persia (*The Harēm*, London, 1966 edn.)

[19] See above Ch. II, n. 40, p. 56.

[20] The text is so corrupt at this point that I can make little sense of it.

of Andarani salt, pepper and ginger compote and brown sugar candy worked into a paste with honey and made up into pills. Or else you can try a mixture of radish seeds and honey. Another recipe is as follows: whip thick honey with an equivalent weight of onion water until the mixture thickens, then mix to a paste with rocket seeds, radish, asafetida and the rennet of a weaned camel. Walnuts, pine kernels, sesame seeds, chickpeas, terebinth, caltrop, manna, ewe's milk, nettles, saffron, galanga, cloves, the ashes of a hyena's pizzle—some go as far as to recommend the use of a stallion's pizzle—and testicles taken with half-boiled eggs and eggshell, bull's horn in honey water or the water of manna, galanga or Chinese ginger, cloves with milk in which they have been soaked overnight—all these things are recommended by specialists in simples for the aphrodisiac properties inherent in them.[21]

The main aphrodisiac foods are as follows: highly seasoned spiced meats cooked with chickpeas and carrots; eggs; ewe's milk; cow's milk; raisins; figs with walnuts and pine kernels; kidney beans; chickpeas.

As regards local applications, the most efficacious are those consisting of onions in the oil of jasmine and narcissus in asafetida. There is also a liniment that is made up of large ants that have been dried in the sun and then left to soak in jasmine oil. Then there is a concoction of pyrethrum, castoreum, euphorbium, costus and garlic. When mixed with jasmine oil, olive oil or the oil of black cumin, it makes a very good embrocation.[22]

Kindi[23] suggests that choice sorghum be cooked with ten dir-

[21] A belief in the aphrodisiac powers of the genitals of stallions, bulls and other animals as well as the horns of bulls and rhinoceroses—powdered for human consumption—is not merely medieval and confined to the Arabs; it is well known in many parts of the world even today. The horn, of course, is symbolic of the erect and rigid penis.

[22] In many parts of the East today one can obtain liniments and embrocations. They are in fact irritants intended to inflame and engorge the penis into a state of erection. Some of these preparations have recently found their way into England through the medium of immigrants. Needless to say, they are apt to set up severe skin conditions with consequent danger of infection, and are therefore to be avoided.

[23] Abu Yusuf Ya'qub ibn Ishaq (c. 800-70), son of a governor of Kufa, came

hams or garlic, five eggs, a handful of cumin, a pinch of salt and thirty dirhams of olive oil. According to him, a man should consume the lot all at once and then rub his back and pubis with the oil of black cumin, though mustard oil will do instead. If he does this, the sexual appetite which he has given up as lost will surge within him once again.

Things which will gradually sap a man's sexual vitality until it is finally exhausted are over-indulgence in intercourse, obesity, too much stair climbing and sitting on stones. A woman's sexual desire is diminished by a number of other things. In particular, we may mention the inhalation of the scent of nenuphar, the wearing of woollen garments, the consumption of foods which induce dryness and the taking of too many baths in hot water.

In both male and female the sexual urge is totally inhibited by hunger, worry, preoccupation,[24] lying on one's side, the consumption of fresh coriander, purslane and rue, the carrying of lead, the wearing of glossy material, the use of roses (this most certainly), blood-letting (to some extent), the use of purgatives, sleeping on bare leather, the consumption of lettuce or anything that has decongestant or carminative action. In cases of hot temperament mint, rue and cumin are contra-indicated since the heat in the pubic region is liable to become excessive and diminish libido. Here cooling substances are the indicated treatment providing they act as maturing agents. Good examples of such substances are milk and peaches.

Provided bodily functions are not impaired the sexual urge is best maintained by keeping the vital organs of the body in good condition since the capacity to experience the sensation of intense pleasure depends on a healthy brain, the capacity of the heart to expand and the liver to secrete moisture. They also say that the secret of a perfectly normal ejaculation resides in healthy

to be known as "the philosopher of the Arabs". He transmitted ancient science and philosophy from Greek writings and made original contributions by way of commentaries and explanations. One of his works on *materia medica* has been translated in recent years by M. Levey, viz., *The Medical Formulary . . . of Al-Kindī* (Wisconsin U.P., 1966).

[24] An accurate observation.

kidneys.[25] The way to keep these various organs in good condition is explained in the appropriate sections of medical textbooks.

Once you are sure that you are in good physical shape and that all you have to do is to strengthen your libido, you need do no more than make use of suitable stimulants. In particular, make free use of such perfumes as musk and amber—they are excellent aphrodisiacs. Also try specific compounds. Of these, the most potent and restorative is a substance compounded of caltrop, garlic and chickpeas. Each of the ingredients should be pounded separately and cooked in milk and fat until they are no longer recognizable for what they are. They should then be mixed with three times their own weight of honey and their own weight of white onion water and manna. The resulting compound is used in just the same way as other aphrodisiacs which are simples. Other recognized aphrodisiacs may be made according to the following recipes. Take as much of a weaned camel's rennet as would equal a chickpea and swallow with a little water. Use a suppository of donkey lard. Use a local application of lion's lard and ostrich oil. Eat asafetida with honey.

Extraordinary sexual sensation may be derived from any of the following procedures. Chew cubeb and rub it on the penis. You may do the same with pyrethrum or with pills prepared from pyrethrum, ginger and cinnamon. The same effect can also be achieved by applying an embrocation prepared from one dirham's weight of asafetida that has been macerated for ten days in ten dirhams of jasmine oil. Another well-tried application is that prepared from the bile of black fowl and oil of cloves.

So far we have only dealt with the male side of the question. Loss of sexual enjoyment may, however, occur in women. Galen writes that perfect sexual ecstasy cannot be experienced by a woman unless the vagina is characterized by three properties, namely heat, tightness and dryness. Later physyicians add a fourth—a pleasant odour. It is also said that other favourable indications are a thick crop of pubic hair, a pronounced pubic eminence and fleshy labia. The absence of any of these character-

---

[25] The kidneys have no connexion at all with the male reproductive system.

istics is said to entail a proportionate loss of sensation, which should then be treated as the condition demands.

If the cause of loss of sensation is internal, draughts to purify the predominating humour are indicated. Then if the temperament is sound, pessaries with an aphrodisiac action may be used. Agents capable of constricting the vagina are present in all astringents such as gall-nut, sukk and pomegranate flower[26] Desiccating agents are present in all dry substances such as musk, black cumin, cloves and sandal, which is the best of all, especially when worked to a paste with myrtle juice. Thermal and cleansing agents act according to their strength. The most effective are walnut, mace, castoreum, myrrh, frankincense, cloves, licorice leaves and resin. Any three of these may be mixed to form a compound suited to need and temperament. According to the ancients, an astringent wine should be used in the mixture. However, we recommend myrtle juice as being better.

The author of the work *Encyclopaedia of Delight* writes: The reason for excessive moisture in a woman may well arise from her inordinate love and affection for her partner,[27] and in such cases treatment is not very effective. The best policy here is to plunge straight into the act of coition without any preliminary petting

Substances which generate heat and dryness include sweet cyperus, pepper and wild caraway boiled in wine and used as a vaginal douche. A draught of opopanax in marjoram juice may also be tried, and this has the added advantage of helping to

[26] Astringents for contracting the vagina—more to give the male sexual satisfaction than to afford the woman any pleasure—have long been used in the Middle East. In more primitive areas a particularly cruel practice prevails even today (though the direct cruelty is self-inflicted): a woman after childbirth will have rock salt packed into the vagina for fear that too large a passage will not give her husband the satisfaction to which he has been accustomed—in which case there is a danger that he will divorce her. Wendell Phillips has reports of the practice in southern Arabia and his informant rightly observes that the practice gives rise to atresia—the formation of inflexible scar tissue which can set up a rigid barrier against delivery in a subsequent pregnancy (*Unknown Oman*, London, 1966, p. 71).

[27] It must be remembered that because of the system of arranged marriages a woman did not necessarily find her husband too sexually exciting.

conserve sexual potential. It is said, moreover, that in the case of women the vaginal use of kohl (eye-black), alum and sal ammoniac and solutions made from such substances exercises a powerful aphrodisiac effect.

On Orgasm, Ejaculation and the Power of Attraction in Different Kinds of Vagina

Delay in the attainment of a climax is another question which arises in the present context. The effect of the activity entailed by protraction of the sexual act is the dissolution of corrupt matter and the regeneration and intensification of natural heat. To delay the orgasm is a very popular practice, but it is mostly met with in people whose constitution is characterized by equable natural heat and excessive dryness and in men who have one testicle that is either retracted or else contracted almost to the point of disappearance. A delayed orgasm may, of course, result from some pathological condition of any one of the organs of the reproductive system. Premature ejaculation accompanied by little pleasurable sensation is a condition that arises in the brain; that accompanied by palpitation is a condition arising in the heart; that characterized by the emission of very little fluid is a condition arising in the kidneys or some nearby organ below them.

In the *Practice of the Art of Medicine* it is stated that, provided the constitution is sound, the time taken to reach the point of ejaculation depends on the power of attraction exerted by different kinds of vagina. The most equable in this respect are Abyssinian women since their power of attraction is that of the perfect mean. After them came women of the fourth clime,[28] who are almost as equable. The coldest of women are negresses and Nubians, for coldness is incarcerated in their system while

[28] The "clime theory" was inherited by the Arabs from the Greeks and elaborated. Basically, there were seven climes, or climates, outside which lay the far northern countries and also those south of the equator. Each was a regional belt on the surface of the earth parallel to the equator and, apart from being characterized by certain physical features, human groups, etc., was subject to a specific astral influence.

heat rises and is dispelled with consequent inhibition of their faculties and delay in the attainment of a climax. The hottest women in this respect are Slavs and Europeans. The reason for this is that by virtue of the cold climates in which they live their external surfaces are well padded and so conserve the heat in the inner recesses of their bodies. The same sort of thing may be observed in wells where water will be found to be warm in winter and cold in summer, though most people suppose the opposite to be true.

Egyptian women are the most sensuous and have a power of attraction that exerts the fastest pull. And so, to delay the orgasm with them is positively injurious. Hejazi women are the coldest and wettest of women. And so with them orgasm is achieved much more slowly. The worst of all are Chinese and Indian women since they undergo eight changes in the course of a year. Persian women from the lands beyond the Oxus are like Indian women, while those from the regions of Iraq are like women of the fourth clime and are indeed even better.

Only when one has a perfect grasp of these basic facts about women should one start looking into the causes of premature ejaculation. If any of the causes are such as we have already indicated, appropriate measures can be taken to remedy the situation. If not, and if the cause is inherent in one's natural disposition, there is no known treatment.

Among specific remedies for premature ejaculation there is a preparation which has marking-nut as its base. To each ounce of marking-nut rind add five dirhams of frankincense, two dirhams of opoponax, one dirham of sandarac and half a dirham of scammony. Simmer the ingredients in oil of terebinth for a week over a low flame from a wick and then make up into pills. Take a half dirham dosage as required. Another preparation that can be tried is the following. Take the pollen of black cumin and the rind of opium poppy in equal quantities and add half the quantity of henbane, sweet cyperus, cloves and mace in equal proportions. Work into a paste with honey. Take about two hours before needed. Alternatively, take equal quantities of galingale, nutmeg, coriander, the rind of opium poppy, the liquid extract of wormwood, the shells of pistachio nuts and opoponax together with half quantities of Indian costus, dry storax, sandarac, thyme and rue seeds in equal proportions. Add to the sum total of ingredients its weight in pistachios. Mix and work to a paste and use when required.

The Timing of Coitus, Frequency of Performance, and the Right Conditions

Suyuti[29] writes: It should be realized that the only suitable occasion for coitus is when the sexual appetite is whetted and the semen is ready for emission. It should then be legitimately discharged from the body in the same way as one discharges harmful waste products which, if retained in the body, will be most detrimental to health. There is no special time for coitus. What matters is the physical state I refer to, even though that state be reached only once a year. This is particularly the case with persons whose temperament is predominantly yellow or black. For them coitus is extremely injurious because of the paucity of moisture in their bodies. For sanguinous and phlegmatic types who are capable of having frequent intercourse, the most appropriate thing is to indulge their appetite once, twice or three times a week. But a man should not have intercourse twice in twenty-four hours since that is extremely harmful. The reason is that semen is the quintessence of nutriment, which is the substance of the spirit. And so, if a man over-indulges his sexual appetite, he will first deplete his store of semen and then go on to tax his nutritive blood and the essential moistures—and that will destroy or wreck him. A man who does over-indulge in sexual intercourse cannot conceal the fact since he will age quickly, grow feeble from decrepitude and go prematurely grey.

The particular way in which sexual union should take place is as follows. The woman should lie on her back and the man mount her. Any other position is useless. The man should gently pet his partner first, all the time embracing and kissing her and

29 A famous writer with an indefatigable pen (1445–1505) who was born in Upper Egypt and wrote on all kinds of subjects.

so fourth. Then, when her passions are stirred, he should thrust his penis into her and leave it inside even after he has ejaculated. He should not quickly withdraw, but rather wait for a while and continue to hold her in a firm embrace. When he is completely relaxed, he should withdraw, moving from his right as he does so. Such a procedure, they say, is one of the things that will ensure male offspring. The best performance is that which is followed by a sense of vitality and expansiveness and some residual desire. The worst, on the other hand, is that which is followed by trembling, breathlessness, listlessness, a sensation of fainting, and intense dislike of the partner with whom one has just had intercourse, even though that partner may be the object of genuine affection.

According to Suyuti, one should not embark on sexual intercourse on a stomach that is either full or empty. Nor is the bath-house the place for coitus. Again, coition should not follow on a period of fatigue or be contemplated after vomiting, diarrhoea or blood-letting. Those who are given to indulgence in sexual intercourse should cut down on tiring pursuits, avoid too much blood-letting and reduce the length of time they spend in the bath-house. They should also ensure that they do not eat too much of those foods which increase the production of semen. Finally, they should cut down on aphrodisiacs.

According to Abu Faraj, once a man has satisfied his sexual urge with a woman, he should bath in hot water—never cold—both in summer and in winter. If possible, this ablution should be taken in a steam bath or in a concealed spot sheltered from draughts. Hot water will moisten the bodily organs from which moisture has been lost and will warm them up again after the dissipation of their natural heat by the emission of semen. To bath in cold water is injurious, no matter whether it is summer or winter, since it will overcool and dry the body's organs. When both the man and the woman have each had a bath, they should make use of pleasant perfumes and vapours, especially musk in large quantities since this is the best scent there is. But they should on no account go near or touch even the smallest amount of camphor [since it is a drying agent]. They should also sit on soft comfortable blankets, which for preference should be red or green since these are the best colours. Such is the opinion of Abu Faraj in his *Women*.

According to Harith ibn Kalada,[30] the Arab physician, if a man wants a long life he should take his lunch early and his dinner late, lie less on women, and never copulate on a belly full of food.[31] It is as the poet says:

> "Three things are causes of an early death and bring
>   maladies on man—
> Continual imbibing, one long life of venery, and a belly
>   stuffed with food."[32]

Yet a sage once said, "There are three things of which a wise man will not deprive himself: eating, walking and coitus. The purpose of eating is to sustain the body. Accordingly, too little will impair its function and too much will end in sickness. Too little walking will result in the loss of the habit, and he who would walk will then find that he cannot walk when he wishes. Finally, coitus may be compared to a well, for when a well is dredged, it will fill again, but, if neglected, its water will run dry. The penis is like an udder, which, if milked, will yield more, but, if left to itself, will dry up."

Ta'abbata Sharran[33] once said, "I love this world for three things: to eat flesh, to ride flesh, to rub flesh against flesh." One of the things that Yazid ibn Muhallab once said was, "I'd love to find a depilatory costing 100 dinars a time, and I'd love to see a

---

[30] The first Arab physician of any repute, Harith flourished in the seventh century and studied medicine at the renowned medical centre of Gondeshapur (now Shahabad in south-west Iran), He died around 634.

[31] This point has been made in the first part of our author's work and A. H. Walton comments: "Coitus after a full meal is never to be recommended, especially in the middle-aged, or older ... Death from heart-failure in certain specifically predisposed persons ... is ... not an impossibility; and cardiac patients should certainly consult their medical adviser regarding the amount of, and conditions for coitus." (*Perfumed Garden*, p. 161, n. 115.)

[32] The first and last causes certainly do shorten life. An active sex life, however, is not likely to do much damage unless one is in ill health from imbibing and over-eating.

[33] See below Ch. XVI, n. 44, p. 282.

woman's vulva on the forehead of a lion, so that only men of rank might afford the depilatory and only a man of courage reach the vulva."[34]

It has also been said that there are four things which cannot manage without another four: A female cannot do without a male, nor earth without water, nor an ear without news nor eyes without sight. Some sage also said, "Every appetite to which a man gives himself up will help to harden his heart. To this there is but one exception, and that is the act of sexual union— this alone will make his heart kinder and purer, and for this reason prophets and sages both practise and enjoy it."

In his *Healing* Judge 'Iyad has this to say: It has long been customary to boast of one's sexual prowess and to take pride in the frequency of one's sexual performance, since it has long been accepted as a sign of perfection and an indication of sound masculinity. In Islamic law the sexual act has long been recognized as an acceptable orthodox practice, and religious scholars have never found it incompatible with a life of asceticism. As Sahl ibn 'Abdullah says, "How can a man renounce women when they were made desirable to the Lord of all Mankind—the Prophet?" In support of his view he quotes a Tradition on the authority of Anas, in which the Prophet declares, "I have been granted four favours which others have not: the qualities of generosity and courage and a capacity for frequent sexual union and the regeneration of my strength."

Bukhari quotes the following Tradition from Qatada on the authority of Anas: The Prophet would circulate among his womenfolk for one hour in twenty-four since he was the recipient of thirty, or rather forty men's sexual capacity.[35] One night when he did his rounds he had union with each of the nine women of his household and performed the major ablution after each act before moving on to the next. "This," he said, "is better and cleaner way of going about such a matter, though it is not obligatory to perform the major ablution after each act of intercourse; it is only recommended."

[34] See above p. 142.
[35] An evident exaggeration to stress Muhammad's position as a superman.

There is another Tradition quoted by Nasa'i on the authority of Hamid, who quotes Anas as saying that the Prophet would go from one of his women to another, performing one major ablution only.[36] This point is not disputed. A difference of opinion arises only in connexion with the following question: Should one who has had sexual union once first perform the lesser ablution before attempting to perform a second time? The Islamic community is unanimously agreed that it is not mandatory.[37]

It is related of 'Umar and his son that both insisted on the lesser ablution such as is required before the ritual prayer. This is also the view of 'Ata' the Traditionist. Ahmad ibn Hanbal's[38] opinion is that, as regards sexual intercourse in the circumstances described, the lesser ablution is recommended, but no blame attaches to failure to perform it.

The reason for the controversy on the matter is the interpretation of the words of the Prophet, "If one of you goes in to his wife and wishes to do so again, he should perform the ablution." Those who interpret the word for "ablution" here in its religious and legal sense of "lesser ablution" insist that the lesser ablution is the same as that demanded before the ritual prayer and, as such, is mandatory, while those who interpret it from a purely lexical point of view insist that what is mandatory is only the washing of the private parts. The lesser ablution in the religious acceptance of the expression is classified by them as recommended, and they make this concession only to avoid controversy. Whether one, two or more women are involved is in their view irrelevant.

[36] On the major ablution and sexual intercourse see above Ch. II, n. 40, p. 56.

[37] The point of unanimity is important because consensus of the community (technically termed *ijmā'*) is, after the Koran and the Practice of the Prophet, the third basis of Islamic religious law. The unanimity of the whole body of Muslims is an infallible source of truth.

[38] Traditionist, jurist and theologian (780–855) and, more importantly, the founder of one of the four Sunnite legal systems, namely that known as the Hanbalite. His teachings exerted a profound influence on Islamic religious and legal thought, and the Hanbalites attracted to their ranks a high proportion of fine scholars. In the first instance he was essentially an authority on Tradition—a foundation on which later scholars built their legal system.

Bukhari on the authority of Ibn 'Abbas quotes the words, "The worthiest members of the Community are for the most part women." In his *Healing* Judge 'Iyad declares that the words are those of the Prophet.

In one of his works Khattabi writes words to the effect that God chose for Muhammad all that was best and combined in him qualities that enhanced his majesty and splendour in the eyes of the Arabs. Now the Arabs would pride themselves on their sexual prowess and, according to all evidence, the Prophet was of strong physique and equable temperament. It follows that any man who could be characterized by such a degree of physical perfection must have had in the highest degree all the requirements that our subject entails. It fell to him to have more than four wives because he was to be trusted. Every other member of his Community, on the other hand, was forbidden to exceed four spouses lest he should not treat them equitably and give them their due.[39] Since concubines do not have the same rights in this respect as free women, all members of the Community have been permitted as many concubines as they desire.

Ja'far ibn Abi Talib once said, "Among those things which characterize the prophets three may be noted—cleanliness, women, and the use of perfume." He then went on to speak of Solomon who had a thousand women—seven hundred concubines and three hundred wives—all in one place. When asked how Solomon managed to cope with them, he remarked, "God gave him the strength of forty men and more, and bestowed the same gift on our Prophet." But when asked about 'Ali he evaded the issue as if too embarrassed to comment on a man so closely related to him and on a woman so highly regarded as Fatima.[40]

In his book *Elegance of Expression* Jahiz quotes 'Abdullah ibn

---

[39] This is Koranic legislation. It permits four wives, but husbands are specifically instructed to accord co-wives equal treatment and not to marry more than one woman if they feel they cannot treat them equally. It is this Koranic injunction which has enabled many Muslim countries in modern times to introduce legislation insisting on monogamy, their contention being that it is not in the nature of a man to love two or more women equally.

[40] 'Ali was Ja'far's brother, and Fatima, 'Ali's wife, was the daughter of the Prophet.

Hasan as reporting that 'Ali once said, "Our family have been specially endowed with eloquence, magnanimity, comeliness and sex appeal." In his testament to his sons he also said, "Do not, my sons, stay too long on your own in the company of women lest they bore you and you bore them. Keep something of yourselves in store, for to hold back from them when they find you with an erection is better than their finding you flat." 'Ali is also quoted as being the author of the verse:

> Happy is he who has a box of dates from which he eats
> but once a day.

In his *Digest* Ibn Sayyid alludes to women in a similar line:

> Happy is he who has a wife whom he can take to bed
> and after union fall heavily asleep.

It has been said that 'Ali's rule was "once only in twenty-four hours", that being the happy medium and hence the most equable. 'Umar ibn Khattab, however, was more stringent: his rule was "once only in each intermenstrual period". There is, nevertheless, no upper limit; it all depends on temperament and capacity. 'Umar's actual words according to 'Abd-ul-Malik ibn Habib were, "It is sufficient for a Muslim woman that her husband should go in to her once each period in which she is ritually clean." In support of his pronouncement he cited a Tradition which he attributed to the Prophet, "Once a month is enough for a woman." In connexion with 'Umar's attitude Muhammad ibn Yahya ibn Hassan observed, "My grandmother once remonstrated with my grandfather because of his lack of interest in sex. 'It's only the ruling of 'Umar that comes between us,' he replied. 'And what's 'Umar's ruling?' she asked. 'He ruled,' came the answer, 'that if a man goes in to his wife once a month during the period when she is ritually clean,[11] he has done his duty to her.' Her comment was, 'Does everyone but you and me ignore 'Umar's ruling?' "

[11] i.e. not menstruating. See Ch. III, n. 11, p. 63.

In his book *For Muwaffaq* Zubayr writes: Ibn Abi 'Atiq[42] had a voluptuous slave-girl who was always out and about followed by admiring young men. One day when Ibn Abi 'Atiq came home he found two youths standing opposite his house. "And how many times a day do you have it, my young friend?" he asked one of them. "Only once and sometimes not at all," came the reply. "And what about you?" he asked the other. "Twenty times a day," he answered. Turning to the first youth, he said "Don't you dare come by my house again!" But to the other he merely commented "You can come and go as you like." The significance of his words is this: the one who claimed he was having it twenty times a day really did not know what it was all about; for had he ever had any true sexual experience, he would never had made such a claim. But the other man's reply was that of an experienced man who really knew what he was talking about. And so he was sent about his business and stopped from going near the house.

In his *Songs* Abu Faraj relates: 'Abbad Bishri, while on the road to Mecca, came to a stage-point called Nubah. There to his surprise he found written on a wall the words, "A ride's a matter of four things—lust and pleasure, cure and malady, and a woman's hole has greater need of two shafts than a shaft has need of two holes." The words were written in the hand of Dananir, a girl who was a client of the Barmecide family.[43] A similar tale is told by Ya'qubi[44] who writes: I was on my way to the house of Hamduna daughter of Rashid when the girl Dafaq, her client, came out with a fan in her hand. On one side was written, "A vagina needs two penises" and on the other "just as a millstone has greater need of two mules than one mule has

[42] Great grandson of the Caliph Abu Bakr. See p. 76.

[43] Or "the Barmak family". The Barmecides were a powerful Iranian family whose members exerted great influence over the early Abbasid Caliphs. Although greatly influenced by them in his earlier years, Harun decided to be rid of them in 803. The reasons for their fall are not as clear as they could be, but it seems likely that Harun had long contemplated their domination over the Abbasid house and decided that their policies were in their own interests and not his. At all events, their name is one of the best known in all Islamic history.

[44] Important historian and geographer of the ninth century.

of two millstones." On this theme a man of culture and letters composed the following verses:

> Fill yourself with pleasure while Time is on your side and
>   grants most generously all that you desire.
> Don't spend your hours beyond the reach of pleasure lest
>   fruitlessly your life should slip away.
> Coitus is the one and only pleasure on this earth—and
>   there's enjoyment for you in the first degree if
>   enjoyment's what you want!
> Don't for a single night deny the joy of coitus to the one
>   you love—and there's advice that's genuine enough,
>   if only you will heed it.
> One act alone with one you love you must not deem
>   sufficient, for once alone does not suffice a man.
> Twice is his due, and twice it must be, for twice is fairest,
>   and a man must have his due.
> And if one night you make it three times, that is a bonus
>   and bounty in pleasure.
> And if you fear parting with the one you love, then make
>   it four times—the more, the better.

In his *Revivification* Ghazali writes: 'Abdullah ibn 'Umar[45] had a voracious sexual appetite. He would break his fast on sexual intercourse, and sometimes he would even have intercourse before the Sundown Prayer, perform the greater ablution, and pray. Once he had intercourse with three of his concubines in one night during the month of Ramadan—in other words, between sunset and the last meal before starting the fast of the following day.[46] It is also said that 'Abdullah ibn Zam'a, an in-

[45] Popular son of 'Umar I (d. 692 or 693).

[46] In order to understand this observation and all that follows something must be known of the great fast of Ramadan, the ninth month of the Islamic year. In general terms strict fasting is obligatory during this month, and this means that a man must not eat, drink, have *sexual intercourse*, or—nowadays —smoke, from about two hours before sunrise until sunset. Between sunset and dawn, however, legitimate needs and desires may be satisfied. Normally the fast of the day is broken with a light snack (our 'Abdullah here preferred sexual intercourse), after which one says the Sundown Prayer, and then eats a full dinner. What 'Abdullah would do would be this: break the fast on

law of the Prophet and one of the most righteous and esteemed members of the tribe of Quraysh, could not wait to have intercourse at any time of the day or night. For this reason he avoided going to the mosques of Quraysh and attending public occasions, but built a mosque in his own house. He would marry a woman, but she would stay with him for no more than a day or two and then run away and go back to her family. A woman from Medina called Zaynab daughter of 'Umar ibn Abi Salama once asked, "What's the matter with these women that they run away from him." "They can't stand up to his excessive demands," she was told. "Well, what's to stop him marrying me?" she asked "I am sturdy, full in the buttocks and well endowed between the legs." Ibn Zam'a came to hear of this and duly married her. She survived his demands and bore him many children.

In his *Songs* Abu Faraj quoting Sha'bi writes: While in Medina Nu'man ibn Bashir, one of the Prophet's Companions, very much wanted to hear some singing. So he went to the house of 'Azzat-al-Mayla' and listened to her. On his way out he was accosted by a woman with complaints about her husband's excessive demands on her. "The judgement I shall give in this dispute," he remarked, "is one against which there can be no appeal. God permits him four wives, so you are bound to oblige him four times—twice during the night and twice during the day,"[47] The full story is a long one.

The following story is told by Asma'i: Once there was a beautiful woman in Basra, and all the best men competed with one another for her hand. But in the end she married a penniless lad who lived with her some time and gave all he had to her five times a night. But then it came down to four times, then three, then two, until in the end he could only manage once a night. When she came to realize that once a night was now his regular

---

sexual intercourse, snatch a snack, sometimes follow this with a second round of sexual intercourse, perform the greater ablution to make himself ritually clean after coitus, and then say his Prayer. The "last meal before starting the fast of the following day" refers to the food one may take about twenty minutes before dawn.

[47] What is implied is that she was his only wife and would have to do duty for the permitted four.

performance, she said to herself, "One fellow who asked my hand was well-to-do and he could manage once a night at least." She then started to make excuses and put him off until in the end she provoked him and could leave and go back to her father's. Her husband went after her and begged her to come back to him, but she refused. "I stayed with you," she said as she pointed to the fingers of one hand, "and accepted you and was quite happy." Then, dropping one of her fingers, she went on, "And there was nothing wrong with you then." As she said that, she dropped another finger and continued, "But you changed." As a third finger went down, she remarked, "And even if you could have gone on like that—meaning union twice a night—I wouldn't have been so cross with you." "But," objected the lad as he pointed to his forefinger, "God will impose upon a man no burden greater than he can bear,"[48] meaning by this that he could manage only once a night.

In his *Songs* Abu Faraj writes: The tribe of Iyad used to boast, "It is we who have produced the most generous of the Arabs as well as the greatest poet and the best copulator," meaning that Ka'b ibn Mama was the most generous, that Abu Du'ad was the greatest poet, and that Ibn Alghaz was the best copulator. Ibn Alghaz, it was said, had such a penis that when erect he could rub it against his knees if he drew them up. There was, in fact, woman who thought very little of the male organ until she was laid by this man. But when he went into her, she cried out, "Is it with your knees that you men of Iyad lay women?" We are told by Jahiz in one of his works that a poet once boastfully wrote of this very same man:

> Among men of old was Ibn Alghaz, and in one thing he'd
>   do he knew no equal:
> He would draw the smooth tip of his organ across a
>   woman's pubic mound, then stop the gap between her
>   legs with a plug of perfect fit.

Abu 'Ubayda relates that Imrul Qays[49] was detested by

48 Koran, ii, 284.
49 See above Ch. IX, n. 2, p. 184.

women. When he asked his grandmother the reason she said, "You're too heavy with your chest, too light with your loins, quick to discharge, and slow to revive." By this she meant that he would ejaculate too quickly, roll on his back, and only get up after a good deal of trouble. It was for this reason that women hated him. It is said also that as an infant Imrul Qays was suckled by a bitch and that when he sweated one could catch her odour from his person.

Abu 'Ubayd Bakri writes in his *Pearls*: According to Arab tradition, children born of a woman conceiving after nocturnal intercourse are nobler than those conceived during the day. The Arabs would also have it that conception following intercourse in the latter part of the night and shortly *after* menstruation and at the beginning of the lunar month never fails to produce noble children. It is to a similar notion[50] that the poet alludes in the following verse:

> To you who were conceived at the end of a night I say
> "I am rich indeed"; for if money is hard to come by,
>   contentment is wealth in truth.

But what he meant here by "you who were conceived at the end of a night" is that his mother conceived him during the last night of her ritually clean period just *before* she menstruated. To beget a child at this stage is held to be bad behaviour on the part of the father and harmful to the child. Good behaviour and the interests of the child demand that he be conceived during the first part of the ritually clean period, for then the child will be born sturdy and be of a healthy natural disposition. In his *Culture of the Secretary* Ibn Qutayba[51] writes: A woman who becomes pregnant during her menstrual period is said to have conceived "carelessly".

---

[50] The notion is similar, but at the same time different as can be seen from the explanation following.

[51] Literary critic, essayist, lexicographer, philologist and historian (828–89). Although of Persian antecedents, he was a staunch defender of the Arabic humanities and aimed at providing the secretarial (administrative) classes with a solid grounding in Arabic culture.

According to Bakri, men used to say that if a woman conceived a boy while in a state of fear, her labour would be easy. Jahiz says that intercourse with a woman in a state of fear or alarm is a most delightful experience as it also is when it follows fatigue or violent movement or takes place between the fifth and seventh months of pregnancy or when after childbearing she once again regains her ritual purity. Asma'i quotes verses by Abu Bakr of Hudhayl which relate to these observations:

> I set out into the darkness of night with a cruel and
>   obdurate young stalwart whom no one had ever cursed,
> A man who was born of such as conceive when tightly
>   bound, and so he gained no weight.[52]
> One dreadful night against her will she conceived the child
>   with her waist-band yet unloosed.
> She brought him into life to be hot-tempered, lean and
>   hungry, and wakeful even in the longest nights,
> But free from the taint of being conceived from menstrual
>   residues and free from the harm that can come from a
>   wet-nurse,
> Or the ill that can follow from sucking the breasts of a
>   woman heavy with child.

Arabic Terms for Sexual Union

Abu Mansur [Tha'alibi] writes: According to expert opinion the terms for sexual union in Arabic may number as many as a hundred. Some are direct and others are metonymic. I shall give details of the various possibilities.

[The following are examples from the list]: *mash* violent intercourse; *za'ab* "pouring forth" the contents of a waterskin, that is the act of driving oneself to the point of exhaustion in coitus; *da's wa-'ard* "piercing through and through", meaning rough and violent coition; *hakk wa-haww* "pounding and grunting", denoting the act of straining oneself in vigorous intercourse; *wisā'* resemblance to a small bird as it treads the

---

[52] The idea here is that constriction of the body during coitus produces lean offspring.

female; *saghm* "giving sips", that is to say the act of going in, then coming out without wanting to ejaculate; *fahz*, a word denoting the act of having intercourse with a girl in one room while another girl listens to one's gasps; *khawq*, a word which means that as one is having intercourse with a girl one can hear a bubbling noise as the penis goes in and out—the actual noise is termed *khāq-bāq*; *ifhār* is the act of sleeping and performing with one girl and ejaculating inside another; *tadlīṣ* is coition outside the vagina; *iksāl* "taking things idly", that is to say falling into a state of fatigue without ejaculation; *khaqkhaqa* is the act of delaying orgasm; *ghayl* is coitus with a woman who is suckling.

Just as the terms for the sexual act and related matters amount to a hundred or so as indicated, so also there are some three hundred consequences of the facts of each case, and these have been collected on the basis of the criteria laid down by Abu Zayd. For instance, one reads: The absence of the glans from the vagina entails such-and-such. A compendium on the subject has been written by Abu Husayn ibn Zarqun. The Imam Abu 'Ali 'Umar ibn Muhammad ibn 'Ulwan Hudhali is the author of a book on this same subject which has been passed from hand to hand and read with unusual interest. In it he goes over all the ground covered by others and corrects many pronouncements extracted from various sources on the basis of much research, inquiry and the acquisition of deep and extensive knowledge. He would regularly maintain that there was hardly any pronouncement on the topic that was not contained in his book. However, the author of the *Bride's Gift* says that he read the book in question and found that a number of pronouncements had been overlooked. Impelled by youth and the desire to show off, so he tells us, he added a supplement in which the emendations come to fifty. Explaining the different versions in detail, he gave the reasons for the variations. The result was an independent work which he showed to Hudhali who expressed the highest opinion of it.

CHAPTER XIII

On Motitation in Coitus

Although we have touched on this subject previously, it is worth reverting to it here since our purpose is to find pleasure in the words that are used and to enjoy reading about it. Under these circumstances repetition will not bore the reader.

It is my view that all movements, sounds, and utterances made by a copulating couple in the course of their performance greatly heighten their rapture and whet their sexual appetite. Ibn Dhakwan[1] says, "I have yet to hear a better reference to such physical reactions than that contained in the following verses":

> And you Umama, cannot know how you excel all women
> by virtue of your heat and the tightness of your fit.
> What I love about you when we couple is the life I find
> in your speech and the look of death in your eyes.

In his *Songs* Abu Faraj quotes Mada'ini[2] as relating the following story on the authority of some women or other: I happened to be in the company of 'A'isha daughter of Talha when she was told that her husband 'Umar ibn 'Ubaydallah had arrived. So I withdrew from view, and her husband came in. I could, however, still hear them talking. He fondled her just once, then mounted her and pushed it into her. She snored and snorted and

---

[1] Possibly one of a Spanish Arab family of Cordova, of whom several members served as judges, the most famous being Abu 'Abbas Ahmad (d. 1022), Chief Justice of Cordova in the time of the 'Amirid Mansur (Almanzor).

[2] 'Ali ibn Muhammad "of Mada'in" ("The Cities"—the name given by the Arabs to the old Persian capital, Seleucia-Ctesiphon) was an early historian and author of a large number of works. Little is really known of him, and even his dates are uncertain (c. 753–840?).

vibrated marvellously as I listened to it all. When her husband had gone I went in and asked her, "And do ladies of your personality, rank, and status do such things as that?" "For stallions such as we have," she replied, "we rouse ourselves to motion as much as we can and do our best to rouse them. What do you find wrong about it?" "I prefer," I said, "to have that sort of thing at night." "All right," she rejoined, "have it during the night and have it even better. But when my husband sees *me* his sexual appetite is instantly roused and his passion is stirred. He then puts out his hand to me, and I respond, and the result is as you now know." " 'A'isha," said I, "you favour 'Umar far more than you ever favoured any of your previous husbands."

It would seem that this woman's rebuke to 'A'isha for what she did was provoked by the copulatory movements which she could hear. This caused her vagina to stream and aroused her sexual appetite to the point where she longed to be bedded herself. Had anyone at that moment been able to look at her vulva, he would have found her like a mare on heat and her underclothes soaked with secretion. And so she took it out of 'A'isha. She did in fact grudge 'A'isha the pleasure of the act and longed to be in her position. Had she only been able to find some man at that very moment, she would have snored and snorted, puffed and panted many times as much as 'A'isha. This is the reason why the Prophet forbade the practice when he got to know that any woman who hears what is going on during some other woman's act of intercourse suffers dreadful pangs.

The author of the *Scattering of Pearls* tells us that on the day when 'A'isha daughter of Talha was conducted to her new husband, Mus'ab ibn Zubayr, a woman who happened to be present in the house heard such snoring and snorting going on between them as she had never heard before. When she mentioned this to 'A'isha, the latter's comment was that horses don't drink unless they are whistled for.

Ibn 'Utba[3] of Asad, addressing Asma' ibn Kharija when the latter married his daughter Hind to 'Ubaydullah ibn Ziyad, had this to say,

[3] Or "Ibn 'Uqba".

"May God reward you, Asma'! You've satisfied the tip
    of the Emir's fine staff
With a chink from which the scent of musk can emanate
    and as large as the callus on a camel's breast.
When the Emir drives home his staff, you'll hear it
    bubbling as he thrusts.
You've married her off as a lovely virgin who will writhe
    on the top of the bed!"

'Ubaydullah was the man who took Hind's virginity,[4] and she loved him dearly. When he was killed, she was shaken with grief at his death and said, "I yearn for the Day of Resurrection when I shall see the face of 'Ubaydullah ibn Ziyad."

A curious story is told by Abu Rayhan in his book *The Multitudes*: The Caliph Mutawakkil was a notorious womanizer. He would often bed a woman and go back for more but then find himself worn out from the writhing of his previous exercise. So a large tank filled with mercury and covered with bedspreads was made for him.[5] After that he always copulated on top of it, and the mercury put him through the motions without his having to use any great effort. He was delighted with this piece of equipment and inquired about the source of the mercury and was told that it came from a place called Shiz in the Province of Azerbaijan. Once he knew this, he sent off to Hamdun Nadim[6] to have him send as much as he could and at the same time wrote him a decree appointing him the governor of Shiz.[7] But Hamdun's reaction was to compose the following lines:

---

[4] i.e. was her first husband. Great importance was attached in law to the question of virginity (leaving aside all question of unchastity). Once deflowered, a woman became second-hand goods, as it were, if any question of remarriage arose. She could not command the same dower, but at the same time she was, in certain respects, less restricted.

[5] The idea of the water-bed of the present day is not as new as it may seem!

[6] Hamdun ibn Isma'il ibn Dawud, court favourite of Mutawakkil seems here to be confused with the Shi'ite *littérateur* Ibn Hamdun Nadim (d. 868) who was also one of Mutawakkil's boon-companions (*nadīm*, in fact, means "boon-companion").

[7] Because of its remoteness from the capital of the empire and all the amenities of contemporary civilization, the place had little appeal. To Hamdun the appointment was as good as banishment from court.

Appointment as governor of Shiz is as good as dismissal—
Dismissal is as good as appointment to the office.
So if you care for me at all, relieve me of my duties!

He kept on pressing to be relieved of his office until in the end he was granted his wish.

In the *Scattering of Pearls* it is related that a slave-girl was once offered for sale to Mutawakkil. "What," he asked, "are you good at?" "Twenty-five artistic squirms and wriggles in bed, Commander of the Faithful," she replied. He bought her on the spot.

The cure for love is kissing and hugging and one belly
    drawn across another
And wriggles and squirms that bring copious tears to the
    eyes and clutching on to forelock and horns.

In his commentary on *The Assemblies* Ibn 'Abd al-Mu'min writes: "A man once went up to 'Ali and said, 'I have a wife, and every time I bed her she screams "You're killing me." ' 'Kill her,' said 'Ali, 'and I'll take the blame.' "

A Bedouin was once invited to join the circle of Yunus ibn Habib.[8] Women were the subject under discussion, and when they came to consider their attributes, they asked the Bedouin what type of women he found best. "One with fair skin who wears scent and is supple, is bashful and yet has all that it takes for coition and who, when bedded, will moan in rapture at the motions, but who, when left on her own, will yearn for one," he replied. "But," they asked him, "do you know what love is?" "Why should I not?" was his answer. "What is it then?" "It consists," he said, "in embracing one's beloved, kissing a mouth with fine white teeth, and a share of conversation." "This," they protested, "is not love as we know it." "What's your idea then?" he asked. "We think of bulging breasts, bringing knee and neck together and noisy squirms that would awaken a seven-sleeper and an act that involves most sins." "That," he objected, "is not the act of lovers but of those who are after children."

[8] Noted philologist and grammarian of Basra (708–98).

Asma'i once asked a woman of the tribe of Beni 'Udhra, "As you folk are great lovers, what do you understand by love?" She replied, "Pinching, kissing and embracing. What about you?" Said Asma'i in reply, "To one of us love means that a man lifts the woman's leg and with all his might thrusts his penis in between her labia." "That," she observed, "is not the act of a man deeply in love but of someone who wants to beget children."

Muhammad ibn Yahya Mada'ini says, "I once heard 'Ata'[9] say: "A man who was in love with a girl once upon a time could hang around her quarters for a year hoping to meet someone who might see her.[10] And if he managed to arrange a meeting, they would spend their time bemoaning their lot to each other. But nowadays a girl indicates her willingness and, as soon as he sees her, he will go boldly up to her, unfasten her clothes and put it in with about as much concern as if he were asking Abu Hurayra and his companions to witness his marriage."[11]

In his *Treasure* Ibn Bassam quotes a poet:

> There was a fair-skinned slender girl—all that one could
>   wish for—who left me wondering what to do either
>   with her or about her.
> Whether she came or went it mattered not— in either
>   case death faced me.
> But when we were alone together and spoke in tender
>   tones, I laid my hands upon her breast,
> And that whose name I dare not utter, like a tube, grew
>   ten times longer.
> Then continually I thrust and struck at her 'Amr and
>   her Zayd[12]

---

[9] 'Ata' ibn Abi Rabah (c. 732–820?) was a jurisconsult of the old Meccan school and is the only one whose doctrines are to any significant degree ascertainable.

[10] See above Ch. IV, n. 33, p. 92.

[11] This is comparable to a Christian saying "as if he were asking St Peter". Abu Hurayra (above Ch. V, n. 69, p. 127) spent much of his time in the company of the Prophet and was devoted to him.

[12] This is a grammatical allusion. Arab grammarians traditionally take the names Zayd and 'Amr together with the verb "to strike" to illustrate syntactical points. Where we would say, "A struck B", "B is striking A", etc., the Arab would substitute Zayd and 'Amr for A and B.

And next our eyes introduced that part of mine to hers
And I gave her my pure silver and she gave to me
  her gold.

In this last line the poet alludes to the male's white fluid and the female's gold.[13] Verses in similar vein are given by 'Umar ibn Abi Rabi'a:

To a girl with jutting breasts I said in unexpected
  dalliance, "Recline upon the ground."
Whereat she said, "On God's own name, your word is my
  command, even though I'm bidden to do what's not
  my wont."
As morning approached, she said, "You've dishonoured
  me, now go. You're not expelled, however, and, if you
  wish, you may stay on for more."

Jahiz relates the following story: In Basra there used to be an effeminate fellow in whose house lovers could meet. Now one of our friends was madly in love with a woman renowned for her beauty, and this homosexual used all his wiles and blandishments to bring the two together. He succeeded, and, when I asked him later how things went, he told me the tale. "When the two met," he said, "they chatted gaily, and one thing led to another. Then that was that—their burning passions were soon assuaged. Once he had it well in and I could hear moaning and groaning and sobbing and heaving, I called out to them, "Have a good time! But may God not hold me guilty for what is of your own doing—just because I was the go-between!" When they'd finished the first round and were at it again, I shouted, "That's

---

[13] The idea that the vaginal secretion of a woman in a state of sexual excitement was female semen and essential to conception was not confined to the Arabs. In Europe this erroneous belief persisted until the seventeenth century. Harvey was one of those who rejected the theory. I have not succeeded in finding any explanation in Arabic sources of the notion that this "female semen" was comparable to gold. It may be worth noting, however, that in unhygienic, but healthy women, a yellow granular material is apt to collect around the clitoris and labia minora. Moreover, certain pathological conditions give rise to yellowish discharges.

enough now—others come here besides you!" "Be a good chap," they called back, "and just leave us till late this afternoon, and then we'll go without any trouble and give you every coin you ask."

CHAPTER XIV

On whether a Man may Gratify himself by Using Other Parts of a Woman's Body than her Vagina

All authorities on religious law are agreed that a man may use any part of a woman's body, the rectum excepted, for sexual gratification. The rectum is a matter on which there is no complete agreement. Most exclude it on the grounds that it is forbidden by certain Traditions of the Prophet and that it is in fact buggery in a lesser degree. But quite a large body of opinion allows it. In his work *On Women* Ibn Sha'ban attributes the permissibility of the practice to the Prophet's Companions and Successors.[1] Malik's view is reported differently by different authorities. He is said to have permitted the practice of rectal intercourse if the woman was not menstruating.[2] Yet, when the point was raised by 'Ali ibn Ziyad, he denied that he had ever given such an opinion and gave the lie to those who attributed

[1] Otherwise called "Followers-on", literally translating the Arabic *Tābi'ūn*, the technical term for the generation following that of the Companions of the Prophet.

[2] In medieval times the system of law that came to predominate in the Muslim West was that based on Malik's doctrines. The question of rectal intercourse with a woman was therefore a real issue, and indeed one of the points taken up in anti-Muslim polemic by the Christians of Europe. There seems to be little doubt that certain Traditionists, in addition to Malik, were —initially at least—prepared to tolerate it and that advantage was taken of the "concession".

such a view to him. Those who permit the practice, do so on the basis of the Koran "So come unto your tillage as you wish."[3] This is taken to mean that no one part of a woman is lawful to her husband to the exclusion of any other. But those who forbid the practice base their opinion on the view that "as you wish" means "adopting whatever position you wish" and that that refers to the position in which the man chooses to copulate (in the supine position, on the side, and so on.)

In support of this interpretation there is a Tradition related by Abu Dawud on the authority of Ibn 'Abbas: Among the Helpers of the Prophet[4] there was a pagan tribe of idolaters who were in contact with another tribe who were of the People of the Book[5] that is to say, Jews. These pagans used to regard the Jews as their superiors in religious learning and therefore adopted some of their practices. Now it was the custom of the People of the Book only to copulate with their women in the sideways position and to keep their partner covered up as much as possible. This was one of their practices which had been adopted by the Helpers. The Quraysh, on the other hand, would strip their women naked and copulate in any position—face to face, from the back, in the supine position, and so on. And so it happened that when the Emigrant Meccans[6] arrived at Medina, one of them married a girl belonging to this tribe of Helpers and began to copulate with her in the manner to which he was accustomed. But she objected, saying "We have been used to doing this on our sides and in no other way. So you do as we do, or else leave me alone."[7] This became a *cause célèbre* which reached the ears of the Messenger of God. God then revealed the Koranic verse "Your women are a tillage for you. So come to your tillage as you wish." This meant to say that you could copulate with your

[3] Koran, ii, 223.

[4] See above Ch. V, n. 50, p. 116.

[5] Originally the Jews and Christians (later the term was extended to others)—so called because they were the recipients of revealed scriptures.

[6] See above Ch. V, n. 50, p. 116

[7] This story is of great interest since it brings out differences between Meccan and Medinese practice. The Arab Quraysh, it should be noted, were Meccan, and the Jews Medinese. The latter no doubt influenced early Islamic practice in matters of the kind under discussion.

women face to face, from the back,[8] in the supine position, on your side, or any way you like, but the part of the body in question must be the birth passage. It is a well-known fact that in Muhammad's community anal coitus is unlawful.

In his *Women* Abu Faraj relates the story of Umm Salama of Hilal, daughter of 'Abd-ul-Rahman ibn Suhayl, who was taken to wife by the Caliph Sulayman ibn 'Abd-ul-Malik ibn Marwan.[9] (She had previously been married to his brother Walid.) When the Caliph was about to penetrate her vagina, he went down a little too low. "Hey, come on up a bit, Commander of the Faithful—not so low!" she cried. "But I haven't gone in there, have I?" he protested. On the other hand, one night he had intercourse with her and felt somewhat weary after it. Notwithstanding he wanted to repeat the performance, and so he asked her if she would lie on her face so that he might support himself on her buttocks and get into her vagina from that position. To this she had no objection whatever. She was, incidentally, his favourite wife and was the only woman ever to marry three Caliphs, namely Walid, Sulayman, and Hisham.

An amusing tale is told by Ibn 'Abd-ul-Mu'min in his commentary on the *Assemblies*: A Bedouin once approached his wife in a state of great sexual excitement and with a strong erection. But, as he bore down on her, she announced she was menstruating. "Well, what about the other place?" he asked and thrust himself in there while she struggled and cursed him as he pressed on with his task. And as he laboured, he sang out:

"By the Lord of the Curtained Sanctuary,[10] I'll wreak havoc on this circlet's rim!"[11]

In his *Treasure* Ibn Bassam has a verse which runs as follows:

> Giddy with wine I rose, and she too rose with a totter
> and sway of her body.
> She put off her shift, lay down by my side, and turned
> her belly to mine.

---

[8] Contrary to Jewish practice.
[9] Seventh Umayyad Caliph (reg. 715–17).
[10] See above Ch. III, n. 23, p. 70 f.
[11] The sense is self-evident.

But then I said, "No, not belly to belly—its your back
to my belly I want."
Turning around coyly, she said, "I'm a shop with two
fronts—come in at the front or the back!"

A woman who makes love on her side is called a *ḥariqa*, and
there is a saying going back to one of the Companions, "A
woman who has made love with you on her side has tricked
you". What they mean by this is "Beware of such a woman; she
is out to allure you". We have already said earlier that this goes
back to Abu Mansur,[12] who says that to mount a woman who is
lying on her back is called the act of *sharḥ* ("opening and ex-
posing to view"). This position, according to physicians, is at
once the most delightful and least harmful.

'Abd-ul-Malik[13] relates that 'Umar would forbid women to
sleep on their backs when not in sexual embrace. "The Devil,"
he said "will forever try to possess women as long as they lie on
their backs." What he meant was that on such occasions the
Devil would encourage them to think of men because such is
the position they adopt for their embraces.

According to a tradition related of Jabir by Muslim, the Jews
used to say that if a man penetrated a woman from behind, the
offspring would be squint-eyed. So God revealed the verse "Your
women are a tillage for you. So come to your tillage as you
wish." This he interpreted as meaning "with back arched or
otherwise", by which, according to Mazini, he meant "with
the woman face downwards". Judge 'Iyad explains, however,
that the bending position is of two kinds: that in which the
woman leans forward with both hands on her knees as in the
bowing position in the ritual Prayer[14] and that in which she
kneels with her head to the floor as in the prostration in Prayer.

[12] Either the author is mistaken or the reference is contained in a missing
portion of the manuscript. No previous mention has been made of Abu
Mansur and this teaching.

[13] Presumably the Malikite jurist Ibn Habib (above Ch. VI, n. 20, p. 140).

[14] This is the *rak'a* (see above Ch. V, n. 54). The bow is made from the hips,
and the back lowered into the horizontal position, the hands being placed
on the knees.

CHAPTER XV

On Jealousy: The Case
For and Against

Daraqutni[1] in his *Weaknesses in Traditions* quotes Ibn Mas'ud as saying, "The Apostle of God said that God is jealous in the interests of His Muslim servants. Every Muslim then should be jealous in his own." The Apostle of God also said, "Jealousy is an ingredient of Faith."

In his *Women* Abu Faraj relates on the authority of Ka'b ibn Malik:[2] The Messenger of God said that there are two kinds of jealousy, one pleasing in the sight of God, the other not. "Which," we asked, "is that which is pleasing in the sight of God, Apostle of God?" "God," he replied, "is jealous when men act in utter disregard of His will and violate things which are sacrosanct." We then asked about the sort of jealousy abhorred by God, and he replied "God abhors jealousy in those who are jealous of the unsubstantial," meaning—but God knows best— "in those who are jealous without true grounds for jealousy," but are merely suspicious of a wife's conduct. We have the same sort of idea in the words of 'Abdullah ibn Shaddad as reported by 'Abd-ul-Malik ibn 'Umayr. "Jealousy," he said, "is of two sorts: that which impels a husband to correct his wife and that which takes him off to Hell."

Writing on marital life in his *Revivification*, Ghazali says that jealousy of one's wife is a matter for moderation. He should not, on the one hand, ignore small beginnings that can end in disaster. Nor, on the other hand, should he be unduly suspicious

---

[1] A well-known Baghdadi authority on the Koran and Tradition (919–95).
[2] One of the Helpers (see Ch. V, n. 50, p. 116.

of his wife, harass her, and spy on her every movement when there is no good reason to doubt her integrity. The Messenger of God himself forbade a husband to be always on the heels of his wife looking for faults. He also said "God abhors unfounded jealousy." Again, he said, "There is the kind of jealousy that is pleasing to God, and that which He abhors. Also there is the kind of pride that is pleasing to God and the kind that He abhors. That sort of jealousy which is pleasing in His sight is that for which there is good cause; that which He abhors is that which is groundless. Likewise the kind of pride which is pleasing in His sight is that of a man in battle or of a man giving voluntary alms. But that which he abhors is vainglory."

In his *Women* Abu Faraj quotes Mu'awiya as saying, "There are three characteristics that are marks of a great leader of men —a bald head, a narrow waist, and a not too jealous nature." Abu Faraj comments that Mu'awiya was taken to task for accounting a not too jealous nature the sign of a great leader of men. But he retorted, "I see nothing wrong in my view. To carry jealousy to excess is to go beyond reasonable bounds—and that to the point at which women become the victims of injustice."

Abu Faraj also relates the following anecdote: Qays ibn Zuhayr once stayed with a certain company of Arabs and happened to comment, "I am jealous, proud, and scornful. But I am not jealous until I perceive, nor proud until I act, nor scornful until abused." He was censured for saying, "I am not jealous until I perceive", but the fact is that he means us to understand the words "cause for jealousy" after the word "perceive" and not the words "the matter proved at law", or something similar. On the same topic Miskin Darimi[3] writes the following:

> I shall not be tied to my hearth and home sitting beside my
> bride neither moving nor budging an inch from her side.
> No oath shall I swear never to let her leave the house,
> and thereby make her house her tomb before her death.
> If her own house is not enough to keep her chastity
> untouched, no castle I can ever build will keep her
> safe from stain.

[3] A contemporary of the Umayyad satirist Farazdaq.

Never shall I give way to jealousy or small talk until
  I know for certain that cause for jealousy exists.
Imagine, if I were to be a man who lived to watch his wife,
  what should I do, once away and far from her side?"

It was also he who wrote:

You there with your burning jealousy, what are you
  jealous of whenever you are not?
Are you jealous that men look? And, if so, is mere
  looking alluring to the chaste?
What value is a bride if all she stirs in you is fear and you
  have to watch her all the while?
If, in her heart, she has no decency, a flailing whip lash
  won't avail her spouse.
And who will watch his bride when he and his mount
  are well away from home?

Zubayr writes as follows in his book *For Muwaffaq*: 'Ali once
said to his son, "Dear son, do beware of unfounded jealousy—
it taxes the health and brings on sickness. Order the lives of your
womenfolk aright. Thus if you see them commit some sin, reproach them for it, be it great or small. But do beware or railing
at them for their misdoings lest your censure lose its sting
through habit."

Certain sages say: Jealousy is a thing inborn and given by God
to man and all that lives and breathes. This is why you see the
wild ass do battle for his mate with any other stallion who dares
approach her. But human nature varies from one man to the
next. At the one extreme you find a man consumed with suspicion, at the other a man that is so complacent that he does
credit neither to religion nor manliness. Both extremes are bad,
and moderation is in all things best.

A man who was jealous in the extreme was 'Aqil ibn 'Ullafa,[4]
whose behaviour with his wives and daughters was that of a
lunatic. It was also said of Ibn 'Abd-ul-Malik that he was the

---

[4] A noted Medinese poet in the early part of the eighth century.

same. In his *Gems* Sâ'id[5] relates the following story on the authority of Ibn Kalbi: The [Umayyad] Caliph Sulayman ibn 'Abd-ul-Malik who was a most jealous creature, once set out for Jerusalem accompanied by his women and retinue. He got as far the Balqa' depression[6] and spent the night—it was full moon at the time—in a certain monastery. Among his soldiers there was a young man by the name of Sinan from the tribe of Kalb. Now this man was endowed with the most handsome of features and the most melodious voice. On this particular night Sulayman invited a group of young warriors to share his hospitality, and he wined and dined them well. When the drink had gone to their heads, Sinan, who was one of the group, raised his voice in song to sing:

> "Behind her veil a girl once heard my voice and fell
>   victim to its charm as she lay at the end of the night,
>   soaked by the dews of dawn.
> Close to her thighs clung a saffron gown, and on her
>   breasts adorning jewels coldly lay.
> Neither locks nor guards can bar my voice as it strikes her
>   ears and calls forth tears.
> So beautiful a girl is she that on a moonlit night when
>   its orb is full, the lover at her side cannot discern
>   which is brighter, face or moon.
> Were she but free, on tender, almost cracking feet she'd
>   make her way to me."

Just at that moment Sulayman was lying with a favourite concubine, and when he heard these lines, he shot to his feet in a burst of thunder, flung back the clothes from her body and saw that she matched the girl described in the poet's verses. Perceiving the anger surge across his face, she knew that it was jealousy stirred by the singer's words. "If I don't throw myself on his mercy" said she to herself, "he will surely kill me, and then kill the man as well." And so she began "To Hell with the man who said,

---

[5] A philologist of Baghdadi origin (d. 1026) who settled in Cordova in 990 and became one of the poets of the circle of the 'Amirid Mansur (Almanzor).

[6] In present-day Jordan.

How many a thrilling voice comes from the mouth of
    some unsightly wretch of lowly pedigree—
Some wretch of stature squat and fingers fat and short,
    the progeny of some slave and scivvy with hands
    well torn from toil!"

"His voice thrilled you, then?" asked Sulayman. "Commander
of the Faithful," she replied, "his voice just happened to catch
me as I woke, and I listened to it." When Sulayman heard these
words, he stood quivering like a palm leaf in a storm wind. He
gripped the hilt of his sword and swore "By God, I'll slay that
damned man or mutilate him as an example to others of his ilk!"
He then sent someone to bring him to him in irons. "Who are
you?" bellowed Sulayman. "May your mother mourn you!" So
Sinan told him who he was, whereupon the Caliph declaimed,

"May Sinan be mourned by his mother, his mother's
    brother, and his father's too, and by all his tribe, the
    Sons of Kalb!
To his mother he was as fragrant myrtle, but now what
    a sorry sight he'll be!"

Then Sulayman rounded on him and said, "You scum! I shall
not kill you; I shall mutilate you as an example to others. He
then gave orders for his genitals to be removed, and thereafter
the monastery in which they were staying was known as "The
Monastery of the Eunuch". This episode was said to be the
occasion of a letter sent by Sulayman to his governor in Medina,
Ibn Hazm, ordering him to castrate all effeminate homosexuals
there. And so the genitals of Dalal ('Coquetry') his friends were
duly removed.

In his *Comparative Proverbs* Isfahani[7] tells the following tale:
When Sulayman gave orders for the person who had sung the
verses to be castrated the future Caliph 'Umar ibn 'Abd-ul-'Aziz
spoke up for clemency. But Sulayman retorted, "Hold your
tongue! What about the neighing of a horse and the response of
a mare on heat? Or the call of a stallion camel and the she-camel's

---

[7] Hamza ibn Hasan of Isfahan, a philologist and historian (c. 893-961).

excited response? In just the same way a man will wing and stir a woman's love in return." With no more ado he commanded that his prisoner be castrated.

In the same work Isfahani relates that Sulayman wrote to his governor in Medina in which he ordered a census (*yuḥṣī*) of dandies in the city. By an accidental blob of the scribe's pen the "ḥ" was changed to "kh" and the verb "to take a census" was read as "castrate". So when the letter reached Ibn Hazm, the governor forthwith castrated them all. But others say this wasn't so. It was the Caliph's intention, they allege, to have them castrated quite straightforwardly and decisively.

When Tuways ('Little Peacock') was castrated he commented, "Now comes a second circumcision.[8] I wish it had been done at the start." But Dalal retorted, "No, this is the Great Circumcision which every queer must suffer." Commented Nasim-ul-Sahar ('Dawn Breeze'), "We're now castrated queers, well and truly done." To which Nawmat-ul-Duha ('Forenoon Nap') replied, "We were queers, by God! But now we are women."[9] Whereat Jami'-ul-Uns ('Complete Companion') merely said, "Well, Nawmat, we shan't have to carry that downspout with us now!" "For God's sake, cut the chatter," retorted Ghusn-ul-Ban ('Ben-tree Branch'), "You're all so damned stupid and silly. What's the point of a useless tool?" Such is the tale of Isfaham.

Sahl ibn Harun[10] once said, "There are three types of fool, however wise they may be: the jealous, the choleric, and the toper." At that point the poet Khali',[10a] who happened to be present, interjected "What about the man with the sexual itch?" "The man with the sexual itch?" he laughed. "Well here's a verse:

[8] Muslims, like Jews, are circumcised for religious reasons.

[9] This would be a clean-cut castration, the penis and testicles being swept off with the single sweep of a razor. There were several types of castration both in antiquity and in the medieval period: some had the testicles removed or crushed; others had only the penis removed and were accordingly left with sexual desire but without the means to copulate; others had the whole lot removed.

[10] Probably the Librarian (d. 859 or 860) of the Scientific Academy (Bayt al-Hikma) of Baghdad.

[10a] "Debauched", nickname of the Basran poet Husayn b. Dahhak (d. 864?).

And yet your friend, whom you deny the dawn-draught,
O Umm 'Amr, is not the worst of the trio."[11]

He also said that jealousy and love of a woman could carry a
man to such lengths that he might make it his last will and
testament to his wife that she should never marry anyone after
his death or that she should never marry such-and-such a person
mentioned by name. He might bind her by oath or bind another
man by oath never to marry his widow. This sort of thing is
utterly stupid and foolish. It could have the opposite effect to
that intended in that it might only urge a woman to marry the
man in mind or cause both parties only to think of one another.

In his *History* Ibn Sa'i[12] relates the following story: Fatima
daughter of Husayn ibn 'Ali and sister of Sukayna, was a
favourite of Hasan, son of Hasan ibn 'Ali,[13] and when he was on
his death-bed he said to her, "You're a very desirable woman,
and, as I lie here, it is as though I see 'Abdullah ibn 'Amr ibn
'Uthman ibn 'Affan[14] at my graveside, having walked behind
my bier reciting his elegies and dressed in his finery. I see him
approach you. I command you—marry anyone you like but him.
Having said this, I can die in peace.' And so he made her swear
an oath to keep her promise and be faithful to her pledge. When
Hasan died, everything came to pass just as he had foretold in
his lifetime. Now 'Abdullah ibn 'Amr ibn 'Uthman was noted
for his handsome appearance and exceedingly good looks. When
he saw the woman beating her face in mourning,[15] he sent a
messenger to her to say "Don't beat your face, we have need of

---

[11] i.e. being a toper—the last-mentioned in the trio—is not the ultimate in
folly.

[12] Abu Talib Taj-ul-Din, an Iraqi historian (1197–1276), who wrote on the
last four Abbasid Caliphs of Baghdad and on the history of that capital.

[13] i.e. 'Ali's grandson and Fatima's cousin and husband.

[14] i.e. the the grandson of the Caliph 'Uthman.

[15] Strict Islamic teaching forbids lamentations, tearing of the hair, and
beating of the face. But these pre-Islamic practices were never wholly sup-
pressed despite repeated condemnations by theologians and jurists. In
Umayyad times women followed funerals doing precisely those things which
were condemned, and as time went on professional women mourners were
often employed.

it, so deal kindly with it." She let her hands drop at these words, and he took note. Later he married her after supplying her with two slaves for every one she had sworn by[16] and giving her twice as much of everything she stood to forfeit. She bore him Dibaj[17] Muhammad ibn 'Abdullah ibn 'Amr ibn 'Uthman ibn 'Affan— the man who was put to death by Abu Ja'far Mansur.[18] Both she and Sukayna died in the same year.

In his *Pivot of Delight* Raqiq[19] relates that Hadi[20] paid 100,000 dinars for his slave-girl Amat-ul-'Aziz, known otherwise as Ghadir. It is also said that she was a present from Rabi'.[21] In her day she was unsurpassable in beauty, and none could sing better than she, nor did anyone combine more talents of the kind required of such a girl. Harun Rashid,[22] it is said, was much taken by her, but he kept the fact a secret. So madly in love with her was Hadi that he had her sleep in his room and would not rouse her until she awoke. One day when Hadi was sitting with her in his room, his brother Harun was announced. At this she quickly slipped away to some nearby hiding place, and Harun then then entered the room, greeted his brother, and seated himself before him. "Harun", said Hadi, "I have a premonition that I just can't get out of my head, and its making my life a misery." "Why, what's the matter, Commander of the Faithful?" asked Harun. "It's my firm belief," said Hadi "that I shall die before very long and that you'll marry my wife Amat-ul-'Aziz as soon as I'm gone." "God make me your ransom and take me before you, Commander of the Faithful!" he exclaimed. "Don't let that worry you—it's not a nice thought. I hope and pray that I neither hear bad news of you nor feel the grievous blow of your death." "Well, there you are—I've told you," said Hadi. "What

[16] These would be self-imposed penalties for non-fulfilment of an under-taking made under oath.

[17] "Dibaj" (brocade) was a common nickname for a very handsome man.

[18] The second Abbasid Caliph.

[19] We should probably identify this person as Ibn Raqiq, a native of Kairouan in Tunisia who enjoyed a high reputation as a historian (d. after 1027).

[20] The fourth Abbasid Caliph (reg. 785–86).

[21] Hadi's vizier.

[22] See Ch. V, nn. 21 and 30.

will put your mind at rest?" asked Harun. "Faith, pledges and assurances," came the reply. At this Harun gave his brother the assurances he required—swearing by divorce, the performance of the Pilgrimage to Mecca on foot, the manumission of slaves, the giving of alms, and indeed every oath that would assure him.[23] And so Hadi's mind was put at rest, and a few days later he did in fact die. Harun immediately sent for the girl and proposed marriage. She reminded him of his oaths, but he merely said, "There's no real difficulty. I shall perform the Pilgrimage, I shall divorce, I shall manumit, and I shall give alms as I said I would." And so he divorced Zubayda and left her, freed the slaves Husayn and Surur, gave 100,000 dinars in alms, and during the same year he went on the Pilgrimage. The latter he performed on foot, treading mile after mile of felt that was laid down before him as he walked. In so doing he went through one whole year from beginning to end. The Pilgrimage over, he married Amatul-'Aziz. She was with him for only a short time when, one night as she was asleep in his lap, she awoke with a start in fear and trembling. "What's the matter?" he inquired. "Commander of the Faithful," she stuttered, "I saw your brother Hadi holding both handles of this door, and as he stood there, he addressed me with these words,

'Any man deceived hereafter by one of your fair sex, having
    seen the facts of *our* case, must be a dupe indeed!
Have you forgotten the pact we made that you could
    disregard your word to me? How ignoble can
    you be! And how few a dead man's friends!
May you never enjoy that wherein you now delight! And
    remember this, that every living creature must soon
    to the grave descend.' "

A year later—some say a month—she died. In his *History* Ibn Kardabus says it was the following verses which were actually spoken by Hadi in the dream:

[23] See above n. 16. Manumission of slaves was a frequent self-imposed penalty for breaking a sworn undertaking.

"Once I had joined the company of those who dwell
in graveyards, you broke your word to me.
To me you swore an oath which then, by sinful lies, you
were prepared to violate.
Traitorously you wed my brother, and truly spoke the
man who named you Traitor.[24]
May your new bedfellow bring no joy to you! May
Fortune beset you with woe!"

A woman's jealousy of a man can never attain the heights of
that of a man for a woman. It was this very reason that God permitted one man to marry four wives and to take as many concubines as he likes. For He knew that a woman's patience is great
enough to bear the burden. But He did not permit a woman to
look into the face of her husband's slave unveiled, for He knew
that the patience of the slave could not stand up to the strain.
Someone once said, "A woman's pleasure in love is proportionate
to her longing for it, and her jealousy proportionate to her
pleasure."

There is a Tradition that the Prophet said: "A jealous woman
does not know the top of a wadi from the bottom."[25] According
to 'A'isha, his wife, Muhammad once brought his son Ibrahim
to her and remarked, "See, 'A'isha, how like me he is." But,
carried away by the jealousy to which women are subject, she
turned to him saying, "I see no resemblance." According to
another Tradition in Muslim's *Corpus of Authentic Traditions*[26]
Muhammad once said to 'A'isha, "I know when you are pleased
with me and when you are annoyed." "But how?" she asked.
"Well, when you're pleased," he said, "you swear by the God of
Muhammad; but when you're annoyed you swear by the God of
Abraham." "You're right," agreed 'A'isha, "I just drop your
name." Judge 'Iyad says in his book *The Perfection*, " 'A'isha's
annoyance sprang from a woman's jealousy—may God forgive
women this sin!"

Malik and other religious scholars of Medina went so far as

[24] *Ghadir* means "treacherous", 'traitorous".
[25] i.e. totally confused and demented.
[26] See Ch. V, n. 47.

to exempt women from the Koranic penalty (*ḥadd*) for defamation if they wrongly accused their husbands of adultery out of jealousy.[27] They based their claim on the Tradition just quoted: "A jealous woman does not know the top of a wadi from the bottom." Had it not been for this, 'A'isha in her annoyance with the Prophet would have merited the gravest stricture; for, to display anger against the Prophet and to drop him [or his name] is a major sin. But the fact that she said, "I drop your name" indicates that she did not drop him from her heart. She only did what she did from jealousy generated by her great love of him. One of Tabari's sayings is: "Jealousy in women is forgivable. It is not a deliberately vicious trait nor one for which they should be punished, and this is so because they are jealous by nature and cannot help themselves." He then quotes the Tradition mentioned above: "A jealous woman does not know the top of a wadi from the bottom."

The author of *The Scattering of Pearls* records that 'Abdullah ibn Ja'far once said to his daughter, "Beware, my pet, of jealousy —it is the key to divorce. Also, take care not to be for ever at your husband's throat, for it leaves a legacy of rancour. One thing you must do is to groom yourself. Eye-black will enhance you most, and you will find water the best perfume." This last point has already been mentioned in the chapter dealing with beauty.

Anecdote related by Hisham ibn Hassan: Hafsa daughter of Sirin, the sister of Muhammad ibn Sirin,[28] used to say, "A free-born woman should consider the expression of jealousy beneath her dignity." She herself was once on the point of entering her own room when she found her husband on the bed with a slave-girl. She closed the door behind them and left. A few days later her husband beat the slave-girl for something or other. "Are you beating the bride?" asked the wife. With a shamefaced smile he

[27] False accusation of unchastity, i.e. unlawful coitus, is technically termed *cadhf*. It consists in an explicit accusation levelled at a free person who has never been guilty of unlawful intercourse. It is a crime against religion punishable by eighty lashes (forty for a slave). In the case of a woman the impugning of her child's legitimacy constitutes *qadhf*.

[28] See p. 117, n. 55.

turned to her and said "I can see you know. Take the girl as your own slave."

The following Tradition is related by Zubayr in *For Muwaffaq* on the authority of 'Abdullah ibn Nafi' ibn 'Abdullah ibn Mus'ab: While Harun was still heir to the Caliphate he complained to me that Umm Ja'far, his wife, had not yet conceived. My advice to him was to stir her to jealousy, and I supported my case by citing the story of Sarah and Abraham.[29] As Sarah had been unable to conceive, Abraham married Hagar and begot Ishmael by her. Sarah, stirred to jealousy, then conceived and bore Isaac. Harun listened to my advice and married Marajil, who conceived and bore him Ma'mun, while Zubayda then conceived and bore him Amin.[30]

Harun used to extol Umm Ja'far to the skies and stand in awe of her. He would say, "I often wish to embrace her in love, but then I feel overawed, and fear grips me so that I can do nothing at all when it comes to the point." Indeed, had it not been for his desire for children, he would not have aroused her jealousy by taking a concubine. She would warn her husband with the words, "Don't put me on the same level as your concubines, who are just there to satisfy your sexual desires and amuse you." Harun once said, "I used to dread even sitting on her bed—I had such great respect for her that she overawed me."

The following verses are from Abu Tammain's *Martial Courage* and are attributed by this anthologist to a poet from the Hejaz, though others attribute them to 'Umar ibn Abi Rabi'a:

> They told her I had married, and inwardly she almost
>   choked with rage.
> Bravely stifling her feeling, she turned to her sister and
>   said, "Would that he had married ten!"
> But to some of her ladies-in-waiting from whom she had
>   no secrets she said in confidence,
> "My heart now feels no longer part of me, and my bones
>   grow weak.
> A dreadful tale has reached my ears, and in my heart
>   I sense a searing burn from the blaze it has set alight."

[29] See Genesis xvi.
[30] Both were to become Caliphs, Ma'mun only after a bitter civil war.

Now the time is approaching when I must bring my book to a close and be done with the great prolixity in which we have indulged—leaving aside, of course, all the inevitable banter, jests, humorous tales, unusual anecdotes, the greater part of which relate to sexual union. There are perhaps few books in which there is no prolixity, but on the present topic such faults are pardonable since the purpose is to provide relaxation and an atmosphere of friendliness. People love unrestrained fun, and this book will undoubtedly cheer the depressed. It will also serve as a stimulant for those whose urge is somewhat flat. So, dear reader, as you dip into this book, treat its author with indulgence and forgive him his shortcomings—repetition and prolixity.

CHAPTER XVI

Diverse Entertaining Tales and Anecdotes

In his *Comparative Proverbs* Hamza ibn Hasan Isfahani relates the following story: Khawwat ibn Jubayr was in the market at 'Ukaz[1] when he came upon a girl who had skin bags displayed for sale. He took one from her, opened it, and inspected it. He then put it into one of her hands. He then took another and put it into her other hand. While both her hands were full, he lifted up her legs and thrust his penis in her. She, for her part, was completely helpless and unable to push him away for fear she might spill the olive oil that was contained in the bags. When he had finished the job and got up from her she cursed him with the words "May you have no joy of it!" It is from this incident that we have the proverb "More preoccupied than the girl with the bags and more scandalous than Khawwat." Another popular saying in the same vein is, "Keep a tight hold of your oil, you there with your bags!"

Khawwat, it is said, was a notorious Arab hooligan, of whom the Prophet once asked, "What have you done with your errant camel?"[2] "Islam", he replied, "has hobbled it."[3] The following verse spoken by Khawwat is quoted by Abu 'Umar in one of his books:

> She fastened a miserly hand on each bag, and so I raped
> her true to my style.

---

[1] A famous place near Mecca where a great fair lasting twenty days was a regular event.　　　　　　　　[2] The background to this remark is given below.

[3] i.e. "The religious precepts of Islam have now checked my outrageous conduct."

We are told that Khawwat was the son of Jubayr ibn Nu'man ibn Umayya[4] and that he served in the Prophet's cavalry.

Ya'qub ibn Sikkit[5] enlarges on the story we have just told. According to his version in the *Correction of Logic* "The Two-Bag Girl" came from the tribe of Taym Allah ibn Tha'laba. Moreover, the following story is related by Rushati[6] in his *Borrowing of Lights* and by 'Umar ibn Shabba[7] in his *History of Medina*: The Prophet was once on a raid and he caught sight of Khawwat chatting to some women under a thorn-tree in a place called Zahran. When asked by the Prophet what he was doing there, Khawwat replied, "I'm trying to find a she-camel for my stallion." Knowing full well that Khawwat had no camel at all either male or female, Muhammad remarked, "Has your camel not stopped its wandering yet?" Khawwat was embarrassed, but ever after the Prophet would repeat the remark in jest. And so it happened that one day when he jokingly asked Khawwat, "What's happened to your errant camel?" Khawwat replied, "Islam has hobbled it, Messenger of God."

Similar to the famous curse uttered by the woman he raped —"May you have no joy of it!" is the one which runs "May the lad not come to manhood nor even bring joy to his mother!" In the following story lies the explanation: Ibn Kalbi[8] relates that Hamama ibn Rafi' of Daws was one of the most handsome of Arabs. He was endowed with exuberant hair which he would regularly wash, and every other day he would let it down and have his attendants drench it with perfume. Whilst riding his horse on pilgrimage to Mecca, he was espied by Khinas of Kinana who was known as "the Beauty" because of her looks. At the time she was already betrothed to one of her own tribesmen who was passionately in love with her. Upon meeting Hamama he was asked by her "Who are you? By God, I have never seen a face more handsome than yours, no hair more glorious, no horse

---

4 The rest of his name is given as "ibn Imrul-Qays al-Ansari al-Awsi".

5 Abu Yusuf Ya'qub ibn Ishaq, an authority on grammar (d. between 857 and 861) and tutor to the son of the Caliph Mutawakkil.

6 A Spanish Arab of Almeria (1075–1147).

7 Abu Zayd, a poet of Basra (d. 876) and authority on historical traditions.

8 A great authority on Arab lore and history (d. between 819 and 822).

more elegant! Who ever can you be?" "I am one of the tribe of Azd," he answered. "You have thrown upon my back," she said, "a burden I cannot bear, and you have found a place in my heart. Please take me with you—I can't bear to be without you." So he took her off to his town, and in due course she bore him a son, 'Umar ibn Hamama. The first man to whom she was betrothed meanwhile had gone in search of her, and when he heard of her and her child, he gave voice to the following lines:

> "Greetings from me to Khinas—for all that she dislikes
> me! Greetings, even though she be gone and far away.
> They tell me she has had a son—may the lad not come
> to manhood nor bring his mother joy!"

On hearing these two verses 'Umar ibn Khattab observed, "Despite the imprecation, the boy both grew to manhood and brought his mother joy."

In his *Borrowing of Lights* Rushati writes: The False Prophet Musaylima[9] was known in the days before Islam as Rahman. When the Prophet called upon him to embrace Islam he refused to drop his claim and said, "Both of us are prophets. I shall believe in those who believe in me. In due course the Prophet died, and the tribe of Tamim argued and disagreed about what action should be taken against apostates.[10] Meanwhile a woman called Sajah daughter of Suwayd ibn Yarbu' appeared among them, laying claim to the gift of prophecy among the warriors of the tribe of Tha'lab. This only made matters worse. In her "Book" she said the following verse had been revealed: "You that are God-fearing and believe, half the world belongs to us and the other half to Quraysh. But Quraysh are a people who deal not justly." So Tamim agreed unanimously to help her. Among them were chiefs and notables such as Ahnaf ibn Qays, Haritha ibn Badr, 'Utarid ibn Habib and others of such standing. The situation is described by 'Utarid in the line:

[9] See above Ch. VI, n. 15, p. 138.

[10] After the death of the Prophet many tribes of the Arabian Peninsula are supposed to have apostatized, though in fact they were probably only being brought into the fold of Islam. Several claimants to prophethood had to be dealt with.

We are left with a woman for a Prophet and her we
circumambulate[11] when the prophets of men who
matter are men.

Sajah's muezzin was Shabath ibn Rib'i. On one occasion she
said to Tamim, "Hearken, mark and inwardly digest what has
been revealed to me, for in it you will find relief from the cares
in your breasts." She also said, "O ye people prepare to mount,
and be ready to plunder and attack Dhiyab[12] who have nothing
to stand between them and attack." She stood firmly in the
battle that followed and slew many of them. Then she followed
it up with another sura "To Yamama". She had been told the
might of Yamama was great and that Musaylima had become a
mighty danger there. And so she said, "These words have been
revealed to me, O tribe of Tamim. To Yamama hasten, and like
pigeons fly. And there strike every herd and burn it with con-
suming fire, and no blame shall fall on you thereafter." So
Tamim went with her to Yamama. And when Musaylima heard
the news he lost his head, became helpless and sought refuge in
the safety of the fort of Yamama. So she was able to surround
him with her army, while he could only send for the notables of
his people and ask their advice on what to do next. "Men of
Thaqif," he said, "What have you to say about this Sajah?"
"We think," said they, "that it is best to concede defeat and
escape while you may. Otherwise we are doomed." To this he
replied, "Let me wait and see." He then sent her a letter from
which the following is an extract: "Each of us—both you and I
—are inspired by God. So come now let us get together and
examine what has been revealed to us. Wherever there is occasion for one to accept the case of the other as better, let the one
follow the other and we shall become one fabric. Then with your
people and mine we shall overwhelm the Arabs." When Sajah
received his letter she wrote back agreeing to his demands.

Next he ordered a hide pavilion to be set up and bade that it
be made fragrant with the burning of aloes wood. "Don't spare

[11] An allusion to circumambulation of the Kaaba (above Ch. XI, n. 19,
p. 203).
[12] Or, more correctly, Dhi'ab, a South Arabian tribe.

the fragrance," he said. "For when a woman takes in fragrance her mind shifts to copulation." And so in due course she came to the pavilion and asked him what had been revealed to him.[13] Whereupon he quoted: "Have you not considered your Lord and His works with the woman in labour? Out of her He brings forth a living spirit, emerging from her inmost tissues and entrails. It is He who gives life and death." "What next?" she asked He went on "Have you not considered God, how He has created us in our several groups and made women to be our wives to go deep within as we wish and to come out therefrom as we desire?"

And then he went off into verse with the words,

> "Come on, let's copulate; the bed is laid. On your back,
>   if it please you, or down on all fours,
> With penis full in, or three parts of the way—in prostrate
>   position or with hands on your knees."

"With penis full in," she replied. "That is the revelation that came to me and which I am bidden to obey." He then coupled with her, and when he had finished she said, "This is not the union for a lady of my standing, for this will besmirch the name of my tribe. I shall surrender to you my claim to prophethood, and when I do so, take me to yourself in marriage." And so it came to pass, and they went out. Then the tribes of Hanifa and Tamim met, and Sajah said, "He recited to me what had been revealed to him, and I found it true and have therefore followed him. So they asked him the bride-price, and his response was "The exemption I grant you from the afternoon prayer." Rushati comments that the tribe of Tamim right up to today—they live in the Raml[14]—do not perform the afternoon prayer, for they argue "It is our right and the bride-price of a sister of ours. Do not repudiate it."

Abu Nukhayla of 'Ukl[15] gives us the following verses in his *Dictionary of Poets*:

---

[13] i.e. in a spurious revelation from God.

[14] 'The Sands' – desert without pasture – a name often applied by the Bedouin to the northern part of the great south desert of Arabia.

[15] A poet of the eighth century who composed in the *rajaz* metre.

Sajah, a prophetess, met the false prophet, and then
  abandoned the Book.
She made her vagina a scabbard in which he sheathed his
  penis deep.

In Mu'awiya's reign she embraced Islam and turned out to be a
good convert.

According to Abu Faraj in his *Songs*, the following story is
told by a man whose narrative runs thus: "Once I went out with
Sayyid Himyari[16] and we met the daughter of Fuja'a.[17] She was
unveiled and radiantly beautiful. Himyari asked her to stop and
listen to him recite some of his verses. Each was much taken by
the other, so he then asked her to marry him. 'How,' she asked,
'can we do this here on the road?' 'It will be like Umm
Kharija's marriage,' he replied. 'Someone said to her, "I ask
your hand in marriage," and she replied, "I accept".'[18] So
Himyari's companion then scratched her head and said, 'I shall
consider the matter further, and keep it in mind. But who are
you?' He then introduced himself, whereupon she exclaimed,
'How remarkable! A man from the Yemen and a woman from
Tamim![19] A Rafidite and an Ibadite![20] How could such a pair ever

[16] Sayyid Isma'il ibn Muhammad, a poet who died before 786.

[17] The full name is given as Ibnat Fuja'a bint 'Amr ibn Qatari ibn Fuja'a.
She was the granddaughter of Qatari ibn Fuja'a, chief of the Azraquite rebels
of East Persia, who led a revolt in 686 and was killed in 698.

[18] Umm Kharija of the Bajila tribe is a legendary or semi-legendary nymphomaniac who is said to have contracted marriages in more than twenty tribes.
The first story related about her here is not told as clearly as it might have
been. What happened—supposedly—is that a man once proposed marriage to
her and that she agreed to contract the marriage without witnesses or legal
guardian (see Ch. IV, n. 17) and to consummate it there and then.

[19] The Himyarites were of Yemen in the south-west of the Arabian Peninsula while Tamim were from the north-east and thus diametrically opposed.

[20] Rafidites—"Rejecters"—an early Islamic group who rejected the first
Caliphs. In time the term became synonymous with "Shi'ites". The Ibadites,
on the other hand, were an offshoot of the Kharijites, an early sect opposing
the notion that the Caliph must be of the Prophet's tribe of Quraysh. They
held puritanical and democratic ideas. In rough terms we could say that the
Rafidites and Ibadites were comparable—in the present context—to the
Catholics and Protestants of Northern Ireland. The Azraqites (above n. 17)
were extreme Kharijites, the latter having split into Ibadites and Azraqites in
684.

unite?' 'There's no problem,' he replied. 'Neither of us will mention the other's religion or lineage.' 'Ah, but I know,' she said, 'that when the curtains are drawn and that which is covered uncovered, the clothes are lifted from what men wish to see.'[21] 'Well then,' he said 'I'll make another suggestion.' 'Go on,' she said, 'There is,' he suggested, '*mut'a* marriage which none will know about.'[22] 'But that's next to adultery,' she cried. 'God forbid,' he rejoined, 'that you should give up your faith.' 'How come?' she asked. So he recited the following verse from the Koran: 'Such as you enjoy thereby, give them their wages apportionate.'[23] 'I am prepared now,' she said, 'to let God decide the issue. I shall obey Him.' She then went with him, and he had his way with her."

The story of her behaviour spread among her people the Kharijites, who threatened to kill her. Yet she kept on meeting him clandestinely and without her people's knowledge whenever she had the opportunity. What a difference between this Kharijite and the other of whom Qatari said,

> "By your life, I am an ascetic renouncing the pleasures
> of this world so long as I don't cross the path of Umm
> Hakim."

This Umm Hakim was noted for her beauty, but she hated men. There was not a Kharijite of rank or station who did not ask her hand. Yet she refused the lot and used to say,

> "Ah, such a face have I, endowed by God with beauty
> fair, that you will find there all the beauty you desire.
> This body I respect too much to yield it to the gripping
> legs of some strapping lad who only wants to ride
> it with his own."

---

[21] i.e. all secrets are revealed upon marriage, and everyone will soon know the truth.

[22] Mut'a is a marriage contracted for a specified term in consideration of a given sum payable to the woman. It is not admissible in Sunnite Islam, but the Shi'ite Twelvers (see above Ch. V, n. 15, p. 103) recognize it.

[23] Koran, iv, 28. In actual fact there is good reason to suppose that Sunnite Islam did not reject *mut'a* marriage till more than a century after the Prophet's death.

As regards the words "like Umm Kharija's wedding" Bakri says that the incident with the man who proposed to her gave rise to a proverb "Quicker than Umm Kharija's wedding". Umm Kharija was good looking enough and much sought after by men, but they just could not keep up with her sexual demands and so divorced her as fast as they could. It is said that after one of her husbands had divorced her she set off with one of her sons back to her tribe. On the way she saw a man riding towards her. At this she turned to her son and asked, "Is this a suitor seeking my hand? Do you think he will undo his clothes before I have him in marriage? Do you think he's getting a move on?" she asked her son. The latter ignored her. It is said that she bore children to husbands of so many different tribes that there was scarcely anyone who did not have some of her blood in him.

In his *Borrowing of Lights* Rushati writes: Hanzala ibn Malik, an old man, married a fair and buxom woman. One night in wind and rain she went out to put her tent right, and all she had on was a bodice. As she leaned over the tent peg she parted her legs, and at that moment she was espied by Malik ibn 'Amr ibn Tamim just as she was bending right over with her vulva bulging from her behind like the lower lip of a camel. He immediately leapt upon her and drove his penis in. She for her part made not the slightest attempt to resist but remained absolutely still. When he had done with her, she turned to him and said,

> "O Hanzala ibn Malik, what heat it has to soothe on a
> night as cold as this!"

[Upon hearing the sound of her voice], out came her sons and her husband. "Whatever's the matter?" they asked. "I've just been stung," she replied. "Where?" they queried. "Just where a witchdoctor shouldn't poke his nose" came the answer. This reply became proverbial.

The following story is related by Abu 'Ali in his *Dictations*: Hammam ibn Murra ibn Dhuhl ibn Shayban had three daughters who were still maidens because he would not give them in marriage. So one day they got together to see what they might do about it. Said the eldest, "The only thing to do is for me to give him a verse of poetry so that we can be off from here." So when her father came in, she put her cheek to his and said:

> "Hammam ibn Murra, my desire is to join those that are
> the possessions of men."

"Men, my dear" said he, "possess dirhams and dinars, and swords and things like that. You don't make yourself clear." The middle girl commented, "Well, you've not got us far." Whereupon she came forward and beckoned her father, saying, "Hammam ibn Murra, I long for that which is slender and high of neck."[24] "Perhaps my dear," said her father "it is a mare or a beast of some kind you are wanting." At that she said no more, and then the youngest came forward and said, "By God, neither of you two has made any progress or done anything to brag about!" So then she approached her father, beckoned him, and said: "Hammam ibn Murra, I long for a penis to stop my waterhole." When the father heard what his youngest had to say no further comment was required. So he forthwith went and married them off.

Another tale of this is told by Abu 'Ali in his *Dictations*: There was once an Arab who had three daughters whom he would not marry off or allow to be espoused to their equals.[25] Said one of them, "If our father persists in treating us thus, we'll lose our chance of marriage. We must tell him how we feel and just hope that he will show some response and come to his senses." Now the Bedouin was in the habit of going to see one daughter one day and another the other day. So the day he visited the eldest she greeted him and paid him due respect, and then they sat down. He talked with her for a while, and then just as he was about to depart she recited to him these two verses,

> "Our playmates chide us—no love is allowed, yet men
> to us are as brothers.[26]

[24] i.e. the penis.
[25] See above, p. 145, n. 31.
[26] The interpretation of these words is given below.

We are buried alive, not once but many times, when
some girls are married and already divorced. Oh, the
injustice of it all!"

The father was deeply hurt by what he heard, and departed in
sorrow and anger. The next day he visited the middle daughter.
She greeted him respectfully, and they then sat and talked. Then
just as he was about to go she made so bold as to recite,

"Young men, your girl feels the call of lovers' talk and
feels a longing.
Take her and find some strong-hearted lad, for, if you do
not, she will feel the urge to take a lover and fall
victim to his passion."

The father was deeply hurt by what he heard, and departed in
sorrow and anger. He went off to his own quarters in a state of
great agitation. He could not sleep, nor did he know which way
to turn. The next morning he went to the apartment of the
youngest who greeted him with due respect. They then sat down
and talked a while. As he was about to leave, she made so bold
as to recite these verses,

"Can my two sisters not coerce a man? Can they not bring
this old man to his senses, if senses he has?
There is either lawful wedlock or the inevitable pursuit
of passion—and that must surely follow. So consider
the course you will take."

When he realized they were in league against him, he married
them there and then.

As to the words "men to us are as brothers" it occurs in a
Tradition of the Prophet reported by Abu Dawud on the
authority of 'A'isha: Once the Prophet was asked whether the
greater ablution[27] was necessary for a man who found himself
wet in the morning, though he had no recollection of a nocturnal
emission. He affirmed that it was. Then he was asked about a
man who had an emission but found himself dry on waking. In

27 See Ch. II, n. 40, p. 56.

such a case, he said that the greater ablution was unnecessary. Umm Sulaym asked, "And what about a woman who experiences such a thing? Must she perform the major ablution?" "Yes," replied the Prophet. "Women are brothers to men."[28]

In his *Songs* Abu Faraj relates the following story: Hind, the daughter of Nu'man ibn Mundhir, was the most beautiful girl of her day. Her mother was Maria of Kinda, who had embraced the Christian religion. Now one Maundy Thursday when she was eleven years old she went to church to receive communion. At that same time 'Adi ibn Zayd[29] had just arrived, bringing numerous gifts from Chosroes[30] to Nu'man. 'Adi was then a strapping young man with broad shoulders, a fine head of hair, soft eyes and a pleasant smile. It so happened that he went into church to receive communion at the same time as Hind, who was well made and buxom. 'Adi spotted her and fixed his eyes upon her as she took her place completely oblivious of his attentions. Her slave-girls had seen him come in but said nothing to her because one of them happened to be smitten by him. When she did spot 'Adi gazing at her she trounced her slave-girls and left them nothing short. 'Adi for his part could not get Hind out of his mind, but for a year he said nothing to anyone.

When Easter Week came round again, Hind prepared to go to church once more, whereupon some of her slave-girls rushed to tell 'Adi ibn Zayd. He rushed off to church, quite unable to believe that he would see Hind, so great was his longing for her. Dressed in his best attire and accompanied by a group of companions from Hira, he entered the church and spotted Hind and her girls. "My lady, just look!" they cried. "Just look at this gorgeous young man. Why, he's so handsome he puts all these images in church to shame." Hind turned and looked at him and asked who he was and all about him. "He's 'Adi," she was told. "How *can* you do this to me!" she cried out to one of her girls. "Why ever bring him and me together when you must know that I'll die if I don't have him!" The girl lost no time in telling

---

[28] i.e. they are of the same species, and, like man, they emit seminal fluid. On this erroneous notion see Ch. XIII, n. 13, p. 245.

[29] A Christian from a noble tribe of Hira and seventh-century poet.

[30] The King of Persia.

Hind's father and recounting the whole tale—how she was madly in love with 'Adi and how she had first fallen for him through seeing him in church on Maundy Thursday. She declared that if he didn't marry Hind to him they would both be at the centre of a scandal. "Go and offer her in marriage to 'Adi," the girl urged Hind's father. "Don't be silly," he replied. "How can I approach him?" "But he's so keen too," she persisted. "I'll do what I can without letting him know that you know anything." With that she departed and went off to 'Adi to tell him the tale. "Invite him round," she said, "and when he's had a drink or two, ask him for his daughter's hand. I'm sure he won't turn you down!" So 'Adi took her advice and got in some food for a gathering. He then went to Nu'man and asked him to go along with some of his friends. Nu'man and his friends accepted the invitation, and when they had drunk sufficiently deeply, 'Adi approached Nu'man and asked his daughter's hand in marriage. The father willingly consented, and three hours later took her in his embrace.

For three years 'Adi stayed in his father-in-law's household until he met his death at his hands—and therein lies a long tale. After her husband's death Hind took the veil and entered a convent which she built for herself on the outskirts of Hira and which was named after her. There she remained until her death, which occurred a long time after the Islamic conquest in the days of Mughira's governorship at Kufa.[31] Mughira sent a messenger to ask for her hand, but she declined his offer by saying, "Had you known that I had still some modicum of youth or beauty, I should have made you desire me. But you merely want me so that you can boast on public high days and holidays that you took possession not only of the kingdom of Nu'man ibn Mundhir but also of his daughter."

The story goes that this Hind fell in love with Zarqa'u-l-Yamama,[32] and that she was the first Arab Lesbian—a point which has already been mentioned.

[31] A marginal note indicates Mughira ibn Shu'ba, who fought in the battle of Qadisiyya in 637 and was later governor of Kufa.

[32] i.e. "The Blue-eyed Girl of Yamama". On this story see Ch. I, where she is just referred to vaguely as the daughter of Hasan Yamani.

An amusing tale is told by ibn Jawzi in his book *The Sharp-Witted*: 'Abdullah ibn Rawaha[33] was in bed with his wife, and, while she was asleep, he slipped out and went to a room where he bedded with a concubine of his. His wife woke up to find him gone. So she took a poker and went after him. She caught him just as he was slipping back and cried, "By God, if I'd caught you where you've just been, I'd have run you through the belly with this!" "But why on earth?" he asked. "Because," she said, you've been with your concubine." "Oh no, I haven't," he protested. "But I saw you with my own eyes," she persisted. "No, no, no, not at all." he kept on. "Well then," she said, "if you are inno-cent, then let me test you by asking you to recite some Koran to prove you're telling the truth, for the Messenger of God forbade anyone ritually polluted[34] to recite the Koran." So 'Abdullah recited the following [fake Koranic] verses:

"Among us is God's Messenger to recite His Book as clearly as the light of the day is scattered abroad at dawn. He has brought light after darkness, and our hearts now believe that, even as He has said, so it has happened. He spends his night away from bed, for only polytheists are held by their couches."

Upon hearing these words she gasped "I believe in God and give my sight the lie. 'Abdullah said, "I went and told the story to the Messenger of God, who, upon hearing it, threw back his head and laughed till his ribs ached."

A similar story is related in the *Songs* of Abu Faraj: Husayn ibn Dahhak[35] recounts the following anecdote.

"Once I was on night duty at Wathiq's palace when a eunuch came and roused me and told me I was wanted by the Caliph. 'Why, what's the matter?' I asked. Whereupon he told me that the Caliph was in bed with one of his concubines when he took it into his head to slip away. Thinking she was asleep, he crept out

[33] An energetic and upright champion of Muhammad's cause in Medina. As second-in-command in the Mu'ta expedition (629) he met his death in the field. He was a vigorous satirist of Quraysh—then hostile to Muhammad, although he was one of them.

[34] As would be the case if he had had intercourse.

[35] Well-known poet (c. 778-864) who started his career as a favourite of the Abbasid Caliph Harun.

to go and bed with another for a short while. When he returned to his bed, the girl had left in a rage and retired to her own room, and so when he awoke a short time later he found her gone. He asked where she was and was told she had left in a temper and gone to her own room. 'That,' said the eunuch, 'is why he has sent for you.'" Ibn Dahhak continued: "I left immediately and on my way I thought up some suitable verses. Upon arrival the Caliph told me the whole story and commanded me to compose a poem. I bowed my head in silence as though putting together a line or two, and then lifted my head and recited,

> 'She was wrathful just because I paid one visit to another.
> I confess I was wrong and will do my best to please and
>   make amends
> O you for whom I'd give my very life it was all a mistake.
> Forgive me, I pray, and let bygones be bygones.
> You have roused me from my sleep, and my heart is
>   consumed with fire.'

"The Caliph was pleased with these verses and commanded me to repeat them until he had them by heart. He then left and quoted them to his concubine, who found them pleasing. Thereafter, whenever I crossed his path he would smile as if to let me know how much my verses had found favour with his concubine."

Mubarrad relates that Ishaq ibn Fadl[36] told the following tale: "I once had a concubine with whom I was deeply in love. Yet, at the same time, I stood in awe of my wife, who was my cousin. One night while on my bed I suddenly thought of my concubine. So I got up, but as soon as I touched the floor I was stung by a scorpion and shot back on the bed with a groan. My wife woke up and asked me what was the matter. So I told her that I had been stung by a scorpion. 'Were you on the bed when it stung you?' she asked. 'No,' said I. 'Well, come on now, tell me the truth. What were you doing?' she inquired. And she went on and on till I told her the whole tale. She burst out laughing and recited,

[36] An early Abbasid poet.

'When those who reside in my house lie fast asleep, it is
   the scorpion that exacts the penalties for sin.
The house's scorpions are there to watch, should someone
   with a craving make a slip.'

"She then called her slave-girls to tell them that she had
resolved to forbid them to kill a scorpion for the rest of that year."

Bayhaqi[37] in *The Calices* recounts the following story:
'Abdullah ibn 'Umar was a most serious man of unblemished
character with no time at all for ribald or bawdy jests. One day
he was brought a piece of paper by Ibn Abi 'Atiq,[38] a humourist
notorious for his jokes. On the paper was written the following
lines:

"The One God has taken away your living. How you have
   gambled with your heart!
How foolishly you have thrown away your substance on
   whores and wine!"

In actual fact the lines had actually been penned by Ibn Abi
'Atiq's wife, 'Atika of Makhzum. "Look at this bit of paper, Abu
'Abd-ul-Rahman," he commented, "and tell me what I should
do with the scoundrel who wrote them." After reading the note
Ibn 'Umar gasped with horror, but said, "Just forgive and forget.
"No," said Ibn Abi 'Atiq, "I shan't. If ever I meet the writer of
this note I'll ride him till my rage is spent!" Ibn 'Umar almost
exploded. Whatever's the matter with you, man? Are you mad?"
"By God," averred Ibn Abi 'Atiq, "I shall do exactly as I've
said." The two men then parted. A few days later Ibn 'Umar
saw Ibn Abi 'Atiq and did his best to avoid him. But Ibn 'Atiq
shouted to him, "By the way, Abu 'Abd-ul-Rahman, I was the
writer of those verses, and I rode that person twice just to keep
my oath." Ibn 'Umar was aghast, but then Ibn Abi 'Atiq went
over to him and whispered, "The writer was my wife." Ibn
'Umar heaved a sigh of relief, and with a smile kissed him on the

[37] A biographer from Bayhaq (west of Nishapur in Iran) who lived 1100–
1169 or 1170.
[38] See Ch. XII, n. 42.

brow. "Well done, good sir." said he. "Carry on with the good work."

Ibn Durayd[39] relates a story told by 'Abd-ul-Rahman, who heard it from Asma'i: There was once a woman who loved to compete with men in posing riddles, and in this game she hardly ever lost. On one occasion a man came up to her and said, "I'll take you on." "All right," she said, "you start." So he said "*Kāda*" [which means in Arabic to "be near to being"]. "The bridegroom was near to being a prince," she continued. Whereupon he took up the same word again, and the way she went on was as follows, "The traveller was near to being a prisioner." So with his move he repeated *kāda*, and she came up with "The rhetoric was near to being magic." The man turned away and was about to leave when the woman caught him and said, "Now I'll take you on." "All right," said he. "I am amazed,' she said. Taking it up, he went on, "I am amazed at stone, for small stones never get bigger and big ones never get smaller." "I am amazed," she repeated, to which he rejoined, "I am amazed at salt marshes, for they neither provide pasture nor do they ever dry up." Again she said, "I am amazed." "I am amazed," he said, "at a hole between your legs, for one can grow weary with digging, yet never reach the bottom." At this she was utterly abashed and gave up her game of competing with men.

A Bedouin once saw a man coupling with a woman and was later asked what he saw. To this he replied, "With the front of his body he drew her, and with the back he dug her, but I saw nothing of the path between them." Another Bedouin answered the same question differently: "I saw he'd gone into her belly, I spotted an anklet in the air, and I heard fast breathing, but that's all I can say."

One of the witnesses who testified against Mughira was asked what he saw. His answer ran: "I saw him lying between the legs of a woman and he rose and fell. I saw two dyed feet,[40] two naked bottoms, and an anklet in the air as he heaved up and

[39] Celebrated philologist and lexicographer of Basra (837-933) whose major work is a monumental dictionary. He was of pure Arab stock.

[40] They would have been treated with henna (see Ch. IV, n. 13, p. 79). The politically motivated sexual charge brought against Mughira, an Umayyad public figure, is, incidentally, historical fact.

down, and I could hear the gasps as they held each other tight. That is all I can say. But were it not for fear of perjuring myself, I would say that he was in as far as the down on her pubis. Again, I couldn't really say that I saw his penis in her passage because his testicles obscured the view. And again, were it not for fear of incurring the penalty for perjury, I'd say he laid her at her own suggestion and hadn't constrained her in any way."

In his *Primary Feather of the Wing* Tifashi writes: Dahna', daughter of Mishal, charged her husband—the son of her father's brother, 'Ajjaj—with impotence, and brought him for judgement before the governor of Yamama. Her allegations was that since her wedding night he had never been near her. She was openly supported in her claim by her father, who, for his pains, was rebuked by the folk of Yamama. "Have you no shame," they cried, "that you demand intercourse for your daughter?" "I want her to bear children," he retorted. "For if they should die before me, I should be recompensed for my patience in the face of loss, while if they survive me, they would be an asset to their mother." When his daughter appeared before the judge, she pleaded that she was still *virgo intacta*. "Maybe you resist the good man's advances" suggested the governor." "Never", she replied. "I relax my vagina and brace my loins.' "She's a liar, Emir!" cried out the husband. I have to wrestle with her in the finest styles of wrestling." To cover up for the husband, the governor deferred judgement for a further year. The husband jauntily left the court reciting,

> "Did Dahna' and her father Mishal think that the Emir
> 　　would pass hasty judgement merely on the grounds
> 　　of inertia,
> When even the sturdiest stallion of unequalled pedigree
> 　　may at times be tardy in mounting his mare?"

He then began to embrace his wife and kiss her like a man. Whereat she commented,

> "By God, don't give me your fraudulent hugs, your
> 　　smothering kisses and snivels!

> Only the glittering blade of a penis can bring me consolation
>   and ease my tension to the point that even rings
>   would slip off and drop into my sleeves."

'Ajjaj took her off to his people and divorced her that very night for fear of exposure.

Bakri in his *Pearls* has verses on the very same theme:

> Neither dalliance nor gifts of robes will profit a woman
> Unless knees are pressed to knees and private parts meet
>   private parts
> And a penis wet with juices comes forth from where
>   it went.

Again we have similar verses by Hudba ibn Khashram,[41] quoted by Jawhari[42] in his dictionary called *The Unblemished*:

> Neither charms nor amulets can soothe the burning
>   passion of a heart,
> Nor talk nor close-togetherness—lovers must embrace
>   and kiss,
> And if they kiss they must unite to consummate their
>   love, and legs must lie on legs.

In his book called *Pleasure* Ibn Abi Waki'[43] quotes the following verses spoken by a woman of the tribe of Dabba:

> To be alone one night and spend one day with Ibn Wa'ili
>   will soothe my heart.
> In some nook or crannie out of sight I'll couch his head
>   on my left arm and leave my right hand free to lift
>   his clothes.
> From the moisture of his mouth I'll suck honey sweet
>   and pure that savours of delight,
> Then push my belly close to his, and, once I lead, the rest
>   will follow easily.

---

[41] A well-known Umayyad poet patronized by the Caliph Mu'awiya (reg. 661–80).

[42] A renowned Arabic lexicographer of Turkish stock (d. *c.* 1006) whose dictionary was greatly esteemed and for long widely used.

[43] The reading of this name is uncertain.

I'll put his hand to a tender spot that rises like a mountain
    to a peak,
And then he'll hold me tightly in his grip till my knees are
    pushed back to my ribs
And he'll sweep me along the torrent-bed till my locks are
    thick with dust.

In the *Songs* Abu Faraj writes: Ta'abbata Sharran[44] was once
much smitten with a girl from his own tribe. For some time he
chased her, but could not get his way. And then one night she
agreed to do as he desired. But when he came at last to consummate their union, he found he could not perform, and
nothing could stir him to action. He was greatly put out and
embarrassed by his impotence. For her part, the girl in her turn
did her best to console him and dispel his depression. But he
addressed his penis and said,

"Wretched organ that you are, may you never again
    have a friend! How could you let me down with a girl
    so comely and buxom?
—A girl who made for you with hasty step even as some
    gazelle makes for water in haste to take a second draught.
Had she been grazing in amongst a herd, you would
    have been as sturdy and thick as any goodly staff."

In a similar vein are the following lines by Tha'alibi:

I have a penis—God deliver me from it!—which has
    brought me nothing but trouble right and left.
When my beloved comes to me, it purposely decides to
    sleep, though upon my word it serves the messenger
    who makes our assignation.
To my utter chagrin the occasion was accounted a lovers'
    tryst, but both went their way with passion unallayed.

Musa ibn 'Isa once went to sleep with a girl of his, but could

---

[44] Famous pre-Islamic poet whose name as given is a sobriquet meaning
"He put a mischief under his arm"—a nickname for which several explanations
are given.

not perform when it came to the point. His verses run as follows:

> What a penis! How helpless it is!
> With my fingers I urge it to rise, and up it comes tightly
> in my grip,
> And then it goes flat once again.

Haytham ibn 'Adi[45] relates the following story: The Umayyad Caliph 'Abd-ul-Malik ibn Marwan was a passionate womanizer. But when he aged, his prowess grew weaker, though his passion for girls grew stronger. One day Ayman ibn Khuraym[46] came in, and 'Abd-ul-Malik asked him, "Well, Ayman, how are you?" "Very well, Commander of the Faithful," replied Ayman. "And how goes your strength?" 'Abd-ul-Malik asked. "Thank God, just as I would wish it," answered Ayman. "I can still devour a young lamb, ride a long run on a difficult camel, and deflower a virgin. Age will not keep me from her nor does the thought of coitus deter me from staying with her." 'Abd-ul-Malik was so enraged and envious that he stopped his allowance and banished him from the royal presence. The matter so disturbed Ayman that his wife asked "Whatever's the matter with you? Have you committed some crime?" "Indeed I haven't," came the reply. "Well, have you had some difference with the Commander of the Faithful then?" "Yes," he said, and he told her the story. "Ah, that's where you went wrong," she exclaimed. "The man envies you of all you said you could do. But I'll scheme to restore you to favour."

She then dressed and groomed herself and went off to see 'Atika, the wife of the Commander of the Faithful. "I beg of you," she said, "to intercede for me with the Caliph against my husband." "What is it that you want exactly?" the Caliph's wife inquired. "Well," said she "I don't know whether I'm living with a man or a stone wall. It's years since he joined me either in discussion or in bed, or removed my clothes. So now I've decided to leave him." So 'Atika went to 'Abd-ul-Malik and

---

[45] An authority on Arab tribal lore and poetry, who came from Kufa (d. 822 or 823).

[46] Poet of the tribe of Asad.

told him the story and asked his advice. At this he sent a message to Ayman setting forth his wife's complaint against him, and Ayman admitted the charges. "But surely," 'Abd-ul-Malik said later, "Did I not question you on this very point? And didn't you tell me all that you could do?" "Yes, I did, Commander of the Faithful," replied Ayman. "A man must put on his best front in the presence of his ruler and in the face of his enemies, and so I exaggerated. But I have said in my verses,

> 'I could have worked wonders with singing girls, had
>   they only caught me in my youth.
> But in one's old age all women of beauty are a great
>   burden to bear.
> If they don't get from him what they want, they become
>   so difficult and obstinate.
> If they are not for ever entertained, they sulk and scowl
>   in anger.
> Why do black-eyed girls adorn their eyes with kohl,
>   and paint their faces, dye their fingers?
> Is it not for you know what? So do not hesitate to
>   copulate.' "

When 'Abd-ul-Malik heard these verses he began to laugh and turned to Ayman saying, "Poor Ayman, women have brought you lots of trouble, but what about your wife?" "I shall ask her not to act too hastily," said he. "I shall plead my impotence, but treat her with tact and kindness, and perhaps in this way I shall be able to hold on to her." "Do just that," the Caliph commented. So he did, and his wife went back to him, and the Caliph made good his losses and he returned to favour.

It is also related that when Ayman had recited his verses, 'Abd-ul-Malik remarked, "No one has ever known women as you have, and none described them in better terms than you."

The Caliph Hisham ibn 'Abd-ul-Malik once asked the ageing and decrepit Abu Najm of 'Ijl,[47] who had just come from the desert, "What's your opinion of women?" "They're no good to me," he replied. "I just look at them askance and they look back

---

[47] Poet who lived in the first half of the eighth century.

at me perplexed." "And what do you think of me?" asked Hisham. "I think the same of you as of myself," replied Abu Najm. "Ah, but you don't know," remarked the Caliph, and he sent for his concubines. "Tell Abu Najm," he commanded "what I am like." "Well," said they, "none of us can ever perform the ritual prayer without performing the greater ablution to cleanse us from the results of coitus with him." At this Abu Najm was taken aback and marvelled. So then Hisham presented him with a slave-girl and told him to come back and give an account of his experiences with her on the following morning. But it was all to no avail. The night passed, and in the morning Hisham asked him how he had gone on. "I could do nothing," he said, and then recited,

> "Looking beneath her bodice, she delighted in her
>   beauteous bosom, and I, too, peered underneath my
>   clothes.
> What she could see were hips lying heavy on her waist
>   and buttocks full and round behind and a swelling
>   pubic mound.
> But all I saw about my penis was shrunken, flabby, thin,
>   outworn.
> Scorpions and snakes would find a better welcome there
>   than shapely knees.
> What's your head, my penis, doing there behind? Do
>   you think that's where the vulva lies?
> Be off! You're dead beyond all hope for ever, no matter
>   what your length of days."

Hisham laughed and gave orders for him to be given a present of a slave-girl.

Hisham once asked Abrash of Kalb to marry him to a woman from his tribe of Kalb. So Abrash did as he was bidden by the Caliph, who then one night some time later said in jest, "I've married into the tribe of Kalb, and I find their women game." To this Abrash replied, "The women of Kalb were made for Kalbites."

A man from the tribe of Kinda once heard another from a different tribe say, "We've found some game ones among the Kindite girls." Whereupon the Kindite commented, "That's because they are like eye-black pots that have lost their sticks."[48]

In his *Necklace* Ibn 'Abd Rabbih[49] writes: Thumama ibn Ashras[50] once said, "I was proud of being able to prove my point of view and see opponents defeated, but God willed that my eloquence should be unequal to that of the most inarticulate. Now I once bought a slave-girl and when I had coupled with her I was stupid enough to remark, "What a vast passage you have!" To which she replied in verse,

"Oh for the man who packed it tight and would often complain that he found it too small!"

An extremely beautiful, but much-divorced woman was once asked, "Why on earth are you so often divorced?" "Because," she replied, "men prefer a tight fit—God fit them tight in their graves!" Then there was another woman who was once asked why her husbands were always leaving her and refusing to stay. "Men", she rejoined, "like openings hot with friction. So may God make their dwelling Hellfire, a bad abode that!"

A man once married a woman renowned for her beauty. After the wedding night he divorced her, but not for any wrong that she had done. Her neighbour asked her the reason, but she withheld the real cause for it all. But her neighbour persisted and vowed to get to the heart of the matter. At last the other gave in and told her questioner that she had married a man who preferred dryness in a copulating woman. "Had you told me of your problem," said the neighbour, "I could have given you useful advice." And with that she prescribed some medicament which her friend then used with success to get rid of excessive secretion.[51] When she thanked her neighbour for her kindness in prescribing a medicament that had cleared up her trouble, her neighbour suggested, "Now I shall contrive to bring you and

---

[48] Eye-black is carried in small pots or phials with a stick inserted for application when required. The penis is often compared with the stick.

[49] A Cordovan poet and man of letters (860–940). His *Necklace* is famous and, as a standard work, has gone into many printed editions.

[50] A Mu'tazilite theologian imprisoned by the Caliph Harun, but a champion of his sect's doctrine under Ma'mun (reg. 813–33).

[51] See above p. 223.

your husband together again." "I've no objection to that," said the woman. So the neighbour went to the husband and said, "Now, good sir, the reason for which you abandoned your wife no longer exists." The husband was astonished at what had occurred and at the same time puzzled as to who had told her, knowing full well that he had never told anyone what had happened. Seeing him thus perplexed, she drew closer and told him the whole story, declaring that if he ever heard otherwise she would take full blame. So the husband went back to his wife, for his heart was still set on her, as he had only left her for the one fault already indicated. He found his wife in excellent condition. For her part, she found great favour with her husband and bore him many children.

It is related that once upon a time a rich Bedouin married a young widow renowned for her beauty. On her wedding night she was disappointed with her new husband for he could just not give her the same satisfaction as her previous husband—her cousin—had given her. He was frigid, could barely get an erection, and would only approach her once a month, and even then without an erection. He might on occasion manage to insert the tip of his penis once or twice, or rub the greater part of it between the labia and forthwith ejaculate, thus leaving her without the pleasure of an orgasm. She lived with him in this fashion for a time consumed with the fire of unsatisfied desire. He would pet and pamper her a great deal, shower her with kisses and embraces, and give her all she wanted in the way of money. Then one day when he had petted her in the usual way, kissing her and embracing her, he went in between her legs, but found himself quite flat. He began to rub his penis on her pubis and between the labia in the hope that this manoeuvre might bring on an erection. But his wife's patience was now at an end as her sexual passion raged. Pushing him off her, she jumped up and cried,

"I've had enough of kisses on cheeks, and sucking of lips
    and breasts—
I wish for nothing but to raise my legs and have you
    in from the root to the tip!

I can find no satisfaction in the tip, or half, of your verge,
  or its rubbing my pubis or vulva.
I want it in right up to the hilt and the meeting of hair
  with hair.
Then you and I could jog to and fro for an hour or two
  at least
As you kiss my cheeks and then my breast and embrace
  me with both your arms.
That's just what I want—forget your gold and silver!"

When he realized she was serious, he left her though the flame of his love for her still burned in his heart.

In his work For Muwaffaq Zubayr relates the following story on the authority of his uncle: Musa ibn Mus'ab once visited a lady of Medina who had a singing-girl whose company he kept. The Medinese lady was a woman of outstanding beauty, demeanour and deportment. In the same house he also happened to see a repulsive young man who was in complete and unfettered control of the place. Musa asked the woman who the man was. "He's my husband," she replied, "and I'd give my life for him." "Good God!" exclaimed Musa, "How frightful a tragedy and how appalling that such a beauty should be linked with the ugliness I see in this man!' At this she retorted, "Oh brother, if you could but see what my husband has to offer me you'd sell everything you'd got for it, and he would greatly increase in stature in your eyes!" "How lucky you are," he said, and took his leave. In this particular case the husband was poor, and all the money was hers. Yet he could do as he liked with it all, nor did his wife do anything without his leave. This was simply because he did what was right by her in the marriage bed.

Once Farazdaq met a slave-girl and fixed his eyes on her. Whereupon she asked, "Why do you look at me like that? Even if I'd a thousand ports of entry, there'd not be one for you!" "Why ever not?" asked he. "Because of your ugly face and dirty mind," came back the answer. "Had you but tried me once," cried Farazdaq, "you would have found that my mind makes up for my face." With this he uncovered himself and showed her a penis the size of a young camel's foreleg. As soon as she saw it, the lust of a hyena gripped her, she watered at the mouth, and began to shake like a leaf, so strong was her desire. She whipped up her clothes and showed him the like of she-camel's hump bulging between her legs.[52] He threw himself upon her and went right in. And when he had finished, he recited the following lines:

> "Into her I thrust a rod the size of a young camel's limb
> —Well shaped at the head and sturdy below, and in length
>   a span and a half.
> And as I thrust it deep inside I felt the heat of an oven."

In the *Dynasty's Reply* the author writes: There was once a woman who was for ever annoying her husband. Whenever they fell out, however, he would part her legs and lay her. "You devil," she once exclaimed, "I'm so helpless when you cross me, for whenever you do so, you bring an advocate whose case I cannot refute!"

In the *Garden of Flowers* we read: Once a husband was at outs with his wife, but when they lay down to sleep she snuggled up to him and his penis rose up. And when he pushed it away with his hand he said to it, "Why have anything to do with those who vex you?" "*We* may have had a row," said his wife. "But what's that to do with our sexual parts? *They're* not at outs." At this they drew closed to each other, and they made it up.

In the *Songs* Abu Faraj relates: Hind of Murra daughter of Harith was once jesting with 'Umar ibn Abi Rabi'a[53] who was greatly enamoured of her and used to rhapsodize his love for her in verse. "Oh, 'Umar," she said. "If you'd only seen me some days ago when I was with my family. I put my head down under my dress and looked at my vulva which I had recently shaved. And there it was—a beautiful handful, all that a man could desire. And as I looked, I called out, "Oh, 'Umar, come on, let's wreck it!" "So," said 'Umar, "I cried out in echo of her sentiments, and she began to smile at me in delight."

---

[52] i.e. the pubic prominence.
[53] See above Ch. IX, n. 6, p. 185.

In the same book we find the following story: Muti' ibn Iyas and Yahya ibn Ziyad[54] and their friends got together and drank for days on end. At length Yahya said to his companions, "Look here, damn you, its days since we performed our prayers. So let's pray together and have this slave-girl lead the prayer.[55] Wearing a light transparent slip and no trousers, she took her place in front to do as she was bid. When she reached the part where worshippers prostrate, her vulva showed up well and could be seen to all behind her. It was newly shaved and smoothe—the most lovely sight ever seen, as rounded as a well-shaped cupola. Beholding such a sight Muti' edged forward on his hands and knees and kissed it. At this the girl sprang back and sat to pronounce the creed. But Muti' came out with the following lines,

> "When, as oblivious she crouched, her vulva came into
>   view as clean as a new-shaven chin,
> Upon it I made my prostation and gave it a gentle kiss
>   like an ascetic in an act of devotion."

Once on his way back from the Pilgrimage to Mecca Husayn ibn Dahhak, in a place called Qaryatayn, saw a slave-girl peering inside her clothes and slapping her vulva and saying, "O what a loss for me and you!" This inspired him to compose the following lines:

> Returning from the place where the pious perform their
>   rites, I passed through Qaryatayn,
> And what did I see there but a girl as comely as a moon
>   when full in the centre of heaven!
> There, with her hand on her vulva, she wailed the lament,
>   "O what a loss both for me and for you!"

When he got up to her, she heard his verses and modestly covered her face out of shame.

---

[54] The first was a protégé of one of the sons of the Caliph Mansur (reg. 754–75) and something of a reprobate. The second was a poet from Kufa (d. c. 776).

[55] As such, she would have been out in front with her back to the worshippers.

In his *Book of Muzaffar* Ibn Aftas[56] writes: The Caliph
Mahdi[57] once entered one of his chambers and espied a slave-girl
stripped to wash. As soon as she saw him she covered her parts
with her hands. Whereupon he tried to recite as follows:

"With my own eyes I saw in the palace . . ."

But there he stopped short, unable to go on. So he asked
which of the poets was in waiting at the door. Bashshar, he was
told, was there. So he told them to show him in and asked him to
carry on the verse where he himself had left off. So Bashshar
recited as follows,

"With my own eyes I saw in the palace a scene to bring
  on my death.
When she saw me she put her hands in front to hide it
  from my sight.
Yet some could be seen beneath her belly's rolls.
Oh, would that I could cover it just for an hour or two!"

On hearing Bashshar's verses Mahdi laughed and chided
"Shame on you! Were you there too?" "No indeed, Commander
of the Faithful." said he. "I'm only sorry I said 'an hour or
two.'" "But what else, then?" asked the Caliph. "A year or two
would be better", came Bashshar's reply. Mahdi then dismissed
the poet and commanded that he be rewarded for his pains.

In his *Songs* Abu Faraj says: Mahdi's concubines requested
him to permit them to sit and talk with Bashshar, arguing that,
as he was blind, there would be no reason for the Caliph to be
jealous. So he let Bashshar go in and talk with them. They found
him witty and urbane and said, "How nice if you'd been our

---

[56] This man—properly Muhammad ibn 'Abdullah ibn 'Abdullah ibn Aftas
—was a member of the Aftasid house, a small eleventh-century dynasty of
Berber antecedents which ruled over a large part of the western region of
Muslim Spain (1045–68) from its capital in Badajoz. He took the regnal style
"Muzaffar", and he is credited with *The Book of Muzaffar*—apparently an
anthology in fifty volumes. Since the book is rarely quoted, it can neither
have been well known nor widely used.
[57] The third Abbasid Caliph (reg. 775–85).

father; we'd never have to leave you." "But," said he, "My religion is that of the old Persian kings."[58] By this he meant that of the Magians[59] which permitted a father to marry his daughters or sisters. When Mahdi heard of this he forbade him ever again to join them in conversation or mix with them again.

A strange story is recounted by Abu Faraj in his *Songs*: A certain person relates: "I once visited Bashshar at a time when he had 200 dinars. He turned to me and said, "Just help yourself to whatever you want. Do you know how I came by all this?" "No," said the man. "A fellow came to me," said Bashshar, "and asked me if I was Bashshar, and when I said I was, he continued: "I solemnly swear to give you 200 dinars. You see, I was smitten with a girl, and so I approached her and spoke to her, but she took no notice of me. I was just about to drop her when I remembered your words:

> Let no curt and wounding words deter you from a girl
> you cannot reach.
> However difficult at first, they all come round at last, for
> even after bolting, a stubborn horse can be ridden in
> the end.

In his *For Muwaffaq* Zubayr tells the story of the father of Sulayman ibn 'Abbas: I once passed through the territory of the tribe of 'Uqayl and saw a fair slave-girl with a walk as haughty as that of a graceful mare. Two large, wide eyes she had and lashes as long as an eagle's pinions—I have never seen any more beautiful. I stopped to speak to her when an old woman appeared and said, "Don't waste your time with this beautiful creature from Nejd—your luck is out!" "Oh, leave him, mother," said the

---

[58] As already noted (above Ch. IV, n. 3, p. 73), Bashshar was of Iranian extraction. His true religious views are uncertain, but he was a sceptic and something of an eclectic. He seems to have had leanings towards old Iranian religious ideas (Manichaean doctrines infused with Zoroastrianism). Be that as it may, he was made the victim of a plot, charged with heretical free-thinking, and put to death. He claimed—probably falsely—that he was descended from the old Persian kings.

[59] i.e. Zoroastrian.

girl. "It's just as Dhu Rumma said: 'Even if there is nought but diversion for a moment, that little will suffice.' "

A man once met a comely girl. She was as beautiful as the moon when full, and, as she was walking along in the company of an elderly woman, he got up and stared at her intently, so struck was he by the beauty of the girl. The old woman rounded on him and cried, "Hey you there! What do you hope to gain—doing her with your eyes you are, but not your tool?"

In Abu Tahir's *History* the following tale is told: The Caliph Mahdi was a love-poet and wencher. Now when he heard of 'Awna daughter of Abu 'Awn,[60] he asked Khayzuran[61] to get her to come along to the palace. This she did, and when 'Awna arrived, Khayzuran asked her if she would like a bath. "Just as you wish", answered 'Awna. So he escorted her into the bathroom. Then all of a sudden Mahdi was upon her as she stood there stripped naked. She dashed behind Khayzuran and tried to hide, but he dragged her away. So she grabbed a chair and threatened him "By God, if you come one step nearer or try to touch me, I'll smash your face in!" "But," said he, "I really only wanted to take a look at you with a view to marriage." "What, marry you!" she cried. "Never!" Without further ado Mahdi left her.

On another occasion this Caliph did the same thing with the daughter of his vizier Abu 'Ubaydullah,[62] and Khayzuran adopted the same tactics. However, when he got hold of her in the bathroom she merely consented with the words," "I am your slave. Do what you like with me." So Khayzuran went out, while her husband lay on the girl and got all he wanted from her. When the girl left she went to her brother 'Ubaydullah

---

[60] Possibly 'Abd-ul-Malik ibn Yazid, an Abbasid general who was appointed governor of Khorasan by the Caliph Mahdi in 775.

[61] His wife, who was the mother of Harun.

[62] Appointed to the vizierate in 775, an office which he held until around 779. The story told here appears not to have been the cause of his downfall. The fact that his son was executed for heresy—a heinous crime in the eyes of the witch-hunter Mahdi—must have played an important part in the matter. He was, however, highly regarded for his honesty and competence, and, even when replaced as vizier, he continued to hold high office as the head of the Caliphal chancery. He died in 786 or 787.

and told him all that had happened. On hearing the tale he told his sister to invite Khayzuran to take a bath with her. In they both went, but no sooner had Khayzuran entered the bathroom than she found 'Ubaydullah upon her. When she saw him standing right there, she tried to hide, but he stopped her and said, "If we wished to do as you with our womenfolk, we could, but we just don't countenance that sort of thing." Khayzuran went off and told her husband what had happened. Later the Caliph trumped up a criminal charge against 'Ubaydullah and had him put to death.

The author of the *Garden of Flowers* writes: Harun was once sitting with two of his concubines. "One of you sleep with me tonight," he commanded. "I'll spend the night with you," said the quicker of the two." "Oh, no," said the other immediately. "I'll sleep with you." "Now how can you argue your case?" he asked the first. "Because," she said, "in the Koran it says, 'And those that are first there—they are those who are nigh [to the Throne]'."[63] "Now," said Harun, turning to the other girl, "your friend made out a good case for herself. What is yours?" In reply she quoted the following verse from the Koran, "The last shall surely be better for thee than the first."[64] "You have each clearly proved your point," commented the Caliph. "So I shall sleep between the two of you." And this he did, and while so doing one of the girls stroked his member, and it rose. But when the other saw this going on, she rapidly mounted him and slipped it in herself (which she could do because he was on his back at the time). When her companion spotted what had happened she cried out petulantly, "I've never seen a dirtier trick! The kill should be mine—it was I who caught the prey for someone else to eat it." "Now then, my girl," said Harun, "did you hear that? She claims you've played a dirty trick and have stolen the prey she hunted." "No, Sire," countered the other. "When I realized she was not driven by hunger to devour her prey on the spot, but wanted to turn it into a well-cooked, spicy dish with all the condiments, I knew she couldn't be starv-

---

[63] lvi, 10 ff.
[64] xciii, 4.

ing. But in my case you can see what I've done. I'm glad to have it just as it is with as little cooking as possible." And with no more ado, she rose and fell on his penis until she came. "This," she said, "is what it's all about." As soon as she had felt the thrill of ecstasy, she turned to her companion and said, "Here's the game you claim you caught. Go on, take it, and Hell to you!" So the other put out her hand to touch it, thinking it was still erect, but not a twitch could she get out of it. "You've eaten the meal, damn you!" she cried.

In his comments on this episode the author of the *Garden* explains that the girl who beat her friend to the mark was stirred to mad passion when she felt Harun's penis erect because it had been some time since she had had intercourse. So she couldn't wait to satisfy her desire with a climax. The other, however, had recently had sexual relations and was not so avid. She only wanted to pet the Caliph as was her wont. This was the point of the girl's saying the bit about cooking a spicy dish with all the condiments meaning petting, kissing, hugging, and so on. The girl who said, "I'm glad to have it just as it is with as little cooking as possible" merely meant that just an erection would do for her since she had a desperate need which needed no preliminaries such as kissing and petting. And so she couldn't wait to quench her burning desire. The truth of the matter is that Harun had recently bought her, and the waiting period[65] [to establish whether she was already pregnant by someone else] had only just come to an end. Up to that night he had been unable to spend the night with her.

In the *Sharp-Witted* Ibn Jawzi quotes the following story told by Mufaddal: [66] "I once dropped in on the Caliph Harun, and there before him were a bowl of roses and the most beautiful

---

[65] In Arabic *istibra'*, a technical term applicable in the case of slave-girls acquired by new owners. The normal period is one month or until the occurrence of one menstruation. It is not obligatory.

[66] This, in all probability, is the scholar of Kufa who compiled the famous *Mufaddaliyyat*—a collection of classical odes—for the instruction of Mansur's son and heir, Mahdi. If the identification is correct, we can only assume that the incident mentioned here took place before the accession of Harun since our Mufaddal died in the year before Harun became Caliph in 786.

girl whom he had just received as a present. Turning to me he said, 'Give us a verse, Mufaddal, telling us what these roses are like.' So I recited,

'They are as the cheek of a girl beloved, kissed by the
    mouth of her lover and still suffused with the blush
    of modesty.'

At this the girl said:

'They are as the colour of my cheek when the hand of
    Harun drives me to that which entails the major
    ablution.'

'Go on out, Mufaddal,' cried Harun. 'This brazen hussy stirs my passions.' So I got up, let down the curtain and left."

The following tale is recounted by Abu Faraj in his Songs: Ishaq ibn Ibrahim said, "One night Harun sent for me, and, while I was with him Fadl ibn Rabi[67] was suddenly announced. He was granted leave to enter and Harun asked him, 'What brings you here at this time of the night?' 'Nothing to worry about, Commander of the Faithful,' replied Fadl. 'It's just that something happened to me tonight which shouldn't be kept a secret. I went to bed with three concubines—a Meccan, a Medinese, and an 'Iraqi. The Medinese girl put out her hand and made my penis rise and swell. Then the Meccan leaped up and grabbed it, whereupon the Medinese protested, 'What dirty trick is this? Don't you know that the Messenger of God once said, "The prey belongs to the hunter, not the beater"?' At this point an Iraqi girl intervened, pushed her Meccan companion aside and took hold of my penis, saying 'I see no end to your wrangle. This is mine and in my possession till you settle your difference and come to terms with each other.' Harun roared with laughter and commanded that the girls be brought to him. Fadl did as he was bidden, and the girls subsequently became

67 c. 758–822. Highly esteemed chamberlain and vizier to Harun and then Amin.

favourites of Harun and completely carried him away." The
following verses are attributed to this Caliph:

> Three young ladies have possessed me and occupied each
>   corner of my heart
> How comes it that, when all mankind obey me, I give
>   obedience to these girls, disobedient though they
>   are?
> Well, I'll tell you—it's the power of love that rules, and
>   through that they reign supreme, the greatest of
>   them all!

It is said that these verses are the work of 'Abbas ibn Ahnaf
since they are more his style of poetry.

As a challenge to them we have the following by Sulayman
ibn Hakam, Caliph of Cordova who took the regnal style
"Musta'in":[68]

> How strange that, when even lions dread my spear's edge,
>   I am cowed by the charm of languid eyes!
> I can do battle with every kind of terror and feel no fear
>   —save when a loved one turns aside and leaves me.
> I am wholly at the mercy of three girls like dolls with
>   rosy cheeks and bodies smooth and soft.
> They shine like stars that twinkle on dark nights when
>   seen by one who gazes above the branches on the
>   dunes.
> One is as fair as the crescent moon, another bright as
>   Jupiter, the third as slender as a ben's slim branch.
> I strove to forget them and find content without them,
>   but power had to yield to power—such was Fate's
>   decree.[69]
> They took by storm the best defended bastion of my heart,
>   and, for all the might of my kingdom, they have left me
>   helpless as a captive.
> Yet what harm to be their slave in love, for, after all, all
>   men alive, themselves included, are but slaves to me!

---

[68] Reg. 1009–10 (first reign), 1013–16 (second reign). By this time the
Umayyads of Spain were on their last legs.

[69] Such seems to be the general sense of a line that is corrupt in the Arabic.

Take not to task a king whom passion humbles, for such
humility is might and a good second sovereignty.
If I, in dearly loving them, both before the power of love, I
am no true scion of Marwan."[70]

In the *Songs* Abu Faraj writes: When the Caliphate devolved
on Mutawakkil people sent him presents, each according to his
means. One of the gifts presented to him was a slave-girl who
could not only write poetry, set it to music and sing it, but also
had a thorough knowledge of scholarship in its various branches.
Her name was Mahbuba, and she so impressed Mutawakkil
that she found great favour with him and finally became second
to none in his esteem. Ibn Jahm[71] records the following encounter: One day I went to wine and dine with Mutawakkil.
When we were all settled in our places the Caliph got up and
went into one of the nearby closets. As he came out he was
laughing. "'Ali," said he, "I've just seen such and such a girl
with the words 'O Ja'far!'[72] written on her cheek in musk. I've
never seen anything so charming. Do give us a line or two on
this theme." Mahbuba was there, continues Ibn Jahm, and after
thinking for a minute or two and gazing at the floor, she took
up the lute and hummed awhile until she had a tune for her
words. She then began to sing.

"I swear by a girl who wrote 'O Ja'far!' on her cheek in
musk, I'd give my very life for the spot where the
letters left their mark.
If she's committed to her cheek one mere line of musk, it's
lines of passion I've committed to the bottom of my
heart!
Oh, what would you give for a slave whose master obeys
his every wish whether in private or in public?

---

[70] i.e. no true Umayyad of the line of Marwan I, Caliph of Damascus (683–
685).

[71] 'Ali ibn Jahm, a gifted Arab poet (c. 804–63), a boon-companion of
Mutawakkil who fell into disgrace.

[72] Mutawakkil's name (as opposed to his regnal style).

What would you give for my eyes, which have beheld the
  like of Ja'far?
May God's refreshing rain ever renew the life of the
  marks tracing the words 'O Ja'far!'"[73]

All this while I was speechless, unable to put a single letter
into verse, and, as I looked helplessly on, Mutawakkil cried out,
"The devil take you, 'Ali, didn't you hear my command?"
"Relieve me of the duty, Sire. I just couldn't say a word nor
think a single thought." Mutawakkil never stopped teasing Ibn
Jahm about this episode.

The author of the *Garden of Flowers* quotes 'Ali ibn Jahm as
saying: "I once called on Abu 'Uthman Mazini. At the time he
had in his company a slave-girl so beautiful that she was the
very image of the moon. In her hand she held an apple, and
there and then she turned to me and asked, 'What did the poet
mean when he said,

"Send me messages with a messenger who spreads no tales
  around."?'

'I don't know,' said I. Throwing me the apple, she cried,
'This is what he meant.' " "By God," said Ibn Jahm, "I've never
found a better answer than the one she gave."

In the *Calices* Bayhaqi relates: As the Caliph Amin was
wandering about his palace at night a drunken slave-girl staggered past him. So he stretched out his arms to her and tried to
seduce her. But she drew back with the words, "Just leave it till
tomorrow, if you please." The following day he sent for her and
asked her to keep her word. Whereupon she demurred with the
comment, "Haven't you heard the saying 'What's said at night
fades with the day'?" But his heart was set on her and so he
committed her to one of the poets-in-waiting at the door with
instructions that he should compose some lines on his encounter
with her. So Mus'ab ibn 'Abdullah Zuhri[74] came up with the
verses,

[73] Water in most Arab countries is highly prized for its life-giving and
refreshing properties. In Arabic poetry, therefore, to wish rain on someone
is to wish him the best things in life.
[74] The text is uncertain, and the name may be wrong.

"Will you reproach me when my heart is shattered,
    despondent, and cannot find repose,
Through love of a beauty who has captured my heart
    with eyes like those of a houri?
When I put out my hands to touch her, she pulled away
    from me.
Then when I asked 'And what, dear lady, of your promise?'
    all she would say was, 'What's said at night fades with
    the day.' "

In the *Dictations* Abu 'Ali writes: One day Harun and his son 'Abdullah Ma'mun were at table together. When they had finished eating, a slave-girl came up to Harun with water to pour on his hands.[75] As soon as Ma'mun saw her he blew her a kiss, but her expression was one of frank disapproval. As a result of this exchange, the girl couldn't help but be slow to pour water over the Caliph's hands. "What's going on?" he asked, threatening to kill her if she didn't come up with the truth. "Abdullah blew me a kiss," she said, "and I frowned my disapproval." At this the Caliph turned to his son—who had meanwhile nearly died of fright—and asked "Do you like the girl, dear boy?" As he spoke he clasped his son to his bosom to allay his apprehension. "Yes, I do, Commander of the Faithful," came the reply. "Then she's yours, my boy" said his father, and let Ma'mun take her into a nearby closet where he had intercourse with her. When they emerged, his father called out "Have you thought of any lines to fit the occasion?" Whereupon the son replied,

"There was a lovely fawn to whom I threw a heartfelt
    message with my eyes.
I kissed her from afar, but her lips would not respond to me;
A frown and a scowl were her sullen reply,
But I held my ground and had her in the end."

'Urayb Ma'muniyya, one of Ma'mun's slave-girls often used to say, "Three Caliphs had me, but I never desired any but

<hr />

[75] See above Ch. V, n. 35, p. 112.

Mu'tazz,[76] for he resembled Abu 'Isa, the son of Harun." In his *Bridegroom's Gift to the Bride* Ibn Hazm comments "If what you said is true she must have been concubine to father and son." 'Urayb was much in love with Abu 'Isa, a most handsome man. According to her herself she was only fourteen years old when Amin bought her. A servant recalls "One day I went into the Women's Palace and saw 'Urayb sitting on a chair with her hair down while she was washing it. I asked who she was and was told it was 'Urayb. She had been summoned by her master that day, and that was the day he first had sexual relations with her. After the death of Amin she passed into the possession of his brother Ma'mun. She completely swept him off his feet, and so infatuated with her did he become that he even kissed her foot. Before she came to Amin from her former master, she had run away under cover of night and gone to live with Hatim ibn 'Adi, with whom she had fallen in love when he was in hiding at her master's house. While he was there, she would exchange glances with him, and he snatched many a kiss from her. And so when Hatim came out into the open again, 'Urayb ran away from her master and went to live with her lover for a time, her whereabouts being quite unknown to her master. On this affair 'Isa ibn Zaynab gives us the following lines:

> Damned bitch that she is, 'Urayb did an uncommon thing:
> On a pitch black night she rode a hard and dangerous
>   mount;[77]
> She dallied with a lover, who was quick to acquiesce and
>   gladly took her in.
> He had his share of this world and indeed much more
>   than his share.

Ahmad ibn Muddabir[78] recounts: "As a boy I once went out on one of Ma'mun's expeditions against Byzantine territory. I was there to earn my daily bread as young people do, and I formed part of a group of lads of my age. We had just left

---

76 The thirteenth Abbasid Caliph (reg. 866–69).

77 A poetical way of saying that she embarked on a most dangerous course.

78 A government official who served in Palestine and Egypt (d. 833).

Raqqa[79] when we spotted a company of women in howdahs. One of my fellows told me that 'Urayb was in one of them. 'Who'll take a bet that I'll get in among the train and sing the verses of 'Isa ibn Zaynab?' One of them took me up on it, so I made over to the camels and their burdens and sang out loud and clear, going right to the end.

"Just as I finished a woman suddenly popped her head out of one of the litters and called out, 'Hey, fellow, you missed the best and loveliest line! Doesn't it go like this,

> " 'Urayb with lips ever moist between her legs had every
> variation on the theme."?

'How could you ever forget that line? Go and collect your bet from the boys.' She then let down the curtain. I realized that it was 'Urayb herself, and so I rushed back to my friends for fear that I should fall foul of one of the servants in attendance."

In his *Songs* Abu Faraj relates: 'Urayb once went to see Muhammad ibn Hamid at the time they were much in love with each other. No sooner had she arrived than he began to upbraid her with having done this, that, and the other. In the end she rounded on him and cried, "Listen, fellow, get on with the job we're here for. Fasten my waist-band round my neck like a necklace, push my knees right up to my jugular vein, get my anklets meeting my ear-rings, and do the job! If you want to grumble tomorrow, write it all down on a scroll so I can reply and just forget what worried you all last night. As the poet says,

> 'Don't count sins when we come together. Let us not
> count, neither you nor I.' "

In his *Multitudes* Abu Rayhan relates: Mu'tadid[80] once had a slave-girl called Durayra ("Little Pearl") with whom he was madly in love. He built a house for her called Buhayra where he could be alone with her. When Ibn Bassam heard of it, he threw out the following lines:

[79] In Syria on the Euphrates.
[80] The sixteenth Abbasid Caliph (reg. 892–902).

"He left men in bewilderment (*bi-ḥayra*) as he went off
    alone to Buḥayra,
There to beat a tattoo on the vulva of Durayra."

When news of these lines reached the Caliph, he gave orders
for Buḥayra to be demolished, and no one knew the reason at
the time. Who can blame the man who commented, "Two
verses drained two treasuries"? For Muʿtaḍid emptied two
treasuries on the building he had constructed.

It so happened that Ibn Bassam[81] who wrote the verses quoted
above once satirized Qasim ibn ʿUbaydallah ibn Wahb.[82] In the
following lines he is addressing ʿUbaydullah, the father of
Qasim, on the occasion of the death of his son Husayn:

"Tell Qasim's father, who had high hopes for his son
    'Fortune's strange vicissitudes are certainly your lot'
You have lost a son who was one of the best and are left
    with one of the worst!
For the one to live is as bad as for the other to die. You are
    never free from life's hard blows."

These verses became so well known and so often quoted that
they became proverbial.

Ibn Hamdun, Muʿtaḍid's born companion was once playing
chess with his ruler when Qasim ibn ʿUbaydullah came in to
seek permission for something or other and then left. Muʿtaḍid
then began to repeat the verses aloud. ʿUbaydullah shortly after
re-entered the room with some other request and caught
Muʿtaḍid reciting them. Muʿtaḍid raised his head, and on seeing
ʿUbaydullāh, was overwhelmed with shame and embarrassment,
and commented, "Why have you never cut out the tongue of
this insolent cur?" (meaning Ibn Bassam). Whereupon Qasim
lost no time in dashing off to look for Ibn Bassam, but he was

---

[81] This is not the author of *The Treasure*, but a satirical poet of Baghdad
(d. between 914 and 916). He had charge of intelligence and communications
under Muʿtaḍid.

[82] Muʿtaḍid's vizier.

unable to find him. Mu'tadid returned to his game, but Ibn Hamdun's hands were shaking. "What's the matter with you?" asked Mu'tadid. "Commander of the Faithful," stuttered Ibn Hamdun, "Ibn Bassam is one of the finest poets, and I'm so afraid that Qasim will cut out his tongue. Before long Qasim returned and Mu'tadid asked him what had happened to Ibn Bassam. "He couldn't be found," remarked Qasim. "Well," said Mu'tadid, "I now command you just to be kind to him and pay him due respect and honour so that you might be delivered from his satires. It was because of him, indeed, that I pulled down Buhayra." Qasim left and was later pleasant to him and treated him most generously.

In his *History of the Yemen* 'Umara[83] recounts: Sayyida Sulayhiyya,[84] the daughter of Ahmad ibn Ja'far ibn Ahmad was renowned for her beauty, perfection, culture, manners, and indeed she combined every good quality. She was called the Queen of Sheba of Islam. When her husband, Mukarram died, he left her in Dar-ul-'Izz, a residence which he had built for her in the Yemenite town of Dhu-Jibla.[85] When Saba' ibn Ahmad ibn Muzaffar seized the throne, he wanted to marry her so that his dominion would be complete. But she turned him down, and he, for his part, therefore decided to put her to death. However, he was advised to write to Mustansir the 'Ubaydite of Egypt[86] and consult him about what to do with her—for the Yemenites at that time supported the cause of Mustansir of Egypt. So he gave in and sent two emissaries to convey his message. After accomplishing their mission they duly returned, accompanied by a eunuch who formulated a plan to speak with her personally. And so it was that he went in to see her in the presence of the notables of the realm who had come in support of him. He ad-

---

[83] Najm-ul-Din 'Umara "of the Yemen" (d. 1175). See H. C. Kay, *Yaman: its Early Medieval History* (London, 1892).

[84] Queen Sayyida Arwa, the Sulayhid, exercised effective authority over the Yemen from 1084 to 1138.

[85] Sayyida Arwa made this place her capital in lieu of San'a'.

[86] i.e. the Fatimid Caliph Mustansir (reg. 1036–94). The Sulayhids ruled the Yemen as the nominal vassals of the Fatimid Caliphs of Egypt and, like them, were Isma'ili Shi'ites (above Ch. V, n. 15, p. 103). Consequently relations between the two countries were cordial.

dressed her as follows: "Greetings from the Commander of the Faithful to the most noble sovereign lady, the acceptable, pure and chaste, the one and only of the age, lady of all kings of the Yemen, pillar of Islam, pure Imam, treasure of religion, confidante of the Commander of the Faithful whose message to her is as follows: 'When God and His Messenger have decided some affair, it is not for a believer—man or woman—to have a choice in their affair. Whoever opposes God and His Messenger has strayed into manifest error.'[87] You are given in marriage by our Lord, the Commander of the Faithful to the Prince of Princes Abu Himyar Saba' ibn Ahmad in consideration of a nuptial gift of 100,000 dinars in gold in cash and 50,000 dinars in kind consisting of precious stuffs and wares." To this her reply was as follows: "As regards the missive of our Lord the Commander of the Faithful I cite in response the Holy Koran 'There has been delivered unto me an honourable letter.'[88] With regard to his command I do likewise: 'O ye nobles, give me an opinion about me.'"[89] She then said to the two emissaries, "As for you two, by God you did not come to our Lord with a true report from Saba', but, rather, perverted his utterances. 'Nay, you have blown up a bubble for yourselves. But patience is a fair thing. God is the one from whom succour is to be sought against that whereof you talk.'"[90]

Her new spouse sought to go in to her at her residence, Dar-ul-'Izz, and she consented. On entering he put out his hand to her, and she did not resist. He then lay with her once, but on the second occasion when he desired her she refused him. But after a while she consented, and he lay with her a second time. He sat a while and tried yet a third time. At this she was angered and left the room which she was sharing with him. It is said that she only had intercourse with him that night and that, while he was with her, he was obliged to quell a group of rebels who had risen against him and that thereafter they had no further sexual relations. Some Yemenites, on the other hand, maintain that he never saw her, and that on that wedding night

[87] Koran, xxii, 36.
[89] xxvii, 32.
[88] xxvii, 29.
[90] Koran, xii, 19.

she substituted one of her slave-girls for herself. When her husband realized the deception, he concealed the fact and never told a soul.

In the *Unique Pearl* Tha'alibi[91] recounts the following: In Hamadan[92] there was once a splendid poetess known as Hanzaliyya whose hand was sought by Abu 'Ali the Secretary. However she declined his proposal. But he was insistent, and to his insistence she replied with the following lines,

> "Your shaft is a shaft that will find no joy in my passage—
> So turn it away from its entrance and take it whence it
>   came."

Abu Mansur Tha'alibi, quoting Sahib ibn 'Abbad, says, "By God, with these two verses she showed herself a better poetess than Kabsha sister of 'Amr [ibn Ma'di Karib] and Khans sister of Sakhr.

In the *Snatched Firebrand* Ibn Hayyan[93] relates: The Emir 'Abd-ul-Rahman ibn Hakam dispatched his emissary Ghazal to the Christian king.[94] Being impressed by what he had to say and finding his company easy, the monarch invited him to drain a cup or two with him. But Ghazal declined with the plea that wine is forbidden to Muslims. One day when he was sitting with the King, the Queen came out adorned like the rising sun in all its glory. As she appeared before them, Ghazal found himself unable to take his eyes off her. The King began speaking to him, but he was just not concentrating on what he was saying. Ghazal nevertheless denied that he was distracted. The King then asked him through the interpreter the reason for his absent-

[91] See above Ch. XI, n. 28, p. 206. The *Unique Pearl* is a very well-known anthology of poets contemporary with the author.

[92] A city in central Iran.

[93] The greatest historian of medieval Spain (987–1076). The work mentioned here (more correctly "The Snatcher's Firebrand") is an important compilation of historical data.

[94] The Emir is the Umayyad ruler of Muslim Spain, 'Abd-ul-Rahman II (reg. 822–52); Ghazal was one of the emissaries he sent to the Byzantine court at Constantinople in 840; the "Christian King" is the Byzantine Emperor Theophilus, and the Queen his wife Theodora.

mindedness. "Tell him", he said, "that what took my mind off what he was saying was the beauty of this queen. I have never seen her equal!" And he began to describe her charms, his wonderment at her beauty, and how she put him in mind of the houris of Paradise.

When the interpreter had explained all this to the King, Ghazal found even greater favour with him, and the Queen was delighted at his compliments. Turning to the interpreter, she said, 'Tell him he shall be my guest today." So Ghazal agreed. She summoned together all her relatives and the great ladies of the realm, giving instructions that they should put on their finest apparel. She arranged an assembly and assigned each his place for that night according to his station. When night fell, they all took their place in the assembly, and, when Ghazal arrived, she commanded that he be seated in the place of honour. She then instructed that musical instruments be brought in according to European custom. They all then began to drink and dance with the Queen circulating among them as radiant as a full moon at its brightest. Then one woman after another started to come up to him, and she said 'This is the daughter of so-and-so, and this is the wife of so-and-so," until she had introduced them all to him. She then asked him. "Which is the best? Do tell me." "Your Majesty," he replied, "they are just like fruit —I can't tell just by looking." It then dawned upon her that he might mean that one can't try fruit without tasting, and so also with women. At this she laughed heartily and said, "Why didn't you liken them to blossoms. The mere act of looking is enough, and beyond that there is smelling?" To this he replied, "You are content merely to see and smell, but we are only satisfied by eating." She went on jesting with him and then asked him through the interpreter why Muslims demanded circumcision and caused such suffering to their boys. "Besides," she concluded, "it's interference with God's manner of creation and useless at that." "Ah," said he, "tell her that circumcision is of the greatest value, for a branch, if pruned, grows strong, and thick, and sturdy. As long as this operation is not carried out, it will remain thin and weak." She laughed at this rejoinder and well grasped its implications.

In the *Treasure-House of History* Ibn Sa'id[95] says of the Emir 'Abd-ul-Rahman ibn Hakam that he set out on an expedition to Galicia. Now at the time he had a concubine in Cordova whom he dearly loved, and one night he dreamed of her and, when he awoke, he extemporized as follows,

> "A vision of the one with whom you are in love came all
> the way from Cordova to pay a call on you."

He then turned to his poet 'Abdullah ibn Shamir and said, "Go on with another line." So he carried on,

> "Had she been there in truth she would have quenched a
> burning thirst, but in fact she was merely a dream."

'Abd-ul-Rahman then appointed a deputy to command the army and went to the girl of his dream in Cordova to do with her awake what he had done in his sleep. After quenching his burning desire he returned to the field.

In his *Elaborator* Hijari[96] writes: One day Mu'tamid ibn Abbad[97] was sitting in one of his residences overlooking Seville when he felt a desire to be with his wife Rumaykiyya. So he sent a message to his wife to let her know, at the same time inquiring of her whether she would like to go to him or whether he should go to her. She wrote back,

> "My wish is that you come to me with speeding steps
> faster than the wind,
> Then mount my bosom and plough my belly with furrows
> clean and true as would a plough.

[95] A well-known Spanish Arab poet, geographer and historian (1213–86). The title given here does not appear to be listed as one of his works.

[96] A Spanish Arab historian (1106–1155) who hailed from Guadalajara (whence his name, which is incorrectly given in the text as "Hijazi", i.e. "of the Hejaz").

[97] Ruler (reg. 1069–91) of a small but notable principality in Muslim Spain. From its capital in Seville this Arab dynasty ruled over the greater part of south-west Andalusia for almost a century.

I beg that when you've had your way on top of me you
will not leave me till the third time round."

Hijari says: He went with speeding steps and gave her three
times round. Rumaykiyya was the one who involved Mu'tamid
in debauchery and a scandalous and notorious way of life until
in the end the Sevillans laid the charge at his door and accused
him of cutting Friday prayers for weeks on end. They then
delivered him to the Commander of the Faithful (the Almoravid
ruler)[98] who dealt with him as he did. As a result Mu'tamid was
imprisoned in Aghmat[99] together with Rumaykiyya who predeceased him there.

The story of Mu'tamid's marriage to Rumaykiyya has as its
point of departure this prince's habit of making trips incognito
with his vizier Ibn 'Ammar to the place known as The Silver
Meadow[100]—a delightful meeting-place for men and women in
search of diversion. One evening when Mu'tamid was on the
river bank a sudden gust of wind sent ripples across the water
that evoked the image of a coat of mail. Turning to Ibn 'Ammar,
he gave him a hemistich and challenged him to complete the
verse. "The wind has turned the water to a coat of mail," he said.
As Ibn 'Ammar paused to think, a woman standing nearby made
up the verse with these words. "What a piece of armour it would
make if the water would only freeze!"

Mu'tamid was speechless with admiration for the words she
had contributed to his verse while Ibn 'Ammar stood inarticulate and helpless. As the prince looked at the woman, he feasted
his eyes on her loveliness and was greatly smitten by her. Before
returning to his palace he detailed one of his eunuchs to keep
an eye on her and told him to fetch her to him as soon as he
could. When she arrived, Mu'tamid questioned her about her

[98] The Almoravids were Touaregs who crossed from Morocco to assist the
Muslims of Spain against the Christians and eventually seized power there at
the end of the eleventh century. They did not create a Caliphate and style
themselves "Commander of the Faithful" as indicated here. Their style was
"Commander of the Muslims".

[99] A small town in Morocco some twenty-odd miles south of Marrakesh.

[100] Marj al-Fidda, on the Guadalquivir near Seville.

birth and station. To this inquiry she replied that her family trained and bred horses and that she herself was unmarried. Whereupon he took her to wife, and for some time the two lived a life of uninterrupted happiness together.[101]

---

[101] Another story about Mu'tamid begins at this point, but it is incomplete and, as such, is hardly worth translating. We must assume a lacuna in the text of indeterminate length.

CHAPTER XVII

Conclusion

Although it is now time to bring this book to an end, the reader will not, I think, find me boring if I draw out my conclusion with one or two anecdotes in light-hearted vein.

Let us begin with the story of a schoolmaster who once seduced a boy in the schoolroom after the rest of his pupils had gone home. No sooner had he penetrated his young victim's person and worked himself into a sexual frenzy than the sound of music could be heard as some players went by outside. Tearing himself away from his master, the lad dashed outside to look at the musicians, while his teacher looked down at a penis as erect as a tent-pole and streaming with secretion as it throbbed up and down at the tip. As he looked at it, he addressed it thus (and may God heap shame upon his head for quoting the Koran!),[1] "When they spot some merchandise or diversion, they scatter away to it and leave you standing."[2]

Then there is the story of a Bedouin who was taken before a judge to testify against a man alleged to have had unlawful intercourse with a woman. When asked what he had seen he said, "I saw his penis as surely implanted in her vagina as a kohl stick in a phial of eye-black." "But you wouldn't have seen as much if you'd been as close as the skin on her bottom," objected

---

[1] Quite apart from his scandalous behaviour and state of ritual impurity—in which a man is forbidden to recite the Koran—the schoolmaster was guilty of an action amounting to blasphemy.

[2] Koran, lxii, 11. Tradition has it that this verse relates to an occasion when all but twelve of the congregation of a mosque rushed out while the Prophet was preaching because they had heard the beating of drums as a caravan entered Medina. In other words, the supposed believers were prepared to leave Muhammad standing as soon as something amusing or profitable caught their attention.

the judge as he told him to stand down.[3] In another case of the same kind the witness was asked to recount what he had seen. "I saw," he said, "a bouncing bottom, the signs of heavy breathing, two feet like an ass's ears, and something hard and solid going into a cavern. I then witnessed an abominable crime."

While speaking of judges, I remember the case of a woman who once brought her husband before one, alleging that he was not doing his duty to her as a husband should. "And if I'm a liar," she declared, "the judge's penis is in my vagina!" The judge was taken aback. "What, my good woman, did you say just then?" he asked. "Repeat what you've just said." So she did as she was bidden. "Now for the third time I'm asking you to tell me what you originally said," insisted the judge. So for the third time she repeated her statement. The judge then turned to the husband, who had been standing there without uttering a word. "And what have you to say, my man?" he demanded. "My wife, sir," came the reply, "gets all her marital rights from me, and if I'm a liar my penis is inside your wife's vagina!" "Arrest this reprobate and chastise him," roared the judge. "Good God above!" exclaimed the man. "Some penises are more favoured than others—the judge's has been in my wife's three times now, and no harm came to him, while mine's been only once inside the judge's wife, and here am I sentenced to be chastised!"

There was once a man who had a most beautiful and charming wife with whom he was deeply in love. She, for her part, was a nymphomaniac who would never refuse a man and who would on occasions even make the first approach. In fact if she could have had her way, she would never have had a penis out of her person. Not unnaturally her behaviour was a source of great grief to her husband, and, although he moved from one town to another, it was all to no avail. Yet, because of his great love for his wife, he could not bear to be separated from her. When he eventually found that he was totally unable to keep

[3] The judge was probably reluctant to convict (which he could not have done in any case on the evidence of just one witness) since unlawful intercourse could entail lapidation.

her under control, he took her to a remote village. One day after he had settled in, he took the opportunity of sitting down and talking to local inhabitants. In the course of conversation he remarked, "I have a rather unusual wife—she has a perfectly normal vagina, but underneath it, she has a male organ. And so, if any man has intercourse with her, he will get the penis slipped into his bottom." With that he went off home to his wife, leaving his audience agape.

Upon his return the man told his wife that all the men of the village were abnormal in that each of them had not only a penis, but also a vagina right under his genitals. His wife was amazed and, as time went on, became increasingly eager to find out the truth of the matter for herself. Eventually she decided to accost one of the men. Now, as it happened, the man she picked had heard her husband describe his wife's supposed abnormality. Nevertheless he agreed to her proposal, but during intercourse remained very much on his guard against anything going into his anus. Meanwhile his partner set about slipping a finger under his genitals to find out what his supposed vagina was like—and, of course, came into immediate contact with his anus. As soon as ever he felt it, the man snatched himself from her without waiting to finish his job and ran as fast as his legs would take him to tell everyone that he had found the woman exactly as her husband had said. From that moment not a man in the village would go near her, and at last her husband found peace of mind.

And now to the blundering Juha.[4] One day after the death of his father, his mother sat up in bed at the crack of dawn when everyone else was fast asleep and began to cry. Hearing his mother weeping, Juha went and asked her why she was so upset. "How can I help crying when I think of your father?" she sobbed. "My heart breaks whenever I think of him." "Ah, now I understand," said Juha, "this is just the time of day when he'd be going up you."

Another story about Juha has it that when he was a child, he

---

[4] Juha is a character about whom there are countless anecdotes and jokes. He is a popular fictional figure who is well known not only in the Arab and Muslim world but also in parts of Europe as well. His mistakes, blunders, and wild schemes are proverbial.

was inordinately attached to his mother and would not leave her even at night. In the end she had to complain to her husband, who decided to bring home some pointed pegs and use them to frighten off the young lad. He left them lying around so that when Juha came home and saw them he would ask his mother what they were for. "Your father," she said when asked, "thrusts those up the bottoms of anyone who talks during the night." That night Juha went off to bed, but later wakened to find his father having intercourse with his mother. "Has my mother been talking during the night?" inquired the curious Juha. "No," replied his father. "Then why are you pushing a peg in her bottom?" he quizzed.[5]

And now as we near the end of this work, let my last few words be as follows. I have collected and arranged all that is contained in my book for the entertainment and delight of others, hoping that I shall be forgiven any prolixity and repetition of which I may be guilty. All items of particular interest which I have included and all humorous tales and anecdotes I have told have been checked by me against the sources, and I have been particularly careful in the matter of prescribing drugs and recommending the treatment of cases where aphrodisiacs are indicated. In this sphere of therapeutics I have devoted much time and attention to the problem of specifying the right treatment for the cases in question. Moreover, I have been at great pains to enumerate the many different positions which may be adopted for coitus. If I am taken to task for having spoken in jest as well as in earnest, my defence is that no blame attaches to a man who mixes sugar with honey. For any mistakes I may have made in this book I beg men of understanding to show me forbearance—my plea is that I have done no more than follow in the steps of those who have gone before and that my work is merely made up of what other authors have said before me. And, if the book contains language that is repugnant and inelegant, I submit that the subject-matter will gladden the heart of the reader and drive away depression because it also contains all manner of light-hearted and amusing anecdotes. Finally, I suggest that, whatever its faults, time will

[5] The state of the text at this point is such that a lacuna may be suspected.

be better spent on reading my book than on calumny and back-
biting.

I beg God the Great to forgive me my sins and to uphold me
on the day of my death, to erase the record of my sins, to overlook my faults and to grant such great mercy as may extend
beyond my own self to all the Muslim faithful. Praise be to God,
Lord of the Worlds.

> O you who read the pages of my book and contemplate,
>   withhold not any blame that you would attach to him
>   who is its author.
> All I ask you is that, if you cannot spare your praise, at
>   least, I beg you, spare a word to say, "My Lord
>   forgive both him and us."

APPENDIX

Genealogical and Dynastic Tables

Since there are frequent references in this book to the Prophet and the Caliphs, the following tables will perhaps help the reader to see the picture as a whole. It should be noted that the Arabs themselves did not refer to their rulers as 'Umar I, 'Umar II, etc., but identified them by indicating of whom they were the sons. If the reader, then, encounters in the body of the text the name Mu'awiya ibn Abi Sufyan, for instance, and it is clear that its owner was a Caliph, he should look for Mu'awiya in the table and find out the name of the father. It will be found that the Mu'awiya whose father was Abu Sufyan was Mu'awiya I. Mu'awiya II will be found to be Mu'awiya ibn Yazid.

I

The "Orthodox" ("Rightly Guided"), or "Patriarchal" Caliphs

Abu Bakr 632–34
'Umar I (ibn Khattab) 634–44
'Uthman (ibn 'Affan) 644–56
'Ali (ibn Abi Talib) 656–61

These Caliphs were four of the Prophet Muhammad's Companions who succeeded him on his death in 632 as head of the Muslim community with the title *khalifa* (whence "Caliph"), i.e. "successor" of the Prophet. 'Uthman and 'Ali (see Table II) were related to the latter by blood—'Uthman by marriage as well. Both Abu Bakr and 'Umar were fathers-in-law of the Prophet, the first through his daughter 'A'isha Muhammad's favourite wife) and the second through his daughter Hafsa.

II

To show the Umayyads and their connexion with the Prophet, the 'Abbasids, etc. The Umayyad capital—which changed frequently—was in Syria, being first transferred to that country from Arabia by Mu'awiya I who established himself in Damascus.

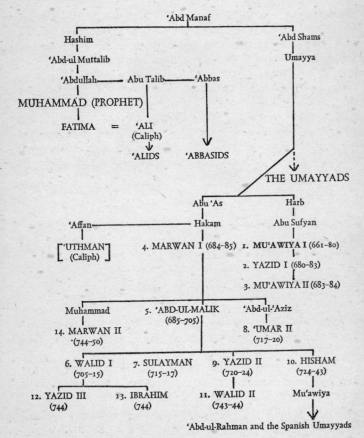

III

The 'Abbasids

With the advent of the 'Abbasids the seat of government was transferred from Syria to Iraq where the second Caliph founded Baghdad. It was the Caliphate of Baghdad that fathered the golden age of Arabo-Islamic civilization—a civilization which attained to extraordinary heights.

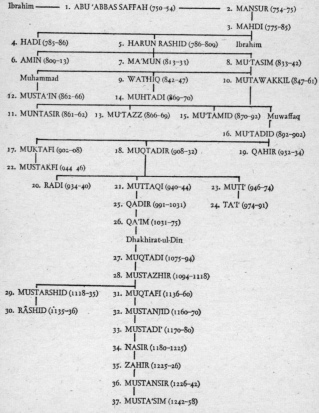

Ibrahim —— 1. ABU 'ABBAS SAFFAH (750-54) —— 2. MANSUR (754-75)

3. MAHDI (775-85)

4. HADI (785-86)   5. HARUN RASHID (786-809)   Ibrahim

6. AMIN (809-13)   7. MA'MUN (813-31)   8. MU'TASIM (833-42)

Muhammad   9. WATHIQ (842-47)   10. MUTAWAKKIL (847-61)

12. MUSTA'IN (862-66)   14. MUHTADI (869-70)

11. MUNTASIR (861-62)   13. MU'TAZZ (866-69)   15. MU'TAMID (870-92)   Muwaffaq

16. MU'TADID (892-902)

17. MUKTAFI (902-08)   18. MUQTADIR (908-32)   19. QAHIR (932-34)

22. MUSTAKFI (944-46)

20. RADI (934-40)   21. MUTTAQI (940-44)   23. MUTI' (946-74)

25. QADIR (991-1031)   24. TA'I' (974-91)

26. QA'IM (1031-75)

Dhakhirat-ul-Din

27. MUQTADI (1075-94)

28. MUSTAZHIR (1094-1118)

29. MUSTARSHID (1118-35)   31. MUQTAFI (1136-60)

30. RÂSHID (1135-36)   32. MUSTANJID (1160-70)

33. MUSTADI' (1170-80)

34. NASIR (1180-1225)

35. ZAHIR (1225-26)

36. MUSTANSIR (1226-42)

37. MUSTA'SIM (1242-58)

Extinction of the 'Abbasid Caliphate *of Baghdad* with the Mongol conquest.

NOTES ON ARABIC NAMES AND OTHER WORDS

Unless there have been special reasons for doing otherwise, no attempt has been made to transliterate Arabic words according to modern scholarly practice. Hence long vowels are not differentiated from short by the usual long stokes (ā, ī, ū).[1] Nor has it been felt desirable to differentiate ḍ from d, ḥ from h, ṣ from s, etc., since the English reader with no knowledge of Arabic would find such distinctions meaningless and the spellings tiresome. In general a compromise has been reached. Thus the letters ' (a strong guttural *consonant*) and ' (a glottal stop, or catch in the breath—also a *consonant*) have been retained because it is undesirable to omit letters which are integral parts of words. Non-Arabists, however, should just ignore them. The same applies to q (which is not always followed by "u" as in English); it may be pronounced as "k" (as in "Koran" which, strictly transliterated, would be Qur'ān).

Except in compound names of the "'Abd-ul-Malik" type and in certain exceptional cases, the article al (sometimes el in some authors) has been dropped—again for the convenience of the English reader. It will be indicated by a hyphen in the index (thus "-Isfahani" will mean that the correct name is "al-Isfahani").

It should be noted that "Ibn" (in the middle of a name "ibn") merely means "son of" and "Abu" ("Abi" when preceded by "ibn") "father of". "'Abd" means "slave" and in compound names it means "Slave of" followed by one or other of the names applied to God.[2] Thus " 'Abdullah" ('Abd Allah) means "Slave, servant of God".

---

[1] In *literary* Arabic there are only six vowels (*a, i, u* (short) and *ā, ī, ū*). Scholars no longer use "o" and "e", etc. There are two diphthongs *ay* and *aw* (of which variants often encountered are "ai", 'ei", "au". The correct transliteration of the word "sheikh" which is now part of the English language would be "shaykh".

[2] Though not invariably.

INDEXES

I

NAMES OF PERSONS, PEOPLES AND PLACES

N.B. (i) Exceptionally, *references to the Koran are included in this index*; (ii) b. = ibn, bt = bint ('daughter of'); (iii) for Caliphs, see in addition to this index, the Genealogical and Dynastic Tables.

'Abbad -Bishri, 233
-'Abbas, Prophet's uncle, 34 & n., 110 n.
– b. -Ahnaf, 193 & n., 297
Abbasids, 110 n., 318 & *passim*
'Abd Manaf, 139. *See also* Appendix
'Abd-ul-'Aziz b. 'Abdullah b. 'Umar b. -Khattab. 204 & n.
'Abd-ul-'Aziz b. -Walid b. 'Abd-ul-Malik b. Marwan, 165
'Abda bt 'Abdullah, 109 & n., 185
'Abdullah b. 'Abd-ul-Rahman b. Abi Bakr, 105 n., 209.
– b. Abi Umayya b. -Mughira, 206
– – 'Ali, 185 & n.
– – 'Amir, 125, 148 f.
– – 'Amr b. 'Uthman b. 'Affan, 257 & n.
– – Harun -Rashid (Caliph -Ma'mun), 300
– – -Hasan, 231 f.
– – Ja'far, 134 & n., 261
– – Khalaf, 173
– – Nafi', 262
– – Qays, 178
– – Rawaha, 276 & n.
– – Shaddad, 251
– – -Shamir, 308
– – 'Umar b. -Khattab, 234 & n.
– – Zam'a, 234 f.
– – -Zubayr, 105

'Abd-ul-Malik b. Habib. *See* Ibn Habib
'Abd-ul-Malik b. Marwan (Caliph), 162, 180 f., 283
– – – – 'Umayr, 251
'Abd-ul-Rahman b. -Hakam (Spanish Umayyad), 306
'Abd-ul-Rahman b. Suhayl, 249
– – – – 'Ubayd, 129
-Âbi, 147, 168
Abraham, 70 & n., 202 n., 262
-Abrash of Kalb, 285
Abu -'Abbas -Saffah, 162, 165 & n., 166, 185 f., 187
– – -Fadl b. 'Abd-ul-Samad. *See* -Raqashi.
– – b. 'Abd-ul-Mu'min. *See* Ibn 'Abd-ul-Mu'min
Abu 'Abdullah Sa'id b. -Musayyib. *See* Sa'id
– 'Abd-ul-Rahman 'Abdullah b. 'Umar, 278
– 'Ali the Secretary, 306
– 'Ali -Qali, 170, 175, 192, 271 f., 300
– – -Zubayr. *See* -Zubayr
– – 'Umar b. Muhammad b. 'Ulwan -Hudhali. *See* -Hudhali
– -'Anbas -Saymari, 47
– -Aswad of Du'il, 134, 173
– -'Atahiya, 36
– -'Awn, 293

Abu Bakr (Caliph), 76 & n., 143, 147, 153 & n., 154, 167 & n., 209 n., 316
- - of Hudhayl, 238
Abu Burda, 186
- Dawud (Traditionist), 128 & n., 137, 143 & n., 152, 248, 273
- Dharr -Ghiffari, 151
- Du'ad, 236
- Dulaf -Qasim b. 'Isa, 178 & n.
- Durayd, 279 & n.
- -Faraj -Isfahani, 106 & n., 108 f., 111, 124, 131, 135, 139, 144 f., 148 f., 162, 168, 170 f., 173, 175, 178, 181, 186, 189 ff., 196, 201, 204, 227 f., 233, 235 f., 240, 249, 251 f., 269, 274, 276, 282, 289, 291 f., 296, 298, 302
- -Fath Kushajim, 136
- Hanifa, 104 & n.
- Hasin, 179
- -Hawari -Wisati, 136
- -Haytham, 128
- Hazim, 201 f.
- Himyar Saba' b. Ahmad, 305
- Hurayra, 127 & n., 128, 201, 244 & n.
- Husayn b. Zarqun, 239
- 'Isa, son of Harun -Rashid, 301
- Ishaq -Zajjaj. See -Zajjaj
- Ja'far. See -Mansur (Caliph)
- Jahl, 74 & n.
- -Makarim, 108
- Mansur. See -Tha'alibi
- Marwan 'Abd-ul-Malik b. Shuhayd, 181 & n.
- Ma'shar (Albomasar), 188
- Muhammad 'Abdullah, 121 & n.
- Mulayka, 170
- Musa, 186
- -Najm of 'Ijl, 284 f. & n.
- Nukhayla of 'Ukl, 187 & n., 268 & n.
- Nuwas, 31, 36 & n., 37 f., 40, 42, 45, 49, 50 f., 58, 64 & n., 69, 111, 188
- -Qattan, 113
- Quhafa, 153 & n.
- Rayhan. See -Biruni
- Sa'id -Khudri, 127 f.
- Salim, 134
- Shayzam, See 'Iqal b. Shabba
- Tahir (Tayfur?), 293
- Tammam, 140 n., 173, 262
- 'Ubayd. See -Bakri

Abu 'Ubaydallah (Mahdi's vizier), 293 & n.
- 'Umar, 264
- Umayya, 119
- 'Uthman. See -Jahiz
- Yasir, 109, 111, 137, 185
- Yusuf Ya'qub b. Ishaq. See -Kindi
- Zayd, 239
- Ziyad of Kilab, 182
Abyssinians, 154
'Ad, 205 n.
Adam, 71
'Adi b. Zayd, 19 n., 274
Afghanistan, 115 n.
'Afra', 67
Agha Khan, 103 n.
Aghmat, 309 & n,
Ahmad b. Abi Tahir, 109
- - Hanbal, 230 & n.
- - -Mudabbir, 301 & n.
-Ahnaf b. Qays, 266
'A'isha (Prophet's wife), 115 f. & n., 130 & n., 133, 135, 144, 153 f. & nn., 175, 189, 197, 207, 217 n., 260, 273
'A'isha bt Abu Waqqas, 141
- - Talha, 96, 105 & n., 114 & n., 201 & n., 204, 209 f., 240 f.
- - 'Uthman, 209 f.
-'Ajjaj, 280 f.
Ajrad. See Hammad 'Ajrad
-Akhfash, 169
-Akhtal, 189 & n.
-Akhyal, 99 n.
'Ali (Caliph), 56, 93 n., 98, 103 n., 113, 127 f. & n., 134 n., 147, 161
- b. -Husayn, 167 f.
- - Jahm. See Ibn Jahm
- - Ziyad, 247
'Alids, 200 & n.
Almeria, 265 n.
Almoravids, 309 n.
'Alqama of Tayy, 148
Amat-ul-'Aziz (Ghadir), 258 f.
-Amin (Caliph), 262 & n., 299, 301
'Amir b. Dharib of 'Adwan, 158
- - Lu'ayy, 139
- - Sa'sa' (tribe), 181
'Amr (a pimp), 81
- b. Ma'di Karib, 306
- - Sa'id b. -'As, 209 & n.
- - Shu'ayb, 124
- - 'Ubayd, 96

'Amran b. -'Attar, 146

Anas, 137, 206, 219, 229 f.

'Anbar (tribe), 169

Ansar. *See* Helpers of the Prophet

Apostle of God. *See* Muhammad the Prophet

'Aqil b. 'Ullafa, 99, 253 & n.

Arafat, Mt., 202 n.

Arberry, A. J., 184 n.

Asad (tribe), 148 & n.

-Asadi ("of Asad"), 141

-A'sha (of Bakr, of Hamdan, of Sulaym, of Taghlib), 191 & n.

-Ashtar (Bishr b. 'Abdullah), 93 ff. & n.

– (Malik b. -Harith), 128, 186

'Asim, 174

Asma' b. Kharija -Fazari, 134, 158, 186, 241

– – 'Umays, 113

-Asma'i, 57 & n., 90 f. & n., 108, 167, 184, 194, 202 f., 235, 238, 244, 279

'Ata' b. Abi Rabah, 118, 230, 244 & n.

– – Mus'ab, 169

'Atid (tribe), 129

'Atika of Makhzum, 278

'Atiyya, 140

'Awf b. Muhallim, 159, 208

'Awna bt Abi 'Awn, 293 & n.

-Awza'i, 134

Ayman b. Khuraym, 283 f. & n.

Azd (tribe), 266

Azraqites, 269 & n.

'Azza (beloved of Kuthayyir), 67

'Azza ('Azzat)-al-Mayla, 209 f. & n., 235

Badiya bt Ghaylan b. -Mughith, 207 & n.

Badr (battle), 74 n.

Badr (client of -Mu'tadid), 199

Baghdad, 68 n., 112, 146

Baha'-ul-Din -Zuhayr, 195 & n.

-Bakharzi, 136

-Bakri, Abu 'Ubayd, 108 & n., 186 f,, 189 f., 208, 236 ff., 271, 281

Balkh, 115 & n.

Balqa' (Jordan), 254 n.

Banu (in tribal names). *See* Beni

Barmecides, 233 & n.

Bashshar b. Burd, 73 & n., 141, 171 & n., 192, 291 f.

Basra (Iraq), 51 n., 73 n., 105 f. & nn., 129, 142 n., 158, 163, 169, 179 n., 188 & nn., 199, 235, 245, 261 n., 265 n., 279 n.

-Bayhaqi, 278 & n., 299

Bayt al-Hikma (Baghdad), 256 n. 10

-Bazzar, 118, 134

Beni Hashim. *See* Hashimites

– Sahm, 145

– Sa'ib, 107

– Tamim, 117 f., 189, 266 ff. & n.

– 'Udhra, 244

Berbers (women), 161 f. & n., 163

Bilal, 107 & n.

-Biruni (Abu-Rayhan), 131 n., 158, 185, 206, 242, 302

Bishr b. 'Abdullah. *See* -Ashtar

– -Hafi, 95 & n.

Bosworth, C. E., 170 n.

Brocade (nickname). *See* Dibaj

Brunschvig, R., 11 f. & nn.

Buhayra, 302 f.

-Bukhari, 116 f. & n., 229, 231

Buktum, 193

Buran, 110 f. & n., 180 & n.

Burdan, 33

Burton, Sir R., 7 ff., 218 n.

Buthayna, 67, 115 & n., 170 & n.

Carrington, C., 218 n.

Ceuta, 116 n.

Chinese (women), 225

Chosroes, 112 & n., 175 & n., 274

Companions of the Prophet, 13, 144, 247 & n., 250

Cordova, 181 n., 240 n., 254 n., 308

Coulson, N. J., 17, 155 n.

Crusaders, 26

Dabba (tribe), 281

Dafaq (slave-girl), 233

Dahna' bt Mishal, 280

Dalal, 255 f.

Damascus, 139, 200

Damra b. Damra, 168

Dananir (slave-girl), 233

-Daraqutni, 251 & n.

-Darimi, Miskin, 252 & n.

Dar-ul-'Izz, 304 f.

David (King), 70 n.

David of Antioch/Dawud -Antaki, 12 n., 214

Dhi'ab/Dhiyab (tribe), 267 & n.

Dhu Jibla, 304 & n.
- -Rumma, 91 f. & n., 174, 191, 293
- -Zahr wa- -Zill (battle), 104
Dibaj ("Brocade"), 200, 204, 258 n. 17
Du'ali. *See* Abu -Aswad of Du'il
Dunlop, D. M., 109 f. & nn.
Durayra (slave-girl), 302 f.

Egyptians (women), 225
Emigrants (Emigrant Meccans), 116, 248
Europeans (women), 161, 225

Fadl the Poetess, 178
- b. -Rabi', 296 & n.
Fam al-Silh, 110 & n.
Farasifa. *See* Na'ila
Farazdaq, 20, 50 f. & nn., 188 f. & n., 252 n., 288
Farra', 175
Fatima (Prophet's daughter), 56 n., 93 n,. 98 & n., 113, 147, 231 & n.
- bt -Husayn, 257
Fatimids, 200 n.
Fuja'a, daughter of. *See* Ibnat -Fuja'a

Gabriel, Archangel, 35
Galen, 212 f. & n., 219
Galicia, 308
Gerard of Cremona, 213 n.
Ghadir. *See* Amat-ul-'Aziz
Ghana (women of), 193
Ghaylan (singer), 203
- b. Maslama, 192
- - Salama b. -Mu'attib, 207 n.
-Ghazal, 306 & n., 307
-Ghazali, 107 & n. 23, 124, 126, 127, 149, 153, 154, 155, 158, 174, 198, 234, 251
Gibb, H. A. R., 17, 117n., 306
Gondeshapur, 228 n.
Guadalquivir, 309 n.

Hababa, 67
Habannaqa -Qaysi, 176 n.
-Hadi (Caliph), 258 & n.
-Hadra' bt Ziq b. Bistam, 188
Hafsa bt Sirin, 261
- - 'Umar (Prophet's wife), 102, 153 & n.
Hagar/Hajar, 70 & n., 262
-Hajjaj b. Farrukh b. Shurayh, 118

- - Yusuf, 98 n., 106 & n., 111, 129, 134, 186
-Hakam b. 'Abdullah, 200
Hamadan, 306 & n.
Hamama b. Rafi' -Dawsi, 265
Hamda (wife of 'Amran b. -'Attar), 147
Hamdun -Nadim, 242 & n.
- b. Isma'il b. Dawud, 242 & n.
Hamduna bt Harun -Rashid, 111, 233
Hamida (wife of Ma'bad -Saliti), 129
Hammad 'Ajrad, 51 f., 181
- b. Ishaq, 201
Hammam b. Murra b. Dhuhl, 271 f.
Hamza b. -Hasan -Isfahani. *See* -Isfahani
Hanbalites, 230 n.
Hanifa (tribe), 268
Hanzala b. Malik, 271
Hanzaliyya (poetess), 306
-Hariri, 145 n., 176 f. & n.
-Harith of Asad, 148 & n.
- b. -'Amr b. Hujr of Kinda, 159, 208 f. & n.
- - Kalada, 228 & n.
- - Khalid, 202
Haritha b. Badr, 266
Harun -Rashid (Haroun al-Raschid), 106 n., 109 ff. & n., 146 n., 258 & n., 262, 294 ff., 297, 300
-Hasan -Basri, 188 & n.
- -Yamani. *See* -Yamani
- b. 'Ali b. Abi Talib, 93, 155, 257 & n.
- - -Hani'. *See* Abu Nuwas
- - Raja', 111
- - Sahl, 110 f. & n.
Hashim b. 'Abd Manaf, 110 n.
Hashimites, 110 n.
-Hasin b. 'Abd-ul-Rahman, 140
Hatim b. 'Adi, 301
Hawt b. Sinan, 129
-Haytham b. 'Adi, 111, 114, 118, 283 & n.
Hayya, 109
Hejaz, 202, 225 (women of), 262
Helpers of the Prophet (Ansar), 116 & n., 122, 135, 248
-Hijari, 308 f. & n.
-Himyari. *See* Sayyid -Himyari
Himyarites, 269 n.
Hind (named in connexion with -Bishr -Hafi), 95

– bt Asma' b. Kharija, 106, 186, 241 f.
– – -Harith of Murra, 289
– – -Mu'awiya, 125, 148
– – -Nu'man, 19 f., 274
Hippocrates, 212 n., 219
-Hira, 19 n., 168
Hisham b. 'Abd-ul-Malik (Caliph), 162 n., 185, 249 f., 284
– – Hassan, 261
– – 'Urwa, 145
Hit, 206 f.
Hudba b. Khashram, 281 n.
-Hudhali ("of Hudhayl"), Abu 'Ali 'Umar, 239
-Husayn b. 'Ali b. Abi Talib, 93 n., 139, 154 n., 204
– – -Dahhak, 276 n., 290
-Husri, 140 & n., 143, 171, 183, 201
Hutay' a, 99 & n.

Ibn 'Abbad, -Sahib, 306
– 'Abbas, 102, 113 & n., 118, 134, 231, 248
– 'Abd Rabbih, 286 & n.
– 'Abd-ul-Malik (Caliph Sulayman), 253
– 'Abd-ul-Mu'min -Sharishi, 145 & n.
– 'Abd-ul-Quddus. *See* Yahya
– 'Abdun, 98 n.
– Abi 'Atiq, 76 & n., 96, 233 & n., 278
– Abi Hakima, 36
– Abi Dhi'b, 202
– – Rabi'a. *See* 'Umar
– – Waki', 281 & n.
– -Aftas, 291 & n.
– -Ahnaf. *See* -'Abbas
– -Alghaz, 236
– 'Ammar, 309
– -Aswad. *See* Miqdad
– Bassam, Abu -Hasan 'Ali (of Santarem), 193, 244, 249
– – – – (of Baghdad), 302 f. & n.
– -Dahhak. *See* Husayn
– -Dhakwan, 240 n.
– Dinar, 113
– Durayd, 279 & n.
– Habib, 'Abd-ul-Malik, 134, 140 & n., 141, 167, 194, 232, 250 & n.
– -Hajjaj, 68 & n.
– Hamdun -Nadim, 242 n., 303
– Hanbal. *See* Ahmad
– Hayyan, 306 & n.

– Hazim, 36
– Hazm, 201 & n., 255 ff. (governor of Medina), 301
– Jahm, 'Ali, 298 f. & n.
– -Jawzi, 101, 138, 145 f., 179, 276, 295
– -Kalbi, 254, 265 & n.
– -Kardabus, 162, 165 f., 259
– Khaldun, 78 n.
– Majashun, 125
– Mas'ud, 197 & n., 251
– -Mu'in, 127
– -Musayyib. *See* Sa'id
– Mutayr, 139
– -Mu'tazz, 36, 183
– Qanbar -Mazini, 199 & n.
– Qutayba, 237 & n.
– -Raqiq, 258 & n.
– -Rumi, 195 & n.
– Safwan. *See* Khalid
– -Sa'i, 257 & n.
– Sa'id, 161
– – -Maghribi, 308 & n.
– -Sayyid, 232
– Sha'ban, 247
– Shabba. *See* 'Umar & 'Iqal
– Shubruma, 184
– Shuhayd, 181 f. & n.
– Sirin, 117 & n.
– Sukkara, 194
– 'Umar, 113
– – , 'Abdullah, 278
– 'Utba of Asad, 241
– Zam'a. *See* 'Abdullah
– -Zubayr, 194
Ibnat -Fuja'a, 269 & n.
Ibrahim (Prophet's son), 260
– b. 'Ali b. Hurrama, 183
-Idrisi, 108 & n.
Imamites. *See* Twelvers
Imrul Qays/Imru'-ul-Qays, 184 & n., 236 f. & n.
India, 103
Indians (women), 225
'Iqal b. Shabba, 187
Iraq, 51 n.
– (women of), 225
'Isa b. Zaynab, 301 f.
Isaac son of Abraham, 262
Isaiah the Prophet, 70 n.
'Isam of Kinda, 208
-Isfahani. *See* Abu -Faraj
– , Hamza b. -Hasan ("of Isfahan"), 255 f. & n., 264

Ishaq b. Fadl, 277 & n.
- b. Ibrahim -Mawsili ("of Mosul"), 146 & n., 296
Ishmael, 71 n., 202 n., 262
Isma'il b. 'Ali, 166
Ismailis, 103 n., 304 n.
Iyad (tribe), 236
'Iyad, Judge (Qadi), 116 & n., 118, 127, 137, 229, 231, 250, 260
Iyas b. Mu'awiya, 179

Jabir, 250
Ja'far b. 'Ali b. Abi Talib, 231 & n.
- - -Mansur, 109 & n.
- - Muhammad, 198
-Jahhaf, 114
-Jahiz, Abu 'Uthman, 129, 180 & n., 188, 231, 236, 238, 245
Jahshawayh, 36
Jami, 97 n.
Jamil, 67, 115 & n., 170 & n.
Jami'-ul-Uns, 256
Jarir, 51 & n.
-Jawhari, 281 n.
Jayda', 93 ff.
Jerez, 145 n.
Jews, 47 n., 248 & nn., 249 f. & n., 256 n.
Jinn, 38 n., 141 f.
Joseph son of Jacob, 70 & n. 22, 97 f. & n.
Judge 'Iyad. *See* 'Iyad
Juha, 313 f. & n.
-Jumahi, 117

Kaaba, 70 & n., 107 n., 145 & n., 203 & n., 267 n.
Ka'b b. Malik, 251 & n.
- - Mama, 236
- - Thawr of Azd, 156 f.
- - -Zubayr, 108 n.
Kabsha, 306
Kairouan, 258 n.
Kalb (tribe), 254, 285
- (Desert of), 124
Karbala, 93 n.
Kay, H. C., 304 n.
Khali' (poet), 256 & n.
Khakh, 207
Khalid b. Safwan, 162 ff., 169 f., 194, 204
- - Zayd, 152
Khans, 306

Khansa' bt 'Awf b. Muhallim, 208
Kharijites, 269 f. & n.
Kharqa', 174
-Khattabi, 128, 147, 231
Khawwat b. Jubayr, 264 f.
Khayf, 178 & n.
Khayzuran (mother of Harun), 293 f. & n.
Khinas of Kinana, 265
Khorasan, 115 n., 129, 213 n.
Khosrau. *See* Chosroes
Khuld Palace, 109
Kinda (tribe), 208, 285
-Kindi, 220 & n.
Koran, 19, 24 n., 34 n., 38 n., 41 & n., 56 n., 63 nn., 68, 70 nn., 71 n., 91 n., 97 n., 123 n., 129 n., 133 nn., 141 n., 142, 144 & n., 150 f., 155, 175, 197 n., 198 nn., 202 n., 230 n., 248 n., 251 n., 270 n., 276, 294 nn., 305 nn., 311
Kufa, 163, 220 n., 275 n., 283 n., 290 n.
Kushajim. *See* Abu -Fath
Kuthayyir, 67, 196 n.

Laghdur, 104
Lakhmids, 19 n.
Laqit b. Zurara, 104 f., 159
Layla (beloved of Akhyal), 99 & n.
- (beloved of Majnun/Qays), 67 & n., 170 & n.
Layth, 134
Levey, M., 221 n.
Lubna, 67
-Lu'lu'i, 143
Luqman b. 'Ad, 205 & n.

Ma'bad -Saliti, 129
Mada'in Salih, 115 n.
-Mada'ini, 105, 186, 240 & n., 244
Magians, 292 & n.
Mahbuba (slave-girl), 298
-Mahdi (Caliph), 109 f., 114, 187, 291 & n., 293
Majnun/Qays, 67 n., 99 n., 170
Makhzum, 74 n., 162, 165
Malik b. 'Amr b. Tamim, 271
- - Anas, 121, 167 & n., 247 & n., 260
- - Asma', 139
- - -Harith. *See* -Ashtar
Malikites, 116 n., 140 n., 167 n., 247 n.
-Ma'mun (Caliph), 34 f., 110 f. & n., 180, 262 & n., 300 f.

Ma'n b. Za'ida, 145 f.
-Mansur (Caliph), 109 n., 166 & n., 258 & n.
- (Almanzor the 'Amirid), 181 f. & n., 254 n.
- b. Zabban of Fazara, 109
Marajil (Harun's wife), 262
Maria of Kinda, 274
Ma'rib dam, 205 n.
Marj al-Fidda, 309 n.
Marrakesh, 309 n.
Marwan I (Caliph), 298 n.
Maryam bt 'Uthman b. 'Affan, 125
Maslama (b. Hisham) b. 'Abd-ul-Malik, 161, 165
Mati', 206
-Mawa'ini, 148
Maymuna, 122
Mayya, 91 f. & n.
-Mazari, 116 n., 208
-Mazini, 56 f., 250, 299
- , Ibn Qanbar. See Ibn Qanbar
Mazyad, 86
Mecca, 57, 70 n., 74 n., 107 n., 116 n., 145 n., 151 n., 170, 178 n., 185 n., 200, 202 f. nn., 206, 233, 248 n., 264 n., 290
Medina, 74 n., 102 f. & n., 115 f. & n., 122, 163, 185 n., 207, 235, 248 n., 255, 260, 265, 288, 276 n., 311 n.
Medinese, 167
Messenger of God. See Muhammad the Prophet
Miqdad b. -Aswad, 56
Monastery of the Eunuch, 255
Morocco, 309
Moses, 70
Mu'ammal b. Jamil, 189
Mu'awiya I (Caliph), 76 & n., 93 n., 125, 127 & n., 148 f., 153, 252, 269
- b. Marwan b. -Hakam, 180
- - -Mughira, 180
- - Salama, 134
- - Yahya, 133
-Mubarrad (or, -Mubarrid), 36, 142 n., 161, 167 f., 194 f., 277
-Mufaddal, 295 f. & n.
-Mughira b. Shu'ba, 275 & n., 279
Muhammad the Prophet, 38 & n., 43, 56, 59, 68, 70 nn., 71 & n., 74 n., 93 n., 102 f. & n., 107 n., 110 n., 113, 116, 118 f., 125 ff., 133 ff.,

143 f., 147, 150 f. & n., 153 f., 156, 164, 175, 182 n., 194, 196 ff., 206 ff. 217 n., 229 ff., 241, 247 ff., 251, 260, 265, 273 f., 276, 296, 311 n.
Muhammad b. 'Abdullah b. 'Amr b. 'Uthman, 204 & n., 258
- b. 'Abdullah b. -Tahir, 169
- b. 'Abd-ul-Rahman b. 'Amr, 200
- - -Fadl -Sakuni, 181
- - -Faraj, 178
- - -Hajjaj, 111
- - -Hatib -Jumahi. See -Jumahi
- - Ma'n, 156
- - -Mundhir b. -Zubayr, 204
- - Sirin. See Ibn Sirin
- - Yahya b. Hassan, 232
- - Yunus, 194
Mujahid, 134
Mukarram, 304
Musa -Kazim, 161 & n.
Musa b. 'Abdullah -Zuhri, 299
- - 'Iqal, 114
- - 'Isa, 282
- - Mus'ab, 288
- - Nusayr, 162 & n.
Mus'ab b. -Zubayr, 96, 105 & n., 114 f., 184, 201, 209, 241
Musaylima, 138 n., 266 & n., 267
Muslim (traditionist), 116 nn., 127, 207, 250, 260
-Musta'in (Cordovan Caliph), 297 & n.
-Mustansir (Fatimid Caliph), 304 & n.
-Mu'tadid (Caliph), 199 & n., 302
-Mu'tamid b. 'Abbad, 308 ff. & nn.
Mutarrif, 167 & n.
Mutarriz, 199 & n.
-Mutawakkil (Caliph), 93, 159 n., 178 f. & nn., 265 n., 298 f.
Mu'tazilites, 286 & n.
-Mu'tazz, 301 & n.
Muti' b. Iyas, 290 & n.

-Nafzawi, 10 ff.
Na'ila bt Farasifa, 124
Najda, 20
-Nasa'i, 117, 125, 147, 230
Nasim-ul-Sahar, 256
Nawar, 188
Nawmat-ul-Duha, 256
Nejd, 292
Niftawayh, 170 & n.
Noah, Children of, 73

Nubah, 233
Nubians (women), 224
-Nu'man b. Bashir, 235
– – -Mundhir, 19 & n., 168, 274
Nusayb, 171
Nusayr b. Tahif of Hilal, 93

Palmer, E. H., 195 n.
Pananti, E., 184 n.
Parvez/Parviz, 112 & n., 175 & n.
Penzer, N. M., 219 n.
People of the Book, 248 & n.
Persian(s), 69, 112, 161, 205, 225
   (women), 292
Phillips, W., 223 n. 26
Potiphar, 97 n.
Prophet. *See* Muhammad the Prophet

-Qali. *See* Abu 'Ali
-Qaryatayn, 290
-Qasim b. Muhammad b. Abi Bakr,
   167 & n.
– – Thabit, 194 f.
– – 'Ubaydullah b. Wahb, 113, 179,
   303 & n.
Qatada, 229
-Qatari, 270
Qays b. 'Amir, 67 & n.
– – Dharih, 67
– – Khatim, 188, 191
– – Mas'ud, 104 & n., 159
– – Zuhayr, 252
Qudama, 114
Quhayf, 174
Qur'an. *See* Koran
Quraysh, 74n., 125, 165, 167, 235, 248,
   266, 276 n.

-Rabi', 258 & n.
Rafidites, 269 & n.
Raghum, 20
-Ramali, 143
Raml, 268 & n.
Ramla, 173
-Raqashi, 188 & n.
Raqqa, 302 & n.
-Rashid, Harun (Caliph). *See* Harun
Rayya bt -Jahhaf, 114
Red Palace (Basra), 106
Rhazes (-Razi), 213 & n.
Rice, D. T., 67 n.
Rizam b. Malik b. Hanzala (tribe),
   129

Rosenthal, F., 42 n.
Rughayb, 114
Rumaykiyya, 308 f.
-Rushati, 265 & n., 266 f., 268, 271

Saba'. *See* Abu Himyar
– b. Ahmad b. -Muzaffar, 304 f.
Sadi b. Isma'il, 118
-Saffah (Caliph). *See* Abu -'Abbas
Safiyya bt 'Isma, 134
Sahl b. 'Abdullah, 229
– – Harun, 256 n.
Sa'ib b. Jubayr, 102
Sa'id b. -Musayyib, 113 & n., 121 ff.,
   167, 202
Sâ'id (of Baghdad), 146, 182, 254 & n.
Sajah, 138 & n., 266 f.
-Sakuni. *See* Muhammad b. Fadl
Salim b. 'Abdullah b. 'Umar b.
   -Khattab, 167 f. & n.
Salman, 118
Samuel (prophet), 70 n. 22
San'a', 304 n.
Sappho, 21 n.
Saqil, 203 & n.
Sarah, wife of Abraham, 262 & n.
Sa'sa'a b. Sahwan, 153
-Sayyid -Himyari, 269 n.
-Sayyida Arwa. *See* next entry
– -Sulayhiyya, 304 & n.
Seville, 308 f. & nn.
Shabath b. -Rib'i, 267
Sha'bi, 118, 235
Shafi'i, 155 f. & n.
-Sharishi. *See* Ibn 'Abd-ul-Mu'min
Shaw, G. B., 195 n.
Sheba, Queen of, 141 f.
Shi'ites, 103 & n., 154 n., 161 n.
   See also Twelvers
Shiz, 242 & n.
Shurayh, 117 & n., 18
Sibawayh, 190 & n.
Silver Meadow, 308 & n.
Sinan of Kalb, 254 f.
Slavs (women), 225
Solomon, King, 97, 141 f. & n., 161,
   231
Spain, 140 & n., 162 & nn., 181 f.,
   306 nn., 308 n., 309 n.
Successors (of Prophet's Companions),
   247 n.
Sufis, Sufism, 32, 75 f. & n.
Sukayna bt -Husayn, 139, 203 f., 257 f.

Sulayhids, 304 & n.
Sulayman b. -'Abbas, 292
– – 'Abd-ul-Malik (Caliph), 249 & n., 254 f.
– – -Hakam. *See* -Musta'in
Sunnites, 103 n.
Suwayd b. Yarbu', 266
-Suyuti, 226 f. & n.

Ta'abatta Sharran, 228 & n., 282 & n.
-Tabari, 261
-Tabi'un. *See* Successors
Taghlib, 159
Ta'if, 206 & n.
Talha b. 'Abdullah, 96, 105
Tamim. *See* Beni Tamim
Taym Allah b. Tha'laba (tribe), 265
Tayy/Tayyi', 148 & n.
-Tha'alibi, Abu Mansur, 206 & n., 238, 250 & n., 282, 306 & n.
Thaqif (tribe), 267
Theodora, Queen, 306 & n.
Theophilus, Emperor, 306 & n.
Thumama b. Ashras, 286 & n.
-Tifashi, 132 & n., 159, 167, 200, 280
Tigris, R., 110 n., 112
-Tijani, 206 n.
-Tirmidhi, 117 & n.
Touareg, 309 n.
Tufawa, 147
Tuways, 256
Twelvers, 103 n., 161 n., 270 n.

'Ubaydullah (son of -Mahdi's vizier), 298 f.
– b. Wahb, 303
– – Ziyad, 106 & n., 241 f.
'Udhra (tribe), 115 & n.
'Ukaz, 264 & n.
Umama bt -Harith of Taghlib, 159
'Umar b. 'Abd-ul-'Aziz (Caliph), 100 & n.
– b. 'Abdullah, 173
– – Abi Rabi'a, 185 & n., 204 & n., 245, 262, 289 & n.
– – Hamama, 266
– – Hamza -'Umari, 127
– – Jawz of Kinda, 104 f.
– – -Khattab (Caliph), 97, 102 f. & nn., 107, 134 & n., 140, 143 f., 147, 149, 153 & n., 155 ff., 161, 168, 177, 201, 207, 230, 232, 266

– – Shabba, 265 & n.
– – 'Ubaydallah, 105 & n., 240
'Umara, 304 & n.
'Umays, 113
Umm 'Amr, 257
– 'Awf, 173
– -Banin, 114
– Hakim, 270
– Iyas, 159
– Ja'far, 262
– Kharija, 269, 271
– Kulthum bt 'Abdullah b. Ja'far, 139
– Manzur, 115
– -Qasim bt Zakariyya' b. Talha, 269 ff.
– Ruman, 115
– Salama (Prophet's wife), 206 & n.
– – (-Saffah's wife), 162 ff.
– – of Hilal, 249
– Shayba, 133
– Sulaym, 274
'Uqayl (tribe), 292
'Urayb, 300 f.
Uriah the Hittite, 70 n.
'Urwa b. Hizam, 67
– b. -Zubayr, 194
'Utarid b. Habib, 266
'Uthman b. 'Affan (Caliph), 76 & nn., 143, 207

Walid (Caliph), 67 n., 249
Wasit, 112 & n.
-Wathiq (Caliph), 35 & n., 276 f.
-Wisati. *See* Abu -Hawari

Yahya b. Aktham, 33 ff. & nn.
– – 'Ali -Munajjim, 199 n.
– – Sa'id b. -Musayyib, 121 & n.
– – Salih b. 'Abd-ul-Quddus, 47 f.
– – Ziyad, 290 & n.
Yamama, 267, 280
-Yamani, Hasan, 19
Ya'qub b. 'Abdullah of Makhzum, 162
– – Salama b. 'Abdullah, 165
– – -Sikkit, 265 & n.
-Ya'qubi, 233 & n.
Yathrib. *See* Medina
Yazid b. 'Abd-ul-Malik, 67 & n.
– – Mu'awiya (Caliph), 139 & n.
– – Muhallab, 228
Yemen 205 & n., 269 & n., 304 & n., 305

Yunus b. Habib, 243 & n.

Zahran, 265
-Zajjaj, 168 f., 180
Zarqa'-ul-Yamama, 275 & n.
Zayd b. -Haritha, 71 & n., 103 f. & n.
Zaynab bt Jahsh (Prophet's wife), 71
    & n.
– – 'Umar b. Abi Salama, 235

Ziyad b. Abihi, 172 f. & n.
Zubayda (wife of Harun -Rashid),
    109 & n., 259, 262
-Zubayr, Abu 'Ali, 118, 159 & n., 208,
    233, 253, 262, 288, 292
– b. Bakkar, 201 & n.
Zuleika, 97 f. & n.
Zuwawa, 11
-Zuwawi, 11

II

SUBJECTS AND ARABIC TERMS, ETC.

Ablutions, 56 n., 63 n., 219, 229 f., 273 f.
Adultery, 24 f. & n., 97 & n.
Akh, 205
Aloes, 110, 136
Aloeswood, 135 & n., 267
Aphrodisiacs, 218, 219 ff.
Arabian Nights, 109 n.
Arak (wood), 136
Arrows (as poetic image), 29 n.
Artisans (disreputable), 53
'*Asor*, 154
Astringents, 223 n.

Bā'a/bāh, 214
Bartholin's glands, 217 n.
Basmala, 118 n.
Beating (of wife as punishment), 152
  & n.
Beauticians (tire-women), 79 & n.
Ben tree (as poetic image), 187, 199,
  211, 256, 297. *See* also Branch
Black Stone (at Mecca), 70 f. & n.,
  203 n.
Book of *Mansur*, 213 & n.
Book of *Roger*, 108 n.
Branch (poetic convention), 43 n., 70,
  171 n., 297
Bride (displaying of), 112 n., (convey-
  ance of to bridegroom's home),
  113 n., 114
Brocade (as a nickname), 200, 204,
  258 n.

Camel (rutting), 87 n.

Camp (deserted, in Arabic poetry),
  61 n.
Camphor, 137 n.
Castration, 256 & n.
Catamite(s), 21 n., 59 ff.
Cemeteries (scenes of illicit sexual
  activity), 98 & n.
Circumcision, 22 n., 47 n., 256 & n.
Clime theory, 224 n.
Clitoris, 22, 23 n., 214 n.
Coitus (medical aspects of), 221 ff.
– interruptus, 156
– , rectal (legal aspects of), 247 & n.,
  248 ff.
Collyrium, 133
Concubines, 14, 161 ff., 231, 276 f.,
  294 & passim
Consummation, 115 & n.
"Crawling". See *Dabīb*
Crusaders, 26 n.

Da 'as wa-'ard, 238
Dabīb, 42 n.
Dallālāt, 77 n.
Dental hygiene, 135 f.
Depilation, depilatories, 26 n., 219
Devil (stoning of), 202 & n.
Dībāj, 258
Divorce, 37 & n., 130 & n.
Dower, 84 & n., 109
Duff, 116 n.

Ejaculation, 224 f.
Evil Eye, The, 210 & n.

Eye-black. See kohl.

Fahz, 239
Farewell Pilgrimage (Sermon of), 151 & n.
Farj, 63 & n.
Fātiḥa, 120 & n.
Female progeny (old Arab view of), 40
Flag (use of by prostitutes), 88 n.
Forensic medicine, 46 n.
Fortune-tellers, 77 f.
Full moon. See Moon.

Gazelle in Arabic literature), 38 & n., 88 & n., 199
Ghayl, 239
Ghusl, 56 n. See also Ablutions
Guardian (of women in law). See walī

Habdara, 104
Ḥadath, 56 n.
Ḥadd, 261
Ḥadīth, 122 n.
Hairdressers (in procuration), 79
Ḥajj, 151 n., 203 n.
Hakk wa-haww, 238
Ḥamāsa, 140 n.
Hann, 63 & n.
Ḥariqa, 250

Height (the ideal in humans), 195 f.
Henna, 79 & n., 133 & n., 134 f., 137
Ḥijāb, 151 f. & n.
Ḥirr, 62 & n., 69
Ḥirs, 69
Horn (bull, rhinoceros, as aphrodisiac), 220
Houri, 35 & n., 68, 175, 198, 307
Humoral theory, 213 n.
Humours, 213 n.

Ifhār, 239
Ijmāʿ, 230 n.
Iksāl, 239
Illegitimates (as disreputable class), 53
ʾIlq, 32
Imam (in mosque), 179; (Twelver), 179
Impotence, 280, 282 ff.
Inbreeding, 107 ff.
Infibulation, 22 n.
Intiʿāẓ, 214

Istibrāʾ, 295 n.
Izār, 54 n.

Janāba, 56 n.
Jealousy, 251 ff.
Jimāʿ, 214
Jinn, 38 n.
Judaism, 63 n.

Kabbalah, 212
Kafāʾa, 145 n.
Khāq-bāq, 239
Khaqhaqa, 239
Khawq, 239
Kohl (kuhl) (eye-black), 133 n., 224, 261, 286 n.
Kunya, 121

Lafūt, 104
Lahbara, 104
Lapidation, 24 n., 36 n., 129 n., 312 n.
Law, Islamic (points of), 19, 24 n., 37 n., 38 n., 56, 63 n., 83 n., 84 n., 85 n., 97 n., 109, 115, 116 & n., 130, 145 n., 152, 156 n., 157 n., 229, 231 n., 242 n., 247 n., 249, 261 n., 312 n.
Lesbianism, 19 ff.
Liber Almansoris, 213 & n.
Lochial discharges, 27 & n.

Madhy, 55
Mahr. See Dower
Malikite law, 140, 247 n. & passim
Marriage, 83 & n., 145 n., 270 f., 292 & passim
Mash, 238
Māshiṭāt, 79
Masturbation, 14, 219
Mawālī, 166 n.
Menstruation, 56 n., 63 n., 66, 173 & n., 180, 217, 232
Merchant classes, 52
Miserliness, 99 n.
Mole (cosmetic value of), 30 n.
Monogamy, 231 n.
Moon as poetic image), 28 & n., 107, 139 & n., 171, 199, 254, 293, 297
Mourning, 257 & n.
Mudarmikāt, 77
Muezzin, 120 n.
Muharram celebrations, 154 n.
Mursal, 143 & n.

Murshid, 33 n.
Mut'a, 270 & n.
Mysticism, 33 n.

Nahbara, 104
Nail polishing, 135
Negresses, 193 f.
Nuptial gift, 84 n., 109, 305

Obesity, 184 ff.
Orgasm, 126, 216, 224 f., 287
Orphans, 53

Paradise, 35 n., 60 n., 147, 156, 175, 198, 307
Parda (purdah), 88 n.
Parturition, 63 & n., 66
Pebble-casting, 78 n.
Pederasty, 19, 32 ff., 60 ff. & passim
Phallus, 48
Pilgrimage. See Hajj
Pimp(s), 72, 81 f., 84 f., 89
Pīr, 33
Polygamy, 231
Prayer (Ritual), 88 n., 120 n., 133, 234 n. & passim
Priapism, 214 n.
Procuration, 72 ff.
Procurers, procuresses, 51, 72, 75 f., 80, 82, 84 ff., 88
Prostitutes, 39 n., 88 n.
Pubic hair, 26 n., 219 n.
Purdah, 88 n., 89, 152
Purgative, 86

Qadhf, 261 n.
Qibla, 126 & n.
Qiyāda, 72 n.

Rain, 299 n.
Rak'a, 117 f. & n., 120 & n., 250 & n.
Ramadan, 234 & n.
Raqīb. See Watcher.
Red (expressing the notion of loveliness), 189 n.

Sadāq. See Dower
Saghm, 239
Sahīh, 116 & nn.
Saliva (in Arabic poetry), 30 n.

Sand-hill (poetic convention), 43 n., 120, 171 n., 184 n., 209
Scorpion, 34 n., 37 f. & nn.
Semen (medieval misconceptions about), 245 n., 274 f. (ritual purity)
Servants (as procurers), 51
Shahbara, 104
Sharh, 250
Sihāq, 21 n.
Slanderer. See Wāshī
Slaves (as procurers), 79
Siwāk. See Tooth-stick
Sufism, 33 n., 75 f.
Sukhf, 68 n.
Sumac, 47
Sunna, 122 n.

Tābi'ūn, 247 n.
Tadlīs, 239
Tattooing, 134 f. & n.
Tawāf, 203 n.
Teeth, See Tooth-sticks & n.
Temperaments, 213
Time (as personalized entity), 62 & n.
Tooth-sticks, 135 n., 136 f. & n.
Torso, 171 n., 184 n.
Tradition. See Hadīth
Tutors (depravity of), 51

Unveiling ceremony (at marriage), 112 & n.

Vaginal secretions, 173 n., 217, 245
Veil, 151 f. & n.
Virginity, 113 n., 180, 182, 242 & n.

Waiting period. See Istibrā'
Walī, 83 n.
Wāshī, 42 n.
Watcher, 43 n., 89
Wife (second), 130 & n.
Wine-drinking (forbidden in Islam), 85 n.
Wine-vendors (as procurers), 80 & n.
Wisā', 238
Wudū', 56 n.

Za'ab, 238
Zinā, 25 n.
Zoroastrianism, 292 & n.

Stimulating Reading from Panther Books

SEXUAL ADVENTURE IN MARRIAGE
Jerome & Julia Rainer 50p ☐
RATIONALE OF THE DIRTY JOKE (VOLUME 1)
G. Legman 75p ☐
RATIONALE OF THE DIRTY JOKE (Volume 2)
G. Legman 75p ☐
THE XYZ OF LOVE   Inge & Sten Hegeler 75p ☐
LIVING IS LOVING   Inge & Sten Hegeler 50p ☐
MY SECRET LIFE   'Walter' 60p ☐
THE SCHOOL OF VENUS Edited by David Thomas 50p ☐
THE KAMA SUTRA Translated by F. F. Arbuthnot 75p ☐
THE PERFUMED GARDEN
Translated by Sir Richard Burton 75p ☐
THE MEMOIRS OF AN EROTIC BOOKSELLER
Armand Coppens 50p ☐
THE LURE OF THE LIMERICK
W. S. Baring-Gould 60p ☐
I, JAN CREMER   Jan Cremer 75p ☐
JAN CREMER 2   Jan Cremer 75p ☐
DRUGS AND SEXUALITY
Edited by David Solomon & George Andrews 75p ☐
BLUE MOVIE   Terry Southern 60p ☐
TROPIC OF CANCER   Henry Miller 95p ☐
TROPIC OF CAPRICORN   Henry Miller 75p ☐
NEXUS   Henry Miller 75p ☐
PLEXUS   Henry Miller 95p ☐
THE RAGIONAMENTI: *The Erotic Lives of Nuns,*
Wives and Courtesans   Aretino 50p ☐

All-action Fiction from Panther

SPY STORY	Len Deighton	60p	☐
THE IPCRESS FILE	Len Deighton	60p	☐
AN EXPENSIVE PLACE TO DIE	Len Deighton	50p	☐
DECLARATIONS OF WAR	Len Deighton	60p	☐
A GAME FOR HEROES	James Graham*	40p	☐
THE WRATH OF GOD	James Graham*	40p	☐
THE KHUFRA RUN	James Graham*	40p	☐
THE SCARLATTI INHERITANCE	Robert Ludlum	75p	☐
THE OSTERMAN WEEKEND	Robert Ludlum	60p	☐
THE MATLOCK PAPER	Robert Ludlum	75p	☐
THE BERIA PAPERS	Alan Williams†	60p	☐
THE TALE OF THE LAZY DOG	Alan Williams†	60p	☐
THE PURITY LEAGUE	Alan Williams†	50p	☐
SNAKE WATER	Alan Williams†	50p	☐
LONG RUN SOUTH	Alan Williams†	50p	☐
BARBOUZE	Alan Williams†	50p	☐
FIGURES IN A LANDSCAPE	Barry England	50p	☐
LORD TYGER	Philip José Farmer	50p	☐

*The author who 'makes Alistair Maclean look like a beginner'
(*Sunday Express*)
†'The natural successor to Ian Fleming' (*Books & Bookmen*)

All these books are available at your local bookshop or newsagent, or can be ordered direct from the publisher. Just tick the titles you want and fill in the form below.

Name ....

Address ....

....

Write to Panther Cash Sales, PO Box 11, Falmouth, Cornwall TR10 9EN

Please enclose remittance to the value of the cover price plus:

UK: 18p for the first book plus 8p per copy for each additional book ordered to a maximum charge of 66p

BFPO and EIRE: 18p for the first book plus 8p per copy for the next 6 books, thereafter 3p per book

OVERSEAS: 20p for first book and 10p for each additional book

Granada Publishing reserve the right to show new retail prices on covers, which may differ from those previously advertised in the text or elsewhere.